Worthy of Freedom

Worthy of Freedom

Indenture and Free Labor in the Era of Emancipation

JONATHAN CONNOLLY

The University of Chicago Press
Chicago and London

The University of Chicago Press, Chicago 60637
The University of Chicago Press, Ltd., London

Published 2024
Printed in the United States of America

33 32 31 30 29 28 27 26 25 24 1 2 3 4 5

ISBN-13: 978-0-226-83362-0 (cloth)
ISBN-13: 978-0-226-83364-4 (paper)
ISBN-13: 978-0-226-83363-7 (e-book)
DOI: https://doi.org/10.7208/chicago/9780226833637.001.0001

Library of Congress Cataloging-in-Publication Data

Names: Connolly, Jonathan, author.
Title: Worthy of freedom : indenture and free labor in the era of emancipation / Jonathan Connolly.
Description: Chicago : The University of Chicago Press, 2024. | Includes bibliographical references and index.
Identifiers: LCCN 2023043810 | ISBN 9780226833620 (cloth) | ISBN 9780226833644 (paperback) | ISBN 9780226833637 (e-book)
Subjects: LCSH: Indentured servants—Great Britain—Colonies. | Contract labor—Great Britain—Colonies.
Classification: LCC HD4875.G7 C56 2024 | DDC 331.5/420941—dc23/eng/20231107
LC record available at https://lccn.loc.gov/2023043810

♾ This paper meets the requirements of ANSI/NISO Z39.48-1992 (Permanence of Paper).

Contents

Introduction

In September 1849, the governor of Trinidad, Lord Harris, wrote to defend a recently enacted labor ordinance that had aroused suspicion in London. The law had authorized five-year contracts for indentured workers the colony sought to recruit from India and Africa.[1] To the colonial secretary, Earl Grey, multiyear contracts of this sort seemed impermissibly coercive; they threatened, in his words, to reinstitute "slavery in a mitigated form."[2] But according to Harris, the law's purpose was not to enslave or unfairly restrict. Instead, it was to make immigrant workers "worthy of freedom."[3] Harris's phrase encapsulated a view that would reappear frequently in official correspondence as post-slavery colonies like Trinidad struggled to define and redefine "free labor" in the early period of emancipation. On this view, freedom was an obligation, not simply a right.[4] Coercion would make migrant laborers industrious, orderly, and valuable. It would civilize "the Coolie and the African."[5] It would make freedom work.

This was 1849, more than fifteen years after abolition. In 1833, Parliament outlawed chattel slavery in Britain's Caribbean and Indian Ocean colonies.[6] There, over the course of two centuries, slavery had built immense fortunes and massive commodity trades, above all in sugar. The cost was an unnamable suffering: the forced migration of more than three million enslaved Africans, and a plantation system characterized by overwork, exploitation, and severe punishment. In the early nineteenth century, that system remained profitable.[7] Yet in 1834, when abolition took effect, the enslaved were "apprenticed," still required to work albeit under new regulations. In 1838, apprenticeship too came to an end, giving rise to a new, under-defined state of social relations: "freedom." For abolitionists, the institution of freedom over slavery marked a triumph over evil, an end to widespread colonial suffering, and an expurgation of national guilt.[8]

Soon after abolition, however, imperial authorities created a transcontinental system of indentured labor migration to bring new workers to plantation colonies. For roughly eighty years, that system operated on a large scale. Between 1834 and 1917, more than a million indentured Indian workers arrived in British colonies in the Caribbean, Indian Ocean, southern Africa, and the South Pacific.[9] Alongside Indian migrants came smaller groups from China and West Africa; during the same period, more than 87,000 Chinese and nearly 40,000 Africans went to work under indenture across the empire.[10] Post-slavery indenture complicates our understanding of the history of emancipation. Slavery gave way to freedom, but ideological and economic conflicts shaped what freedom meant.

This book is about the idea and practice of free labor in the early period of emancipation. Its focus is Indian indentured labor in the three British colonies most transformed by migration: Mauritius, British Guiana, and Trinidad. In each, indenture bolstered sugar production after the rupture of abolition. Migration was organized, not spontaneous: supervised and facilitated by the imperial state, an indenture "system" was built. As a tool of legal, social, and economic engineering, that system helped shape the particular form of freedom that followed abolition. In the process, indenture became a touchstone for contemporary debates on race, non-European free labor, and the legacy of emancipation.

At the heart of my analysis lie questions of normalization. In the 1830s and 1840s, indenture sparked public scandal and official conflict. The colonial secretary, John Russell, warned that indenture might soon produce a "new system of slavery."[11] At the same time, a rapidly changing economic landscape made indenture unstable in practice, as abolition, free trade, and freedpeople's efforts to forge new economic lives reshaped the colonies. Yet by the mid-1860s, all this had changed. A new consensus had emerged in Britain: indenture was now a legitimate form of free labor, not a betrayal of abolition. In Parliament, a new colonial secretary, Edward Bulwer Lytton, extolled the system as a means of preserving, not subverting, "the sublime experiment of negro emancipation."[12] As he spoke, in 1859, indenture bolstered the sugar economy as production matched and then *surpassed* pre-abolition levels. At this stage, Britons saw indenture as a force for progressive development—not a covert revival of slavery, but instead a legitimate, natural, and necessary part of the modern world.

Why did indenture become less controversial over time? How and why was the indenture system consolidated, legally and economically? These are the questions that this book answers. It is at once a study of ideas and of structure, of free-labor ideology and of labor relations in practice. It is also a study of law—of the ways colonial law shaped the historically contingent category of post-slavery free labor, and of the related but distinct ways law responded to and was applied in local social contexts.

The Colonial Office disallowed the Trinidad ordinance that Harris defended in 1849.[13] But over time, Harris's conception of freedom ascended over Grey's fear of neo-slavery. In analyzing this transformation, this book explains how intertwined notions of race and class and related assertions of state power shaped post-slavery freedom. It explains, in other words, how indenture became free labor.

* * *

Indian indentured labor is the subject of a large, multifaceted historiography, with emphasis on both administrative structure and lived experience.[14] Much debate has focused on the relation between slavery and indenture, and the extent to which the latter resembled the former. Beginning with Hugh Tinker's pioneering work, many have argued that indenture covertly perpetuated unfree labor relations.[15] Others have rejected Tinker's "new system of slavery" thesis, arguing instead that indenture was a form of voluntary migration.[16] David Northrup's prominent synthesis suggested a "median position"; in his view, indentured laborers faced plantation conditions similar to those of formal slavery, but the system as a whole had much in common with broader patterns of nineteenth-century migration.[17]

Moving away from these debates, this book focuses on a related but distinct topic—the relationship between indenture and emancipation. Efforts to evaluate the relative coerciveness of the system as a whole have too often masked complexity and variation. Here, alongside others, I seek not to make claims about the overall character of indenture but rather to explain how it changed over time.[18] Just as important, I treat "freedom" and "free labor" as historical constructs, not analytic metrics.[19] Though undeniably valuable, much prior scholarship portrayed slavery and freedom as unproblematic, objective categories, "outside of history itself," as Radhika Mongia has written.[20] By engaging in typological debate, such an approach leaves unexamined broader questions about the meaning of freedom in post-emancipation context. If, as Northrup explained, many nineteenth-century officials ultimately concluded "that indentured labor was free labor," it is important to ask *why* they did so.[21] What exactly did the term "free labor" mean? How was it shaped by shifting constellations of other ideologically charged concepts, such as race, civilization, and progress? How did those cultural formations relate to changing social and economic dynamics in the colonies? Understanding indenture should involve more than weighing hardships against benefits. It should also lead us to consider how the meaning of free labor was constructed in a particular context, as part of the long history of emancipation.

This study is an attempt to meet that challenge. As such, it draws inspiration from a separate historiography on the history of emancipation.[22] Often focused on Jamaica, where Indian labor migration played a smaller role than it did elsewhere, that historiography rarely addressed indenture.[23] But it created an analytical framework that remains central here. Theoretically, it proposed that freedom should be understood as a "social construct" rather than a mere "conceptual foil to bondage."[24] Empirically, it showed that profound ambiguities marked the project of emancipation. If abolition ended formal slavery, it did so without resolving broader questions about socio-economic transformation, citizenship, and equality. Those questions provoked what Thomas Holt called the "problem of freedom" in post-emancipation societies.[25] New struggles over land, labor, and representation defined that freedom. Emancipation was a contested process rather than a triumphal event.

Indenture played a crucial role in this process. Over the course of the nineteenth century, new modes of thinking about society and economy reoriented perceptions of the "experiment" of emancipation.[26] Even as abolition remained sacrosanct as a moral cause, the political economy of emancipation grew increasingly controversial. Indenture was part of that conversation—part of the way contemporaries debated and understood the purpose of emancipation. Meanwhile, if justifications for indenture were fundamentally linked to perceptions of emancipation, the indenture system also restructured the underlying socio-economic dynamics of post-slavery freedom. In Mauritius, British Guiana, and Trinidad, indenture sustained monocultural export production, foreclosing the possibility of radical economic transformation raised by abolition. And within the sugar economy, indenture reshaped labor relations. The importation of thousands of immigrant workers annually made planters less reliant on Creole labor and reduced the bargaining power of the working classes as a whole.[27] An increasingly severe legal apparatus then structured the terms of wage labor for indentured immigrants. The study of indenture thus reveals how state power was used to structure post-emancipation society—to "construct" a particular kind of freedom—in the aftermath of abolition. In this broad sense, indenture remade emancipation during the second half of the nineteenth century.

* * *

To illuminate these themes, I develop three interconnected arguments. The first concerns public debate on indenture in Britain, traced from daily newspapers, antislavery pamphlets, published reports of inquiry, and parliamentary speeches. It explains how Britons came to see indenture as a legitimate form of free labor during the 1850s and 1860s, despite widespread public criticism during the 1830s and 1840s. I argue that new forms of social-scientific analysis centered on race, political economy, and demography transformed debate on indenture, displacing older antislavery modes of conceptualizing long-distance trade and labor. Above all, a growing consensus that emancipation had failed fueled support for indenture. By the 1860s, though some criticism remained, the center of debate had shifted dramatically. No longer a betrayal of emancipation, indenture adopted a refashioned antislavery language of its own. This is the story of indenture's "normalization" in public discourse—a story about the decline of antislavery and concomitant rise of new ideological poles associated with free trade and race.

The second concerns law and legal ideology. Here I argue that the laws of indenture became increasingly restrictive over time, as officials diluted or abandoned provisions originally designed to preserve voluntariness and competition, and intensified penalties applied against workers. My goal, however, is not to suggest that indenture replicated slavery in an absolute sense. Instead, it is to explain how and why British imperial authorities eventually perceived indenture, despite its severities, as an acceptable form of free labor. In addition to examining statutory development, then, I also reconstruct an extensive set of debates among officials tasked with overseeing the indenture system in the colonies, in India, and in Britain. Though not identical, the trajectory of these debates mirrored that seen in broader public discourse. Serious disagreement over the nature and limits of free labor resulted in persistent legal conflict during the 1840s. But over the course of the next two decades, economic and ideological change underpinned the gradual imposition of harsher laws. In analyzing this transformation, I insist on two claims: first, that shifting notions of race and civilization reshaped the category of post-slavery free labor between 1838 and 1871; and second, that the legal ideology espoused by key officials consistently reframed particularized economic interests in terms of generalized and neutral forms of social good.

Finally, a third line of analysis considers practical applications of the law and ideology of indenture in local colonial contexts. Here I show that local dynamics shaped the indenture system in important ways; that the laws of indenture were in many cases not applied as written; and that variation, informality, and everyday resistance frustrated state regulatory structures during the 1840s and early 1850s. Enforcement mechanisms hardened in the following two decades but continued to face challenges raised by changing social dynamics, particularly in Mauritius, where Indian population growth transformed the social order. This mode of analysis underscores the distinction between theory and practice emphasized by the law and society movement.[28] But more broadly, it focuses attention on sugar production and the political economy of emancipation, meaning, as Eric Foner has written, "how political power . . . redefine[d] class relations in the aftermath of slavery."[29] Though perceptions of economic decline initially justified indenture, labor migration was used to dramatically expand export production in Mauritius, British Guiana, and Trinidad beginning in the 1850s. This pattern continued during the 1860s, by which point indenture had become similarly essential to newly established plantations elsewhere in the empire.[30] Alongside the ideological normalization of indenture, I argue, there was also a substantial legal and material consolidation, a movement from crisis to confidence. In these terms, "consolidation" and "normalization" reinforced each other. Shifting notions of race and political economy remade indenture, and indenture remade the political economy of emancipation.

* * *

The cultural turn breathed new life into imperial history by focusing attention on discursive logics underlying assertions of state power.[31] The study of political culture in this context is important in its own right—it is important for historians to dissect and analyze the language used to justify violence, even when that language is stylized or obviously misleading.[32] It is similarly important to explain how "the activities of the modern state are shaped by the cultural imagination," as Priya Satia has put it.[33] Historians of indenture have paid too little attention to these concerns.[34] Part of my project, then, is to interpret shifting ideological commitments surrounding emancipation, and to show how they affected state policy on indenture. This is especially the case in my discussions of law. To understand legal change, in this and other contexts, it is necessary to consider historically contingent cultural conceptions that influenced legal reasoning.

None of this goes to minimize the importance of economic interest on the indenture system's development, however. Integrating cultural, legal, and socio-economic perspectives allows for sustained reflection on the relation between ideology and structure, a question of longstanding interest to historians of antislavery. Sparking decades of debate, Eric Williams famously argued that changing economic circumstances, not antislavery ideals, underpinned the rise of British abolitionism.[35] Scholars subsequently revised

Williams's empirical conclusions regarding economic decline and reattributed causal importance to the political and religious content of antislavery thought.[36] At the same time, many remained committed to untangling the nuanced connections between capitalism and antislavery.[37] These developments influenced my decision to view language as an agent of historical change rather than a byproduct. But they also magnify the potential importance of understanding connections between "economic" and "cultural" history as industrial capitalism transformed the world.[38]

In what follows, then, it should be clear that economic structure influenced but did not determine ideological change. Here and elsewhere in the book, I use the term "ideology" in a deliberately broad manner to refer to representations that give meaning to political power.[39] In this usage, ideology is normative but not systematic; it is not *an* ideology with precisely defined contours, but rather a realm of activity that the book subjects to historical analysis. When ideology is juxtaposed with economic "structure," it is not to suggest that one has inherent, constitutive priority over the other but rather to reveal historically specific relationships between the two.[40] Indenture functioned to sustain plantation production, and perceptions of economic need precipitated major shifts in indenture policy. But ideology also mattered from an economic perspective; ideology motivated and justified patterns of state action that quite clearly shaped economic activity. By physically transporting hundreds of thousands of workers across the ocean, by subsidizing the cost of such migration, and by lowering import tariffs (and therefore prices) on the home market, the state radically changed the economic "conditions" in which indenture was perceived. Those changes, in turn, reflected back into both public and official debates. Economic "necessity" was malleable in this context, not absolute. Economic success and failure were themselves part of an ideological formation—part of the overall vision of progress that turned decidedly in favor of indenture in the 1850s.

* * *

Worthy of Freedom is about indenture in theory and practice, but it also shines light on the structure of the imperial state. To do so, the book adopts an imperial frame. My methodological goal is not comparison, though I do discuss some of the ways indenture differed in the Caribbean and Indian Ocean. Instead, it is to explain the making of indenture as a connected, imperial phenomenon.[41] This approach is "trans-colonial" in seeing patterns of historical change as the result of forces and ideas emanating from multiple poles rather than a single, geographically bounded space.[42] Public debates on indenture—and the logics of labor and trade they generated—abstracted disparate Caribbean and Indian Ocean locales into a stylized entity: the "sugar colonies." Specific officials, meanwhile, shaped indenture in multiple places. This was true of imperial officials in Britain and India, who oversaw the system as a whole, but also of local officials who held posts in several indenture colonies at different points in their careers.[43] More broadly, the legal structure of indenture developed in an interconnected manner, as individual colonies responded both to each other and to centralized directives from above.

Given these dynamics, understanding imperial policy involves reconstructing long-term multipolar conflicts. This requires integrating the Indian Ocean and Atlantic worlds, as scholars of the former have long called for.[44] It also shifts attention from the colony/metropole binary toward more diffuse forms of circulation and influence.[45] Changes in indenture policy involved triangular patterns of communication between Britain, India, and the colonies, as well as additional lines of exchange among the colonies themselves. What emerges, in tracing such exchange, is a layered view of imperial praxis. From this vantage, imperial power appears ubiquitous but decentralized. Policy formed not in a unified "official mind" but rather through conflict across distinct levels of imperial administration, in London, Calcutta, Port Louis, Georgetown, and Port of Spain.[46]

Why Mauritius, British Guiana, and Trinidad? After all, the indenture system operated in many British colonies, not just these three. First, scale: they were the largest British indenture colonies in terms of Indian arrivals. Many more Indian workers came to British Guiana and Trinidad than to Jamaica—Britain's wealthiest Caribbean colony before abolition. Meanwhile, more Indian workers arrived in Mauritius than in all the West Indian colonies combined.[47] Indenture assumed a central economic importance in Mauritius, British Guiana, and Trinidad, in a way it did not in other parts of the empire. Contemporaries, both imperial officials and the wider public, paid special attention as a result; debate on the indenture system centered on these three colonies.

A second consideration is time: the indenture system began and largely took shape in the Caribbean and Indian Ocean. Later it would be extended—to South Africa in 1860, and Fiji in 1879. Because I focus on the early period of emancipation, Mauritius, British Guiana, and Trinidad are necessarily central to my argument. It was there that the regulatory structures surrounding indenture first developed. Laws and principles produced through rough negotiation in the 1840s and 1850s were later transferred wholesale, as models, to other parts of the world. Because of its relative proximity to India, Mauritius had particular primacy, and Mauritian precedent frequently justified reform and expansion elsewhere. But the process of transformation at the heart of

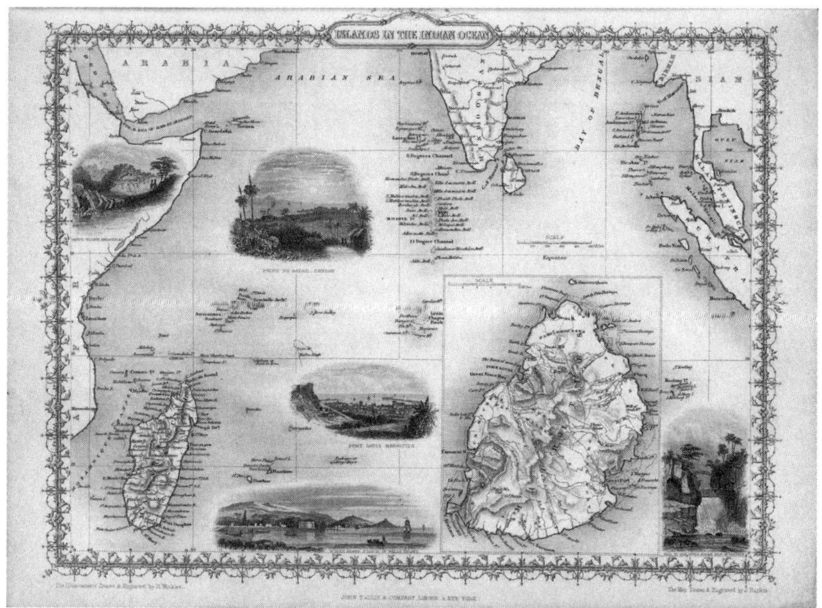

FIGURE 1. Islands in the Indian Ocean with inset map of Mauritius, from *The Illustrated Atlas* (London and New York: John Tallis and Company, 1851). David Rumsey Map Collection, Stanford Libraries.

this study occurred in all three colonies. In each, indenture was conceived of as a response to and remedy for the "experiment" of emancipation.

Finally, there were key structural similarities among the three colonies. Britain captured Mauritius, British Guiana, and Trinidad from foreign powers (France, the Netherlands, and Spain, respectively) during the Napoleonic Wars. By the early nineteenth century, each had become a "sugar colony," but at the time of abolition, none was a fully developed plantation society. Compared with the largest sugar colonies of the eighteenth century—Jamaica and Saint-Domingue—British Guiana and Trinidad had smaller populations and more uncultivated land. Beyond British Guiana's arable coastal plain, where sugar production was concentrated, the colony encompassed tens of thousands of square miles.[48] At 1,841 square miles, Trinidad was smaller, but still much larger than other Lesser Antilles colonies where indenture was used. Mauritius was the smallest of the three, at 788 square miles, but it was nonetheless the largest sugar economy. In the late eighteenth century, less than a quarter of the island's arable land had been brought under cultivation.[49]

The combination of these factors gave Mauritius, British Guiana, and Trinidad shared characteristics that shaped the development of indenture in the post-emancipation period. The existence of undeveloped land suitable for cultivation made expanded plantation production possible after abolition.

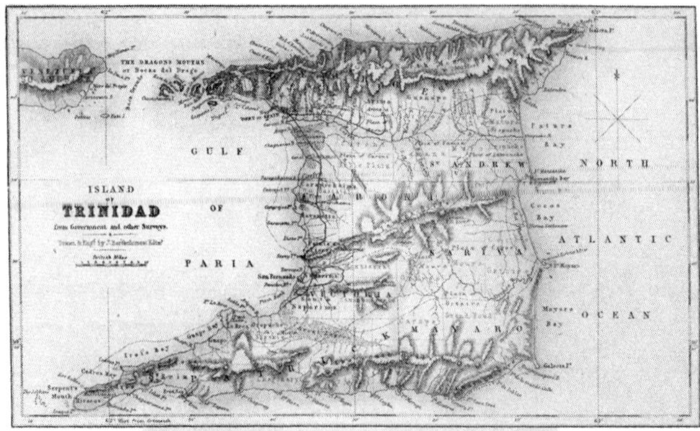

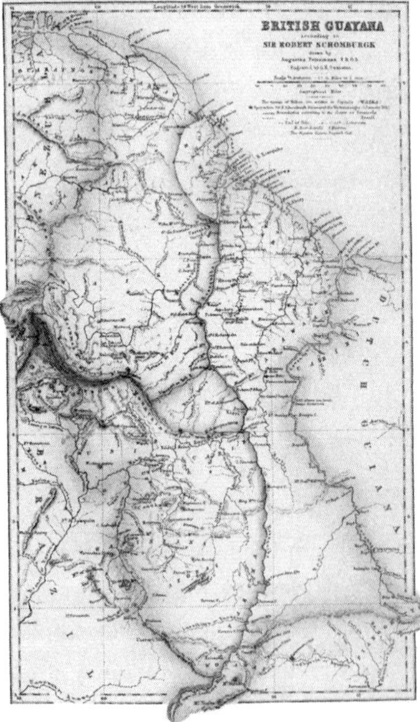

FIGURE 2. Maps of Trinidad and British Guiana, from *The Royal Illustrated Atlas of Modern Geography* (London: A. Fullarton & Co., c. 1864). David Rumsey Map Collection, Stanford Libraries.

Conversely, smaller pre-abolition populations, coupled with the availability of land, created problems of labor supply and control. After abolition, freedpeople could leave the plantations (if not the sugar economy entirely) and establish greater independence in newly built villages. Planters and local officials, in turn, fixated on "labor shortage," a concept that renewed itself as new land was developed for sugar production.[50] Such concerns and conditions motivated the imposition of increasingly stringent terms of indenture. It was no accident that the indenture system focused so significantly, in terms of migration flows, on these large, newer colonies. They were the frontier, and increasingly the heart, of the British imperial sugar economy during the nineteenth century.

These similarities considered, Mauritius, British Guiana, and Trinidad were hardly identical. As indicated, the three colonies had different colonial legacies—French, Dutch, and Spanish—and, as a result, different legal traditions, customs, and planter elites. British Guiana and Trinidad, in the Southern Caribbean, were also of course distinct geographically from Mauritius, which lies deep in the Indian Ocean, south of India and east of Madagascar. The journey from India to the Caribbean was significantly longer than it was to Mauritius. Partly as a result, the scale of indentured labor migration was significantly larger there, and the indenture system transformed the Mauritian population more completely than it did elsewhere.

These distinctions matter when studying law in action. Local context—in three different societies—clearly influenced the making of indenture in practice, as well as the lived experience of indenture in each place. Scholars have explored the formation of diasporic identities in Fiji, South Africa, and the Caribbean.[51] Others have shown that Indian knowledge networks structured migration patterns in the Indian Ocean.[52] Recent work has done much to uncover the particular experiences of indentured women in Mauritius, British Guiana, and Malaya, while a further body of scholarship focused on the late nineteenth century has illuminated links between indenture and the emergence of Indian nationalism.[53]

My focus is different for both practical and theoretical reasons. This is a study of the early period of emancipation, from which relatively few individualized testimonies of indenture survive. It is also a study of state power—of the use of state power to structure the imperial economy, and of the conceptual transformations that led contemporaries to justify to themselves and others the persistence of labor coercion in the aftermath of abolition. As such, the book focuses on state officials as much as it does indentured workers. My intention is not to undermine the humanity of individual workers or imply that migrants labored passively; indeed, part of my argument is that variation and informality marked labor relations, and that many managed to evade or alter strict terms of control. But it is my intention to show that the imperial state shaped the legal and economic conditions under which indentured laborers worked, and to explain how and why those conditions changed over time.

As a study of state power, *Worthy of Freedom* addresses two additional broad themes: race and free-trade liberalism. Scholars have long sought to explain an apparent hardening in European attitudes toward race during the nineteenth century. Historians of science, among others, have pointed to scientific racism and the emergence of a fixed, biological conception of race in tracing this shift. By displacing the biblical theory of monogenesis, racial science made race an immutable identity, and a cause (rather than an effect) of social difference.[54] Historians of empire, by contrast, have emphasized a different set of causal factors. Work on missionaries in colonial contexts has shown how cultural conflict motivated a turn from universalism to fixed notions of racial difference during the second half of the century.[55] Other important scholarship has linked the transformation to major episodes of violence and political upheaval. The Indian Rebellion of 1857 and the Morant Bay Rebellion of 1865 are often seen as turning points in this regard; both events helped precipitate the rise of essentialized conceptions of permanent non-European difference, and both marked the rising influence of such notions on imperial policy.[56]

My analysis of debates about indenture allows for a related appraisal of the diffusion and salience of transformations in race-thinking in Britain and the empire. In both public and official discourse, notions of fixed racial difference supplanted antislavery commitments and helped legitimize indenture. This shift began early, from the late 1840s onward, and it was linked not to political violence but rather to economic concerns. Above all, a belief in emancipation's economic "failure" drove contemporary observers to invest new explanatory significance in race. Assertions of inferiority were bound up with economic struggles surrounding wage-labor dependency. Race was grounded in the political economy of emancipation. And shifting conceptions of race gradually restructured the legal structure of indenture.

In illuminating this shift, the book makes a set of related arguments about liberalism and empire. From the early twentieth century, theorists of empire traditionally associated mid-century liberalism with anti-imperialism; that is, with an expansion of international trade but not direct imperial rule.[57] Subsequent scholarship undermined that view by showing that the empire continued to expand, directly and indirectly but always by force, throughout the century.[58] Yet this scholarship made the seeming paradox of liberal empire even more pressing: how could liberalism, with its devotion to political liberty and economic freedom, coexist with imperial rule? On one view, notably argued by Uday Singh Mehta, there was no paradox; hierarchy was immanent within liberal thought, and it was the logic of liberalism itself that justified imperial expansion and political exclusion.[59] According to others, the nineteenth century witnessed a "turn" to empire, as Jennifer Pitts has argued, while liberal theorists of the late eighteenth century had remained broadly opposed to imperial expansion.[60]

Focused on officials rather than theorists, my work answers this question from a different vantage point, one more attuned to the effects and adaptations of liberal ideas on the "practical terrain of imperial politics."[61] Like Mehta, I argue that a particular conception of historical time acted to legitimize subordination in colonial contexts. Local colonial officials frequently argued that labor regulations would improve non-European workers not yet "ready" for unrestricted freedom. In this manner, liberal theories of progressive social development—what Dipesh Chakrabarty has called "historicist thinking"—supplied the impetus for ostensibly illiberal policy.[62] In a post-slavery context, liberalism and paternalism not only coexisted but were mutually reinforcing.

At the same time, in discussing law and legal ideology, I argue that there was a definite turn away from liberal principles at mid-century. In the 1840s, the Colonial Office insisted that non-European immigrant workers would respond rationally to free-labor incentives. On that basis, London repeatedly disallowed local proposals for heightened indenture restrictions—most notably fixed, multiyear labor contracts—which it viewed as both inefficient and unjust. During the 1850s and 1860s, the Office's position changed; abandoning its earlier, universalist stance, it accepted the view that non-European workers were incapable of productive social and economic development without regulation. The boundaries of acceptable "free labor" thus shifted; there was a transition from liberal universalism to race-based justifications for labor coercion.

Again, race has crucial explanatory force in this account; race-thinking helped shape and legitimize the legal development of indenture. But race was always linked to questions of class, and to economic interest more broadly. The racialized legal ideology that emerged in the 1850s undergirded a particular economic order centered on wage-labor dependency. That order appeared in official discourse in broad, moral terms, linked to wider concepts of self-improvement and social progress. I refer frequently to this process of translation as "moralization." Linking economic and moral ideals, its effect was to redescribe particular economic interests in the neutral terms of social order. This was of crucial importance to the development of indenture: heightened restrictions on workers could be presented as a mutually beneficial form of social management, delivering "progress" to workers and employers alike. As such, legal discourse connected the imperatives of race and class; race was a language through which class interests were subtly articulated and maintained alongside the state's commitment to economic liberalism.

All of this concerns imperial power and liberal *thought*, yet the book is equally engaged with questions of liberal *policy*. The mid-nineteenth century saw the enactment of the world's first free-trade policy, which contemporary proponents enshrined with a set of broader ideals. Of key importance was the notion of the minimal, non-interventionist state, renewed by and responsive to a middle-class, anti-corruption ethos. Small government, in this popular conception, was to free the state from vested interests. By the same token, tariff reform was to lower food costs to the benefit of domestic consumers. This vision led generations of historians to view the mid-nineteenth century as an era of "classical liberalism," to be followed by a distinctly late-century era of "imperialism."[63]

Against this backdrop, the history of indenture reveals a different side to the liberal state. From the perspective of the post-slavery empire, the state continued to structure trade and labor markets despite, and in some cases because of, its commitment to economic liberalism. Over the course of the century, the imperial state remade ostensibly free markets by regulating, funding, and facilitating indentured labor migration, which in turn sustained colonial export production. It did so, crucially, because state power attached workers, directly and indirectly, to the plantation system.[64] In short, free trade at home depended on labor coercion abroad. The repeal of trade tariffs did strike at entrenched landed interests and benefit domestic consumers. But it also set in motion a course of dynamics that bolstered and legitimized the indenture system. Lower prices led planters to demand lower wages. The prospect of economic decline led officials toward heightened labor controls. In the empire, free trade resulted in a retrenchment of elite economic interests, which were themselves newly linked to a competing view of progressive social development. My argument in this regard is not about hypocrisy or selectivity. It is rather that the logic of labor control traced over the course of this study legitimized state intervention in colonial economic relations during the ostensibly non-interventionist era of free trade.

While free-trade ideology idealized the self-regulating economy, free-trade policy depended on state power. When it came to labor, the market was not self-regulating. As Karl Polanyi argued, labor is more than a mere commodity; it is a human activity shaped by and inextricably connected to social life.[65] Emancipated populations sold their labor not in perfect accordance with market laws, but rather in line with their needs, desires, and sense of dignity as people. When free trade lowered sugar prices, "labor" resisted planters' attempts to lower wages. In this context, the state intervened forcefully, creating patterns of wage labor where markets alone failed to support them. In the post-slavery empire, the transition from slave to wage labor involved the systematic importation of new workers. The state controlled that importation by regulating the indenture system and, as we will see, by subsidizing it. To achieve the domestic goals of free trade in Britain, the state wielded its power in the empire, actively structuring the "market" for colonial labor.

* * *

These arguments unfold across six chapters. Chapters 1 and 2 examine the initial scandal of indenture, the creation of a state-regulated indenture system, and the conflicts—ideological and material—that bisected state policy through the 1840s. Chapter 3 explains how free-trade policy deepened those conflicts while laying a groundwork for the system's eventual consolidation. Chapters 4 and 5 explain the conceptual processes that legitimized indenture during the 1850s and 1860s, and the concomitant means by which indenture restructured the imperial sugar economy. Chapter 6 underscores these transformations through analysis of renewed scandal and formal inquiry during the 1870s, which temporarily questioned but ultimately reaffirmed the logic of indenture built over the previous thirty years.

Each of the chapters has a distinct chronological focus, but together they illustrate an overall pattern of change, from controversy to acceptance, instability to solidity. In brief, then, the following arguments run throughout the book. State power structured post-slavery labor markets and bolstered particular private interests despite (and in certain cases because of) Britain's commitment to free trade and economic non-interventionism. Over the course of three decades, state regulation and new forms of social-scientific analysis centered on race and political economy transformed the public image of indenture from a covert reincarnation of slavery into a modern, progressive, mutually beneficial form of economic development. In the same period, the conceptual boundaries of post-slavery free labor shifted significantly, underwriting increasingly stringent and centralized laws of indenture. These ideological shifts made possible a material consolidation of the indenture system, which in turn reinforced the emerging pro-indenture consensus. During the 1850s and 1860s, indentured labor migration allowed for substantial growth in the sugar economy, and export production and revenue came to exceed pre-abolition levels. All of these developments marked an astounding process of normalization by which modified forms of labor coercion were legitimized ideologically and solidified in practice.

The book's epilogue flashes forward to describe the eventual end to indenture during the early twentieth century. But it does so to restate and etch in greater relief the book's core arguments about the *making* of indenture from the 1830s through the 1870s. As will become clear, the conflicts that built indenture during that period fundamentally altered the meaning of emancipation.

1

The Scandal of Indenture and the Making of State Regulation, 1834–1845

In the spring of 1835, the secretary to the Government of Bengal reported that 151 Indian workers, referred to as "Dhangur Coolies," had contracted to work on a sugar plantation in Mauritius.[1] Signed in Calcutta before a magistrate, the contract bound the workers to a particular Mauritian planter, John Shaw Sampson, for five years. Wages were set at five sicca rupees per month, along with rations, medical care, and clothing. According to the magistrate, the workers had engaged "voluntarily"; a list of names was appended, an "x" next to each signifying agreement.[2]

This was 1835, before full emancipation. The Abolition Act passed in 1833 created an intermediate state, "apprenticeship," which required the formerly enslaved to continue working on the plantations. But even before the end of apprenticeship, planters and colonial elites sought new labor from abroad. Many recruitment schemes failed, but some, particularly those involving India, resulted in the migration of large numbers of workers. This chapter is about this early history of indenture, the public controversy it produced, and the subsequent creation of a state-regulated indenture system.

During the 1830s and early 1840s, indentured labor migration caused a public scandal in Britain and India. Critics decried what came to be known as the "coolie trade" as news of private recruitment efforts spread. In antislavery circles and beyond, many portrayed indenture as a thinly veiled reincarnation of slavery. A smaller but vocal group of radical critics argued that indenture threatened to undermine emancipation for migrants and freedpeople alike. In the scheme of this book, the scandal of indenture introduces a larger story about the notion of free labor in the era of emancipation. Free labor was made, not received, and its meaning changed significantly over time. Gradually, the scandal would fade; once maligned, indenture would gain approval and even celebration. But initially, many Britons rejected it. The story of indenture's "normalization," its eventual public acceptance, begins with the controversy it first produced.

Ultimately, the scandal of indenture only delayed the economic project of post-slavery labor migration. Under public pressure, imperial authorities investigated and eventually banned privately run migration from India. But soon after, in the 1840s, they re-established indenture. New regulations served to justify this reversal of policy. The result was a state-regulated indenture "system," administered by officials in Britain, India, and the colonies. That system originated in Mauritius in 1842, expanded to British Guiana, Trinidad, and Jamaica in 1845, and then continued to grow—to Natal in 1860 and Fiji in 1879.[3]

As we will see, state regulation helped legitimize indenture. Officials claimed that a state-led system would prove mutually beneficial to impoverished migrants and imperial trade. Emphasizing the protective functions of regulatory personnel, they distinguished indenture from slavery and the scandalous "coolie trade." Plans for state regulation thus combined a liberal ideal of labor redistribution with an emphasis on state power. Like earlier efforts to "ameliorate" slavery, regulation for indenture purported to limit unbridled private authority—to transfer power from local plantation owners to officials of state.

Yet beneath this presentation lay a more complex social reality, in which private interests shaped the state's regulatory capacities. Lobbying groups representing both Mauritian and West Indian sugar producers quietly embraced the cause of regulation, and their persistent advocacy influenced both the rules ultimately put in place and the officials appointed to implement them. In the process, private lobbies secured public support, not just to permit but to facilitate migration. There was no clean division between "state" and "economy," public authority and private interest. Instead, state power was porous, and intimately connected to particular private interests. At the broadest level, then, several strands of argument lead to a composite conclusion. In public, state regulation legitimized indenture by framing disinterested state power as a check on private exploitation. In private, that power was shaped by and most responsive to the interests it sought to control. Planter elites helped design state regulation, and the state subsequently helped planters continue the economic project of importing new labor into post-slavery societies.

The Scandal of Indenture: Early Indenture and Public Outcry

In the 1830s, as emancipation approached, planters and colonial authorities scoured the globe for new labor. Many schemes were hatched, but only in India did recruitment succeed. In 1836, British Guiana tried but failed to recruit

African *emancipados* from Cuba, as well as "liberated Africans"—Africans taken from slave ships captured by the Royal Navy—recently settled in Sierra Leone.[4] Though such migration would later take place with government approval, in 1836 the Colonial Office rejected the idea, warning that it would appear as an "African Slave Trade in a new and mitigated form."[5] Other labor migration schemes foundered for more practical reasons. A group of Mauritian planters financed a quasi-diplomatic mission to Madagascar but failed to secure permission to recruit laborers.[6] Between 1834 and 1845, Jamaica attempted to recruit European workers, but many of those who arrived either abandoned plantation labor or succumbed to disease.[7]

Early efforts to recruit Indian labor were more effective, especially in Mauritius. Beginning in 1834, a stream of reports reached the colony notifying the governor of contracts signed in Calcutta, indenturing groups of Indian workers. The size of these groups varied from the mid-thirties to nearly five hundred.[8] Precise contract terms also varied, but the basic arrangement was the same: five years of indenture on a sugar plantation, wages of five rupees per month along with food rations, and transportation to Mauritius and back to India after completion of the contract.[9] Between 1834 and 1839, when emigration from India was temporarily prohibited, 25,468 Indian workers arrived in Mauritius on these terms.[10] Starting in 1836, an additional 396 went to British Guiana.[11]

Many though not all of these workers came from the hills of the Chota Nagpur plateau, where colonial rule had destabilized formerly independent tribal polities. As the East India Company took control of the frontier, members of these polities began to migrate into the plains of Bengal. The commercialization of property in land undermined their independence; if they had formerly come to raid the plains, they now came as migrant laborers. During the 1820s, many worked in British indigo factories in Calcutta. Later in the century, many more would travel to the tea plantations of Assam. In these contexts, they became "Dhangars," "Kols," and "coolies."[12]

These terms revealed more about what planters sought than the shifting relationship between the hills and the plains. The "Dhangar" was an ideal type: strong yet easily managed, without caste and inherently mobile; male, primitive and "docile," that is, governable. This image soon circulated among planters and merchants around the empire, from the tea gardens of Assam to settlements in Australia, to those interested in sugar in the Caribbean and Indian Ocean. By the 1830s, the notion of the "hill coolie" had coalesced as imperial conventional wisdom.[13] A proposal for Indian labor in New South Wales cited Mauritius; the proposal's author, a former indigo planter from Bengal, claimed: "Dangurs entertain no prejudices of Cast or Religion; and they are willing to turn their hands to any labour whatever."[14]

It was this kind of worker that planters wanted in the sugar colonies. Inspired by reports from Mauritius, John Gladstone became a prominent early sponsor of Indian migration to British Guiana.[15] A former MP and the father of the future prime minister, Gladstone was an important absentee proprietor. His correspondence, which later became the object of parliamentary scrutiny, reveals just how central notions of primitiveness were to early claims for indenture. Responding to Gladstone's inquiries, the Indian shipping and trading company Gillanders, Arbuthnot & Co. suggested that certain "Hill tribes" north of Calcutta were ideally suited for field labor: "well limbed and active," they had "hardly any ideas beyond those of supplying the wants of nature." Once arrived, these workers would be "docile and easily managed," the letter continued; after all, they reportedly had "no wants beyond sleeping," and were "spoken of as more akin to the monkey than the man."[16]

While this supposed primitiveness made Indian indenture attractive, fears of economic decline drove efforts at recruitment. Even before full emancipation, planters predicted that labor shortages would cripple plantation production. Gladstone argued that immigration was needed to ensure "regular continuous labour," noting the "risks to which our Properties in British Guiana will be exposed when the Expiration of the Apprenticeship takes place."[17] In 1839, a petition signed by nearly 800 Guiana planters and merchants claimed that without new labor, the colony would "speedily degenerate into a state of barbarism."[18] These fears had a longer lineage in Mauritius, where sugar production had expanded rapidly in the 1820s, just as the Indian Ocean slave trade, illegal but still active, began to collapse.[19]

From the beginning, then, two concepts underpinned Indian indenture: the primitiveness of the "hill coolie," and the urgent inevitability of "labor shortage." Like the image of the hill coolie, labor shortage was an ideological construct.[20] That is to say, it was a formulation of reality that made a particular course of action appear natural and objectively necessary—a formulation that naturalized the political.[21] As a justification for indenture, the concept of labor shortage was anticipatory: it emerged before its ostensible cause, full emancipation. And it was flexible: it outlived the perceived crisis of emancipation to describe very different economic conditions in the 1850s and 1860s. As its meaning changed, its ideological core stayed the same: labor shortage served to justify, to make necessary, migration designed to support the plantation system and export production.

The idea of the coolie served the same purpose and was similarly imprecise.[22] In the 1830s, the "hill coolie" signaled a particular, stylized group, renowned for primitiveness and docility. Yet the reality of migration was far more complex. Indian migrants came from a variety of caste and class backgrounds, as men and women, Hindus and Muslims, from north and south.[23] Over time, the word "coolie" shed its association with the Chota Nagpur hills and became increasingly generic, as a marker of difference between Indians and Europeans, not status within or across Indian regions or social groups. In the United States, where Chinese workers became archetypal "coolies," the term assumed additional meanings.[24] What remained, in the British imperial world, was the term's ideological function. The notion of the coolie, whether it signaled primitive indigeneity or more generalized non-European deficiencies, served to naturalize legal restrictions associated with indenture.

As several historians have shown, Gladstone was hardly the first to bring indentured workers to the West Indies. A plan for Chinese recruitment brought nearly two hundred migrants to work in Trinidad (via Penang and Calcutta) as early as 1806.[25] Precedents in the Indian Ocean were more extensive. Some 1,500 Indian convicts arrived in Mauritius between 1815 and 1837, where they built roads, bridges, and other public infrastructure as part of a wider system of penal transportation used by the East India Company.[26] Planters in Mauritius and Réunion recruited several thousand more Indians to work in sugar cultivation in the late 1820s.[27] These efforts likely influenced the post-emancipation turn to indenture, particularly at the level of recruitment, where existing networks were mobilized to new ends. They also likely shaped what migrants themselves made of indenture, as Clare Anderson has argued.[28]

Yet these early experiments differed from what emerged in the mid-1830s. Most of the Chinese workers brought to Trinidad in 1806 had left the island by 1808; from the perspective of sugar production, the episode had little effect.[29] Mascarene efforts to employ Indian contract labor in the 1820s similarly "faltered."[30] Convict transportation dramatically decreased in scale in the 1830s, nearing its end not only in Mauritius but in the far more numerous transit from Britain to Australia.[31] Most important, abolition dramatically changed the context in which indenture was pursued and perceived. Planters fought with new urgency, and the scale of migration, in Mauritius at least, increased sharply. For abolitionists, meanwhile, indenture suddenly appeared as a threat—as an effort to undermine the project of emancipation.

Indeed, the salient point for our purposes is that in the 1830s and early 1840s, indenture caused a scandal. Though migration to Mauritius had begun earlier and occurred on a larger scale, Gladstone's efforts became a particular flash point in Britain. After traveling to British Guiana, the antislavery activist John Scoble accused Gladstone of organizing a "Coolie Slave Trade."[32] According to Scoble, each aspect of Gladstone's project was illegitimate; recruitment depended on misinformation and fraud, transportation was unsanitary, and plantation life was marked by coercion, corporal punishment, and high mortality rates.[33] Other prominent antislavery advocates and publications condemned Indian indenture in similar terms. Indenture was "a new slave-trade in likeness of the old," in Thomas Clarkson's judgment.[34] According to the *British Emancipator*, the newspaper published by the Central Committee for Negro Emancipation, indenture was "a *legal shelter*, under which may be imported and destroyed, as many *slaves* as they please, under the name of Hill Coolies of Calcutta!"[35]

Equally stringent attacks appeared in India, in newspapers that self-consciously sought to engage with and influence metropolitan debate.[36] Beginning in 1838, the evangelical *Friend of India* published a string of critical accounts which, like Scoble, portrayed indenture as a "mitigated form of slavery," run by "kidnappers" and marked by persistent "fraud and injustice."[37] Around the same time, Anglo-Indian antislavery advocates began to petition the Government of India to protest against indentured emigration. "If the present system be continued," warned one such petition, "the Coast Ports of India will soon resemble the slave marts of Africa and the Mauritius become a slave emporium for the world."[38] Taking particular aim at the Gladstone controversy, the petition further decried the "inhumanizing views" of those "who in private and confidential communications state them [Indian indentured laborers] to belong to the race of the Monkey rather than the man."[39]

Extending beyond the antislavery press, the burgeoning critique of indenture unleashed a wider public scandal. In the summer of 1839, the *Times* condemned Indian labor migration in particularly direct terms. According to the paper, "the fate of these unhappy beings" was "almost too horrible to be contemplated." "Even on the voyage from east to west," the *Times* suggested, "the sufferings of the Hill Coolies were actually worse, it seems, than those of the Africans in the middle passage." For Britain's leading daily, not only was Indian labor migration insufficiently free, it was also productive of "atrocities."[40] In the early 1840s, the *Times* continued to publish attacks on indenture, citing the domestic and social dislocation caused by labor migration, and warning that indenture could result in "virtual slavery."[41]

Indenture also became a scandal for imperial officials, as well as in Parliament, particularly as pressure mounted to abolish apprenticeship in 1838. In Parliament, Lord Brougham denounced indenture as Scoble had, portraying it as a covert revival of the slave trade. Mocking what he identified as the "soft language of bringing over free men," Brougham declared: "nothing but slave trading is, and . . . nothing but slave trading can be, the meaning and the result of all that is thus doing."[42] In India, meanwhile, officials sounded alarms, now convinced that migrants were being deceived and exploited. Lord Auckland, the governor general, warned of the possibility that laborers would be "subjected to much suffering from interested deceit and imposition."[43] Soon after, W. W. Bird reported to fellow councilors in the Government of India that despite efforts to prevent involuntary emigration, "a system had been organized by means of crimps," with the result that "simple and unsuspecting people were decoyed from their homes on false pretences, plundered, and betrayed."[44] Upon arrival in Mauritius, Bird continued, they faced "unsurmountable" difficulties, such that their well-being "practically depended on the personal character of their employers."[45]

Bird's language reveals a strange mirror: like their antagonists, critics of indenture tended to portray Indian migrants as helpless victims. "Simple and unsuspecting"; acted upon: this was the willing, unthinking worker that planters lauded, in reverse. Antislavery critics deployed the image to different ends, but they too imagined a stylized, primitive "hill coolie." Defined by ignorance, Indian migrants appeared as an "undifferentiated mass," as Andrea Major puts it, without knowledge or agency.[46] This image was distorted, as contemporary historians have argued.[47] It remained blind to the ways in which subaltern networks shaped migration patterns, as well as the varied range of experiences that hundreds of thousands of migrants incurred over the indenture period as a whole.[48]

Yet it is important to understand the antislavery critique of indenture, not as objective historical evidence, but as a structure of thought that influenced metropolitan opinion and imperial policy. After all, the result of growing official concern was an outright ban on emigration. In response to Scoble's reporting, the governor of British Guiana, Henry Light, instituted a commission of inquiry, which condemned neglect and violence against indentured workers on two plantations.[49] In the summer of 1838, the Government of India appointed its own committee to investigate allegations of mistreatment in Mauritius. Its report gave official credence to the scandalous portrayal critics had advanced. Recruitment, the Calcutta Committee concluded, depended on "misrepresentation and deceit," while most workers were "incapable of understanding the nature of the Contracts they were said to have entered into."[50] In the colony, planters failed to pay wages and rations as agreed, further undermining workers' contracts in practice.[51] While debate on the issue continued in Parliament, the Court of Directors instructed the Government of India to suspend migration to the sugar colonies.[52] The Government acted immediately, discontinuing emigration permits then required under British-Indian law.[53] India Act XIV of 1839 subsequently made labor migration illegal.[54]

By the end of the 1830s, then, indenture had been rejected on multiple levels. Recruitment efforts by planters in Mauritius and British Guiana produced a public scandal, and as that scandal grew, many portrayed indenture as being profoundly unfree. Antislavery advocates in Britain and India attacked indenture as a covert means of perpetuating slavery. General-interest newspapers like the *Times*, alongside prominent government officials, condemned labor migration in similarly strong terms. Though many argued that migration was needed to confront perceived labor shortages resulting from emancipation, an emerging public consensus rejected the notion that indenture would benefit migrants. Indenture was marked, on this view, by deceit and mistreatment by "atrocities," as the *Times* put it in 1839.[55]

Legitimizing Indenture: Liberalism and State Regulation

The period 1839–1842 was thus of crucial importance for debate on indenture. Indian labor migration had been denounced, and migration to both British Guiana and Mauritius had been banned. But the question was far from settled. Petitioning in favor of labor migration persisted, and by 1840, the Colonial Office began to consider new measures to sanction and regulate migration. In 1840, Lord Russell proposed an amended Colonial Passengers Bill, which would have permitted Indian migration to Mauritius. That effort failed, but in 1842 Lord Stanley, who was then colonial secretary, successfully approved state-regulated labor migration to Mauritius. In 1845, the system expanded to the West Indies.[56] Between 1842 and 1850, a total of 115,562 indentured Indians left for Mauritius, British Guiana, Trinidad, and Jamaica.[57]

This reversal of policy turned on state regulation.[58] Mauritius and British Guiana had proved the unregulated, private "coolie trade" a failure. In response, those who saw labor migration as a vital means of bolstering sugar production argued that a state-regulated indenture system could eliminate abuse and prove mutually beneficial for workers and employers. A liberal notion of mutual benefit clearly emerged in this context: "free" emigration, key officials suggested, would rationally redistribute labor power as workers followed demand abroad. Thus as Henry Light reported evidence of mistreatment in British Guiana to the Colonial Office, he nonetheless remained convinced that "under proper regulations, as to sexes and location, the natives of India might safely be introduced here to the great amelioration of their own condition, and the undoubted benefit of the province."[59] For Light, the moral of the Gladstone scandal was not that labor migration was unworkable. Instead, it was that new regulations were needed both to protect workers from mistreatment and to expand the system of transportation. In his account, as in others, protective regulation legitimized indenture, distinguishing it conceptually from slavery.

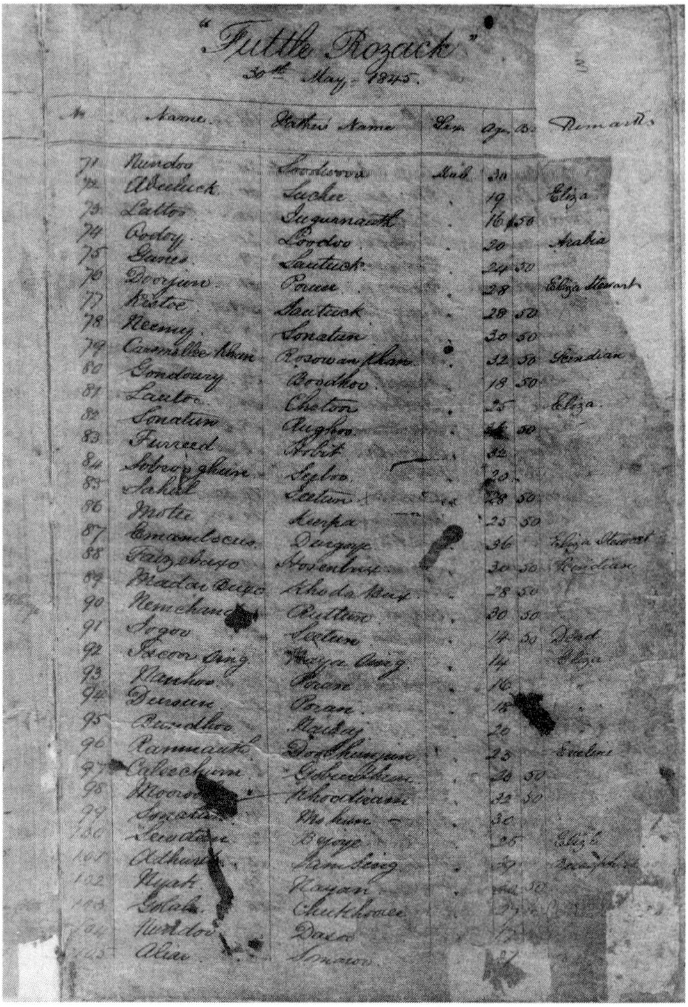

"Futtle Rozack"
30th May 1845.

No. Name. Father's Name. Sex. Age. Remarks

FIGURE 3. Register of the *Futtle Rozack* (*Fatel Razack*), 1845. Courtesy of the National Archives of Trinidad and Tobago.

In India, state regulation similarly shifted official debates in favor of re-authorizing emigration. The mark of liberal political economy, if never absolute, was readily apparent.[60] For H. T. Prinsep and A. Amos, councilors in the Government of India, an absolute prohibition on emigration was both unsustainable and objectional in principle.[61] Like Light, Amos emphasized the notion of mutual benefit, suggesting that regulated "free emigration" could prove "eminently beneficial" to laborers themselves.[62] James Grant, a dissenting member of the Calcutta Committee, argued that the ban violated the rights of Indians as British subjects.[63] Lord Auckland's view was more conflicted; he feared that, on a large scale, regulation would fail to prevent deceptive recruitment practices. Still, he thought that a permanent prohibition would unreasonably "restrict the freedom of labor," and by 1841 cautiously favored resuming migration to Mauritius.[64]

This "freedom of labor" was clearly different from that of indenture's many critics. It was freedom *from* state interference—in this case, the emigration ban—alongside an assumption that such release would lead to opportunity rather than exploitation. "Negative liberty," as Isaiah Berlin called it, proved influential far beyond indenture, as a tenet of liberal political economy in the nineteenth century, and in Anglo-American jurisprudence well into the twentieth.[65] For our immediate purposes, it reveals the deep multiplicity of free-labor discourse in the post-emancipation period.[66] As debate continued in Parliament, some framed the emigration ban as an infringement, shifting attention from the plantations to famine and poverty in India. Would the Commons "prevent men subject to the chance of such misery from emigrating?" asked one MP in June 1840.[67] These conditions, it should be emphasized, were treated as natural, extra-political events, an assumption that contemporary historians have undermined.[68]

In the spring of 1842, the colonial secretary, Lord Stanley, presented the House of Commons with a plan for regulated indentured labor migration that combined the liberal ideal of mutual benefit with an emphasis on the reformist power of the state. Stanley conceded that previous immigration experiments had resulted in mistreatment. But he argued that the root of the problem was private management without sufficient oversight. If the Indian laborer had been "deluded and smuggled from India," it was chiefly because "he had been brought over for the private interests of the planter—for the private advantage of those who brought him over."[69] If, in Stanley's words, privately managed immigration was marked by "injustice," a state-regulated system would in fact benefit immigrants—by allowing peasants "starving on 1½ d. a day in India" to better their economic standing in other parts of the empire.[70] As we will see, this rigid distinction between public and private was misleading, but it helped create a new, more favorable image for indenture.

In suggesting that state-regulated migration could serve the interests of capital and labor simultaneously, Stanley spoke to a theme already prominent in the context of liberal colonization theory. From the early 1830s, Edward Gibbon Wakefield's National Colonization Society promoted "systematic" colonization, a scheme for state-sponsored migration to Australia and New Zealand. Such migration, Wakefield argued, would improve the lives of poor emigrants from Britain and Ireland. By creating new export markets for British goods in the colonies, it would also grow the imperial economy. Wakefield's ideas circulated widely; the Society's membership included John Stuart Mill as well as Charles Buller and Sir William Molesworth, who advocated for assisted migration in Parliament.[71] While Indian labor migration to the sugar colonies differed from British migration to the South Pacific, the theory of systematic emigration took shape, in part, through Wakefield's reflections on the economics of Caribbean slavery.[72] After abolition, the post-slavery labor question, like Wakefield's theory, helped promote a crucial idea across the empire: the notion that state-regulated imperial migration could prove equally beneficial to individual laborers and to investors of capital and imperial trade.

Stanley's turn toward state regulation also bears contextualization in a sphere of practice centered more solidly in the Caribbean. After all, efforts to regulate and thereby justify plantation labor long preceded indenture. In the 1810s and 1820s, after the abolition of the slave trade, colonial authorities sought to "ameliorate" slavery by limiting its worst violence. Pioneered in Trinidad, amelioration put legal limits on punishment and established a new office, the Protector of Slaves, to serve as a legal advocate in plantation disputes. It also instituted a system of slave registration designed to monitor and reduce mortality rates and illegal slave trading. Amelioration had a humanitarian impulse, but it was also defensive—as a means of preserving the institution of slavery against the threat of abolitionism, at a point when high death and low birth rates threatened production. For the antislavery leader Thomas Fowell Buxton, amelioration was a step toward gradual emancipation. For the West India Committee, as for John Gladstone, the goal was to renew slavery in a sustainable, profitable form.[73]

State regulation for indenture can be seen in a similar light, as part of a long effort to create a regulated, acceptable labor system in the face of antislavery pressure. A key office of the post-1842 system, the Protector of Immigrants, was the institutional descendant of the Protector of Slaves.[74] Both oversaw protective regulations in the context of a broader administrative mandate to maintain order and facilitate export production. In British Guiana, the office took the name Immigration Agent General, which reflected the role more accurately. In both India and the colonies, the agents installed to safeguard basic well-being simultaneously (and more assiduously) served to facilitate recruitment and distribution. In this sense, regulation brought about "state formation," as Diana Paton has argued with regard to apprenticeship.[75] When the state imposed regulation on the "coolie trade" of the 1830s, it transferred authority from private to public, from owners and overseers to new officers of the state. This was a continuation of a process begun earlier, through amelioration and apprenticeship, by which the state sought to curb the private authority of plantation owners over enslaved workers.[76]

The argument for state regulation, then, seamlessly combined a liberal view of "free" labor distribution with a new apparatus for state power. Migration itself was framed as natural, spontaneous, and rational: as a liberal means of improving impoverished lives. But like systematic colonization theory, the turn toward regulation belied classical assumptions about the role of the state. Far from disclaiming interventionism, administrators embraced state power as a means of regulating migration and structuring the imperial economy. In regulating indenture, state personnel assumed the authority to coordinate and coerce, not just to protect.

Yet the discursive effect, for Stanley and others, was to legitimize indenture by distancing it from slavery. As Stanley explained to Parliament, government agents would be installed in India to protect against deceptive recruitment practices and ensure that ships carried adequate provisions. In Mauritius, another set of agents would verify the number of disembarking workers and perform inspections. Labor contracts would be signed in Mauritius as opposed to India and limited to one year (one of many aspects that would change by the end of the decade). After five years, workers would be entitled to free passage back to India. These measures, among others, led Stanley to conclude that the new indenture system—unlike the old, private system—would have nothing "in the slightest degree indicating the most remote approach to slavery or forced labour."[77] Regulation was thus a means of justifying indenture—of refiguring it as a form of free labor against the scandals of the 1830s.

Regulating Indenture: Private Interest and the State

From the middle of the nineteenth century onward, imperial officials regularly referred to the 1830s as a distinct phase in the history of indenture, separate from the state-regulated system that took shape during the 1840s. On this view, the temporary prohibition on emigration issued in 1839 marked a radical disjuncture. An early, unregulated system—"entirely under the direction of private enterprise," as the Court of Directors put it—ended.[78] In its place there emerged, beginning in 1842, a government-controlled system, in which the "strict superintendence of Government Officers" protected migrants.[79] Contemporary historians have often reinforced this periodization in separating the early history of Indian indenture from what subsequently occurred across the nineteenth century.[80]

State regulation was important, but our inherited tendency to conceptualize the 1830s and 1840s as distinct phases is misleading. Doing so served an instrumental purpose for officials, as we have seen: by emphasizing the novelty of regulation, officials distinguished "immigration" from the widely condemned "coolie trade." Yet in reality, important lines of continuity bridged the apparent divide of 1839. From the beginning, state power facilitated private immigration. With the formal creation of a state-regulated system in 1842, that power was used not only to protect workers, but also to expand the economic project begun in the 1830s. In this sense, the line between public and private blurred. Regulation was not imposed top-down; instead, organized lobbying helped shape the rules ultimately put in place. What becomes clear is that the invention of state regulation served to facilitate particular private interests. Those interests, in turn, shaped the state's regulatory aims and capacities.

To begin to see continuity across the prohibition of 1839, it is first important to recognize that the state did play a meaningful role in the 1830s. When Gladstone sought to bring Indian workers to British Guiana, he petitioned the Colonial Office for permission to engage in multiyear contracts, then illegal under local law. The colonial secretary, Lord Glenelg, obliged.[81] Though Glenelg's decision soon attracted criticism, it demonstrated the willingness of state institutions to accommodate labor migration during the purportedly private period. The Government of India began regulating emigration in 1837, when it introduced transport restrictions and a licensing system for recruiters, who were prohibited from engaging workers without government approval.[82] In Mauritius, meanwhile, the local government enacted a law requiring those seeking to hire immigrant labor to request and receive permission from the colony's governor.[83] Permission under this process was routinely granted.[84] But the point remains that the home, Indian, and colonial administrations all helped structure the process of indentured labor migration during the 1830s, before the formal creation of a state-regulated system. After 1842, this early history of state involvement was forgotten.

Second, though it would be wrong to minimize the importance of the prohibition on emigration instituted by the Court of Directors and Government of India in 1839, many Company officials, including those who loudly criticized the apparent mistreatment of indentured laborers, viewed the prohibition as a temporary measure. Lord Auckland, whose misgivings about the capacity of regulation to prevent abuse were persistent, nonetheless saw complete prohibition as "most objectionable in principle" and argued that Act XIV of 1839 "should not be regarded as permanent."[85] W. W. Bird, the Government of India councilor who objected most strenuously to "unrestricted emigration," similarly acknowledged that the prohibition "was intended only to be in force until adequate measures for the protection of such persons could be devised by the Legislative."[86] The ultimate goal of the Indian administration, then, was to modify rather than end indentured labor migration. The prohibition of 1839 was an important reaction to the growing scandal of indenture. But it was not instituted as an attack on the ends of labor migration—creating a new labor force to sustain recently emancipated plantation economies. In this sense, it was not a radical rejection of indenture, but rather part of a planned transition toward a reformed system of migration.

Most important, the manner in which specific regulations were devised revealed that the state worked with, not against, the very interests that had propelled indenture in the 1830s. State regulation was not forced on planting interests by decree, as implied by the stark division between private and public in official accounts of the history of indenture. Instead, regulation emerged through a process of exchange between private actors and colonial officials—a process that began during the late 1830s. As indenture became a public scandal, some proponents argued that employers had the right to engage labor without government interference. But organized planting interests eventually adopted a different strategy, embracing the cause of regulation as a means of facilitating further migration. The influence of these interests on the regulatory apparatus that eventually developed was significant: private groups helped shape specific regulatory mandates as well as official appointments made to effect state supervision.

Integral to this process was the formation of organized lobbying groups in Mauritius and London. In December 1839, months after the Indian government's formal ban on emigration went into effect, an Emigration Committee was created in Mauritius with the express purpose of re-establishing Indian migration to the colony.[87] Though technically private, the Committee had close links to local government from its inception. Composed mainly of prominent planters, several of the Committee's members also served as elected members of the colony's Legislative Council. In January 1840, after the organization received official recognition, Governor Nicolay appointed the colony's colonial secretary, George F. Dick, to serve as a member of the Committee.[88] Between 1839 and 1841, the Committee corresponded with the governor, regularly apprising him of its activities and recommendations.

The Committee, which renamed itself the "Free Labor Association" in March 1840, did more than simply advocate against the Indian ban on emigration. Assuming quasi-public functions, the organization developed immigration plans with increasing specificity, which were then sent to the local and imperial governments.[89] In formulating these plans, the Free Labor

Association embraced the cause of state regulation. Writing to several London trading houses invested in Mauritian sugar, the group explained that it had devised "a scheme for the introduction of Labourers from abroad under regulations calculated to prevent . . . abuse."[90] In subsequent correspondence, it consistently emphasized its interest in devising "every guarantee for the due protection of the Emigrant."[91] Dissatisfaction with the results of emancipation undoubtedly underlay these efforts. To its many correspondents the Association repeatedly complained of labor shortages, which it viewed as the result of "the abrupt abolition of the apprenticeship of the Negroes" and of a general "withdraw[al]" of freedpeople from the plantations.[92] But in pursuing new sources of immigrant labor, the lobbying group advanced rather than rejected the need for government regulation.

Minutes of the Free Labor Association's meetings reveal that in various respects its regulation plans were similar to those adopted concurrently by the Colonial Office. In early 1840, Charles Anderson—a committee member and future official in the regulated system established in 1842—proposed that recruitment be centralized in a "regular system" and "brought under the comptrol [*sic*] and surveillance of a public office, or Body such as the Emigration Committee."[93] A detailed plan produced in May recommended the appointment of resident recruiting agents in Calcutta and Madras; transport regulations in line with those set forth in the Colonial Passengers Act; and a fixed scale of wages and rations.[94] These features all figured in the proposal for renewed labor migration that John Russell presented to Parliament during the same period.

Intensifying its lobbying efforts, the Free Labor Association enlisted paid advocates in England and India to distribute its plans for regulated migration and petition the home and Indian governments on the subject. In January 1840, the Association sent Charles Anderson to London to coordinate advocacy efforts with a group of absentee proprietors.[95] In September, the group retained Thomy Hugon, a civil servant in Bengal who had previously investigated the treatment of immigrants in Mauritius, to pursue a similar advocacy program in India.[96] Both agents received copies of the Association's immigration plans to present to Colonial Office and Government of India officials. To Anderson, the Committee reflected on its mission in a manner that emphasized its quasi-public role. "You are aware," they wrote,

> that the Committee which you represent, although authorised by the Governor of the Colony[,] is really a private Body, which in its own Interests, as well as those of the Colony at large, has undertaken a task, which brings with it, a great degree of responsibility, inasmuch as the publick has not been consulted

> on the plan which we have adopted, and which nevertheless, in consequence of the countenance we have received from the Local Government, is likely to be adopted, by the Secretary of State for the Colonies, and thus affect the public at large.[97]

This may have exaggerated the Committee's influence, but as a statement of intention it is nonetheless striking: the Committee's goal was to write state policy.

To that end, the Committee took pains to shape the information officials relied on. In London, Anderson did indeed correspond with the secretary of state, Lord Russell. Arguing that indenture was both necessary and moral, Anderson laid out an account of labor relations that the Colonial Office would ultimately accept: the end of apprenticeship had produced a drastic "scarcity of labourers"; state regulation would "completely remove" the kinds of abuse found to have permeated the "former system" of labor migration; and indenture would improve the "state and condition of the emigrants" themselves, relieving British Indian authorities from "the expense of supporting many thousands of her starving population."[98] By 1841, anticipating a reversal of policy at the Colonial Office, the Association pressed Governor Smith to prepare for the arrival of Indian immigrants and advocate for the removal of the ban on Indian emigration.[99] In the spring, it developed a parliamentary strategy for the same purpose, which involved distributing its regulatory plans "to all members of both Houses" and attempting to convince specific MPs to support Indian labor migration.[100]

In London, meanwhile, the Free Labor Association's correspondents were hardly alone. From the early 1840s onward, the West India Committee—the influential voice of the Caribbean sugar interest in London—engaged in persistent advocacy in favor of re-establishing Indian indentured labor migration. From the time of the American Revolution, the Committee had centralized lobbying efforts on behalf of West Indian planters and merchants.[101] Funded through self-imposed assessments on imported sugar, the organization steadily opposed abolitionism through the early nineteenth century, and subsequently pushed to increase compensation payments for slave owners after abolition.[102] The Committee failed to prevent abolition, but its ongoing activity helped shape the process of emancipation.

In correspondence with the Colonial Office, the West India Committee deployed a range of arguments in favor of indentured labor migration. A memorial drafted by the organization's specially appointed Immigration Committee claimed an abstract right to "hire free labourers wherever they may be found" and argued that limitations on free migration hurt workers as well as employers.[103] Alongside such claims was the persistent assertion that economic decline was inevitable without additional labor. "Such is the lamentable state of the principal West India Colonies," the Committee claimed, "that unless a considerable number of laborers be introduced without delay, very many more estates must be abandoned."[104] In this context, only "continuous immigration" could "restor[e] beneficial cultivation."[105]

But like the Free Labor Association, the West India Committee eventually came to support the idea of creating a government-regulated immigration system, especially after Indian migration to Mauritius was legalized in 1842. Again, the state did not impose regulation from above; planters' lobbying groups embraced the idea as a means of reviving indenture. In May 1844, the West India Committee developed a detailed proposal for regulated migration from India to Jamaica, British Guiana, and Trinidad.[106] In June, a subcommittee led by Henry Barkly met with G. W. Hope, the undersecretary of state for the colonies, who shared the Colonial Office's own strategy for regulated migration from India to the West Indies.[107] The Colonial Office plan, which was then sent to the Board of Control for the Affairs of India as part of ongoing negotiations on the subject, was strikingly similar, although more detailed, to what the West India Committee had suggested.[108]

Recent scholarship has emphasized the importance of networks across seemingly separate regions in shaping imperial rule.[109] By facilitating the circulation of people and ideas, these networks created not only "radial" links between Britain and individual colonies, but "transverse" or "trans-colonial" connections among colonies.[110] Cementing these connections was the fact that career administrators moved frequently through term postings on multiple continents.[111] With regard to indenture, the study of lobbying helps us understand not just *that* but *how* imperial networks were formed. For in addition to shaping regulatory rules, private lobbying also influenced the appointments made when the regulated system was instituted. At the heart of the Colonial Office's plan for West Indian migration was the assertion that public officers paid by colonial governments, rather than private recruiters and others motivated by a desire for individual gain, would oversee each aspect of the system. "The principle of the plan," the Colonial Office assured the Indian authorities, "is that it should be entirely conducted by public officers."[112] This was true, but it was also true that many of the public officers ultimately appointed to oversee the system had close links to the private planting interests described above.

Regulatory expertise and private lobbying were thus connected. In 1843, Charles Anderson, the paid advocate of the Free Labor Association in London, was named Acting Protector of Immigrants in Mauritius. He subsequently became Protector of Immigrants, the chief government officer responsible for overseeing the indenture system in the colony. His successor, in 1847, was Thomy Hugon, the Association's former agent in Calcutta. Hugon held the position through the late 1850s. The officer appointed emigration agent for Madras, meanwhile, was recommended to Lord Stanley by the West India Committee.[113] Henry Barkly, who during the early 1840s actively petitioned for the resumption of immigration as a member of the Committee, later oversaw large expansions of the indenture system, first as governor of British Guiana between 1848 and 1853, and then as governor of Mauritius, between 1863 and 1870. Not only did planters' lobbying groups have access to imperial decision-makers, they also had influence over, and in some cases exercised themselves, the practical implementation of regulatory functions. In this sense, too, the boundaries, sources, and instruments of state regulatory power were fluid, not distinctly separate from the ostensibly private realms of trade and industry.

Meanwhile, if regulation put limits on working conditions, it also helped make larger-scale migration possible. Transport from India was expensive, particularly to the West Indies. Both the Free Labor Association and the West India Committee argued that public funds should be used to subsidize costs. Their appeal depended partly on the assertion that indenture was "a matter of great public interest."[114] But they also framed financial assistance as a necessary exchange for regulatory concessions made to protect immigrants. If binding contracts were limited in time, the Association argued, then the state should bear the cost of transportation.[115] The West India Committee went further, calling for Parliament to guarantee immigration loans—that is, for funding indenture with public debt.[116]

Both measures—local government funding and parliamentary loans—became important features of the regulated indenture system. In consultation with the Free Labor Association, the government of Mauritius instituted a tax on spirits to create an immigration fund.[117] In the West Indies, colonial governments incurred large public debts to pay for migration, particularly in the 1840s and 1850s. British Guiana borrowed £170,000 from private creditors in 1845 and an additional £250,000 guaranteed by Parliament beginning in 1850. Trinidad received nearly £200,000 in similar loans, and, like British Guiana, used import taxes to subsidize long-term costs.[118] Debt financing had regressive redistributive effects, as we will see in greater detail in chapter 3. Here, the simple point is that public funding allowed for migration on a larger scale than would otherwise have been possible. In 1843 alone, 34,525 Indian immigrants disembarked in Mauritius, more than the combined total from the 1830s.[119] In British Guiana and Trinidad, nearly 18,000 indentured Indians arrived between 1845 and 1848.[120]

In this respect, too, the transition from unregulated to regulated migration was marked by continuity rather than disjuncture. In the crucial period between 1839 and 1841, the private interests responsible for unregulated labor migration successfully petitioned for financial support from the state. In a broad sense, then, the establishment of state regulation bolstered the economic project begun in the 1830s. The goal was to use immigrant labor to restructure post-slavery labor markets and to restore and eventually increase colonial sugar production. Government regulation was protective, but it was also enabling. It reinforced the economic aims of labor migration, which remained consistent across the divide of 1839.

That lobbyists sought to influence policy should come as no surprise; parliamentary lobbies became common in the eighteenth century, and the West India Committee's campaign against abolition is familiar to historians of Britain and the Atlantic world.[121] What is surprising is the fact that sugar interests embraced state regulation in the ways we have just seen. Indeed, the point worth underscoring concerns the disjunction between public debate and private advocacy as the regulated indenture system was created. In public, regulation was framed as a check on private exploitation by an impartial state. Yet behind the scenes, there was no such distinction between public power and private interest. Lobbyists helped shape both the rules put in place and the appointments made to implement them. "State" power was hybrid, and it contained within it a continuity of interests even as its assertion distanced indenture from slavery in public discourse.

Regulation, Emancipation, and the Radical Critique of Indenture

As these proposals for state regulation took shape, antislavery critics continued their appeals. As we have seen, a wide range of observers—from the antislavery activist John Scoble to the liberal-conservative *Times*—argued that indenture resembled slavery. But "antislavery" was a constellation of ideas and commitments, not a unified policy.[122] At the same time, a different and more radical line of critique emerged in response to proposals for regulated migration. This radical critique has generally escaped the attention of historians focused on the relation between slavery and indenture.[123] Yet its recovery is worthwhile, for in revealing horizons of conceptual possibility, it shows us how competing notions of *emancipation* structured early debate on indenture. An expansive view of emancipation—as a process of socio-economic, not just legal, change—underlay the radical critique of indenture. For these writers, as for Walter Rodney years later, indenture threatened to undermine that process for both indentured immigrants and freedpeople.[124]

By 1839, the key issue was not whether labor migration had produced unseemly abuse but rather whether state regulation could curb that abuse. In this context, the British and Foreign Anti-Slavery Society called into question the very idea of government regulation in post-slavery society. The critique that resulted was systemic. New laws would have little effect in unreformed plantation societies, radical critics argued. Individual instances of abuse could not simply be stamped out; mistreatment was the normal and necessary product of plantation production. Indeed, this was a critique of plantation society, where "the spirit and usages of slavery" remained despite formal abolition.[125]

In early 1840, Joseph Sturge, the Quaker activist who helped found the British and Foreign Anti-Slavery Society, introduced this argument to the readers of the *Anti-Slavery Reporter*, the Society's bimonthly newspaper.[126] Sturge's approach to indenture and emancipation was strikingly anti-formalistic; his basic premise was that law did not transform society on its own. "Although slavery is legally abolished in our colonies," he wrote, "its spirit yet remains in full force." Thus, laws enacted in the metropole would do little to protect migrant laborers. "The free emigrant would find too late," he warned, "that the enactments in this country of the most impartial and humane laws would not save him from oppression, in the present state of colonial feeling."[127]

Underlying these claims were two more specific arguments about the relation between indentured labor migration and emancipation. First, the *Anti-Slavery Reporter* portrayed immigration as a scheme designed to thwart the progress of emancipation by reinforcing asymmetries in the labor market. In this view, altering the terms of that market was a central part of the project of emancipation. As an article published in February 1840 explained, "If there be a sufficient demand for labour, bad masters will get no work-people; and thus, in order to get work done, they will be obliged to become better masters." In this sense, a "healthy state of the market for labour" was "the practical cure for habits of oppression."[128] Labor migration, meanwhile, was a calculated effort to prevent the labor market from reaching this "healthy state." Importing additional labor would decrease demand, solidifying planters' control over the terms and conditions of employment. "If the planters can dictate the terms of labour," the *Reporter* concluded, "they will perpetuate the habits of slavery." Their "love of ease and power" would "never yield but to necessity."[129]

The second key argument was similarly anti-formalistic and skeptical with regard to the capacity of legal reform to safeguard the interests of indentured immigrants. Its core proposition was that since white minorities controlled both politics and the administration of justice in the West Indies, the law—as a process rather than as a body of doctrine—would ultimately fail to protect freedpeople and indentured laborers. In this context, "no substantial justice" could be expected for "the Asiatic labourer, or the emancipated Negro."[130] Drawing attention to the relationship between civil and political rights, the Anti-Slavery Society argued that regulation would necessarily fail because Indian immigrants, like the formerly enslaved, lacked "social and political equality."[131]

These arguments questioning the power of imperial regulation drew on related critiques of apprenticeship, which forced that system's early end in 1838.[132] The connection was no mere coincidence. Sturge had published an important critique of apprenticeship after traveling to the Caribbean in 1836.[133] Lord Brougham similarly emphasized the relationship between class and the administration of justice in debate on the subject in the House of Lords.[134] In the sugar colonies, "pretended ameliorations" were necessarily specious, wrote the *British Emancipator*.[135] Slavery had to be abolished "root and branch"; only then would "absolute and unrestricted freedom" be achieved.[136] From this perspective, indenture, like apprenticeship, was part of a larger effort to "reduce the nominal freemen to a condition of serfs" and "circumscribe the market for free labor."[137] Any attempt to create a "middle state between slavery and freedom" was an unacceptable subversion of the principle of emancipation.[138]

Similarly structural critiques emerged in India around the same time.[139] Focusing particularly on deceptive recruiting practices, the report of the Calcutta Committee warned that "scarcely any human precaution would avail to prevent a repetition of abuses."[140] The *Friend of India*, meanwhile, cast doubt on the ability of regulation to protect indentured emigrants. "No agency which Government can establish," the paper claimed, "will be adequate to prevent a repetition of those scenes of fraud, violence, and villany [*sic*], which have filled the minds of men with horror."[141] Like the *Anti-Slavery Reporter*, the *Friend of India* saw indenture as a means of structurally subverting the project of emancipation by reshaping post-slavery labor markets in favor of plantation owners. The ultimate goal, the paper suggested, was to "deprive those negroes of the just price of their labour at the period of emancipation, by the introduction of five years' apprentices from India, upon lower wages."[142] On this view, the purpose of regulation was not protection but rather legitimization. Repeatedly the paper warned that state regulation would only serve to "legalize" what would otherwise seem blatantly improper—"a *trade* in the sinews, and muscles, and blood, and bodies of men!"[143]

Meanwhile, the radical critique of indenture also took aim at state subsidies for indenture. Such subsidies depended on colonial taxation, whose burden fell primarily on the formerly enslaved.[144] This was "an act of gross oppression," argued one petition organized by the London Missionary Society, for it would redistribute wealth from the poor to the rich.[145] At the very same time, migration would create a "glut of labour" and decrease wages, according to the *Anti-Slavery Reporter*.[146] This was the crux of the argument: emancipated populations were being taxed to support an immigration system decidedly against their own economic interests. In the spring of 1842, responding to a proposal for recruiting labor from the west coast of Africa, the *Reporter* criticized "the avowed purpose of reducing the wages of labour paid to the lately emancipated slaves."[147] In 1844, citing the "deep injury it [immigration] will inflict on the emancipated classes," Thomas Clarkson condemned immigration subsidies as a matter of "inhumanity as well as injustice."[148] These arguments the Society would consistently restate and expand over the course of the decade.[149]

It is sometimes assumed that legal formalism shaped British views of post-emancipation societies around the middle of the nineteenth century, differentiating slavery from freedom in an unambiguous manner.[150] But like the outcry against apprenticeship, attacks on state subsidies for indenture reveal a systemic approach to post-slavery freedom. For the *Anti-Slavery Reporter*, condemnation of indenture was intimately related to a broad vision of emancipation as a process of social and political transformation. At this early stage, the *Reporter* argued that, in addition to legal freedom from bondage, emancipation was meant to institute "real equality with the whites."[151] From this premise, indentured labor was cast as a structural subversion of the process of emancipation. It would preserve asymmetries in the West Indian labor market and maintain the class structure of plantation society. The radical critique of indenture did not merely suggest that indenture resembled slavery. It also suggested that without civil and political rights, exploitation would necessarily persist, and the meaning of freedom would be significantly circumscribed. Radical critics understood "freedom" and "free labor" in a particularly expansive manner. Their vision did not last.

2

Free Labor Contested: Indenture and the Limits of Freedom, 1838–1849

As we have seen, early indenture experiments created a significant public scandal. Observers from within the antislavery movement and beyond portrayed Indian labor migration not as free labor but rather as a covert revival of slavery. State regulation helped quiet that scandal, but not the deep moral, social, and economic ambiguities latent in the project of emancipation. The "problem of freedom" remained unresolved. In private official correspondence, the scandal of indenture persisted in a different register, as imperial administrators struggled to articulate and uphold competing visions of post-slavery free labor.

This chapter examines the conceptual and practical implications of legal conflicts surrounding the meaning of free labor as the indenture system developed during the 1840s. While planters and imperial authorities both used state regulation to justify the resumption of labor migration in 1842, profound disagreements over the proper scope and content of regulation remained. For much of the decade, officials in London prevented local colonial authorities from intensifying legal restrictions on indentured workers. Underlying these conflicts, as this chapter shows, were competing conceptions of freedom and free labor. Planters and local authorities argued that non-European workers were naturally inclined to "Sloth" and therefore unfit for "unbounded Independence."[1] The Colonial Office rejected this theory, at least initially, and the restrictive laws it implied. Instead, London insisted on a universalistic conception of free-labor efficiency. This perspective set limits on the category of free labor: laws that directly compelled workers to stay on the plantations for long periods of time were not free enough.

Like the public scandal of indenture, these legal conflicts were part of the broader pattern of change explained over the course of this book. Over time,

London's resistance to long contracts and strict absence penalties would diminish. Race-based justifications for direct legal compulsion would in turn displace the liberal universalism that underpinned regulation in the 1840s. Chapters 3, 4, and 5 detail these transformations in law and legal ideology. But that result should not be taken for granted. The category of free labor was made and remade, through negotiation and conflict, over the course of three decades. In the 1840s, the Colonial Office did not simply acquiesce to local demands for heightened labor discipline. Competing views of the colonial subject, of the Indian, "coolie" worker, divided the category of free labor.

After examining the statutory effects of these conflicts, the chapter then turns to their practical implications. In this and other contexts, it is wrong to assume that doctrine determined practice. What, then, did free labor mean on the ground? How did legal-ideological conflict affect the reality of labor control in the colonies? Local authorities failed to enforce strict labor discipline as the indenture system took shape. As London disallowed heightened indenture restrictions, state weakness further limited enforcement in practice. At the same time, local environmental, demographic, and economic factors fractured labor relations. Many indentured workers left the plantations; for some, that meant more freedom, but for others it meant deprivation, even death. Thus the everyday enforcement of labor control remained unstable, like the law's ideological contours. As we will see in the next chapter, this material instability played an important role in shaping ideological beliefs and priorities during the late 1840s and 1850s.

Legislative Structure: Colonial and Imperial Lawmaking in the Sugar Colonies

Before proceeding, it is important to turn briefly to legislative structure and the nature of the archival sources used to make the arguments that follow. British Guiana, Trinidad, and Mauritius were Crown colonies taken from foreign powers during the Napoleonic Wars (Guiana from the Dutch in 1796, Trinidad from the Spanish in 1797, and Mauritius from the French in 1810).[2] In contrast to Jamaica, which had an elected assembly, British Guiana, Trinidad, and Mauritius had only limited rights of self-government. As Crown colonies, each had a legislative council composed of "official" and "unofficial" members, as well as a governor appointed by the Colonial Office. Official members of council were appointed senior officeholders such as the attorney general. Unofficial members were prominent residents, often planters, who were either appointed or elected.[3] In British Guiana, an additional elected body of "financial representatives" had special authority over appropriations decisions.[4]

In this context, colonial lawmaking was both centralized and decentralized. Legislative councils had the authority to enact ordinances regulating local matters, including labor, taxation, and policing. As a result, British Guiana, Trinidad, and Mauritius each had formally separate bodies of law regulating contract terms and penalties for absence throughout the period of indenture. To remain valid, however, local ordinances had to be submitted to and approved by the Colonial Office, the department of the home government responsible for colonial administration. The Colonial Office could either confirm or "disallow," that is, repeal, the ordinances it received. London also had authority to legislate directly for the colonies, through either acts of Parliament or ministerial decrees (known as "royal orders" or "orders in council") issued by the Colonial Office. Finally, the Government of India had authority to regulate emigration; over time it set out increasingly detailed restrictions pertaining to recruitment and transportation.[5]

Colonial laws of indenture were thus subject to two levels of imperial oversight, in Britain and India.[6] The Colonial Office could disallow local laws directly, while the Government of India could refuse to allow migration to colonies whose laws were deemed inadequate. These pressures produced an informal tendency toward centralization. When one colony received permission to enact a certain kind of provision, others made claims for the same privilege on the basis of precedent, often borrowing explicitly from the text of laws already approved.[7] Legal norms circulated not only between metropole and colony, but through more complex channels, between Britain and India, and among the several indenture colonies. Like goods and people, law "traveled," as the unsteady product of negotiation across these multiple spaces.[8]

These bureaucratic processes produced large amounts of regular reporting, from which we can now reconstruct extensive official debates about the nature of free labor.[9] Local colonial governments engaged in lengthy correspondence with the Colonial Office each time new labor laws were enacted. Some laws occasioned parallel correspondence between the Colonial Office and the Court of Directors of the East India Company. These records—dispersed among the separate files of each colony—are the primary source material for the first half of this chapter, as well as later discussions of legal change in chapters 3, 4, and 5. Archivally, this material allows us to reconstruct statutory development. But just as important, it serves as a window into the kind of reasoning, legal and otherwise, that motivated conflict and change. What follows, then, is an analysis of "legal ideology," or the sociocultural perceptions underlying legal decision-making. Instead of assuming that law fulfilled pre-existing needs, the goal is to show how ideological debates regarding race, personhood, and the nature of freedom structured legal change.

Legal Foundations: A Framework for Free Labor

Abolition ended formal slavery without defining freedom. The dismantling of slave codes thus left a legal void. The Abolition Act of 1833 set out terms for apprenticeship, requiring freedpeople to continue working on plantations while regulating labor conditions and forms of punishment.[10] But beyond apprenticeship, London intentionally delayed lasting legal reform.[11] In Mauritius and the West Indies, local authorities enacted a range of new laws making wage labor mandatory and imposing strict anti-vagrancy penalties.[12] Deemed unacceptably coercive, these laws the Colonial Office refused to accept.[13] Instead, the colonial secretary, Lord Glenelg, sought to purge local law of "vestiges of racial discrimination," as Thomas Holt has explained, and to guarantee "personal freedom" in a "full and unlimited sense."[14] By the summer of 1838, as apprenticeship neared its end, there was little agreement over the nature of post-slavery free labor.

It was in this context that the laws of indenture initially took shape. Convinced that "the old slave code exercised a very powerful influence" on existing colonial laws, the Colonial Office decided to legislate directly.[15] Between 1838 and 1842, it issued a series of orders in council creating a new framework for contract labor in the colonies. As part of a larger effort to prepare for complete emancipation, these orders aimed to establish principles of employment law (the law of "master and servant") applicable to both freedpeople and indentured migrants.

In the fall of 1838, the task of drafting these orders fell to James Stephen, the permanent undersecretary of state. The son of a prominent abolitionist, Stephen had significant ties to the Clapham Sect. He began working for the Colonial Office as a legal adviser in 1813 and became permanent undersecretary in 1836, a post he held until 1847. Throughout his tenure, he had primary responsibility for reviewing West Indian legislation. His knowledge of colonial labor law was extensive and his influence on policy was quietly forceful, as suggested by the derisive moniker used by some of his critics, "Mr. Oversecretary."[16] In 1833, Stephen was the primary author of the Abolition Bill, which he drafted in a single forty-eight-hour period.[17] Afterward, his internal memoranda on legal matters frequently became dispatches sent (nominally by the colonial secretary) to individual colonies.[18] Though rarely given to public advocacy, Stephen was an abolitionist. Within the Colonial Office, he was the figure most wary of veiled attempts to perpetuate forced labor after abolition. Stephen refused to sanction stringent labor laws enacted in the colonies, which he feared would "reestablish under the shelter of new titles, the Offices, and much of the authority, which are the peculiar characteristics of

Slavery."[19] As apprenticeship drew to a close, Stephen favored direct intervention in colonial affairs as a means of safeguarding the rights of freedpeople.[20]

Stephen's 1838 orders pertaining to employment and vagrancy embodied the Colonial Office's effort to define a workable form of free labor in the early period of emancipation. They also created a framework that would initially control the legal terms of indenture. From the outset, this framework proved unacceptable to planter elites and local colonial officials, setting the stage for extensive debate over the nature of free labor. In short, Stephen's orders revealed principles thought to be essential to freedom in the period in which indenture began. Against this baseline, one can track competing visions of that illusive notion, and the process by which Stephen's original vision was gradually displaced.

No longer in use, the term "master and servant" referred (in 1838 and throughout the period) to employment relations in the context of wage labor. In Stephen's order on the subject, the "servant" in question was any person contracted to perform "bodily labour in agriculture or manufactures."[21] The order, sent to the colonies in September 1838, set forth restrictions on the kind of contracts that could be made and the appropriate means of enforcing those contracts. With regard to the first imperative, the order limited the maximum length of verbal contracts to four weeks and that of written contracts to one year. Suspicious of efforts to recruit immigrant labor with deceptive promises, it further stipulated that only contracts made "within the limits and upon the land of the colony" be valid, and that written contracts be signed "in the presence of a stipendiary magistrate." These terms the Colonial Office viewed as the outer limits of free labor. Longer contracts, and contracts signed overseas, were outlawed. All existing law in conflict with the order, the Office explicitly repealed.[22]

Meanwhile, Stephen's master-and-servant order limited the kinds of penalties that could be used to enforce contract terms. Workers found by a stipendiary magistrate not to have completed stipulated tasks could be punished by either fine (in an amount not to exceed one month's wages) or imprisonment (for up to fourteen days, with or without hard labor).[23] Conversely, the punishment for nonpayment of wages by employers was compensatory money damages.[24] Importantly, the order gave exclusive jurisdiction over labor disputes to the stipendiary magistracy, a special judicial body created during apprenticeship and paid for by the Crown.[25] Stipendiary magistrate decisions were final, and no right of appeal was given to local colonial courts, which Stephen distrusted.[26] The broader principle, which Glenelg explained in announcing the orders, was to limit "domestic" or self-enforcement by employers, and to guarantee the "disinterested administration" of the law.[27]

A separate order in council issued on the same day, 7 September 1838, instituted a new code for the prevention of vagrancy. Though significant penalties remained, the order rejected expansive definitions of the offense. Under the new law, failure to secure employment was not enough; the crux was criminality tied to a refusal to work (in a manner deemed respectable). Thus, to be punished as an "idle and disorderly person," an offender would have to engage in begging, prostitution, or "riotous and indecent" behavior.[28] A second-order offense, that of the "rogue and vagabond," required a higher level of disorderly behavior, like public exposure, gambling, weapons possession with felonious intent, or violent resistance to arrest.[29] The punishments for these offenses were fourteen and twenty-eight days' imprisonment with or without hard labor, respectively.[30] But the order made it impossible to prosecute those unwilling to work on plantations and capable of supporting themselves independently for vagrancy. In Stephen's view, "mere indolence, unattended with positive criminality, or direct injury to others" was not "an offence properly falling within the cognizance of human laws."[31]

When indentured labor migration resumed under state regulation, Stephen's orders applied to newly arriving Indian workers in addition to freedpeople. In 1842, as the home government sanctioned Indian labor migration to Mauritius, the Colonial Office issued an additional order setting out foundational legal principles for the regulation of indenture.[32] The bulk of that order concerned recruitment and transportation, including the appointment of salaried emigration agents in India and the supplies required for individual ships.[33] But the order also imposed important restrictions on labor. First, it prohibited labor contracts signed in advance, in India; only contracts signed in Mauritius forty-eight hours after initial arrival would be valid.[34] Second, the order stipulated that contract terms and disputes be governed by existing master-and-servant law, that is, Stephen's 1838 orders.[35] The same arrangement applied when the indenture system was extended to British Guiana and Trinidad in 1844.[36]

As a framework for free-labor relations, these orders should be interpreted in the wider context of English master-and-servant law. Certain provisions that appear anomalous from a modern standpoint were in fact familiar features of the English legal landscape dating back to the fourteenth century. Penal sanctions for breach of contract, for example, were first instituted under the Statute of Laborers (1350–1351), which was enacted in response to labor shortages caused by the Black Death.[37] The Statute of Artificers (1562) reconstituted a similar employment framework, fixing wages and rendering workers who failed to complete their contracts liable to imprisonment.[38] Like the Statute of Laborers, the Statute of Artificers also made labor compulsory under certain circumstances for those unemployed and without apparent means.[39] From this point onward, master-and-servant laws, which proliferated not only in England but throughout the empire, commonly provided for summary enforcement of contract provisions by lay magistrates and punishment of workers for breach not by damages but rather imprisonment, forced labor, and other seemingly criminal penalties.[40]

As Robert Steinfeld has argued, the rise of market society did not immediately undermine the legal underpinnings of Tudor labor relations.[41] During the eighteenth century, Parliament passed a series of acts extending master-and-servant law to new trades. In 1720, one such act made it illegal for journeymen tailors to leave their employers before finishing their contracts, under penalty of two months' imprisonment with hard labor.[42] In 1766, Parliament extended similar penalties to calico printers, handicraftsmen, miners, colliers, pitmen, and others.[43] These statutes remained on the books and (to varying degrees) continued to be enforced well into the nineteenth century, until their repeal in 1875.[44] In this context, the imposition of fourteen days' imprisonment for certain forms of breach in Stephen's 1838 order was not aberrant; it was in fact a penalty less stringent than some in force in England at the time.

Alongside these developments was of course the important phenomenon of European indentured servitude in colonial America and the Caribbean during the seventeenth and eighteenth centuries. The basic indenture relationship—an agreement to work for a fixed period in exchange for transportation—figured prominently in migration to North America during this period. Scholars originally estimated that between one-half and two-thirds of the European migrants who arrived in the American colonies during the pre-revolutionary period were indentured servants.[45] Christopher Tomlins has revised these figures downward, to between 39 and 49 percent of the total, with a gradual decline during the eighteenth century.[46] But even considering his lower estimates, it is clear that significant numbers of European migrants arrived under indenture and that indentured migration continued, though on a decreasing scale, until the early nineteenth century.[47]

With these histories in mind, one can argue that pre-existing ideas and practices shaped the indentured labor system that emerged in the sugar colonies during the nineteenth century.[48] Certainly the notion of indenture was not new; the legal concept used to hire and bind Indian migrants was a variant on that long used to bring Europeans to the Americas. The penal apparatus used to enforce indenture contracts, meanwhile, had extensive precedent in English employment law. From the fourteenth century onward, significant legal coercion had coexisted with "voluntary" contract labor. Given this context, one might interpret nineteenth-century indenture as a continuation of longstanding practice, as part of a European and imperial landscape in which free labor (in the modern sense) simply did not exist.

But it is also important to bear in mind the differences between nineteenth-century Indian, Chinese, and African indenture, on the one hand, and long-present forms of coercive labor elsewhere, whether under indenture in the Americas or mere contract in England.[49] The existence of these legal forms and practices did not, in and of itself, explain the appearance or eventual public acceptance of indenture in the sugar colonies. Though clearly related at the level of doctrine, these histories followed divergent trajectories in practice. European indenture in the Americas was primarily a seventeenth- and eighteenth-century phenomenon; by the 1820s, it had become highly controversial, and by the 1830s, it ceased to play a role in US labor relations.[50] Around the same time, trade unions began to resist penal master-and-servant laws in England. By the late eighteenth century, a series of decisions at King's Bench had narrowed the scope of such laws, excluding domestic service and task work from their control.[51] In 1844, a well-organized campaign led by Chartists and trade unions pressured Parliament into abandoning a proposed bill that would have expanded existing master-and-servant law.[52] Though older laws continued to be enforced in the 1850s and 1860s, they were ultimately repealed in 1875 under similar forms of public pressure.[53] It was during this same time period that the Indian indenture system was created. During the nineteenth century, as master-and-servant doctrine was questioned and reformed in England and North America, it simultaneously expanded in the empire, and in the former slave colonies in particular. That divergence was important: the legal coercion of post-slavery indenture depended on concepts of race and conditions of production whose history was distinctly imperial.

Equally important, it is clear that contemporaries—both imperial officials and observers from the wider public—viewed post-slavery indenture apart from European indenture and European labor relations more broadly. Nineteenth-century indenture was distinctly non-European; by that stage it was widely believed that Europeans were physically incapable of working the fields in tropical climates.[54] Over the course of the century, concepts of race inapplicable in the domestic context would shape the indenture system, often serving to justify increasingly restrictive laws. In the 1830s and early 1840s, as we have seen, indenture produced a scandal. Despite the prevalence of similarly coercive practices at home, indenture did not simply appear as free labor. This was because indenture was consistently perceived in relation to colonial slavery, not domestic contract labor. Slavery left its own legal legacy—in the form of slave codes—which complicated straightforward comparison between English master-and-servant law and the laws of indenture.

Indeed, the legacy of slavery shaped official thinking on indenture and colonial free labor. Stephen had rejected overbroad vagrancy restrictions effectively rendering labor compulsory as falling outside "the cognizance of human laws." Compulsory labor regulations were part of the Statute of Artificers. But that did not mean the Colonial Office would allow the sugar colonies to enact them after abolition. Glenelg's circular dispatch announcing the 1838 orders referred pointedly to the "very peculiar condition of society existing" in the West Indies.[55] That peculiar condition convinced the Colonial Office that special restrictions were needed to protect free labor against a historical and institutional tendency toward labor coercion.[56] In post-emancipation context, indenture was not simply seen as free labor. That category, as we will see in the next section, remained highly contested.

Free Labor Contested: Legal Conflict in the 1840s

Conflict over the substance of colonial labor law marked the 1840s. That is to say, as the indenture system was built, the notion of free labor was the subject of fierce debate. No uniform "official" view of the laws of indenture held sway. To the contrary, legislative proposals originating in the colonies—which, as a rule, aimed to heighten controls over labor—met resistance and outright disapproval in London. Underlying the conflicts that ensued were distinct views of the boundaries of free labor. From the beginning, local authorities argued that Indian and other non-European workers were racially predisposed to idleness and disorder. Officials in London rejected that assertion, insisting instead on the general applicability and efficiency of market-based work incentives. In short, competing views of the colonial subject—one universal, the other premised on difference—produced sustained disagreement over whether and how law should be used to compel work on the plantations.

As we have seen, the Colonial Office imposed a new legal framework for post-slavery free labor between 1838 and 1842. Its terms, which banned multiyear labor contracts and limited penal sanctions against workers, soon proved unacceptable to planters and political elites in the colonies. In Mauritius, the colony's Legislative Council argued strenuously in favor of longer mandatory contracts. A consistent racial theme underlay these arguments; according to the Council, the Indian worker was incapable of steady, orderly labor without legal compulsion. In July 1845, a special committee tasked with studying labor reached the conclusion that Indians were "by nature averse, and by habit unaccustomed, to steady labor." Marked by a "capricious and roving disposition," indentured Indians would "absent themselves continuously from the Estates, wandering about in idleness." Increased labor coercion was thus perceived as necessary; according to the planters who testified before the committee, only "a prolongation of Engagements to five or three years" could counteract the Indians' supposed predisposition to vagrancy.[57]

Equally important, the committee argued that liberal assumptions about economic behavior could not be applied to Indians (and non-Europeans more broadly). Citing London's initial justification for one-year contracts, the committee argued that Indian habits of idleness undermined free-labor incentives. In 1840, the colonial secretary, Lord Russell, had argued that short contracts would increase labor efficiency by allowing workers and employers to "meet and act towards each other in the spirit, and under the motives, of free men."[58] The committee plainly rejected this line of thinking; in its view, it was "abundantly proved" that Russell's understanding of free labor "d[id] not apply to an Indian population."[59]

Scholars have sometimes assumed that imperial officials acquiesced to local demands in shaping indenture policy.[60] In this early period, however, it is clear that the Colonial Office frequently disagreed with and overruled local proposals. Indeed, when the governor of Mauritius sent the Council's committee report to London, the Colonial Land and Emigration Board dismissed the report's findings. First, the Land Board rejected the notion that Indians were naturally predisposed to vagrancy, emphasizing instead their "orderliness" and "industry." Second, the Board refused the committee's demand for five-year contracts. Long contracts, the London officials argued, would unjustly "fetter those who might find themselves on ineligible Estates or subject to harsh treatment." Meanwhile, the problem of desertion the Board reframed as the "justifiable exercise of the independent choice of free men." In this sense, long contracts appeared as a threat to free labor; the Board rejected the Mauritian proposal because it substituted "the power of enforcing a contract by compulsion for the willing exertions of labourers who make their own bargains."[61]

When William Gladstone became colonial secretary in 1845, he proved similarly unwilling to sanction multiyear contracts for Indian and African workers. In response to lobbying by the West India Committee, Gladstone agreed to permit three-year contracts for Portuguese laborers recruited from Madeira, the Azores, and the Canaries.[62] But he rejected the Committee's more significant requests regarding Indian and African migrants, emphasizing his opposition to "new principles of increased stringency" in the enforcement of existing contracts.[63] In all cases, Gladstone insisted that long contracts were likely to sow discord and prove unenforceable absent physical punishment. “Such inflictions,” he warned the Committee, “are not within the principles of the existing laws, and the enactment of a new law to authorize them, is forbidden by motives of the highest and most conclusive nature.”[64]

Beneath Gladstone’s ambivalence lay concerns regarding “natural” and “artificial” forms of society. Gladstone was not particularly close to the anti-slavery movement, and as we have seen, his father was one of the progenitors of Indian indenture in British Guiana. But like the Anti-Slavery Society, Gladstone understood “freedom” in relation to post-slavery social structure. Sex, religion, education—a range of social factors affected his analysis of indenture, not just legal punishments and safeguards. These concerns he raised particularly in relation to Mauritius, where the scale of Indian migration was largest.[65] At the time, the colony’s Indian population was only 15 percent female.[66] Emphasizing this imbalance, Gladstone feared that indentured Indians were “simple organs of labour,” without opportunities for broader social development.[67] Beginning in 1855, rules requiring fixed percentages of women in the recruitment of new workers would partially insulate indenture against such fears.[68] But here, gender imbalance threatened the civilizing mission Gladstone otherwise believed in. In his view, Mauritius had failed “to bring into action any social and moral influence upon [indentured Indians] for good.” Premised on ongoing temporary migrations rather than permanent settlement, the entire indenture project appeared suspect. It produced a system of labor that was, for Gladstone, “not natural, but artificial”—at odds with the “order of nature” and the “regular constitution of society.”[69]

Gladstone’s tenure as colonial secretary was short lived; in 1846 he was replaced by Earl Grey after the fall of Peel’s second ministry.[70] Grey, who remained colonial secretary until 1852, exercised considerable influence over the indenture system.[71] He did not oppose indenture, but he too had strong views about the nature and limits of free labor. Under his direction, the Colonial Office continued to reject local proposals to heighten vagrancy controls and impose multiyear, fixed-term labor contracts. Grey’s concept of free labor, which depended on universalizing, liberal assumptions about efficiency and self-interest, led to frequent collisions with local officials and planters who increasingly cited non-European difference as a justification for legal coercion.

Such conflicts were manifest in Trinidad as the colony sought to reorganize its labor laws in the summer of 1846.[72] In July, Lord Harris, the colony’s governor, proposed that Indian workers be indentured for ten years in exchange for transportation.[73] James Stephen’s response was to suggest that such an extension “would be a great step towards the introduction of a new kind of slavery,” and the idea was dropped.[74] Around the same time, however, Harris approved a series of new regulations that heightened vagrancy controls used to keep indentured Indians on the plantations.

Called the "Coolie Regulations," these rules aimed simultaneously at protection and coercion.[75] They required that housing provided for indentured Indians meet certain requirements, and that wages be paid on a regular schedule.[76] In addition, they fixed specific rates of wages, along with food and clothing allotments, and set required hours of work.[77] But the "Coolie Regulations" also imposed new restrictions on Indian movement. In particular, they mandated that Indian workers present certificates of discharge before finding new jobs and changing employers.[78] They similarly prohibited indentured workers from leaving their plantations without a signed ticket of leave from an employer, and empowered the police to "take charge of, and send back to their respective Estates, any Coolies they may find wandering over the country unprovided with the above mentioned tickets of leave."[79]

As Harris explained to the Colonial Office, the "Coolie Regulations" were drafted by Major James Fagan, a former Indian military official recently appointed as Trinidad's "Coolie Magistrate."[80] Fagan's role, as Coolie Magistrate, was to superintend indentured Indians, and he framed the regulations in consideration of what Harris described as "the interests of both parties."[81] That framing exemplified a key feature of the emerging ideology of indenture, which tied labor control to the ideal of mutual benefit. Meanwhile, Fagan's experience as an Indian official lent credence to the notion that such control was necessary. Justifying the restrictiveness of the new anti-vagrancy provisions, Harris suggested that the Indian workers who had arrived in Trinidad were "naturally dissolute and depraved in their habits" and therefore "much inclined to fall into habits of drinking and of wandering idle about the country." Though "stringent," the rules were thus necessary, Harris argued; "the close supervision of Government" was needed to prevent "public cases of vagabondage and licentiousness."[82]

Assertions of racial difference did specific work in this context. The "docile" coolie that had featured so prominently in early appeals for indenture disappeared in Harris's account of Indian personhood. Transformed in the face of labor conflict, the notion of the coolie now served to highlight an apparent indisposition to work and a pressing need for special control. Detached from specific geographic referents (Chota Nagpur, for instance), Harris's portrayal emphasized more generalized forms of racial incapacity leading to indolence, vice, and disorder. This altered image of the Indian worker blended with related negative appraisals of African characteristics; what was emphasized in both cases was the racial incapacity of non-European workers. Indeed, a generalized racial logic underlay Harris's subsequent claims in favor of multiyear contracts for freedpeople as well as indentured Indian and African migrants. Only those who lived in the West Indies, Harris wrote, had "a true idea of the careless and desultory habits of the African and Creole races." For Harris, long contracts were "very necessary" as a means of "procuring continued labor"; general theories of free-labor incentives were inapplicable. Special restrictions were needed to combat a special "disinclination to constant employment or continued exertion."[83]

The Colonial Office disallowed Trinidad's "Coolie Regulations" on technical grounds, but "grave objections" of principle bolstered Grey's decision.[84] In particular, Grey rejected Harris's assertion that Indian and African laborers were inherently different and naturally incapable of steady work. "With reference to your statement as to the 'careless and desultory habits of the African and Creole races,'" Grey told Harris, "I believe that this indisposition to regular labour does not arise from any thing peculiar to these races, but that it is owing to the circumstances in which they are placed."[85] Rational, free-labor incentives did apply to non-European workers, Grey further insisted: "when subjected to the influence of the same motives by which men in other countries are impelled to industry, the African is capable of steady and vigorous exertion."[86] If freedpeople had purchased land and leveraged demand to reduce the amount of wage labor needed to subsist in the wake of emancipation, they acted not on particular racial imperatives but rather just as "the European Labourer, who, when enabled by any sudden increase in the demand for labour to obtain a large increase of Wages, almost invariably avails himself of this to diminish the number of hours, or of the days in the week, which he devotes to labour."[87] Applying this framework of analysis, Grey rejected not only the vagrancy restrictions embodied in Fagan's regulations but also Harris's ongoing calls for longer contracts.[88]

These views Grey reinforced in correspondence with Mauritius, where the local government similarly attempted to enact heightened master-and-servant laws in 1846. According to William Gomm, the colony's governor, the Legislative Council's particular aim in revising Stephen's 1838 order in council was to suppress a "disposition" among indentured laborers to abandon work.[89] But Grey disallowed the amended law they enacted—Ordinance No. 1 of 1846—arguing that local attempts to restrict workers' freedom were "unjust and oppressive." The ordinance contained "tacit consent" clauses that provided for the automatic renewal of verbal contracts absent affirmative nonconsent. These clauses Grey saw as subjecting Indian workers, "ignorant alike of the language and habits of the country," to a "perpetual engagement." Like Fagan's regulations, the ordinance required a certificate of discharge in order to change employers; this measure Grey similarly condemned as a method of "compel[ing] the Laborer, whether he would or not, to re-engage with his former Employer." Additional fines imposed by the ordinance for neglect of work and absence, meanwhile, Grey considered "unnecessary and unadvisable."[90]

In elaborating these and other objections, Grey explicitly rejected the race-based logic previously promoted by the Mauritian Legislative Council as well as by Governor Harris in Trinidad. In its place, Grey asserted a more universal theory of free-labor efficiency. "Where the motives of self-interest are properly brought to bear upon their conduct," he wrote, "there are few, if any, among the various races of mankind, who may not be stimulated to industry."[91] The "original error" of the proposed law, then, was the "principle of endeavouring by Law to enforce upon the Immigrants the due performance of the obligations to labour." No level of compulsion short of slavery, Grey argued, could "succeed in enforcing really efficient labour." In this sense, the "true policy" of indenture was to promote labor discipline through self-interest rather than legal coercion—to create a "situation in which they [indentured Indians] might be acted upon by the same motives by which men are impelled to labour in countries in which industry flourishes."[92] Applying these principles, Grey strictly prohibited contracts lasting longer than one year. "The full liberty of making the most he can of his labour," he asserted, "is absolutely essential to give the labourer an adequate stimulus to render, by his skill, and his industry, that labour as valuable as possible." Longer contracts, in his view, were both impermissibly unfree and unacceptably inefficient. Only short contracts would result in "real industry, from free labourers."[93]

Similar fault lines dividing the category of free labor appeared in correspondence between the Colonial Office and British Guiana. In February 1848, British Guiana passed a new immigration ordinance that substantially altered the existing terms of indenture.[94] The new ordinance centralized the colony's system of recruitment and "allotment" (that is, its system for assigning newly arrived workers to individual plantations). Under the law, planters seeking to hire Indian immigrants would apply directly to the colony's chief immigration official, the Agent General of Immigration.[95] Eliminating competitive bargaining among employers, the law then directed the Agent General simply to assign newly arrived immigrants "to the various applicants."[96] In addition, it authorized fixed, three-year contracts.[97] Both of these changes represented substantial departures from the legal framework created by the Colonial Office in 1838.

The response of the Colonial Office was unambiguous disapproval. According to Earl Grey, mandatory three-year contracts plainly amounted to "interference with the freedom of labour."[98] Writing to disallow the ordinance, Grey argued that long contracts should not be used to lower the prevailing rate of wages for agricultural labor.[99] And he affirmed once again a liberal, universalistic view of labor efficiency. "Legal coercion," Grey told British Guiana's governor, was necessarily inefficient. Instead, law should "make it the interest of the Immigrant to be industrious."[100]

The core conflict, then, concerned what we might call "political anthropology": competing accounts of human nature and governance. Grey's was universalistic and "liberal" in a particular sense: its premise was that non-European workers were not inherently different.[101] In British Guiana, local officials consistently rejected that premise. In July, Lieutenant Governor Walker told the Colonial Office that "the difficulty regarding the three years' engagement [was] likely to prove insurmountable" in light of strong support remaining for the idea among elected members of the Legislative Council. Defending the disallowed law, Walker argued that three-year contracts would prove mutually beneficial to employers and workers, actually improving "the welfare of the people." Sustaining this view was an assertion that Indian workers were incapable of rational decision-making. "Scarcely any of the people who arrive whether Africans or Coolies are in a position to decide for themselves," Walker wrote. Legally, they could and should be treated as minors, with the state "standing in loco parentis . . . as their legal guardian," and assigning to them employment contracts "calculated to promote their own well doing."[102] Like Harris, Walker grouped Indian and African migrants together to produce a racial taxonomy that emphasized non-European difference rather than specific social origins. The result was a reframing of restrictions on labor as protective social management, with the state assuming a paternal role over a dependent workforce.

Debate over the validity of multiyear contracts remained similarly unresolved in Trinidad, where local authorities framed freedom as an obligation, wage labor as a condition of subjecthood. In 1849, the colony enacted an immigration ordinance that extended the length of the initial indenture contract from one to five years.[103] Like British Guiana's proposed law, the new ordinance also gave the governor power to assign immigrants directly to plantations, eliminating the existing process in which individual employers had competed to hire new laborers upon their arrival in the colony.[104] Writing to justify these changes, Governor Harris claimed that earlier attempts at facilitating labor migration had failed "in consequence of there not being sufficient restraint imposed on the immigrant." In his view, tying indentured immigrants to specific plantations for longer, fixed periods was necessary to avoid "lawlessness and disorder" and to maintain the plantation system. It would also, he suggested, benefit the workers themselves, "inasmuch as it would tend to give them regular habits, attach them to certain localities and give them the

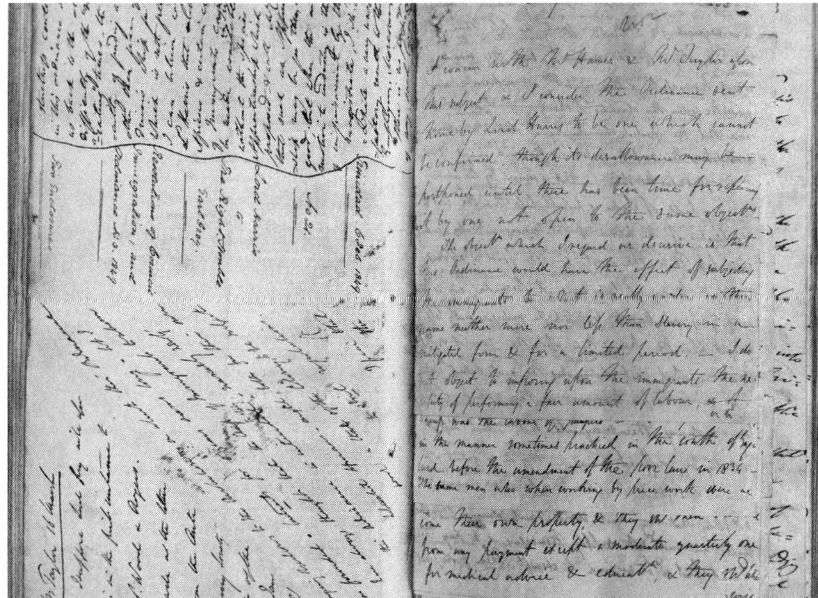

I concur with Mr Hawes & Mr Taylor upon this subject & I consider the Ordinance sent home by Lord Harris to be one which cannot be confirmed, though its disallowance may be postponed until there has been time for replacing it by one not open to the same objection.

The objection which I regard as decisive is that the Ordinance would have the effect of subjecting the immigrants to what is really under another name neither more nor less than Slavery in a mitigated form & for a limited period.

FIGURE 4. Earl Grey, Minute, 7 April 1849. The National Archives, London, CO 295/166.

opportunity of becoming intelligent and industrious men."[105] Progress for the laborer was the virtue of industriousness, the imperative of work.

Despite these entreaties, the Colonial Office disallowed the ordinance. Henry Taylor, a senior clerk, wrote privately to his colleagues: "The word 'contract' is scarcely a fair word to designate the transaction contemplated by the Ordinance, which is not a voluntary agreement between Labourer and Employer, but an assignment of the one to the other by the Gov[ernment]."[106] Earl Grey made the point more directly. In his view, the law "would have the effect of subjecting the immigrants to what is really under another name neither more nor less than Slavery in a mitigated form and for a limited period."[107] Grey's criticism echoed that of John Scoble, who, writing on behalf of the Anti-Slavery Society, called the ordinance "a renewal of the former Slave Code of Trinidad" and a "violation of human rights and of Constitutional law."[108]

Yet after the disallowance, local officials and colonial elites continued to argue that five-year contracts were necessary. A committee formed by the Council to respond to Grey's dispatch argued that stricter laws were needed to counteract the indentured laborers' "constitutional propensity to a wandering course of life."[109] In Trinidad, as in Guiana, officials used the language of industriousness to moralize restrictive labor discipline, framing the state's intervention as a form of training, and as a benefit not to narrow class-based interests but rather to the social order as a whole.[110] As Harris wrote, his aim in sanctioning the five-year contract had been not to reinstitute slavery but rather to make immigrant workers "worthy of freedom."[111]

Harris's words underscored the essential ambiguity of the concept. Even after state regulation distanced indenture from slavery, the meaning of freedom remained unclear. To officials in London, efforts to bind workers to the plantations appeared to violate free-labor principles. But for many others, including Harris, freedom implied a class-based duty to work for wages in an economic order centered on export production. Difference served to justify legal compulsion in this context. Law would correct a racial indisposition to work; it would make immigrant laborers "worthy." That logic, as we will see, would reshape the category of free labor over the course of the next decade.

Free Labor in Practice: Disease, Desertion, and State Weakness

As these legal and conceptual conflicts raged, a host of institutional, demographic, and environmental dynamics further complicated the problem of post-slavery free labor in practice. In the 1840s, limitations on state capacity made it impossible for colonial authorities to prevent indentured workers from leaving the plantations. Alongside these limitations, outbreaks of disease frustrated efforts to increase and order labor supply. Although Indian migrants faced various legal restrictions, many resisted the state's overall aim of stabilizing labor on the plantations. By switching employers in search of higher wages, and by leaving agricultural employment for short and long periods, some Indian workers effectively renegotiated the terms of indenture, even as others faced significant privation, including disease, hunger, and corporal punishment. In short, local authorities struggled to enforce strict labor discipline in these years. If indenture remained fraught ideologically, it was also unstable in a material sense.[112]

In both Mauritius and the West Indies, planters and local colonial authorities often complained that indentured laborers refused to work consistently, and that many left the plantations altogether as "vagrants" and "deserters." These complaints featured from the beginning of the regulated system. Writing in early 1846, the governor of Mauritius, William Gomm, warned that reports of "daily and protracted absenteeism continue[d] to be prevalent."[113] A year later, Governor Harris similarly claimed that in Trinidad indentured Indians were "utterly disorganized," with many "wandering over the country in a wretched condition."[114] Statements like these should be appraised with caution; many served an instrumental purpose as the colonies continued to petition for stricter labor laws, which the Colonial Office was unwilling to sanction. But read carefully alongside other records, these claims suggest a broader point: during the 1840s the laws of indenture did not succeed in tying indentured workers systematically to the plantations. Refusals to work—generally portrayed as absenteeism, desertion, and vagrancy—were a normal feature of the indenture system in this early period, one which local, colonial governments struggled to control.

Returns filed in Mauritius in 1846 stated that 7.7 percent of the colony's contract laborers had "deserted," that is, remained absent from work for more than two weeks. At the same moment, an additional 6.2 percent were recorded as absent for two weeks or less, while 5.1 percent were sick and unable to work.[115] Taken together, 19 percent of the island's estate labor force was thus unavailable. These figures fluctuated but remained significant for the rest of the decade. Returns from 1848 showed roughly 16 percent of the Indian workforce unavailable due to desertion, absence, and sickness.[116] The percentage was 17 at the end of 1849.[117]

As the relative stability of these figures suggests, the colonial state had trouble preventing unauthorized absence and finding those who left their contracts behind. In 1845, Charles Anderson—acting now in an official capacity as Protector of Immigrants in Mauritius—emphasized a "firm conviction that the Indian Immigrant who has once had recourse to desertion and vagrancy is lost for ever to agricultural labor."[118] Referring to the 36,000 indentured workers who arrived in 1843 and 1844, Anderson argued that it would be "impossible to retain such people on Sugar Plantations" without additional means of legal compulsion.[119] As the decade wore on, London's refusal to sanction heightened restrictions on labor limited local enforcement capacities in both Mauritius and the West Indies. After the Colonial Office disallowed the "Coolie Regulations" implemented in Trinidad in 1846, Governor Harris reported a general increase in unauthorized absence, suggesting that many Indian workers had left the estates and were "wandering about the country in bands."[120] By 1848, he further suggested, few remained on the plantations to which they had originally been sent; most had changed employers.[121] In British Guiana, Lieutenant Governor Walker similarly complained that Stephen's 1838 order in council was "insufficient as a means of discouraging vagrancy."[122] As we have seen, Stephen thought it imperative that "vagrancy" connote criminality, not mere unemployment. According to Walker, departed workers rarely engaged in the kinds of behavior—begging, for instance—required under the order to be punished as vagrants. As a result, many who arrived in the cities, within view of local police, were not arrested.[123]

If conflict with the Colonial Office obstructed local efforts to maintain labor discipline, institutional limitations also played an important role. Indeed, during the 1840s and 1850s, state weakness was a prominent albeit paradoxical feature of colonial administration in the sugar colonies. In many ways, the study of indenture illuminates state power; after all, the imperial state successfully transported more than a million migrants over the course of the century, dramatically expanding colonial sugar production as a result. But from a localized perspective it simultaneously calls attention to the relative weakness of individual colonial governments. Overburdened policing and judicial structures, coupled with a general reluctance to increase fixed colonial expenditures, made it difficult to enforce the laws of indenture that did exist evenly and regularly.[124] In Mauritius, the acting chief commissary of police reported in 1847 that the colony's rural police force was marked by "utter ignorance" and a "total want of discipline." Small, disorganized, and mired in its responsibility to guard and assist magistrates, the police remained "in a state of inaction" outside the capital, Port Louis.[125] The stipendiary magistracy, the judicial body responsible for adjudicating master-and-servant claims, was similarly understaffed across the sugar colonies.[126]

This was not the prototypical modern state. It was instead one in which colonial officials concentrated in Port Louis struggled to "broadcast power," to use Jeffrey Herbst's term, into unevenly developed rural territories.[127] To be clear, indentured workers who left the plantations were arrested and punished.[128] But many others escaped the law's reach. After the passage of a new vagrancy ordinance, Ordinance No. 7 of 1849, Governor Anderson reported that fifteen Indian workers had been arrested for desertion in October, along with twenty in November and five in December.[129] Though not insignificant, these arrest figures paled in comparison with the number of deserters reported by employers during the same period, which exceeded 950.[130]

Officials in British Guiana and Trinidad faced similar institutional limitations. In contrast to older, smaller Caribbean colonies like Barbados, British Guiana and Trinidad contained, like Mauritius, large amounts of undeveloped land. As Governor Harris explained, Trinidad's sugar plantations collectively occupied some 32,000 acres "scattered over an area of 1,200,000," and connected by roads that became "almost impassable for horsemen" during the rainy season.[131] In this setting, the expense and difficulty of filing complaints with the stipendiary magistrates sometimes outweighed the potential benefit of reclaiming indentured workers who breached their contracts. In 1848, Harris claimed to be aware of "only one instance" in which a proprietor had attempted to "recover" employees who had deserted.[132] The availability of land made it easier for departing workers to elude detection, and harder for local authorities to police the full extent of their territories.

In addition to illegal absence and desertion, colonial authorities struggled to control the manner in which indentured immigrants found and changed employers. As noted, the Colonial Office had refused to allow contracts lasting longer than one year. Without multiyear contracts, relatively few workers re-indentured with the same employer for long periods of time.[133] Some left soon after engaging, abandoning their contracts and moving to different plantations. According to Governor Harris, many Indian workers left their employers "within a week" of signing initial contracts.[134] Trinidad's Superintendent of Immigrants, Henry Mitchell, similarly reported that Indian workers traveled great distances, often in groups, not to abandon field labor but rather to change employers.[135]

Officials generally viewed this phenomenon as irrational disorder stemming, like vagrancy, from an "erratic tendency" supposedly natural to the Indian character.[136] Read against the grain, however, their reports suggest that changing plantations was rational market behavior—that Indian workers switched employers in search of higher wages and better treatment.[137] Harris's dispatches after the repeal of the "Coolie Regulations," for example, suggested that many Indians left their estates "because they heard that higher wages or more food were to be obtained in some other quarter."[138] Mitchell's discussion similarly implied that the phenomenon was organized, not haphazard: workers departed and re-engaged in groups in response to information received from neighboring and distant districts.[139]

The suggestion that Indian laborers frequently switched employers to secure higher wages comports with what we know about the unevenness of plantation finance during this period. The effect of free-trade policy on the plantation economy will be explored in greater detail in the next chapter. But suffice it to say here that during the 1840s, liquidity crises affected sugar plantations across the Caribbean. After the repeal of the sugar duties in 1846, the price of sugar declined on the British market, reducing revenue for colonial producers. With declining revenue came a tightening of both imperial and local credit. The combined result was decreasing solvency for plantations unable to obtain loans and a fragmented local economic landscape in which some but not all plantations struggled to pay wages at regular intervals. In Trinidad, where interest rates on domestic credit "approached 45%," delayed wage payments were a common problem.[140] By 1848, Governor Harris reported that nonpayment of wages was "almost universal" as a result of the "inability of the planters to procure money."[141] In British Guiana, Governor Light also expressed concerns regarding financial "distress" and nonpayment of wages.[142] In this context of uneven financial stability, it makes sense that indentured laborers would remain unsettled, refusing to contract for long periods and moving across districts in search of regular wages. In so doing, Indian migrants actively sought to improve their working lives.

If the disorder of this early period created space for Indian agency, however, it also set the stage for significant privation. Limited state power alongside everyday acts of resistance made the imposition of strict labor discipline impossible. But outbreaks of disease also played a role in destabilizing labor relations during the 1840s. Epidemics simultaneously disrupted the state's economic goals and subjected immigrant workers to widespread suffering. In Mauritius, the chief commissary of police reported in 1843 that Indian immigrants were being found in "a state of disease as to require immediate medical treatment" on an "almost daily" basis.[143] Similar claims appeared in Trinidad in 1846 and 1847, shortly after Indian migrants began to arrive. According to the *Trinidad Spectator*, a local newspaper that opposed immigration as a costly mistake, immigrant workers "in the greatest state of destitution" filled the colony's hospital.[144] By 1847, Governor Harris had created two additional temporary hospitals, which similarly became overburdened.[145]

These dynamics complicate our understanding of agency and control in this setting. These terms, of longstanding interest to scholars of both indenture and slavery, appear frequently in opposition to one another, as a means of conceptualizing resistance to domination.[146] Confounding this binary, epidemics disrupted the "order" of the plantations, but did so through immiseration. In British Guiana, the spread of disease prompted an official inquiry into mortality on estates in 1848. Its results showed that epidemics ravaged several of the colony's immigrant populations. Nearly 16,000 Portuguese immigrants had arrived since 1841, principally from Madeira, where crop failures prompted mass emigration in 1846 and 1847. By 1848, some 7,730 of these migrants had either died or left the colony, and only 5,853 continued to live and work on plantations. The primary cause of death was yellow fever, which proved particularly fatal among migrants weakened by famine in Madeira.[147]

Rates of death and disappearance among Indian immigrants varied but were also notable, especially among those who arrived from Madras.[148] Assessing data collected during the 1851 census, Henry Barkly—who was then the colony's governor—noted that of the 6,654 immigrants who arrived from Madras between 1845 and 1848, only 3,665 remained, according to state records. Barkly did not conclude that the roughly 45 percent apparently missing had all died; some, he suggested, had merely left the colony's developed agricultural and urban sectors and subsequently become invisible. But he did suggest that the group's rate of mortality had exceeded 8 percent annually, "nearly twice as great as that among the natives of Calcutta."[149] Of the 5,233 indentured Indians who arrived from Calcutta during the same period, 983 were similarly unaccounted for.[150]

Scholars of indenture have argued that extralegal mistreatment—physical violence, wage and ration withholding, and other illegal forms of coercion—figured particularly during the early period, in the 1830s and 1840s.[151] Widespread disease, on the one hand, and limitations on institutional capacity, on the other, intertwined with this phenomenon. Beginning in 1847, James Fagan, Trinidad's Coolie Magistrate, reported with increasing urgency that certain employers had severely mistreated laborers unable to work because of sickness. Fagan claimed to have found one worker, named Kunduppa, "rotting away to death" in the mill house of a plantation called Clydesdale Cottage, whose owner had illegally withheld medicine and rations and subjected workers to corporal punishment.[152] On another estate, L'Envieuse, Fagan found forty Indian workers starving, suffering from dropsy, and housed on an "earthen floor saturated with animal filth."[153] More generally, he accused plantation owners of casting "sick and helpless Coolies from Estates, to die like dogs on the road side."[154] Disabled women and others unable to work were subjected to "brutal inhumanity," he insisted.[155]

Fagan's tenure in Trinidad was fraught and short lived. After drafting the "Coolie Regulations," he was shocked by what he witnessed and became one of the colony's more vocal critics of mistreatment associated with Indian migration. Dismay with the government's inaction led to a series of personal conflicts with other officials, including with Governor Harris, and ultimately to Fagan's removal from office in 1848.[156] After that, the Colonial Office routinely dismissed Fagan's accusations. But Fagan was not the only observer who pointed out mistreatment in connection with sickness and hunger. Harris's own reporting confirmed what Fagan wrote about Clydesdale Cottage, and the governor ultimately removed the indentured Indians from the estate.[157] Like Fagan, the *Trinidad Spectator* reported that Indian immigrants were treated in an "inhuman manner," and continued to complain in 1849 of the "murderous cruelty inflicted on the ignorant and pliant children of the East."[158]

In British Guiana, meanwhile, missionaries affiliated with the London Missionary Society publicly accused planters of turning out sick immigrants and the government of ignoring rampant mortality. In a letter published in the *Leeds Mercury*, Joseph Waddington, a missionary in Berbice, claimed: "A monster in human form, who lived near me, used to send his sick Coolies away in a boat."[159] As in Trinidad, government officials denied these reports; Lieutenant Governor Walker told the Colonial Office that Waddington's account was "grossly exaggerated."[160] It is difficult to appraise Walker's dismissal since no further inquiry took place. But the frequency of accusations suggests at the very least that some Indian workers suffered significant mistreatment in the face of sickness and starvation.

Overall, the key point is that dispersal from the plantations figured prominently in all three colonies. Taken together, the multiple factors discussed thus far—state weakness, desertion, and disease—prevented local governments from imposing strict labor discipline during the 1840s. Indenture did not imply, at least initially, rigid control over labor. By the end of the decade, a large proportion of the indentured workforce brought to the Caribbean had either left the plantations to work in various trades or perished. In Trinidad, Governor Harris estimated in early 1848 that, of the 4,359 Indian laborers landed since 1845, only 2,110 still worked on the plantations.[161] Some 11,887 Indians arrived in British Guiana between 1845 and 1848, 5,233 from Calcutta and 6,654 from Madras.[162] Of these, only 8,410 still lived and worked on estates by 1849.[163] And in 1851, official returns showed only 7,670 remaining in the colony.[164] Before the arrival of Indian labor, the colony had recruited large numbers of freedpeople from neighboring islands, principally Barbados. Rates of dispersal among these workers were even higher; responding to an official inquiry in 1845, the president of the colony's Agricultural Society estimated that only a third of those introduced since 1838 still worked as field laborers.[165] And, as we have already seen, only 5,383 of the nearly 16,000 Portuguese immigrants who came from Madeira remained on plantations by 1848.[166] "Preferring the counter to the cane-field," as the royal commission held to investigate indenture in Guiana in 1871 put it, many more left to become shopkeepers during the early 1850s.[167]

These losses alarmed officials, so much so that the system plunged into crisis. Harris's reports became increasingly pessimistic. Instead of praising indenture, as many had between 1840 and 1845, he warned the Colonial Office of the "general failure of the Coolie immigration."[168] In the West Indies, that sense of failure was augmented by mounting financial difficulties. Immigration expenses attracted increasing controversy, particularly in British Guiana, where elected members of the Court of Policy came into serious conflict with the Crown over the local government's budget.[169] In the midst of these conflicts, Indian labor migration to both Guiana and Trinidad temporarily stopped in 1848.[170] It would not resume until 1851.

In this respect, Mauritius differed from Trinidad and British Guiana. In Mauritius, the scale of migration had been substantially larger, and no suspension occurred in 1848. By that time, Indian workers had already become the primary source of plantation labor. But in Mauritius, too, dispersal was a widespread phenomenon. In early 1846, Governor Gomm reported that

7,000 Indian immigrants imported since 1844 had "betaken themselves to other employments distinct from agriculture."[171] From 1846 to 1849, between 15 and 19 percent of the colony's Indian plantation workforce was unavailable because of desertion, absence, or sickness, categories that covered a range of life experiences, from everyday resistance to immiseration.[172] This did not debilitate production; to the contrary, sugar exports increased from an average of 34,707 tons per year between 1840 and 1844, to 56,069 between 1845 and 1849.[173] But in Mauritius, as in British Guiana and Trinidad, the state was unable to rigidly tie indentured laborers to the plantations.

* * *

The early period of indenture was thus marked by conceptual and practical instability. State regulation distanced indenture from slavery, but controversy persisted as imperial authorities struggled to redefine the boundaries of free labor. The law of indenture was a site of constant conflict and change in this context. London refused to allow long contracts and other restrictions deemed unjustifiably coercive. In spite of local appeals, many officials viewed direct legal compulsion as an infringement of freedom.

At the same time, a range of contextual factors compounded the problem of free-labor discipline in practice. The Colonial Office's refusal to sanction strict vagrancy laws limited the ability of local authorities to control indentured workers. More important, institutional limitations—"state weakness"—prevented colonial police and judicial systems from aggressively enforcing labor contracts. Of the thousands of indentured immigrants who arrived in the 1840s, many left the plantations. Dispersal was both a form of resistance and an effort to obtain higher wages. But in other cases it reflected widespread sickness and disease, which, in this early period, were rarely met with medical treatment. The creation of the indenture system, then, did not resolve the "problem of freedom." In practice and in theory, "free labor" was unstable and riven by conflict.

Beginning in the late 1840s, further economic change put new pressure on the indenture system. That change stemmed from Britain's free-trade policy, which altered the imperial sugar economy at both local and global levels. Free trade gradually turned public and official opinion in favor of indenture. At the same time, it deeply unsettled colonial labor relations. These dynamics—and the many effects of free trade on indenture—are the subject of the next chapter.

3

Indenture and Free Trade, 1846–1853

As we have seen, conceptual, legal, and material instability marked the early period of indenture. Beginning in the late 1840s, a new force deepened that instability while simultaneously laying the foundation for the system's expansion. That force was free-trade policy, which Britain adopted to dramatic political and economic effect in 1846. Though the process was hardly straightforward, free trade gradually bolstered public support for labor migration. More practically, trade liberalization reshaped the imperial sugar economy and, in turn, the development of post-slavery free labor. This chapter takes up both themes in the late 1840s and early 1850s; that is, soon after the repeal of the sugar duties. It explains the conceptual and social conflicts produced by free trade while showing how those conflicts led to an increasing reliance on indenture. As such, the chapter serves as a bridge between the two halves of the book. It continues to explore the conflict that marked the making of post-slavery free labor. But it also sets up the sustained argument about the consolidation of the indenture system that unfolds in chapters 4, 5, and 6.

What was free trade? The term refers variably to an economic philosophy, policy program, and social movement. In the British context, its intellectual origins trace to the eighteenth century, most recognizably to Adam Smith. But it was not until the nineteenth century that free trade gained momentum as a concrete political force. Evangelical revival helped disseminate and popularize free-trade ideas. Middle-class growth fueled demand for lower-cost consumer goods while, in the aftermath of the Napoleonic Wars, urban poverty and an economic depression raised the specter of social unrest. In response, Parliament introduced incremental reforms liberalizing trade relations in 1828. This process continued to more dramatic ends in the late 1830s and early 1840s as free trade became a social movement. The Anti-Corn Law

League catalyzed extra-parliamentary pressure against the protective tariffs that increased food prices. Though working-class protest did not always align with the League's program, the Chartists joined in support of tariff reform as a means of raising living standards.[1]

Seemingly technical, tariff reform portended rupture, politically and economically. In 1846, the Conservative prime minister, Robert Peel, endorsed free trade in spite of significant opposition from within his own party. The subsequent repeal of the corn laws split the Conservatives, aiding in the rise of the Liberal Party. Repeal also marked the enactment of the world's first free-trade policy, a milestone in the history of globalization. That policy reshaped trade relations in the empire and beyond. For our purposes, its most important aspect was the repeal of the sugar duties—a set of tariffs formerly imposed on foreign-grown sugar. The sugar duties had inflated the price of imperial sugar on the British market; repeal benefited British consumers but imperiled plantation capital in the empire.[2]

In Britain, a set of popular ideals underlay the turn to free trade. Domestically, the goal was to lower food prices to the benefit of middle- and working-class consumers. Internationally, advocates presented free trade as a means of ensuring long-term peace through trade. For the prolific free-trade campaigner Richard Cobden, both causes stood against entrenched aristocratic interests, which profited, through landownership and patronage, from high prices at home and imperial expansion abroad. So too did a third—the ideal of small government embodied by William Gladstone and the Liberal Party. In this milieu, economic non-interventionism and fiscal conservatism became political virtues. Though laissez-faire never applied uniformly, liberal economics gained support as part of the "assumptive world" of the mid-Victorian era. Stripping away the forms of privilege and mismanagement commonly known as "old corruption," fiscal conservatism was to free the state from vested interests. Without state intervention, the supposedly natural laws of political economy would then rationalize class and trade relations.[3]

In the empire, however, these ideals had little bearing. Despite Cobden's anti-imperialism, the empire continued to expand, formally and informally, through the middle of the century.[4] As the Opium Wars made particularly clear, "free" market expansion frequently depended on military force.[5] In Britain's former slave colonies, as we will see, free-trade policy led to the imposition of heightened forms of labor coercion. By lowering sugar prices, the repeal of the sugar duties reduced plantation revenues, destabilizing the imperial sugar economy.[6] Freedpeople resisted efforts to lower wages—the resulting, local effect of free trade—and sought to lessen their dependence on the plantations through landownership, a longer-term trend dating to the end of apprenticeship.[7] Though the process was indirect, the imperial state intervened, using indenture to reassert wage-labor dependency in the colonies.

Indenture should thus be seen as a form of "free trade imperialism," to use and perhaps add to Bernard Semmel's term.[8] The notion of the self-regulating economy played an important role in free-trade ideology, but state power undergirded the adjustment to free-trade in practice. In response to reports of decline and disorder, the Colonial Office introduced legal reforms designed to tie workers indirectly to the plantations. State subsidies, meanwhile, increased the scale of Indian migration, and planters in all three colonies began to rely increasingly on indentured labor. The ends of free trade—lower commodity prices and a redistribution of productive labor—depended on state intervention.

Yet the road was uneven; at both the abstract level of public debate and the local level of labor relations, free trade produced conflict. New market forces bore down on the cost of labor, but labor*ers*, who were never fully commodified, valued their work in less impersonal terms.[9] When free trade lowered sugar prices, freedpeople resisted planters' attempts to lower wages. When colonial authorities heightened legal penalties for absence, indentured workers found ways to evade enforcement. As free trade reshaped the sugar economy, it created new forms of legal and social instability. But in so doing, it set the stage for the expansion and consolidation of the indenture system over the course of the next two decades.

Repeal, Protection, and the Fragmentation of Public Debate

In the 1830s and early 1840s, indenture experiments drew public outcry, as we saw in chapter 1. But beginning in the late 1840s, free trade reshaped public debate on indenture. Heightened fears of economic decline eclipsed the scandal of neo-slavery and strengthened claims for labor migration. At the same time, however, protectionist opponents of free trade turned against indenture. In other words, when free trade split conservative interests, it fragmented public debate on post-slavery free labor. Free trade moved the London press away from the Anti-Slavery Society's radical rejection of indenture. But it also created a new, conservative critique, which adapted antislavery language to its own purposes. Competing views of the merits of indenture—and the nature of post-slavery freedom—continued to clash.

Even before the repeal of the sugar duties, declining sugar production helped shift debate in favor of indentured labor migration. Between 1834 and 1846, average annual sugar production in the West Indies fell from 184,060 to 131,177 tons.[10] This decrease led many to conclude that the colonies faced an economic crisis. Prominent newspapers began to portray labor migration as a necessary means of preventing collapse. The *Morning Chronicle*, for example, argued that emigration "ought by all means to be encouraged" in order to increase production.[11] "Let us not run into the mistake of conceiving that justice to the emancipated slave demands the ruin of his late master," it warned even earlier. "The material interests of Great Britain are greatly dependent on the prosperity of the sugar colonies."[12] Though the *Times* did not at this stage support indenture, it too argued that "prompt and vigorous measures" were needed to stem economic "deterioration" and the "utter annihilation" of British capital in the West Indies.[13]

Official inquiries from the period affirmed a similar logic. Facing pressure from planters' groups, Parliament convened a select committee to assess the condition of the West Indian colonies. Chaired by John Pakington, a Conservative MP who later served as colonial secretary, the committee concluded that a lack of "steady and continuous labour" had led to "diminished production and consequent distress." The solution proposed for this indiscipline was labor migration. "One obvious and most desirable mode of endeavouring to compensate for this diminished supply of labour," the committee wrote, "is to promote the immigration of a fresh labouring population, to such an extent as to create competition for employment."[14] Evidence for these conclusions came mainly from owners and managers of sugar plantations, and the committee's final report masked dissenting views expressed during its investigatory proceedings.[15] As Madhavi Kale has argued, official reports like Pakington's helped produce, not merely discover, a theory of labor shortage that would remain integral as a justification for indenture.[16]

As trade liberalization gained political momentum, free trade paved an additional ground of support for indenture among those fearful of West Indian decline. As leader of the Whigs, John Russell endorsed the policy of total repeal (as opposed to partial diminution) in 1845.[17] Soon after, upon the outbreak of famine in Ireland, Peel steered the Tories (and the government) toward the same goal. These events strengthened claims for labor migration. Petitions from planters' groups in the colonies and Britain argued that repeal threatened profitability beyond repair. The Agricultural Society of Trinidad predicted "irretrievable ruin" and "inevitable destruction."[18] Investors faced "the utter loss of the capital which ha[d] been embarked in the British West India Colonies," claimed a similar petition organized by the West India Committee in London.[19] In short, free trade bolstered the argument, initially made on the basis of falling production, that indenture was an economic necessity.

In this context, West Indian commercial interests adapted antislavery language to their own ends, as a cudgel against free trade. Petitions like those cited above argued that trade equalization would reinforce slavery in foreign colonies by undermining British imperial production. If repeal was "extremely injurious" financially, it was thus also a threat to the international project of antislavery: "the continuance of slavery will be encouraged—and the free Colonies will be destroyed," the West India Committee warned Parliament in 1848.[20] The Anti-Slavery Society clashed with the Anti-Corn Law League over the same issue.[21] Yet for the West India Committee, unlike the Society, an antislavery critique of free trade served an additional, instrumental purpose—as an argument for indenture.

Both ideas—financial ruin and antislavery—served as justifications not just for indenture, but also for state financial assistance to subsidize the cost of migration. According to a committee appointed by Trinidad's Legislative Council, only with a greater ability to obtain cheap labor could the colony successfully "compete with the Slave grown Produce of Cuba and Porto Rico."[22] "Restrictions" placed on labor migration were thus decried.[23] But in addition, new claims for state funding rang out. According to the West India Committee, the colonies were "incapable of raising a sum sufficient to cover the expense of introducing a large and immediate addition to their laboring population."[24] With the effects of free trade in mind, the Committee argued that the home government should guarantee loans to make labor migration possible.[25]

Indeed, free trade reignited plantation owners' claims for financial compensation. As the *Legacies of British Slave Ownership* project has emphasized, the British state paid £20,000,000 as compensation to slaveholders when slavery was abolished.[26] In the mid-1830s, this was a momentous sum—"the largest single financial operation undertaken by the British state to date," as Nicholas Draper has explained.[27] But after 1846, planters' associations nonetheless argued that they had been undercompensated. A public meeting held in British Guiana in late 1848 called for "full indemnity"—an additional 11 million pounds for losses of capital and infrastructure, as well as 7 million for allegedly undervalued slaves. The group similarly claimed state aid for labor migration: "unrestricted Emigration on an extensive scale, at the expense of the British Government."[28] Free trade became a justification for state immigration funding, now framed as an additional form of compensation.[29]

Still, at this stage, indenture remained mired in controversy. As repeal split conservative interests, it also fragmented the debate on indenture. Among anti-Peelites, protectionism survived.[30] From their perspective, tariffs were needed to bolster destabilized colonial economies, and indenture was a mere panacea. Through the mid-1840s, the scale of Indian labor migration to the Caribbean had remained relatively small. In 1848, moreover, transports ceased temporarily because of financial difficulties.[31] In this context, before the system's effects on production had been fully realized, protectionists turned against indenture.

Indeed, between 1844 and 1847, prominent conservative newspapers hostile to repeal went from supporting indenture to condemning it. In 1844, the *Standard* praised indentured labor migration as a means of "support[ing] the free colonies of the empire" against the "human flesh dealers of the Brazils and of Cuba."[32] But in 1847, after the abolition of the sugar duties, the paper's position changed dramatically. "The truth," it now argued, "is that free labour never can compete with slave labour."[33] A return to protection was needed; African immigration was a "godless scheme," Indian immigration a "Coolie delusion."[34] A similar pattern of criticism was apparent in the *Morning Post*, also a conservative daily. In the summer of 1844, the paper suggested that the West Indies needed protective tariffs but also a means "to supply the place of that labour of which they have been deprived by the Act of the British Legislature [the Abolition Act]."[35] After the passage of the Sugar Duties Act, the *Post*'s assessment of emancipation grew increasingly grim. Arguing that emancipation, a "desperate experiment,"[36] had failed, the *Post* rejected labor migration as a misguided free-trade policy and as a poor substitute for protection. Indenture was a mere "fallacy."[37] Only protective tariffs could save the colonies from economic collapse.

As these conservative critiques of indenture and free trade developed, they acquired a highly pronounced antislavery vocabulary. The *Standard* warned of a "smuggled slave trade" and condemned free traders for promoting "a traffic in men, women, and children, Coolie or African."[38] According to the conservative *Quarterly Review*, the repeal of the sugar duties was a "measure for increasing the production of Brazil sugar" and therefore the cause of "wholesale murder and torture."[39] Such language underscored the untethering of antislavery from its original orientation and aims, as a form of authoritative argument that could be deployed across the political spectrum toward a variety of ends, both for and against indenture.[40] "We should be deeply guilty were we to shut our eyes and refuse to see the truth," the *Review* declared.[41] Adopting antislavery language to their own ends, protectionists condemned indenture and demanded regulation of global trade—highlighting the potential dangers of an unregulated free market.

In short, free trade split public debate on indenture in new ways. Fears of economic decline, amplified by trade liberalization, moved many observers away from the Anti-Slavery Society's strong condemnation of indenture. At the same time, free trade led some conservatives to reject indenture. Antislavery language proved malleable in this dynamic context. The radical critique of indenture, which questioned the structure of plantation society, receded.

Protectionists used antislavery differently—to reject free trade and preserve the traditional structure of the sugar economy. Still, in the late 1840s, antislavery remained a means of challenging labor migration. Over time, as we will see, that would change: antislavery language would gradually serve to make indenture acceptable as free rather than forced labor.

Free Trade and Indirect Labor Compulsion

As free trade reshaped public debate on indenture, it also influenced the officials in charge of the system. In turn, the laws of indenture—and the legal category of free labor—began to change. As the previous chapter showed, significant legal conflict over the nature of free labor marked the 1840s. Local officials argued for multiyear, fixed indenture contracts, insisting that free-labor principles did not apply to non-European workers. Rejecting these proposals, imperial officials in London outlined an alternative, more universalistic vision of free labor: their position was that Indian workers would respond to rational labor incentives and that direct legal compulsion was inefficient.

Free trade challenged that position, initiating a larger process through which London would gradually accept increasingly restrictive labor laws. The repeal of the sugar duties convinced both local and imperial officials that the cost of labor had to be lowered. London continued to reject certain local proposals for direct compulsion, but not the general notion that law should be used to structure the labor market. Beginning in the late 1840s, the Colonial Office introduced revised laws designed to tie indentured workers to the plantations. In this context, free trade was an impetus for increased labor coercion.

In 1846, Earl Grey and the Colonial Office disallowed a Mauritian master-and-servant law—Ordinance No. 1 of 1846—as an "unjust and oppressive" attempt at labor compulsion. Appealing to liberal free-labor principles, Grey argued that self-interest rather than legal punishment was the key to labor efficiency.[42] These principles he reasserted in disallowing revised indenture laws enacted in British Guiana and Trinidad, which attempted to impose mandatory, multiyear contracts on Indian workers. But if Grey proved unwilling to sanction certain kinds of restrictions, he remained concerned about dispersal from the plantations. Emphasizing his agreement with local authorities, he maintained that changes to the existing indenture system were "urgently required."[43]

Thus, when Grey disallowed Ordinance No. 1 near the end of 1846, he forwarded his own set of proposals aimed at securing "continuous labour."[44] Grey's model made two related innovations, which together moved the Office closer to local demands for five-year contracts. First, it conditioned the right of return passage to India on the completion of "five years' *industrial* residence."[45] By "industrial residence" Grey meant either plantation labor under written contract, or payment, in monthly installments, of a portion of the original cost of transportation.[46] These monthly payments were the second innovation: labor taxes, charged at the rate of five shillings per month, against workers who chose to leave the plantations after fewer than five years.[47]

Taken together, these changes signaled an initial departure from the free-labor framework set out by the Colonial Office between 1838 and 1842. Under Glenelg, James Stephen had explicitly rejected the use of labor taxes as a means of directing freedpeople toward wage labor.[48] In late 1846, after the repeal of the sugar duties, Grey's response was different. Grey continued to reject the direct modes of labor compulsion advocated in the colonies—five-year fixed contracts, for example. But he accepted the notion that law should be used to encourage (or indirectly force) immigrants to work on plantations for a full five years. Under Grey's instructions, then, the boundaries of free labor began to shift.

In Mauritius, the local government soon enacted Ordinance No. 22 of 1847, a modified version of Grey's model. The law required five years of industrial residence to be completed either under written contract "with a sugar Planter" or through payment of a four-shilling monthly tax.[49] Meanwhile, the law increased the monetary penalties imposed on indentured workers for unauthorized absence. In addition to forfeiting wages and rations, Indian workers would be liable to pay their employers one halfpenny per shilling of monthly wages for each day absent.[50] In other words, daily fines for absence were to exceed daily wages.[51]

These measures met with strong disapproval among Indian officials. In correspondence with the Colonial Office, the Court of Directors objected to the notion that "industrial residence" should specifically require plantation labor "in the cultivation of sugar."[52] Citing Grey's own language, the Court argued that such an arrangement repeated the "original error" of the colony's disallowed Ordinance No. 1 of 1846—that is, seeking to instill labor discipline through legal restrictions and penalties rather than free-labor incentives.[53] More broadly, it accused the Mauritian authorities of seeking to reduce wages by oversupplying the labor market, creating "a competition for labour instead of the present Competition for Labourers."[54] Again, law was subject to triangular negotiation, as imperial, Indian, and colonial officials disputed the boundaries of free labor.

Debate among these officials made the nature of Grey's liberalism—and the manner in which it helped define post-slavery free labor—clear. The Colonial Office agreed that it was wrong to require sugar labor as a condition of industrial residence; doing so would violate "the principle that legislation should not be used for the direction of labor and capital into one Employment in preference to another," as well as the "free agency of the laborer which is essential to the efficiency of his labor." But the Office nonetheless maintained that a more general industrial residence requirement, stipulating "labor of one kind or another," did not run afoul of free-labor principles. Such a requirement would leave "free range for the ordinary motives by which industry is stimulated." Imposing labor taxes, and conditioning the right of return passage on contract labor, meanwhile, would create additional motives for "continuous industry."[55] If the Office insisted that Indian workers could react rationally to free-labor incentives, it simultaneously allowed that law could be used to adjust those incentives without invoking the specter of unfair coercion.

In short, Grey's liberalism hardly implied non-interference in employment relations. Deeply hierarchical, it allowed for structuring the labor market in a manner that effectively restricted the choice of the worker.[56] Free labor meant an ability to choose one's employer and (to a certain extent) employment, not a right to reject wage labor altogether. Inasmuch as dispersal from the plantations was seen as a manifestation of idleness, measures taken to encourage wage labor could be framed as promoting the general good as opposed to particular class interests. In this sense, the Colonial Office came to view legal inducements like labor taxes as benefiting "the true interests both of the masters and of the Immigrants."[57] Wage labor was associated with civilization, other forms of economic life with disorder.

Grey's public writing on colonial policy elaborated the same view. The goal of his model ordinance, he later wrote, was to create an "effective obligation to work."[58] Free labor implied such an obligation, and when societal pressures failed, the state needed to intervene. For civilization depended on labor; the alternative was a "relapse by degrees into the savage state."[59] That was Herman Merivale's diagnosis of Haiti, and his warning for Trinidad and Guiana. Officials like Merivale, the permanent undersecretary of state, wrote works of political economy that articulated this view of freedom quite openly.[60] For Marx, these accounts revealed that "free" wage labor was a lie: capital depended on pressures, whether of population or of law, to force labor into "productive" channels.[61] Merivale made the same observation but drew the opposite normative conclusion. In the larger post-slavery colonies, where land remained available and where labor's dependence on capital was incomplete, the goal of migration—the "*sine qua non*"—was to bolster that dependence by increasing supply.[62]

To meet the Colonial Office's position, Mauritius passed a modified law eliminating the specific requirement that only sugar-plantation labor count toward industrial residence.[63] The four-shilling monthly tax remained, as did stiff monetary penalties for unauthorized absence.[64] Under pressure from the home government, the Court of Directors eventually agreed, first to the principle of industrial residence and then to the use of labor taxes.[65] Grey's model ordinance, meanwhile, was sent to the West Indies.[66] In 1850, Trinidad enacted an ordinance based on Grey's instructions for Mauritius, which similarly required either five years of contract labor or payment of monthly taxes.[67]

British Guiana pushed further, however, enacting a stricter version of Grey's system. Guiana's ordinance—No. 21 of 1850—raised the monthly tax on new immigrants not working on plantations and rendered those in default liable to imprisonment.[68] The Court of Directors rejected this arrangement, finding it "more unfavorable and in some instances much more severe" than the law sanctioned in Mauritius.[69] Even after British Guiana enacted revisions, the Indian authorities continued to object.[70]

The response of the Colonial Office exemplified how official attitudes toward free labor had begun to change in this period. If labor taxes had previously appeared coercive, they now seemed rational and fair. T. W. C. Murdoch and Frederic Rogers, the emigration commissioners charged with reviewing all indenture law, justified increased monthly taxes in light of the relatively high cost of transportation from India to the Caribbean.[71] More broadly, Murdoch and Rogers evinced a rising paternalism in their analysis of indenture, which diminished their concern for expansive freedom of choice in employment relations. The government of Madras had complained that immigrants would fail to understand the increasing complexity of British Guiana's law, particularly as it pertained to return passage, taxation, and wage penalties. Though much indenture law was premised on contract theory—and the idea that Indian migrants voluntarily accepted specific terms, like industrial residence—the commissioners discounted this concern. "In no civilized Country would it be possible to explain to an uneducated person the details of the law under which he lived," they argued. What mattered, then, was simply that employment law "is found by those capable of understanding it to be just," and that "the person affected by it is capable of understanding its main outline and general bearing on his own interests."[72] The Victorian notion of freedom of contract was a formalist ideal, as P. S. Atiyah argued; its basis was the agreement of individual parties rather than an overriding principle of justice or fairness.[73] Murdoch and Rogers followed that logic in their unwillingness to consider the power imbalances at work in indenture contracts. Yet they also departed from the ideal in their conscious discounting of individualized choice, and in their statist reference to the judgment of elite policymakers like themselves. Pure theories of autonomous choice had little bearing on questions of labor, even in the era of classical liberalism.

If Murdoch and Rogers's remarks on contract relations applied generally to Europeans and non-Europeans alike, the commissioners also endorsed local claims regarding a *particular* need for close control of Indian workers in the Caribbean. There, they suggested, the primary threat to immigrant labor was not "oppression" but rather wandering, disease, and poverty amplified by a lack of "foresight and discretion." "Experience has shown that it is against himself that the Cooly requires to be protected," Murdoch and Rogers wrote. In their view, the Indian worker needed to be kept "for a time at least in a position which implies surveillance." Special restrictions and penalties were designed with this end in mind, not for "punishment" but instead to preserve order.[74] In short, their paternalism was racialized, and the result was a reframing of coercion as protection. Herman Merivale, the undersecretary of state, called the commissioners' report "extremely satisfactory."[75] Despite the complaints of the Indian authorities, the 1851 ordinances were allowed to stand.[76]

As these exchanges occurred, petitions arriving from the colonies relied increasingly on race-based justifications for heightened legal compulsion. In early 1851, the governor of British Guiana, Henry Barkly, wrote to the Colonial Office to dispute charges made by the Anti-Slavery Society against indenture. While the Society criticized what it perceived as racially discriminatory legislation constraining the freedom of Indian workers, Barkly responded by openly endorsing the policy of "accustoming men to freedom gradually for their own sakes."[77] Abolition, in his view, had produced "complete freedom," but racial inferiority and a cultural predisposition to idleness nonetheless necessitated strict regulation of labor conditions.[78] To bolster this argument, Barkly enclosed portions of a letter written by the colony's emigration agent in Calcutta. Claiming to speak with authoritative knowledge on the "Hindoo character," the agent wrote: "The natives here are so broken to the rule and control of others, that they absolutely require for their own benefit, as well as for the benefit of the Colony, some moderately coercive regulations on their first arrival in a new country."[79] Like Murdoch and Rogers, the emigration agent ascribed a protective function to special restrictions and penalties that applied to indentured immigrants alone.

In Mauritius, Governor Higginson similarly argued—in the course of proposing changes to Mauritian law—that Indian laborers should not be entitled to equal treatment, at least during their initial period of industrial residence. "Vagrancy may be repressed by coercive laws," he suggested, since it was "difficult to prevent the infection of a sloth which is protected by the forms of law." In this formulation, vagrancy appeared as a disease, though one whose etiology remained vague. The salient point, then, is that the language of disease, like the language of race, naturalized labor indiscipline and the necessity of legal coercion. This was the foundation for a racially inflected civilizing rhetoric used to justify Higginson's restrictive legal policy. In his view, indenture was a form of "emancipation"—a means of civilizing primitive workers. "A system of order and discipline," he argued, would protect Indians from "the temptations of idleness and drinking" and in fact "improv[e] their condition." "Emancipated from the influence of bad society or unguided caprice," indentured workers were free to become industrious.[80]

Such a view underscores not only the essential ambiguity of post-slavery freedom but the shifting conceptual terrain on which officials conceived of indenture. Early critics saw indenture as a betrayal of emancipation; now, for Higginson, labor control *was* emancipation, for purportedly primitive migrants. This reversal deepened over the course of the decade, as did its influence on policy. In Trinidad, Governor Harris's legal reports similarly emphasized non-European difference. "They are not, neither Coolies or Africans, fit to be placed in a position which the laborers of civilized countries may at once occupy," he wrote. "They must be treated like children, and wayward ones too."[81] These assertions served as an argument against expansive concepts of liberty as applied to indentured laborers. Active state management of labor was justified, on this view, as a means of protecting and civilizing the primitive wayward. Of making, as we saw earlier, indentured workers "worthy of freedom."[82]

At this stage, the Colonial Office did not endorse these arguments fully. It continued, moreover, to reject aggressive proposals for legal reform sent from the colonies. Despite the concessions made in 1850 and 1851, British Guiana enacted a new labor ordinance in 1853 binding indentured immigrants to fixed five-year contracts on arrival.[83] The Colonial Office disallowed the change, arguing that it was "hardly compatible with personal freedom."[84] In other words, though important concessions had been made, some distance remained between local demands and London's conception of free labor.

But as we have already seen, the Colonial Office did during this period move away from its earlier, highly skeptical regulatory stance. In 1849, the Colonial Office allowed Mauritius to legalize three-year initial contracts—abandoning its longstanding refusal to permit contracts lasting longer than one year.[85] In approving the law, Grey "continue[d] much to doubt whether such agreements w[ould] be found of advantage."[86] But there is evidence that Grey's universalism faded in these years. Facing increasingly negative reports, he drew closer to the view that Indians were naturally predisposed to vagrancy. Writing to the governor of Trinidad in 1848, Grey questioned the sufficiency of Stephen's 1838 orders, suggesting that they had failed to prevent "the Coolies from falling into fatal and dissolute ways of life." Though he had disallowed them himself, he wondered whether stricter regulations, like Fagan's "Coolie Regulations," were necessary. Beneath these thoughts lay an apparent belief that "immigrants belonging to savage or half-civilized races" were unfit for "unrestrained liberty."[87]

Thus, in 1849 and 1850, the Colonial Office began to approve stricter vagrancy laws alongside Grey's labor taxes arrangement. In 1849, Mauritius enacted an ordinance authorizing warrantless arrests for contract laborers accused of desertion.[88] Existing law had prevented the police from making such arrests without first obtaining a warrant from the stipendiary magistrates, a process that leading planters considered "absolutely insufficient."[89] Governor Anderson agreed; he directed the colony's procureur general to draft a new law, which the Colonial Office soon confirmed.[90] British Guiana's revised immigration laws of 1850 and 1851 similarly authorized the warrantless arrest of suspected vagrants. Ordinance No. 20 of 1851 empowered both the police and employers to apprehend and return immigrant workers found more than two miles from their plantations on working days.[91] Ordinance No. 21 included additional provisions applicable to indentured Indians. Those unable to prove either completion of industrial residence, engagement under written contract, or current payment of monthly taxes were to be taken by police to the stipendiary magistrates and imprisoned with hard labor.[92]

Ultimately, then, the laws of indenture became more restrictive between 1846 and 1852. In 1838, James Stephen and the Colonial Office had resisted attempts to use law to forcibly direct workers toward plantation labor. After the abolition of the sugar duties, that changed. Though Grey continued to reject direct measures like mandatory five-year contracts, he introduced reforms indirectly designed to keep indentured workers on the estates. Most notably, these reforms included labor taxes for indentured immigrants who left the plantations before completing five years of "industrial residence." Under Grey's authority, the Colonial Office also approved optional three-year contracts and warrantless arrests for vagrancy and desertion.

Contract theory played a role in justifying these changes. Industrial residence, for instance, was premised on the notion that indentured immigrants had agreed to work for a specific period in exchange for transportation from India. But Grey's reforms also reflected a larger conceptual and ideological shift. Without fully endorsing race-based accounts of vagrancy emanating from the colonies, the Colonial Office became increasingly convinced that Indian workers needed heightened controls—"surveillance," as Murdoch and

Rogers put it. From this perspective, increasingly restrictive laws came to be seen as a means of preserving the social order rather than enforcing labor discipline and defending particular economic interests.

Both lines of argument assuaged the government's liberal commitment to free-market principles. The Colonial Office rejected specific attempts to require sugar-plantation labor as undue interference in private relations of labor and capital. But Grey accepted the use of labor taxes as a means of directing workers toward contract wage labor, both because immigrants under indenture had (in theory) privately agreed to the arrangement and because wage labor was itself conceived as a mutually beneficial activity—in the service of the social order, not just private gain. In other words, liberalism did not prevent the Office from using law to structure the labor market. Underlying all of this, of course, was the fact that the Office's vision for post-slavery free labor contracted during these years, as Grey came to doubt whether "unrestrained liberty" was appropriate for "half-civilized races."

Sugar Revenue, Wages, and Labor Relations in Practice

As free trade affected the law and ideology of indenture, it also reshaped labor relations on the ground. By lowering prices, revenue, and wages, free trade altered the structure of the sugar economy. In so doing, it produced local conflict and new patterns of landownership among freedpeople. These complex dynamics restructured post-slavery free labor in practice. They frustrated state attempts at totalizing labor control, but they also changed the relation between Indian and Creole labor on the plantations.[93] In the process, they set the stage for an eventual expansion of the indenture system.

For both critics and supporters of indenture, wages had long caused controversy. As early as 1840, the Anti-Slavery Society had portrayed indenture as a scheme for saturating the labor market and reducing wages.[94] In British Guiana, missionaries and freedpeople similarly argued that state subsidies for indenture were "iniquitous" and "oppress[ive]."[95] Their appeals focused not only on the well-being of indentured immigrants but also on the relation between immigrants and the formerly enslaved. Labor migration, they argued, would dilute the bargaining power of emancipated workers, restructuring the terms of emancipation.

Colonial governors and other supporters of indenture routinely denied these charges. They insisted that immigrants would receive the same wages as Creole workers for plantation labor.[96] Later, emphasizing the savings brought by some migrants back to India, many would argue that colonial wages were in fact generous.[97] Such arguments shifted the terms of debate, making the relevant comparison wages in India and the colonies as opposed to in the colonies with and without indenture.[98]

In the late 1840s, the colonial state did in fact use indenture to lower wages and restructure the labor market, although not exactly in the way assumed by the Anti-Slavery Society. The key factor was repeal. The Sugar Duties Act of 1846 ended protection for imperial sugar, first by reducing existing import duties on foreign sugar and later by repealing protective tariffs altogether.[99] In London, the price of sugar fell from forty shillings per hundredweight in 1841 to twenty-three shillings in 1851.[100] The effect in the colonies was to suddenly and dramatically decrease the value of sugar exports.

This decrease in value, more so than decreases in raw production, damaged colonial sugar economies. After the end of apprenticeship, production decreased, but only temporarily. By the late 1840s, sugar production was once again on the rise. In 1847, British Guiana exported 47,208 hogsheads of sugar, still less than it had produced in 1830, but nearly 9,000 hogsheads more than its total for 1839.[101] In Mauritius, average annual production was 66 percent higher between 1845 and 1849 than it had been before abolition, between 1830 and 1834.[102] In the late 1840s, then, the primary threat was price rather than production. While declining production was often attributed to abolition, declining prices were the result of free trade.

Between 1846 and 1850, the falling price of sugar on the British market lowered export revenues in the colonies, erasing gains made in raw production. In 1846, Trinidad exported 37,901,800 lb. of sugar with a value of £414,158.[103] In 1847, even though raw production increased to 44,665,600 lb., export revenue dropped to £386,124.[104] The trend continued in 1848 and 1849, as production figures remained relatively steady while revenues fell further to £219,761 and £242,296, respectively.[105] The phenomenon was equally apparent in British Guiana. In 1844, the 38,521 hogsheads Guiana exported carried a value of £717,895.[106] By 1847, production had increased to 47,148 hogsheads, but revenue decreased to £688,422.[107] In 1848, prices fell further; Guiana exported 46,237 hogsheads to Britain with a value of only £586,968.[108]

These figures reflected revenue without expenses, not profit. At reduced prices, sugar planting became decreasingly profitable. In early 1848, Governor Harris argued that production costs largely absorbed export revenues.[109] Later that year, he claimed that Trinidad's plantations had sustained net losses since 1838.[110] Bankruptcies became common, especially as lending slowed during an 1847 commercial crisis in Britain.[111] From British Guiana, Governor Barkly reported that twenty-three estates were sold through sequestration in 1848.[112] Records from some of these estates showed production costs—money spent on labor and other expenses—exceeding export revenues.[113] All told, nearly one hundred estates went to execution sale between 1847 and 1850.[114]

In this context, free trade motivated renewed appeals for imperial assistance and lower wages. In the summer of 1846, the governor of Mauritius reported that a deputation of prominent planters and merchants had asserted the "necessity of lowering the rate of Wages by a vast and immediate additional introduction of Labour."[115] In 1848, planters in British Guiana demanded a general 25 percent reduction of wages, citing the "frightful fall in the value of British Plantation produce" caused by the repeal of the sugar duties.[116] In resolutions fashioned as a petition to the House of Commons, the Court of Policy similarly argued that twin "*crises*," abolition and free trade, made current wages for plantation labor unsustainable.[117] Privately, at least, colonial officials suggested that immigration would play a role in making wage reductions possible. As Governor Barkly asserted in 1850, a "further reduction of wages" would lead to "deplorable results" without a larger laboring population.[118]

Surviving wage records show that, in practice, wages were systematically reduced in the late 1840s following planters' demands. But the process was not straightforward, and early attempts to lower wages failed. In Mauritius, a group of merchant houses that managed estates attempted to fix wages in 1844, agreeing not to pay indentured immigrants more than five rupees per month.[119] The plan was only partly successful, however, as indentured workers refused to renew their contracts (after the initial one-year period) without wage increases.[120] In the Caribbean, meanwhile, wages rose in the years immediately after the end of apprenticeship.[121] A brief attempt to reduce wages was made in British Guiana in 1842, but it proved "futile" according to Governor Light, and wages once again increased as planters attempted to discourage emancipated workers from leaving the plantations.[122] In 1844 and 1845, average daily wages for field labor reached 3s. 6d. in British Guiana.[123] The reported figure for Trinidad in 1846 was even higher—4s. 2d. per day.[124]

After 1846, however, wages declined sharply in all three colonies.[125] In Trinidad, average wages dropped to 1s. 5d. per day in 1848, 1s. 3d. in 1849, and further to 1s. in 1850.[126] These reductions followed the decreasing price of sugar in these years. But when sugar prices began to rebound in the early 1850s, wages remained low. In 1857, the average daily wage for field labor was still 1s. 3d., even though by that point sugar export revenue had more than tripled.[127] The pattern in British Guiana was similar. There, the average rate of wages fell from 3s. 6d. per day in 1845 to 1s. 4d. in 1848—a 62 percent decrease.[128] The figure remained there, between 1s. 4d. and 2s., in 1849 and 1850, before rising to 2s. 6d. in 1853.[129]

In Mauritius, too, where wages were lower to begin with, average rates dropped significantly between 1846 and 1852. In late 1847, planters lowered the wages offered to newly arriving workers from 10s. to 8s. per month, a development that Governor Gomm described as "manifestly the result of Combination among parties exercising a commanding influence over the labour market of the Colony."[130] Overall, average wages for field labor fell from 14s. per month in 1846 to 11s. per month in 1852. While in 1846, 31.3 percent of plantation workers received 16s. per month, by 1852 only 3 percent of workers did so. New immigrants under indenture—those who had not yet completed the five-year period of industrial residence—consistently made less than other workers. Thus in 1852, when the overall average was 11s. per month, new immigrants received 9s. 3d. The result was substantial savings to owners. In 1846, wages paid to more than 47,000 sugar workers totaled £400,956. According to the Legislative Council's immigration committee, the same number of workers paid at the rates prevailing in the second half of 1852 would cost only £295,944.[131]

Though initiated by employers, efforts to reduce wages received state support. As we have seen, local officials tacitly sanctioned wage fixing in Mauritius. Meanwhile, in British Guiana, the governor instructed the colony's stipendiary magistrates, whose official function was to adjudicate labor disputes impartially, "to induce a consent to a reduction of wages."[132] The justification for this rather illiberal interference in private employment relations was of course free trade—a conviction that wage reductions were necessary because of the "great and unusual depreciation of the value of its [the colony's] staple productions in the markets of the Mother Country."[133] Earl Grey approved the governor's decision in early 1848.[134] Free trade, premised on a liberal view of international trade relations, required more active intervention in colonial labor relations.

This was also the case on a macro scale, as state subsidies for indenture increased to offset the effects of free trade. A parliamentary select committee created to study those effects warned of "ruin" and called for "relief."[135] To supply new labor, the West India Committee argued not only for permission but also for financial support.[136] To that end, Parliament made £500,000 in guaranteed loans available to British Guiana, Trinidad, Jamaica, St. Lucia, and Grenada in 1848.[137] These loans came after additional, one-time payments from the Treasury to Guiana and Trinidad, and alongside other, private loans raised by the two colonies' local governments.[138] What emerged was a system of state subsidies for indenture, financed using public debt. In British Guiana alone, the cost of labor migration, including interest on loans, reached nearly £850,000 between 1841 and 1858. Of this, the state paid more than 80 percent.[139]

As small groups of freedpeople and missionaries began to argue in the early 1840s, state subsidies for indenture indirectly transferred wealth from formerly enslaved populations back to the plantations.[140] After abolition, British Guiana and Trinidad enacted highly regressive systems of indirect taxation. Property and export taxes paid by plantation owners were repealed and reduced; import duties on a broad range of common consumer goods were increased. By increasing the price of food and clothing, import duties fell on the population at large, the majority of which had once been enslaved. In other words, after abolition, tax burdens shifted from planter elites to newly freed majorities. "Public" revenue, the money used to repay immigration loans, depended on import and sales taxes and the people who paid them.[141] Given the structure of the loans, this meant repaying substantial interest in addition to the actual cost of migration.

State subsidies, meanwhile, allowed for labor migration on a much larger scale than would otherwise have been possible. The months-long journey from India cost roughly £15 per person. At scale, that meant hundreds of thousands of pounds, as the Caribbean colonies realized during the indenture system's first fifteen years. Immigration soon became the largest single item in British Guiana's annual budget; it comprised close to 30 percent of total government expenditure in 1847 and 1848. Migration costs were too expensive to simply pay on existing revenues. Using loans, Trinidad and Guiana recruited more than 18,000 and 38,000 new workers, respectively, between 1845 and 1860.[142]

A continuing influx of new labor was important because wage reductions met with serious resistance from Creole laborers, particularly in the Caribbean. That resistance, in turn, reshaped labor relations on the ground, setting the stage for an ongoing expansion of the indenture system. In 1846, officials in British Guiana reported organized acts of violence against owners and managers who attempted to reduce wages.[143] Arson in particular became a tool of protest. In 1847 and 1848, workers repeatedly burned down estate storehouses containing megass, a highly flammable sugar byproduct, in response to decreasing wages.[144] Six such burnings occurred in January 1848 alone.[145] The response of the Colonial Office was to authorize collective punishment for crimes against property.[146] But in 1849, reports of fires and other disturbances similarly began to arrive from Trinidad.[147]

On a larger scale, workers in British Guiana went on strike, refusing to accept lowered wages. The main strike, which affected the entire colony although not each plantation equally, lasted nearly three months, from December 1847 to February 1848. Stipendiary magistrate reports from the period described a "general suspension of labor," and in some districts hundreds of

Creole workers left the plantations.[148] In February, Governor Light told the Colonial Office that the "great majority" of formerly enslaved workers had stopped working, though some indentured migrant laborers had continued.[149] Missionary reports similarly documented the strike's magnitude. According to James Scott, a member of the London Missionary Society (LMS), seven-eighths of the plantations on the west coast of Demerara stopped production altogether, "the planters standing out for a reduction of wages amounting to 50 percent or more—and the people refusing, I think not unreasonably, to submit to so large a reduction."[150]

Unlike official reports, LMS accounts also suggested that workers suffered because of the strike. The price of basic food items, many of which were imported, remained high. Without wages, some workers—especially newer immigrants without savings or access to land and alternative food sources—went hungry. According to Scott, some Indian immigrants in Demerara began to starve in January, "having nothing to subsist on but roots and wild fruit."[151] In March and April, many workers returned to the plantations at reduced wages. By April, districts where nearly all Creole workers had participated in the strike reported that significant numbers had returned.[152]

Historians have generally viewed Indian indenture in relative isolation, apart from formerly enslaved Black working populations. Walter Rodney's classic *History of the Guyanese Working People* is an important exception.[153] His perspective—emphasizing connections between the class positions of indentured and non-indentured workers—is essential to understanding the strikes and wage conflict described above. Indenture did not itself cause the sudden drop in wages—that was free trade and the declining price of sugar on the British market. But once wages fell, indenture made it easier for planters to overcome strike action and other forms of labor negotiation. Special legal restrictions "immobiliz[ed]" indentured immigrants, as Prabhu Mohapatra has written, making it difficult for them to reject wage labor.[154] Unlike freedpeople, many of whom moved to newly created villages, indentured workers generally lived on the plantations and lacked access to alternative resources. In some cases, competition undergirded additional hostility toward Indian migrants, as emancipated workers positioned their economic grievances and status as free, Christian men against that of the foreign, "heathen Coolies."[155]

For advocates of indenture, the purpose of labor migration was not explicitly to force local workers from the plantations. As many officials protested, their aim was to increase the overall size of the working population, not maintain it through displacement. But in introducing new workers under indenture, planters and local officials did explicitly intend to diminish the Creole population's control over the market for wage labor. Governor

Light argued that increased competition would prevent Black workers from indulging in "irregular" labor practices. This economic pressure he framed as "moral influence," understanding morals through the prism of class, as "the practice of the duties of life—amongst which in a laborer are industry in various shapes."[156] As Rodney argued, indenture was about labor discipline, not just labor supply.[157] This was the case because the laws of indenture required certain forms of labor from indentured immigrants, but also because the presence of indentured immigrants limited the bargaining power of unindentured Creoles. Both dynamics were apparent in the wage struggles of the late 1840s. It was impossible to hold out for high wages when, as one LMS missionary observed, immigrant labor made certain plantations "quite independent of our people's services."[158]

All of these developments—wage struggles, strikes, and partial displacement—took place alongside a broader phenomenon frequently referred to as Creole "withdrawal," the process by which many freedpeople left the plantations and full-time plantation labor.[159] Beginning in the early 1840s, many moved from the plantations to newly created villages, which were themselves frequently built on former estates.[160] Stipendiary magistrate returns from British Guiana recorded 25,852 people living in villages built since emancipation by the end of 1845.[161] By 1853, the figure had nearly doubled, to 48,991, or roughly 36 percent of the colony's total population.[162] In Trinidad, meanwhile, Governor Harris estimated that only 3,166 Creole workers continued to live on estates by 1848, down from a pre-emancipation total of roughly 20,000.[163]

In this context, landownership was part of a broader conflict over wage-labor dependency and the meaning of freedom itself. Scholars of Jamaica have mined this theme to reveal the centrality of land and family structure to freedpeople's conceptions of the term.[164] There and elsewhere, movement to new villages did not necessarily imply a rejection of wage labor, but it did provide freedpeople with greater control over the terms by which they worked. As one Guiana magistrate complained, lapses in labor discipline stemmed "not so much from scantiness of people as from the independent position of the general body of the old labouring population." No longer dependent on owners for housing and other basic necessities, Black laborers remained "willing to work," but only "on their own terms."[165]

Indeed, Creole landownership increased workers' independence from the plantation-based market for wage labor by creating alternative means of subsistence and commerce. From the early 1840s, freedpeople began purchasing large amounts of land in small plots. The process intensified in the late 1840s, as the effects of free trade took hold.[166] Reduced wages led more workers from export agriculture toward local food production. Reduced revenue and credit, meanwhile, led some landowners to sell land at relatively low rates. In some cases, groups of formerly enslaved people purchased failing estates for the construction of new villages.[167] There and on estates, women sought greater autonomy for themselves and their children.[168] Local officials reported, often with dismay and disdain, that Creole populations had come to view landownership as an essential component of freedom.[169] By creating new forms of economic life, land offered freedom not just from slavery but from the rigid demands of the plantation system. According to one missionary writing from British Guiana in 1849, the formerly enslaved saw landownership as "an indispensable acquisition to their enjoyment of real freedom."[170]

Officials, by contrast, interpreted these developments as an indication of social and moral regression. Governor Barkly saw landownership and small farming as a social malady, an "internal hemorrhage," as he put it.[171] A rejection of wage labor was thus framed as "secession," a turn away from "productive industry" and "civilization" itself.[172] In this manner, Barkly's discussions of withdrawal emphasized the extent to which class-based economic imperatives were transposed in civilizational and racial terms. Concepts of the general social good—progress, development, industry—reflected particular economic interests. In other words, an ideological preference for wage-labor dependency colored official accounts of Black landownership in the post-emancipation period. New settlements away from the plantations meant for Barkly a "relaps[e] into barbarism of the deepest dye."[173]

However useful in terms of parsing ideology, this kind of condemnation masked the complex dynamics that underlay Creole "withdrawal."[174] In Mauritius, the formerly enslaved had acquired the means to begin purchasing land by the very early 1840s. As Richard Allen has shown, landownership among formerly enslaved people (referred to as "ex-apprentices" in Mauritian records) and free people of color (*gens de couleur*) significantly altered the Mauritian economy, fueling the process known as the *petite morcellement*, by which certain estates were subdivided and sold in small tracts.[175] Freedpeople leaving the estates engaged in a variety of new occupations, including truck farming, crafts and trades, and non-sugar-estate labor.[176] And by the late 1840s, many formerly enslaved women, who had played a significant role in the colony's labor force under slavery, had stopped working on plantations.[177] In addition, high rates of mortality—the result of epidemic disease and an aging population—contributed to patterns of apparent withdrawal from plantation labor.[178] These precipitants of change—economic, social, demographic, epidemiological—tend to be marginal in official sources focused primarily on export agriculture and labor supply. By 1861, census officials had stopped recording "ex-apprentices" as a distinct segment of the population altogether.[179]

Taking these developments together, what was changing in the era of free trade was the *relation* between un-indentured Creole and indentured Indian working populations. Between 1846 and 1853, indentured immigrants came to provide an increasingly large proportion of the plantation labor needed for sugar production. This was the case most dramatically in Mauritius, where the scale of Indian migration was largest. Between 1846 and 1851, the colony's recorded Indian population increased from 56,245 to 77,996.[180] Some 64,383—more than 80 percent of the total—were men, and of these, 44,942 worked on plantations as agricultural laborers.[181] At the same moment, only 6,292 ex-apprentices (5,472 men and 820 women) still worked on estates, out of a total ex-apprentice population of 48,330.[182] By 1851, in other words, the Indian population exceeded the emancipated population in size, and Indian workers vastly outnumbered the formerly enslaved on the plantations.

The Caribbean colonies witnessed a related shift, though on a smaller scale. In the early 1850s, Indian immigrants continued to make up a relatively small proportion of the total population—5.82 percent in Trinidad[183] and 6 percent in British Guiana.[184] Nonetheless, there too indentured workers began to comprise a growing proportion of plantation laborers. By 1851, Indians accounted for approximately 16 percent of Guiana's sugar-estate labor force, according to Walton Look Lai.[185] The 1851 census did not reflect new waves of Indian migration, which resumed in that year after a three-year suspension. By 1853, Governor Harris claimed that sugar estates in Trinidad relied primarily on immigrant labor, with freedpeople "preferring to retire to small plots."[186] Harris was exaggerating, but the proportion of Indians in the labor force would continue to rise over the course of the decade. By 1858, Indians made up nearly 35 percent of Trinidad's sugar workforce.[187]

Following the crisis of free trade, all three colonies became increasingly reliant on indentured labor. In Mauritius, the scale of Indian immigration was such that Indian workers greatly outnumbered Creoles on the plantations by the early 1850s. In the Caribbean, where Indian and African immigrants remained minority populations, indentured labor became increasingly important as freedpeople acquired land and capital outside the plantation system. By lowering wages, the repeal of the sugar duties intensified Black resistance and "withdrawal" from the plantations, creating new problems of labor supply and control. Facing these dynamics, the imperial state sought to re-establish wage-labor discipline by subsidizing labor migration and enforcing indenture contracts. Shrinking export revenues served to justify

FIGURE 5. Felix Morin, "Trinidad: Coolies," c. 1870s–1880s. Getty Research Institute, Los Angeles (97.R.50).

this remaking of labor relations. While the formerly enslaved sought land to establish what they viewed as "real freedom," the state turned to indenture to bolster a more circumscribed vision of free labor within the plantation system. In short, as free trade altered the structure of the sugar economy, the plantation system depended increasingly on indenture.

Labor Taxes, State Weakness, and Everyday Resistance

The year 1846, as we have seen, marked a turning point in the willingness of imperial officials to sanction indirect modes of labor control. In particular, the Colonial Office introduced a program of labor taxes designed to encourage indentured workers to remain under contract for a five-year period of industrial residence. Yet these efforts failed to stabilize labor relations in practice. Disorder and variability marked the implementation of labor taxes in Mauritius, and state weakness undermined effective enforcement in the West Indies, particularly in British Guiana. As free trade fragmented abstract debates about the nature of freedom, it also produced a practical context in which strict labor discipline remained elusive.

Labor taxes were first implemented in Mauritius, when the colony enacted Ordinance No. 22 of 1847 in response to Earl Grey's model. Local records in the Mauritian archives, particularly reports written by stipendiary magistrates, provide an unusually detailed view into the law's implementation. These reports provide more than interesting detail; they alter our understanding of what the law was. In addition to revealing tremendous variability, they demonstrate the ongoing importance of local, non-state factors in shaping practical outcomes even as the laws of indenture became formally more restrictive.

Collecting labor taxes (as opposed to simply imposing them) was hardly straightforward. In Mauritius, magistrates reported divergent results. Some magistrates and tax inspectors did manage to recover monthly taxes from immigrants who chose not to enter into written labor contracts.[188] Others, however, revealed that it was impossible to enforce the monthly tax requirement given limited state resources. One magistrate called the law a "dead letter," noting that the single tax inspector in his district was overworked and ineffective.[189] Citing the small size of the police force, the magistrate for Black River similarly argued that "active surveillance" of the immigrant population was "impossible."[190]

In authorizing monthly taxes, Earl Grey had emphasized the law's contractual logic: indentured workers who chose not to fulfill industrial residence would be required to partially repay their initial cost of transportation. Local magistrates, by contrast, clearly viewed the law as a tool for pressuring immigrants to continue working on estates—"to induce the Immigrants to return to the cultivation of the cane."[191] In this regard, many argued that the law was a failure. Stipendiary Magistrate Henry Self claimed not to be aware of any cases in which payment of the tax led immigrants "to quit the small culture and return to that of a Sugar Estate."[192] In his view, the law had the opposite effect, allowing sugar laborers capable of paying the tax to leave.[193] Others echoed this notion that labor taxes effectively served to license "sloth and idleness" by making it legal for indentured immigrants to reject plantation labor.[194] More generally, magistrates argued that the law did little to combat the broader phenomenon of vagrancy.[195]

Yet if the law failed to prevent vagrancy on the whole, it nonetheless pressed upon the individuals it ensnared. First, some Indians were incorrectly charged the tax, even while working under contract, while many others were mistakenly arrested despite not owing the tax. "Every day some one is committed to prison who has paid his tax," wrote one magistrate from Port Louis.[196] Another writing in the spring of 1848 identified three immigrants under contract who had been "erroneously required to pay the monthly tax since Ordinance No. 22 went into effect."[197] Another magistrate, Maguire, highlighted the "arbitrary and harsh manner" in which labor taxes had been imposed, emphasizing that workers who failed to pay became liable to long prison sentences with hard labor.[198] His records showed that of the 3,474 Indians arrested in his district for nonpayment of taxes between July 1847 and May 1848, 1,729 were summarily released.[199] That so large a proportion of those arrested were discharged without penalty suggests that many were arrested without cause, either by accident or as harassment. This result was in a sense unsurprising, given the wide latitude for warrantless arrest afforded by the law. Indians who did not carry proof of industrial residence, written contract, or monthly tax payment were at all times liable to arrest.[200] State authorities struggled to distinguish between indentured and un-indentured Indians—a problem that would only increase as the Indian population grew in the 1850s and 1860s.

Though fragmentary, individual case records also indicate that nonpayment of wages by employers was relatively widespread and frequently unpunished. Unpaid wage claims made up a large proportion of Maguire's case log in the fall of 1848.[201] Self repeatedly claimed that workers in his district were being discharged without receiving full wages due for work already performed.[202] A report written by the procureur general concluded that in multiple districts large estates employing thousands of immigrant workers had delayed wage payments "for 3, 6 and even 9 months."[203]

Apart from the monthly taxes, these records also revealed significant variability in the manner in which magistrates enforced vagrancy penalties under Ordinance No. 22. Some arrested for illegal absence were simply sent back to their employers, while others were first fined and then sent back.[204] Still others faced prison. Two, for example, arrested in Moka without "Tickets papers or employment" were sentenced to twenty days with hard labor.[205] A key variable was whether the employers of those arrested were known or ascertainable. But other practical considerations shaped outcomes as well. As one magistrate reported, some employers chose to deduct daily wages alone for unauthorized absence, less than what the law allowed, in an effort to maintain positive relations with their workers.[206] At the same time, there is evidence that the punishments of other workers exceeded what the law permitted.[207] One worker named Mootoosamy was fined twelve shillings and sentenced to fourteen days in prison with hard labor for illegally leaving work for approximately three weeks.[208] All the while, magistrates continued to report relatively large numbers of desertions, claiming that they had no means of effectively tracking those who departed.[209]

The Caribbean colonies faced similar complications when they attempted to implement Earl Grey's model. This was most clearly the case in British Guiana, where labor taxes were widely pronounced a failure by 1853. The colony's local government had introduced significant administrative reforms to bring the law into effect. In the summer of 1852, Governor Barkly appointed twelve subagents of immigration, a new office, under the Immigration Agent General and the stipendiary magistrates.[210] These new officers were to assist their superiors with the allotment of new immigrants and recording of industrial residence. Perhaps more important, their task was to collect monthly taxes from indentured workers and contract (stamp) duties from their employers. For these services, each was to be paid £200 annually.[211]

This bolstering of the state's administrative apparatus had some effect. After news of the appointments spread, roughly 800 Indian workers returned from Georgetown to their former plantations, according to Governor Barkly.[212] Several subagents similarly declared that the threat of monthly taxes led Indian workers in their districts to accept fixed contracts. Again, many viewed this as the law's real purpose—"to enforce the Coolies into contracts with the estates, instead of their paying monthly sums."[213] John Brumell, a subagent in Essequibo, claimed that the great majority of affected immigrants in his district chose to re-engage rather than pay the tax, "without the slightest hesitation."[214] Another subagent, who struggled to collect monthly taxes, nonetheless reported re-engaging Indian workers whose contracts had finished on seven plantations in his district.[215]

Most subagents, however, reported with increasing frustration that their efforts to enforce the law and collect monthly taxes failed in the face of resistance. After being informed of their obligations under the new law, some Indian immigrants simply "disappeared."[216] Others refused to pay. Forty-six workers on the Ma Retraite estate in Berbice argued that they could not be compelled to pay the tax because it had not been explained to them (or existed by law) when they emigrated in 1848.[217] In another district, immigrants "universally declared they had no money," leaving their subagent with a "very meager collection."[218] According to the agent, many subsequently appeared with certificates of exemption (showing completion of industrial residence), which he suspected were fraudulent.[219]

Facing these forms of everyday resistance—avoidance, refusal, an emerging black market for exemption papers—subagents and magistrates had limited means of enforcing the law. Problems of identification were frequently cited; subagents struggled to muster the personal information needed to lodge complaints and compel appearance in the magistrate courts.[220] In some cases, administrative disputes made things worse; at least one magistrate resented and refused to share information with his subordinate.[221] Further complicating the situation was the fact that some immigrants who technically owed monthly taxes continued to work on plantations as day laborers, without written contracts. According to one subagent, *employers* resisted wage withholding—another apparent means of collecting the taxes—for fear that their day laborers would reject them and leave.[222]

The result of these many difficulties was that officials recovered relatively little money through monthly taxes. In 1852, the colony's twelve subagents collected $573.50 combined, far less than they received in salary.[223] In the years in which the law continued to be enforced, the colony collected little more while spending nearly $9,000 in administrative costs.[224] These results led many to proclaim the law a failure. In a formal protest sent to the Colonial Office, the elected members of the Court of Policy called the effort to collect labor taxes a "ruinous experiment."[225] Nearly twenty years later, the royal commission of inquiry sent to investigate conditions of indenture in Guiana concluded that Grey's system had been an "egregious failure."[226]

Such condemnation served particular interests as local elites continued to petition London for permission to require five-year fixed contracts.[227] But the negative consensus that led to the rejection of labor taxes emphasizes an important point embedded throughout this chapter. After the repeal of the sugar duties threatened to undermine the plantation economy, officials in London began to accept and themselves promote indirect modes of labor coercion, changing the nature of the indenture system and abandoning an earlier, more robust vision of free labor. Nonetheless, relative state weakness, resistance, and practical difficulties continued to prevent local authorities from enforcing the law strictly.

The changes initiated after the repeal of the sugar duties did not, then, stabilize the legal structure of the indenture system. Nor did the extensive official debates traced over the course of this chapter quell underlying disagreements over the nature of free labor. Despite the concessions made, local officials and elites demanded more. Having denounced labor taxes as a "great error," the elected members of British Guiana's Court of Policy argued that indentured Indians were not "fit to be left entirely free agents" and called for stricter labor controls.[228] Underlying these claims was an increasing conviction that the "experiment" of emancipation was failing. Looking back at the wage struggles and economic difficulties of the late 1840s, and the "apparent retrogression" of the formerly enslaved who left the plantations, Governor Barkly spoke of the "comparative failure of Emancipation."[229] In the 1850s, the Court of Policy similarly criticized what it viewed (in a clearly exaggerated manner) as the Creole population's "complete emancipation from labour."[230] As this sense of moral, social, and economic regression gained prominence, the notion of emancipation itself became suspect. It had produced an "indolent freedom," a freedom needing to be remedied.[231] As we will see in the next chapter, that sentiment—rejecting the project of emancipation—became the basis for further changes and a more dramatic consolidation of the indenture system during the 1850s.

4

Consolidating Indenture, 1848–1862

The 1850s witnessed the ideological and material consolidation of the indenture system. The disruptions of free trade amplified public fears about economic decline, and by the late 1840s, many believed that emancipation had failed economically. The supposed failures of emancipation transformed debate on indenture, galvanizing public support for labor migration. Yet as this occurred, Mauritius, British Guiana, and Trinidad all experienced substantial economic growth. Ever malleable, the relation between economic conditions and public discourse thus changed during the 1850s. If economic crisis had initially served as the foundational basis for indenture, economic growth was by the end of the decade a new primary justification. This chapter explains this transformation in three related registers, through analysis of public debate, legal ideology, and local and global economic structure.

As free trade made imperial export production less profitable, longstanding observers like the *Times* came to view post-slavery freedom from a new vantage point. The triumph of abolition had been moral; the failure of emancipation was economic. Economic "decline" and the perceived failure of emancipation were one important catalyst in the British public's turn toward indenture. Free-trade political economy was a related, equally important cause. During the 1850s, political economy and demography displaced older modes of conceptualizing labor and long-distance trade, subverting antislavery critiques of indenture. The result was a new image of labor migration as a progressive, modern, and mutually beneficent form of development.

At the same time, the conceptual boundaries of free labor continued to shift, and the laws of indenture became increasingly restrictive. Moving further from the liberal framework of the early 1840s, the Colonial Office agreed to permit centralizing allotment reforms and mandatory five-year indenture contracts. Like the broader public, imperial officials came to view post-slavery free labor through the prism of racial difference, and evinced a greater willingness to approve direct forms of legal compulsion as a result. An ideological tendency to "moralize" particular economic interests was important in this regard: reforms designed to reduce competition and variability in the labor market were framed as a means of promoting the general social order rather than elite interests. Meanwhile, changes in the law also reflected competing foreign policy priorities and growing internal momentum, as precedent served to routinize the spread of legal norms concerning indenture.

The consolidation of the indenture system during the 1850s was material, not just ideological and legal. After declining sharply after the repeal of the sugar duties, the price of sugar rose again during the late 1850s. As this occurred, planters used indentured labor to expand sugar cultivation. By the end of the decade, export production and revenue exceeded pre-abolition highs, particularly in Mauritius but also in British Guiana and Trinidad. These changes reflected back into public discourse: economic growth solidified the emerging consensus in favor of indenture. In this context, crucial concepts like labor shortage and economic necessity assumed new meanings. As sugar economies grew, the economic logic of indenture became self-reinforcing.

Emancipation, Social Science, and the Normalization of Indenture

From the late 1840s through the 1850s, the center of public debate shifted decidedly in favor of indentured labor migration. New forms of social-scientific analysis associated with liberal political economy played an important role in publicly legitimizing indenture. So too did a growing consensus that emancipation had failed economically. Over time, that consensus made race a primary lens through which non-European labor was appraised. Notions of racial inferiority, in turn, made restrictions on labor like indenture appear necessary. Finally, economic expansion during the mid- to late 1850s bolstered support for indenture, realigning former critics. By 1860, most observers in the press as well as in Parliament lauded indenture as a clear success.

In 1838, Lord Brougham's critique of labor migration had featured a self-conscious rejection of political-economic reasoning. "Let their laws of political economy fare how they may," he proclaimed. "I am abiding by the law of God and the law of the land."[1] A decade later, Brougham's moral viewpoint lost ground in public debate. The crucial context was free trade. As we have seen, the protectionist response to free-trade policy resulted in new attacks on indenture. But at the same time, free-trade publications played an important role in publicly legitimizing the system as it grew. Particularly notable in this regard was the *Economist*, founded in 1843 to support the Anti-Corn Law League.[2] Alongside other publications, it helped disseminate free-trade arguments, which soon spread to daily newspapers like the *Morning Chronicle* and the *Times*. The result was a reinterpretation of both indenture and emancipation. Seen increasingly as an "experiment," emancipation was subjected to social-scientific analysis.[3] As this occurred, new arguments concerning political economy and demography solidified public support for indenture.

Prompted by the apparent failure of the Royal Navy to suppress illegal slave trading by foreign powers, free-traders developed a broad re-evaluation of the political economy of the slave trade, with important implications for perceptions of indenture.[4] Antislavery advocates had long condemned the slave trade as an "unnatural traffic." Arguing from the perspective of political economy, free-traders adopted a radically different position: the slave trade was in a certain sense "a natural trade," logically derived from the economic progress of the West. In late 1848, for example, the *Economist* argued that even after abolition, an overseas trade supplying Europe with basic agricultural goods produced using non-European labor would inevitably remain. This was because, in the paper's view, "the extent and activity of the slave trade have been mainly governed by the *demand* for the products of slave labor in Europe."[5] Europe's burgeoning population and wealth sustained and increased this demand despite abolition.

Quite dramatically, this argument broke with core antislavery principles. The advocates who became the movement's first historians portrayed abolition as the triumphal result of rational and religious awakening.[6] From this perspective, slavery was pre-modern, uncivilized, and cruel, while abolition was coterminous with European progress. By contrast, the *Economist* suggested that the slave trade was the logical outcome of European economic growth. As such, overseas trade (including the slave trade) was distinctively *modern*. And progress itself had sustained the slave system. Equally important, the *Economist*'s reading naturalized the slave trade. Incorporating a logic of racial difference into its economic analysis, the paper portrayed labor migration from Africa to the West Indies (whether slave or free) as "a great natural fact," affording no cause for moral reprobation. "We do not apologise for this any more than we apologise for earthquakes," it noted.[7] Thus reconfigured, the slave trade could be seen as a historical necessity rather than an immoral aberration.

This rereading mirrored proslavery arguments that circulated beyond the British imperial world. In the United States, as Matthew Karp has shown, southern newspapers similarly portrayed slavery as an integral and inevitable part of modern economic development—an "inexorable necessity," as the *Southern Literary Messenger* put it in 1854.[8] Dulling the moral force of abolitionism, proslavery writers saw forced plantation labor as an economic necessity. International commerce depended on unfree labor, argued the *Charleston Mercury*; demand was "a law inherent in the nature of society."[9] Southern critics read post-emancipation conflict in the West Indies as evidence for this view.[10] Britain, the paragon of antislavery, and the US South, still a bastion of formal slavery, produced convergent discourses of labor at mid-century.[11]

For British debate on indentured labor migration, the implications of this economic account of slavery—of slavery's supposed modern necessity—were profound. The question was no longer whether indenture resembled slavery. "The interchange of the products of temperate for tropical climes" was simply a "natural traffic." For the *Economist*, it followed that "the inhabitants of western Africa should be employed as labourers within the tropics by more civilised and skilful men."[12] Labor migration was now seen as a logical means of bolstering an inevitable pattern of global trade.

If liberal political economy made labor migration appear necessary at a macro level, a civilizing discourse advanced by the same publications cast the potential experience of individual migrants in a new, positive light. This discourse depended on a decidedly negative assessment of non-European societies and tended to abstract Africa and Asia to highlight non-European difference rather than specific geographic or cultural referents. Such abstraction changed the meaning of the term "coolie," which shed its prior association with Chota Nagpur in favor of a more generic sense of primitiveness. It similarly allowed for a blending of assertions of inferiority drawn from a variety of imagined African and Asian contexts. Thus the *Economist* simultaneously supported "Coolie emigration from India" and "a more extensive emigration from the coast of Africa" on the basis that the British West Indies were more advanced, socially and politically, than either vast region.[13] In so doing, the paper figured labor migration as a form of "emancipation"—as a means of civilizing primitive peoples. As the same article explained, emigration from Africa "would practically be emancipating a whole race of men who are at present held in the most brutal and debased state of slavery," putting them instead "under a mild and good government."[14]

Civilizing languages featured in multiple colonial contexts and across time periods, from the *mission civilasatrice* of the French Empire under the Third Republic to the triad of "commerce, Christianity, and civilization" associated with British imperial expansion from the late nineteenth century. What was distinctive in the early era of emancipation was a civilizing mission that undermined the conceptual foundations of existing critiques of indenture. Indeed, an image of moral and economic improvement made it possible for the *Economist* to invert the polarities of antislavery discourse and more firmly distinguish between slavery and indenture. Among the "privileges and advantages of civilisation" attributed to West Indian society were "a perfect security for political and personal freedom" and "institutions for the extension of education, and religious instruction."[15] These features stood in dramatic contrast to the supposedly dominant characteristics of African society, which had "hitherto baffled every attempt to civilise or improve it," and was "sunk in the most abject poverty and slavery."[16] In this rhetorical universe, indentured labor migration shed former associations with slavery and the slave trade, and instead assumed the mantle of freedom and progress.

By locating non-European societies in a primitive, inferior past, liberal publications like the *Economist* thus reframed indentured labor migration as means of emancipatory advancement.[17] As we saw in chapter 1, similar notions had appeared in official discussions of state regulation. Over the course of the 1840s and in the context of free trade, newspapers elaborated related ideas with less emphasis on state protection and a greater reliance on a deeply hierarchical global sociology. In the summer of 1845, the *Friend of India*, which had fiercely opposed indenture in the late 1830s, suddenly came to support it. It did so on the basis of reports suggesting that migration to Mauritius "improved" Indian workers formerly mired in poverty and superstition.[18] Not only did indenture bring greater "comforts of life," it also worked against the "prejudices of caste" and helped create "independence of character," the paper asserted.[19] By 1848, meanwhile, multiple newspapers joined the *Economist* in portraying migration from Africa to the West Indies as a form of "emancipation."[20] Indentured Africans "would simply lose Africa and slavery," argued the *Examiner*, "and gain the congenial climate of the West Indies and freedom."[21] According to the *Times*, African migrants "would find themselves much happier, and certainly more in the road to civilisation, than in their own miserable country."[22]

In the context of ongoing political conflict over repeal, parliamentary proposals for African migration stimulated such speculation, temporarily capturing the attention of the London press.[23] Yet at the same time, many proponents applied the same civilizing logic to India and China. For Lord George Bentinck, a key figure in these debates as the chair of an 1848 parliamentary select committee on sugar and coffee planting, it was "impossible to doubt that the condition of Africans, Chinese, or Hindoos, would be greatly improved by their transport" to the Caribbean.[24] Despite its imprecision, this kind of thinking, based on a very general sense of non-European backwardness and improvement through empire, helped redeem indenture from antislavery and protectionist critiques alike. It also reframed the question, minimizing arguments over cruelty and exploitation while providing an alternate sociological basis for the notion that indenture was itself a form of emancipation.

Comparative sociology was similarly important to a third key element of the social-scientific reinterpretation of indenture: demography. Beginning in the 1850s, press accounts turned increasingly to population dynamics as a means of explaining economic productivity in post-emancipation societies. The emerging consensus was that low population densities in the larger Caribbean colonies—Jamaica and British Guiana in particular—produced a shortage of labor discipline.[25] This notion reprised a core tenet of liberal colonization theory: that density, whether natural or imposed, was necessary for industry.[26] Seen in these terms, the post-emancipation Caribbean portended dispersion and decline. Freedpeople in the larger colonies retained an important measure of independence from the colonial economy; they could reject wage labor on plantations in favor of small farming and other modes of support.

On this seemingly scientific basis, newspapers used demographic theory to argue that labor migration was necessary to avoid economic collapse. Comparing Barbados and Jamaica, the *Morning Chronicle* argued that low population density had doomed the larger colony to economic failure.[27] Making the same comparison, the *Morning Post* held that only high population densities could secure "a continuous supply of labour at a moderate cost."[28] For both papers, labor migration became a demographic necessity. As the *Morning Chronicle* put it, "decided measures for the repression of squatting, and for the encouragement of immigration," were "the most valuable boons that could be conferred on the West Indies in the present crisis of their destiny."[29]

Additionally—and of particular importance—analysis of population dynamics gave rise to a re-evaluation of the relationship between coercion and "free" wage labor. Comparing the West Indies with England, the *Times* argued that free labor was both voluntary and forced. "Labour is never given without a motive," an editorial published in 1850 explained. Population pressure in England had forced peasants to work in order to secure "the first wants of nature—food, clothing, fuel, and shelter." The English free laborer evinced "a steadiness and continuity of exertion" not simply by choice, but "under the penalty of actual want." In the West Indies, the *Times* complained, the situation was different. There, an abundance of fertile land made it possible for freedpeople to survive without working for wages. According to the paper, the now free, formerly enslaved worker needed "little shelter, less clothing, and scarcely more food than can be found above his head or at his feet." On this view, small farming was a sign of social regression; freedpeople became "vagrants" who squatted "in true barbarian fashion." But in terms of debate on indenture, the key inference drawn from the paper's racialized demography was that emancipation had produced a drastic shortage of labor and labor discipline. "The planters can never reckon with any security either upon sufficient labour at a remunerative price," the *Times* maintained, "or upon vigorous or continuous labour at any price at all."[30]

Labor migration—efforts to "introduce labourers from foreign ports"—was seen as a potential solution to this problem. But the broader conclusion with implications for both free Black and indentured labor was that "free labor" in the West Indies was distinct from its English counterpart. According to the *Times*, special coercive measures were necessary in the West Indies as a substitute for the pressures of population found in England and Europe more broadly. The fundamental conclusion was that Black laborers "liable to no wants beyond those of a savage," "amenable to no laws of vagrancy," and "on whom terms of hiring are not to be obligatory" could not be trusted to work consistently. Free labor in the Caribbean would require additional coercion.[31]

Race, Emancipation, and Economic Change

As liberal economic and demographic theory bolstered support for indenture, an additional, closely related transformation played an equally important role in legitimizing labor migration. This was a shift in attitudes toward race, which similarly turned on the ambiguous, contested meaning of emancipation. By the late 1840s, still in the throes of repeal, prominent British newspapers turned against emancipation. Between 1848 and 1858, it became increasingly common to assert that emancipation had failed—economically, socially, and morally. This consensus anchored support for indenture, now framed as a necessary means of correcting the supposed failures of emancipation.

Public denunciations of emancipation focused on freedpeople, whose partial resistance to plantation labor was interpreted as a sign and result of racial inferiority. The formerly enslaved had refused to become modern wage workers, and an industry central to imperial trade had purportedly been debilitated. Emancipation, on this view, had produced social regression, backward movement from civilization to wilderness. According to the *Spectator*, emancipation created a "fool's paradise of half-civilised Blacks." Freed "not only from slavery but also from industry," freedpeople were now "indolent" and "luxurious." Rejecting the "obsolete romances" of Exeter Hall, the paper denounced the "experiment" of emancipation as a failure.[32] This kind of pronouncement marked a hardening of racial attitudes and a deliberate rejection of antislavery principles.

Indeed, newspaper accounts denouncing the supposed failures of emancipation demonstrated the increasing salience of race-thinking in the British public sphere.[33] A significant body of scholarship has argued that British (and European) conceptions of race transformed during the nineteenth century. This argument begins with the work of scholars who have persuasively charted the mutability of early modern notions of race. As they have shown, race was linguistically multivalent during the eighteenth century, and it was frequently understood as the contingent product of environment and culture.[34] Against this backdrop, many have sought to explain a hardening of racial categories and a new, "modern" notion of race, as an immutable identity and cause of social difference. Historians of anthropology and science have shown how a biological conception of race displaced the biblical theory of monogenesis, which had posited a common origin for mankind.[35] Work on a variety of colonial encounters has emphasized social and religious conflicts between missionaries and indigenous peoples.[36] Still other work on empire has seen larger-scale acts of revolt like the Indian Rebellion of 1857 and the Morant Bay Rebellion of 1865 as turning points that precipitated the rise of fixed notions of inherent racial difference.[37]

Alongside these explanations, debate on indenture and emancipation reveals that assertions of racial inferiority were also, and from an earlier stage, bound up with economic conflicts surrounding wage-labor dependency in the post-slavery empire. A "sociological" approach to race, as Stuart Hall termed it, rejects economic determinism.[38] Such a standpoint informs this book and much of the work outlined above. Yet one result, perhaps unintended, is a tendency to dissociate race from economic context.[39] The study of emancipation challenges us to reunite these realms without reducing racial attitudes to economic relations or an ahistorical functionalism.[40] This becomes visible, as we are seeing, when we ground race-thinking in particular conflicts over labor and export production. Additionally (and newly for a historiography that often omits indenture), we should understand that "modern" race-thinking reoriented public debates on and lent legitimacy to state-sponsored labor migration. Doing so allows us to join the intellectual and cultural history of race to "the concrete historical 'work' which racism accomplished under specific historical conditions."[41]

Assertions of African inferiority were hardly new in this context; they had long accompanied formal slavery.[42] But if the mid-century hardening of racial attitudes reassembled old materials, it produced a new hegemonic complex in the process, one which proslavery writers had failed to sustain. The racism of the *Times* in 1850 meant something different from the racism of a plantation owner like Edward Long, for instance, fighting the tide of antislavery in 1774.[43] By the 1850s, press accounts of emancipation purported to demonstrate racial inferiority on a new, seemingly objective basis. That basis was the perceived failure of freedpeople to meet the unequal requirements of commodity production as wage workers.[44] Race, in other words, became an explanation for perceived economic failure. "Indolence" was thus linked to savagery; resistance to labor discipline attributed to racial incapacity. Like the *Spectator*, the *Morning Chronicle* condemned the formerly enslaved for "their love of idleness" and their "natural disinclination to work."[45]

This was the beginning of the "Quashee" stereotype, which Thomas Carlyle named but did not by himself invent.[46] The *Times* labeled emancipation a failure in the same key moment in 1848, as sugar prices fell in response to the repeal of the sugar duties, and as labor protests broke out in Jamaica and British Guiana in response to falling wages.[47] In so doing, the *Times* similarly combined perceptions of economic and civilizational, or moral, decline. Emphasizing a profound ambivalence regarding the status of non-European free labor, the paper's editorial simply concluded: "We have made a desert and called it freedom."[48] A desert, the once verdant Caribbean, green in the British imagination since Sir Walter Raleigh. Economic change turned the ideal. A possible retreat from export agriculture impugned emancipation; "freedom," for the *Times*, had dried the land.

Over the course of the next decade, this new consensus that emancipation had failed amplified public support for indenture. This factor was perhaps most important in explaining the dramatic reversal of the *Times*'s position on the issue. By the end of the decade, the paper was even more strident in its condemnation of emancipation. The great experiment it portrayed quite simply as a "failure": "it destroyed an immense property, ruined thousands of good families, degraded the Negroes still lower than they were, and, after all, increased the mass of Slavery in less scrupulous hands."[49] In this context, labor migration appeared necessary. "Not a word can now be said against a process which, natural as it seems, was loudly protested against only a few years ago," the same article affirmed. Indeed, the transformation of the *Times*'s position was complete. In the late 1830s and early 1840s, the paper strongly criticized the use of Indian indentured labor for reviving slavery's "most odious horrors."[50] That system it now proclaimed a success. "It has answered, and the mouths of all adversaries have been stopped."[51]

The *Times* was not alone: the later 1850s witnessed a dramatic consolidation of the logic underpinning indentured labor migration. As we have seen, race-based justifications for indenture hardened in a context of economic conflict over wage labor in the plantation system. By the later part of the decade, a related but contrasting set of economic developments proved equally influential in shaping public debates. The prospect of economic failure had been a catalyst for indenture from the beginning. But starting in the mid-1850s, a new economic story—a story of growth rather than decline—altered the material basis of support for indenture. By the end of the decade, nearly 370,000 Indian workers had arrived in the colonies.[52] In Mauritius, British Guiana, and Trinidad, the impact was transformative. Against the "failure" of emancipation, indenture soon stood for economic success.

Alongside indentured labor migration, increases in both price and production drove the material growth of imperial export economies. After falling precipitously because of the repeal of the sugar duties, the market price of sugar once again increased during the 1850s in response to the Crimean War and unexpected contractions in European supply.[53] Planters in the colonies, meanwhile, increased production by bringing new land under cultivation and importing new laborers. In Mauritius, sugar production nearly doubled between 1850 and 1856.[54] Because of both production and price increases, the colony's sugar export revenue rose from roughly £1,110,546 in 1852, to £1,687,826 in 1856, to £2,038,682 in 1857.[55] On a smaller scale, the same trend was apparent in the Caribbean. In Trinidad, for example, export revenue increased from £387,999 in 1855, to £546,296 in 1856, to £1,013,414 in 1857.[56] We will return to these changes in greater detail later in the chapter. But here, the key point remains discursive. It was no coincidence that production increased in the three colonies where labor migration had occurred on a large scale. As it did, metropolitan support for indenture found additional backing.

Dramatic export growth added to indenture's public appeal even as it conflicted with the foundational belief that emancipation had failed economically. If indenture had initially been portrayed as a means of preventing economic collapse, in the later 1850s it became a means of promoting growth above and beyond pre-abolition levels. Mauritius, where the scale of Indian migration was largest, was a particularly important symbol in this regard. Supporters of indenture frequently juxtaposed Mauritius with Jamaica, where labor migration had featured less prominently and where sugar production had decreased.[57] Many distinct factors contributed to Jamaica's changing economic landscape. But in newspaper accounts the comparison furnished an increasingly direct argument in favor of Indian migration. As an editorial published in the *Morning Post* explained:

> Since the year 1842 down to the present time there have been imported into Mauritius no fewer than one hundred and seventy-four thousand two hundred and thirty free immigrants. This striking fact enables us to account for

> the immense increase of production which has since been witnessed in that island, and, we may add, for its present prosperous condition. Let us now, by way of contrast, turn to our principal West India colony, Jamaica . . . In one word, we know that Jamaica has suffered more and that Mauritius has suffered less from the effects of emancipation than any of our sugar colonies. What is the cause of this striking contrast? It is to be found, as we have shown, in the simple fact that free labour has been withheld, or very scantily afforded, to one, while it has been abundantly supplied to the other.[58]

For the *Post*, "free labour" was migratory; it was the freedom of colonial employers to import migrant labor without government restriction.[59] But more broadly, the paper's heralding of Mauritius signaled the extent to which debate on indenture had shifted since the early 1840s. After all, for the early critics of Indian labor migration, Mauritius was a primary antagonist. It was in Mauritius that the clandestine slave trade persisted longest after 1808. It was similarly Mauritius where the private recruitment of Indian laborers aroused the greatest scandal between 1834 and 1838. By the late 1850s, however, Mauritius's symbolic function in indenture debates had transformed completely. Indenture was now regarded uncontroversially as free labor. And Mauritius was now portrayed as an uncommon success. Citing the colony as an example, the colonial secretary, Edward Bulwer Lytton, told Parliament in 1859: "Where immigration has been continued, prosperity has followed."[60]

Export growth also helped explain the eventual realignment of conservative interests around indenture. As we have seen, protectionist newspapers rejected indentured labor migration as a poor substitute for tariff protection after 1846. In the 1850s, by contrast, they abandoned protectionism, joining the *Times* and the *Morning Chronicle* in support of indenture and the apparent boom it had enabled. From 1854 onward, the *Morning Post* steadily supported labor migration, arguing that it was demographically necessary to make sugar production viable.[61] The same shift was apparent in the *Standard*, only several years later. "The whole arable surface [of the West Indian colonies] would have been overrun with weeds," claimed one editorial, "had not labour been obtained from India and China."[62] If free trade had initially fragmented conservative interests surrounding indenture, the cleavage proved temporary.

Some criticism of indenture remained. Throughout the late 1850s, the *Anti-Slavery Reporter* continued to oppose the indentured labor system.[63] Though clearly in the minority, a few other English newspapers did the same. The abolitionist *Daily News*, founded in 1846, published articles critical of labor migration in 1858 and 1859.[64] In 1859, it argued that an immigration bill proposed in Jamaica would "re-establish slavery in the West Indies under another name."[65] And the *News* actively disputed the negative assessment of emancipation propagated by the *Times*. In its view, freedpeople did work and the post-emancipation labor shortage was a myth. "Such people as these," the paper declared, "the sons of slaves, and the makers of their own independence, are certainly not lazy."[66]

But by the end of the decade, a public consensus supporting indenture had formed. The notion that emancipation had failed economically led prominent newspapers like the *Times* to abandon their former opposition. New forms of social-scientific analysis reshaped debate on indenture by undermining antislavery conceptions of free labor, long-distance trade, and progress. From the perspectives of free-trade political economy and demography, indentured labor migration was a modern economic necessity rather than a pre-modern revival of slavery. Dramatic economic growth spurred by the rise of sugar prices during the 1850s then solidified public support for indenture. Protectionist critics realigned as the boom occurred, joining Peelites and Liberals who had long supported indenture. By the end of the decade, with Mauritius as a particular example of economic success, indenture would assume a stylized antislavery language of its own. As we will see in the next chapter, supporters would increasingly portray indenture as a tool of antislavery—as a means of competing with slavery in foreign territories. In this triumphal image, indenture became not a perversion but rather an integral piece of the project of emancipation.

Moralizing Economic Interest: Indenture, Social Order, and Civilization

Over the course of the 1850s, as public discourse embraced indenture, the system's legal structure continued to change. In important ways, the laws governing labor relations became increasingly coercive. At the level of legal ideology, justifications for coercion reflected changing conceptions of non-European free labor: like the broader public, imperial officials came to view indenture through the prism of racial and cultural inferiority. At the same time, officials "moralized" particular economic interests as they continued to debate the law. Through this process, heightened terms of indenture were framed as a form of "order" that would benefit labor and capital equally. This was important because it allowed colonial officials to treat labor discipline as part of the general social good; the language of order was, as Adam McKeown has argued in a different context, a "seemingly neutral vocabulary" that "redeploy[ed] principles of hierarchy."[67] Taking these strands together, the

1850s saw a turn away from the liberal universalism the Colonial Office had insisted upon in the 1840s. In its place, there emerged a belief that direct labor coercion was necessary in the face of racial incapacity, and right as a means of promoting social order.[68]

As we saw in the previous chapter, attempts to enforce Earl Grey's model laws of indenture met with significant difficulty in practice. As a result, legislative conflict persisted despite the Colonial Office's concessions. Unable to impose labor taxes effectively, colonial elites began to petition once again for more direct legal compulsion. By 1852, the Protector of Immigrants and governor of Mauritius had both rejected labor taxes, which the governor argued had "entirely failed" to raise revenue.[69] In 1853, British Guiana's Court of Policy repealed Grey's system without permission, replacing it with an ordinance that simply allowed for five-year fixed contracts.[70]

The Colonial Office rejected Guiana's new law as an infringement of "personal freedom."[71] But several months later, the Duke of Newcastle, who was then the colonial secretary, issued a new model ordinance that made additional concessions to local demands. Abandoning Grey's system of labor taxes, Newcastle's model called for three-year initial contracts.[72] At the end of three years, it gave indentured workers the choice of either re-indenturing under one-year contracts for an additional two years, or paying a commutation fee to redeem the remainder of industrial residence.[73] In addition, the model authorized imprisonment with hard labor for up to fourteen days as punishment for absence from work, as well as warrantless arrests for Indian, African, and Chinese workers found away from the plantations without written tickets of leave or certificates demonstrating the completion of five years of plantation labor.[74] After circular instructions were sent to the colonies, these proposals became the basis for consolidated indenture laws enacted in Trinidad and British Guiana.[75]

Though Newcastle's instructions explicitly rejected harsher alternatives suggested in the colonies, they nonetheless demonstrated an increasing acceptance of long-contested claims—most notably, the notion that five years of indentured labor should be required of immigrants.[76] They also reflected a growing sense that Indian workers benefited from indenture, morally and economically. In connection with Newcastle's model, the Government of India agreed to extend the period before which Indian immigrants were entitled to return passage, from five to ten years. Noting "very favourable" official reports on the condition of Indian immigrants in British Guiana and Trinidad, one councilor saw "no objection" to such an extension.[77] For Mauritius, where the cost of transportation to India was lower, the Indian authorities agreed to abolish the right to free return passage altogether.[78]

As these changes occurred, local and imperial authorities portrayed indenture ever more frequently as a mutually beneficial enterprise. As an engine of economic growth, labor migration was presented not only as a means of supporting the *plantations* but also, and more generally, as a means of spreading order and civilization. This civilizational rhetoric served an ideological function: it translated particular economic interests into a general and seemingly neutral ideal of the social good. In Mauritius, for example, claims that labor migration was necessary to sustain production turned into broader arguments about protecting civilization from anarchy. "Without Indian Immigration," the colony's Chamber of Agriculture maintained, "the ruin of this colony would long since have been consummated."[79] In this context, "ruin" was understood in relation to entwined notions of economic and civilizational progress. By early 1855, Mauritian officials warned the Colonial Office of "universal stagnation if not universal Anarchy," summoning an image not only of lost capital, but also of social regression.[80] Without legal restrictions on labor, "the island would be subjected to the tyrannical license of men who, emancipated from the thralldom of disciplined industry, had learned that subsistence on such a soil and in such a climate could be procured without toil, and without wages."[81] This vision of a world without toil was conjured as a nightmare, not a utopia. Small farming portended a retreat from civilization. At stake in legal debates about labor discipline was a broader vision of the social order—and the idea of "civilization" itself—centered on wage labor and economic dependency.

Appeals to this concept of social order were often framed negatively, in response to the possibility of economic decline. But they were also made positively, in terms of social "improvement." When British Guiana modified its immigration laws in response to Newcastle's model, Governor Wodehouse justified both interference in private employment relations and legal restrictions placed on immigrants as tools of civilization. According to Wodehouse, government in fact bore a "duty" to put indentured workers "under such regulations as will promote their eventual social improvement, without reference to their own immediate wishes." His logic depended on a theory of tropical social development that emphasized both demographic pressure and ingrained habits. Comparing the tropics with England, he argued that the availability of land undermined labor discipline in the colonies, creating a "natural tendency to idleness and self-indulgence." Raising non-European plantation workers "in the moral and social scale" could thus only be achieved through government control. "I should little expect to see any where any such progressive improvement of the native population," Wodehouse continued, "if it were to be the result of their own free choice alone, or still less of their own continuous, steady labour." From these premises, and for the sake of social order and moral improvement, the colony would "legislate between him and his employer" and "ensure his continuous labour."[82]

This vision of improvement served to justify the use of law to control labor. Before abolition, antislavery reformers sought to enlarge the powers of the imperial state to combat the unbridled authority of slaveholders.[83] That private power—in particular the power to punish the enslaved—was seen as a kind of despotism, free from law and justice.[84] Against this despotism, Crown officials would mediate between "masters" and "servants"; magistrates and public law would reform colonial slavery, protecting the enslaved from extralegal tyranny. In the post-emancipation period, public power assumed a new function. As Diana Paton has argued with regard to Jamaica, abolition transferred private power to the state, such that "the state, symbolized by the notion of law, became in a sense a new type of bond."[85] In the context of indenture, the province of law similarly grew. Between employers and their indentured workers, law now served to police the order of wage labor—to ensure "continuous labour," as Governor Wodehouse put it.

This dynamic found particular expression in efforts to reform the recruitment and distribution of indentured workers over the course of the decade. When, in 1842, labor migration resumed under government supervision, Lord Stanley stipulated that labor contracts committing individual workers to specific plantations be signed in the colony, rather than in India.[86] Stanley and the Colonial Office further required that such contracts only be signed after a forty-eight-hour waiting period, rather than immediately on arrival.[87] The principle underlying both rules was voluntariness; the aim was to allow workers to choose among different possible employers and protect market dynamics in hiring by forcing employers to compete over workers. In 1842, these rules were part of what made indenture free labor.[88]

During the 1850s, planters' associations and local colonial authorities rejected this arrangement. To do so, they appealed to superficially neutral concepts of order like those we have already begun to trace. In such appeals, competition in the hiring process appeared as irrational disorder. Centralization, by contrast, was a mutually beneficial means of ensuring growth. In other words, the language of social order served to delegitimize market dynamics that disfavored employers. Sirdars—Indian labor brokers who mediated between newly arriving workers and employers—were an early target in this regard.[89] Sirdars played a variety of roles, as recruiters, overseers, and moneylenders, and as overseers they aided planters in enforcing labor discipline.[90] But as labor brokers, some sirdars also acted in the interest of workers,

FIGURE 6. "Coolies on arrival from India, mustered at Depôt," Trinidad, c. 1890. The National Archives, London, CO 1069/392.

negotiating wage increases collectively.[91] Such negotiation was particularly important on arrival, where "fierce competition" took place before individual migrants had committed to particular plantations, as well as after the expiration of individual contracts.[92] Inasmuch as sirdars increased competition, their bargaining power was delegitimized in moral terms. "No possible good can result either to employers or employee" from allowing workers to organize in groups under sirdars, the Mauritian Chamber of Agriculture argued. Such an arrangement "operate[d] from the outset to the serious prejudice of that respect which is due by the inferior to his superior."[93] A moralized, hierarchical sense of order made laws designed to minimize competition appear to serve the common good.

With these concerns in mind, the Mauritian government introduced centralizing reforms between 1851 and 1854. Without repealing the forty-eight-hour rule, new laws gave the governor power to determine the number of newly arriving indentured immigrants each of the colony's plantations was entitled to hire annually.[94] Reducing active competition among employers, these laws rationalized the hiring process, predetermining rough distribution in relation to sugar production rather than individualized market incentives.[95] Though routinely referred to as "immigration," indenture was in this and other respects a state-run labor system, a reality that laws regulating distribution did much to produce.

In 1858, the colony went further, passing a law that legalized labor contracts signed in India.[96] Ordinance No. 30 of 1858 allowed for three-year initial contracts committing workers to specific plantations before arrival in the colony.[97] In addition, it gave the governor power to "allot" workers without pre-signed contracts to individual plantations on arrival.[98] Neither London nor Calcutta objected. The Government of India noted that "engagements may with advantage be permitted to be formed between employers in Mauritius and Indian laborers before the latter quit India," and the ordinance was approved.[99] From this point onward, hiring in the colony was in essence a distribution process organized by government officials. The Colonial Office abandoned its previous insistence on competition at the hiring stage as a means of preserving voluntary contract principles.

Other forms of economic restructuring followed, similarly framed as neutral methods of preventing disorder. In addition to legalizing contracts signed in India, Ordinance No. 30 created a fixed wage scale to eliminate competitive bargaining.[100] Under this arrangement, the government would set wages for the initial three-year contract period, using past averages as a guide.[101] In 1860, the colony extended this system of wage fixing for the full period of industrial residence. Absent affirmative non-consent, initial labor contracts were automatically renewed for a fourth and fifth year, with small stipulated wage increases on each renewal.[102]

These changes drew on a system of "tacit consent" pioneered in British Guiana, where planters and officials had continued to demand fixed, five-year contracts in place of Newcastle's model. In both colonies, supporters of automatic contract renewals portrayed them, in moral terms, as a means of containing disorder and as a tool of civilization. Rather than rational market behavior, delays between engagements reflected and resulted in "vice and immorality."[103] The ability to change employers after the third year, meanwhile, "unsettle[d] and demoralize[d] the immigrant."[104] Broader issues of competition and choice in the labor market receded in this language, appearing instead as moral failing and administrative disorder. From this viewpoint, choice was "the very reverse of advantageous" to indentured workers rather than a marker of their freedom.[105] Though the Colonial Office still refused to allow for simple five-year contracts, it allowed British Guiana, and then Mauritius, to enact tacit-consent re-indenture provisions for the final two years of industrial residence. In other words, expiring contracts would automatically renew unless workers actively reported to a stipendiary magistrate to decline or change employers.[106] Trinidad's consolidated immigration law of 1862 similarly provided for automatic re-indenture for workers who failed to either request new employment or pay a commutation fee.[107]

All of these measures—centralized allotment, wage scales, automatic contract renewals—aimed to minimize unpredictability in labor supply, but also to control competition and unwanted labor bargaining. The contrast with un-indentured labor was notable; as we have seen, freedpeople had explicitly contested these kinds of contract terms in the late 1840s. Yet efforts continued to prohibit sirdars from acting as labor brokers and to undermine mediating forces between labor and capital. According to the governor of Mauritius, it was important to "destroy that system of middle agency" which provided the "germ" of what might become "a very serious affliction to the Country."[108] Regulations issued under Ordinance No. 30 of 1858 prohibited the allotment of workers to "middlemen" and allowed the colony's Protector of Immigrants to ban from the Immigration Depot those suspected of "inducing" new arrivals to contract with employers other than those for whom they were initially recruited.[109] The resounding Victorian binary of "industry" and "idleness" hovers over this discussion: "moralization" transformed economic imperatives into moral duties. In the process, it served to justify the state's ostensibly illiberal efforts to shape and control labor markets. And it bolstered the ideologically important conviction that indenture served general, not just particular, interests—that "all classes benefit by Immigration," as the governor of British Guiana put it in 1860.[110]

Foreign Policy, Imperial Precedent, and the Five-Year Contract

As ideological change influenced the law, so did two other factors, which depended on both the relationship between British and foreign colonies during the era of emancipation and the circulation of legal texts within the empire as the indenture system grew. In 1862, after years of dispute and refusal, the Colonial Office allowed the colonies to impose mandatory, five-year contracts on newly arriving indentured workers. The process underlying this change reveals the ongoing importance of Britain's foreign antislavery policy on the development of indenture. It also demonstrates an increasingly salient set of internal legal dynamics, mainly concerning precedent, on the approval of restrictive labor norms. Statutory precedent made the spread of new legal norms across colonial boundaries routine. And, importantly for the broader sweep of my argument, it weakened London's resistance to direct forms of legal coercion.

By the early 1850s, planters in French sugar colonies had begun actively to recruit Indian workers under a form of indenture known as *engagement*. *Engagisme* had existed since the seventeenth century, and it persisted alongside formal slavery during the eighteenth. In the early nineteenth century, after the abolition of the slave trade, *engagisme* facilitated illegal importations of enslaved Africans, particularly to Réunion. After 1848, when France abolished slavery, *engagisme* experienced a revival. Mobilizing pre-abolition recruitment networks in Madagascar, Mozambique, East Africa, and India, French planters brought thousands of new workers to the colonies. Between 1849 and 1859, 43,958 Indian workers came to Réunion under *engagement*.[111]

Observers in British colonies objected frequently to these developments. They argued that French planters operating under fewer formal restrictions enjoyed advantages that British planters were denied. P. N. Bernard, a merchant active in Trinidad, complained that the system of indenture permitted in French colonies was "vastly preferable and superior" to those the home government had sanctioned in the British Caribbean.[112] The governor of Trinidad forwarded Bernard's complaint to the Colonial Office, noting in particular that Martinique and Guadeloupe bound Indian immigrants under five-year contracts.[113] Allegations of preferential treatment would persist, invariably to support demands for additional concessions.[114]

As these complaints accumulated, British officials entered into diplomatic negotiations that would eventually lead to the five-year contract in both British and French colonies. Imperial authorities were keenly aware of French migration patterns. After all, Indian workers embarked from Pondicherry were frequently recruited from British territory. As early as 1852, French officials petitioned the Government of India to make migration to French colonies legal.[115] Several years later, the Foreign Office opened negotiations on the issue as migration flows expanded without official recognition.[116]

Motivating the Foreign Office, in part, was a conviction that emigration, legal or illegal, could never be fully stopped. But Britain's antislavery policy also played an important role. Alongside Indian migration, French planters had turned to African contract labor, which British authorities viewed as "essentially [a] slave-trade."[117] For John Russell, then serving as foreign secretary, the key object to be attained in allowing Indian migration was a renewed commitment on the part of the French to stop African recruitment mired in "men-hunts and other atrocities which belong to Slave Trade."[118] From a diplomatic perspective, Indian indenture was an antislavery compromise—a means of discouraging African slavery in foreign territories.

In this sense, the extension of the Indian indenture system to Réunion and other French colonies reminds us that antislavery was throughout the post-emancipation period a question of both imperial and foreign relations, shaped by related but different strategic aims and forms of administrative oversight.[119] To understand the laws of indenture within the empire, it is important to see the indenture system in the broader context of Britain's ongoing efforts to suppress the slave trade internationally. Such measures took different forms over time. From the British abolition of the trade in 1808 through the end of the Napoleonic Wars, the Royal Navy captured foreign slave ships as prizes. Shortly afterward, Britain signed bilateral anti-slave-trade treaties with Portugal, Spain, and the Netherlands. The Palmerston Act of 1839 and the Aberdeen Act of 1845 authorized the navy to intercept suspected slave ships beyond the strict limits of the treaties.[120] Much debated, often maligned, these efforts persisted, and in some cases antislavery diplomacy contributed directly to important changes in indenture policy.

Russell's goal—stopping French recruitment from West Africa—was only partially attained.[121] But in its service the Foreign Office proved willing to meet French demands on multiple regulatory provisions. The result of the negotiations, a convention signed in 1860, conceded long-contested prohibitions still enforced in British colonies.[122] Most notably, the convention allowed for five-year fixed contracts.[123] In addition, it loosened the Government of India's standing transportation requirements, allowing more workers to be sent on individual ships.[124]

Thus, just as it evinces interconnection across foreign and imperial policy, the French convention also stands as further evidence of ideological shift among the imperial administrators tasked with overseeing the indenture system. Frederic Rogers, the official sent to Paris to negotiate the convention, had previously served as an emigration commissioner within the Colonial Office. Responsible in that capacity for systematically reviewing proposed changes to the laws of indenture, Rogers was clearly aware of the longstanding prohibition on five-year contracts. So too was John Russell, who, as colonial secretary during the early 1840s, had insisted on limiting contracts to one year. By 1859, both viewed the longer contracts as acceptable. Rogers criticized Newcastle's system of renewable contracts as unnecessarily "complicated."[125] Deferring to colonial opinion, he suggested that five-year contracts could be implemented without "any serious disadvantage to the Cooly."[126] As late as 1849, Earl Grey had condemned the five-year contract as part of an attempt to reinstitute "Slavery in a mitigated form."[127] Ten years later, that had changed. No longer a marker of unfair coercion, the multiyear fixed contract had become a harmless tool of administrative convenience. The conceptual boundaries of free labor had shifted.

Once the five-year contract had been conceded in the French context, British colonies demanded the same privilege. The West India Committee lobbied the government, securing a commitment that lesser restrictions should not apply to French as opposed to British colonies.[128] Leveraging that commitment, Mauritius enacted a law legalizing five-year contracts in 1862.[129] Later that summer, the Colonial Office issued circular instructions explicitly authorizing the Caribbean colonies to follow suit. British Guiana and Trinidad did so by the end of the year.[130]

Britain's agreement with France created a new ground for argument in the sugar colonies: fairness, in a legalistic sense. In so doing, it demonstrated a broader process by which precedent came to generate a specifically legal logic for indenture restrictions. As we have seen, local proposals for legal reform frequently provoked extensive debates in Britain and India. These debates, in turn, focused on external, or social, consequences, and on the relation between given rules and the concept of freedom. Legal arguments based on precedent, by contrast, tended to ignore external consequences. When the governor of Mauritius wrote to the Colonial Office to announce the imposition of five-year contracts, he did not argue that long contracts were *better* than short ones. He simply argued that the precedent set by the French convention justified the extension of five-year contracts in Mauritius.[131] Precedent obviated the need for social argument.

Scholars attuned to the mobility of law have debated the importance of "legal transplants"—the transposition of legal rules from one jurisdiction, country, or territory to another.[132] For Alan Watson, the prevalence of such transplants disrupts the notion that law responds to particular social circumstances.[133] In contrast, Renisa Mawani and Iza Hussin propose a multivalent framework for examining the "travels of law" in imperial and global contexts.[134] Drawing on work that emphasizes "webs" of connection among colonies, they point to contestation and circulation across overlapping imperial networks rather than diffusion from metropole to colony.[135]

My claim with regard to legal borrowing is related but distinct. Over time, statutory precedent and conscious legal borrowing played an important role in the law of indenture, generating internal as opposed to social forms of legitimacy. This dynamic highlights the trans-colonial nature of the indenture system—the extent to which legal texts circulated not only between metropole and colony but across multiple colonial sites, from the Caribbean and Indian Ocean to South Africa. Like imperial officials, legal norms moved across the empire.[136] As that occurred and as the 1850s progressed, a particular kind of statutory precedent gave the laws of indenture internal momentum. Local legislative councils did not operate in isolation. Rather, they borrowed deliberately from each other, importing (often verbatim) legal rules enacted in neighboring colonies. Their aim in this respect was strategic. Laws approved by the Colonial Office in one context were hard to resist in another. In London, imperial officials tended to approve transplanted legal rules without re-evaluating their social consequences. Administratively, this procedure was logical enough. But as the indenture system expanded, it quieted official debates about the propriety of formerly controversial laws, even as they were exported into new, very different social contexts.

Perhaps the most dramatic example involves the extension of the Indian indenture system to Natal, in southern Africa, in 1860.[137] Natal was unlike the former slave colonies where the indenture system had been created. But while Natal was different—geographically, demographically, socially—its laws of indenture were not. The Colonial Office forwarded immigration ordinances already in place in British Guiana, St. Lucia, and Trinidad as models.[138] The laws Natal ultimately enacted were based on ordinances from St. Lucia and Mauritius.[139] Few modifications were made; according to the colony's lieutenant governor, the new laws were "little more than a transcript" of the borrowed ordinances.[140] As such, London approved them without lengthy consideration.[141] The key point, then, is that legal borrowing shielded the law of indenture from controversy. Once sanctioned, legal principles and texts gained authority that did not depend on particularized consideration of political and social circumstance. That authority further separated the law of indenture from the specter of slavery and exploitation. Precedent made indenture appear normal and unchanging, even as the system continued to expand.

Economic Growth and the Material Consolidation of Indenture

In the shadow of free trade, a sense of crisis motivated indenture policy in important ways; as we have seen, fears of economic collapse bolstered public support for indenture. In the 1850s, however, even as such arguments continued to proliferate, the material reality of sugar production changed. The dislocation of tariff reform proved temporary. After dropping sharply in the late 1840s, global sugar prices rebounded and then increased in the late 1850s. At the same time, imperial sugar production increased as planters in Mauritius, British Guiana, and Trinidad brought new land under cultivation. Large-scale labor migration was crucial to this development: new labor facilitated production, and newly developed land called for new labor. In these respects, the 1850s witnessed the economic consolidation of the indenture system. Facilitated by the imperial state, labor migration did far more than stave off "decline": it helped produce a dramatic expansion of plantation production. For both Indian and Creole workers, indenture reshaped the political economy of emancipation. As it did so, economic growth further solidified the ideological consensus supporting indenture.

Beginning in the late 1840s, planters and other supporters of indenture portrayed abolition and tariff reform as twin disasters. Abolition, on this view, had created a drastic labor shortage as freedpeople left the plantations for newly formed villages. Free trade, meanwhile, undermined profitability by reducing the price of sugar in Britain. These claims persisted, as did the notion that state-supported labor migration should be used to compensate plantation owners for lost labor and profit. But during the 1850s, they became increasingly misleading. In terms of both raw production and export revenue, sugar economies grew. From the 1830s onward, indenture had been justified as a means of *repairing* economic damage. By the late 1850s, it had become something else. In Mauritius, British Guiana, and Trinidad, sugar production came to exceed pre-abolition levels. Solidified, indenture was about expansion, not just revival.

Global sugar prices fluctuated over the course of the nineteenth century, with important implications for the imperial sugar economy. The century's long-term trend was toward decreasing prices, particularly as beet sugar production increased overall supply. But the 1850s saw significant and in some cases sudden price growth on the British market. After declining during the 1840s, the average price of raw sugar in London rose from a low of twenty shillings per hundredweight in 1852 to twenty-four shillings in 1855, twenty-eight in 1856, and thirty-four in 1857.[142] The Crimean War, which took place between 1853 and 1856, fueled this price increase by reducing overall supply.[143] The trend was impermanent; by the end of the century, the price was closer to ten shillings.[144] But it was nonetheless significant during the 1850s, and it helped the indenture system grow.

As prices rose, planters in Mauritius and the West Indies cleared new land and expanded cultivation. In Mauritius, the amount of land devoted to sugar planting roughly doubled between 1851 and 1857.[145] Increases in the Caribbean were similarly impressive. Trinidad had 28,507 acres growing sugar in 1845; by 1861, it was 36,739.[146] In British Guiana, the figure rose by roughly 60 percent in ten years, from 31,354 acres in 1851 to 52,163 in 1861.[147] In terms of planting, none of the three colonies had been a "mature" sugar colony before abolition, and large tracts of arable land remained undeveloped in the 1840s. During the 1850s, under indenture, much more of that land became cane-field. As it did, raw sugar production rose to match and then exceed pre-abolition levels.

Indeed, export records, which were collected more regularly than land-use surveys, illustrate a striking process of economic expansion. As early as 1850, Trinidad produced more sugar on an average annual basis than it had in the late 1820s and early 1830s.[148] Production continued to rise over the course of the decade, from roughly 43,000,000 lb. in 1850 to more than 50,000,000 lb. in 1854.[149] In 1858, the colony exported 68,286,450 lb. of sugar.[150] Between 1842 and 1858, then, raw production had nearly doubled.[151] The same trend was apparent in British Guiana, where the underlying figures were consistently larger. In 1844, the colony exported 38,521 hogsheads of sugar.[152] That number rose sharply during the 1850s—to 55,700 hogsheads in 1852 and 56,253 in 1854.[153] By the end of the decade, production growth was even more apparent. The colony exported 62,198 hogsheads in 1860 and 72,347 in 1861.[154]

In Mauritius, too, export production increased rapidly, nearly doubling over the course of the decade. But there, the scale was even larger. Between 1845 and 1849, the colony's annual exports averaged 56,069 tons.[155] In 1851, the colony produced 75,000 tons of sugar, and the number rose steadily, from 80,500 tons in 1852, to 100,000 in 1853, to 110,000 in 1856.[156] By 1859, the crop was estimated at 115,000 tons.[157] At this point, Mauritius was producing close to 9 percent of the world's total cane sugar.[158]

Equally if not more important, rising prices on the British market elevated export revenue. In Mauritius, revenue rose from roughly £1,110,546 in 1852, to £1,848,090 in 1855, to £2,209,076 in 1858.[159] In 1859, it increased further, to roughly £2,559,699, more than double what it had been less than ten years earlier.[160] Though on a smaller scale in absolute terms, export revenue nearly tripled in Trinidad. Roughly £387,999 in 1855, it rose to £546,296 in 1856, and £1,013,414 in 1857.[161] In British Guiana, too, revenue gains were dramatic. In 1848, the colony's sugar was valued at £589,160.[162] That figure, in 1855, was £826,026.[163] In 1860, it was £1,088,465.[164]

Rising prices meant that revenue rose even faster than raw production. More important, they made sugar planting increasingly profitable. As we have seen, falling sugar prices after 1846 greatly reduced profit margins, driving some plantations into bankruptcy.[165] By the mid-1850s, that had changed. In some cases, revenue increased even when production declined.[166] In 1857, the Governor of Mauritius reported that "fully one half" of the previous year's sugar revenue—estimated at more than £2,000,000—was "clear profit."[167] If free trade had undermined plantation economies, the disruption was temporary. By the late 1850s, production, revenue, and profit were all increasing.

This dynamic is under-recognized, perhaps because of the prominence accorded to Jamaica in the historiography on the British Caribbean. In Jamaica, where indentured migration occurred on a smaller scale, sugar production did gradually decrease after abolition.[168] By contrast, the nineteenth century saw the dramatic rise of Cuban production, fueled by the importation of hundreds of thousands of newly enslaved Africans before 1867.[169] Cuba's surpassing of Jamaica as the region's preeminent sugar colony suggests a broader interpretive periodization, in which Saint-Domingue, Jamaica, and Cuba appear as a temporal sequence in the history of Caribbean slavery, marked by three different abolitions.[170] Because of indenture, however, parts of the British Empire followed what we might see as the Cuban pattern, of continued export growth (though on a smaller scale) through the middle of the nineteenth century.

This remarkable economic expansion depended on indentured labor. Indeed, as production increased, so too did the scale of labor migration. More than 12,000 Indian workers arrived in Mauritius each year during the 1850s.[171] Toward the end of the decade, migration spiked: 29,946 Indians arrived in 1858; 44,397 in 1859.[172] Fewer made the journey to the West Indies. But there too the late 1850s saw a significant increase in the number of newly arriving indentured workers. Between 1856 and 1860, 16,206 Indian immigrants arrived in British Guiana, as compared with 9,981 between 1851 and 1855.[173] Over the course of the decade (1851–1860), an additional 16,262 Indian workers arrived in Trinidad, nearly three times as many as the colony had received during the 1840s. Overall, more Indian migrants ventured to sugar plantations abroad between 1858 and 1860 than in any other two-year period between 1831 and 1920.[174]

This pattern was neither natural nor spontaneous. Rather, it was the result of state efforts to restructure the political economy of emancipation. As argued in the previous chapter, large-scale migration to the Caribbean colonies depended on state subsidies for transportation. Guaranteed by public revenue, these subsidies were regressive; they redirected wealth from freed and working people back toward the plantations. They also made the expansion of the system possible. In the Caribbean as well as in Mauritius, where the scale of migration was even larger, a key result was an increasing reliance on immigrant rather than Creole labor. That process, which began in the late 1840s, continued with different causes during the 1850s. In the immediate aftermath of free trade, independent landownership and decreasing wages led some freedpeople to leave the plantations, changing the proportion of indentured and un-indentured workers even when Indian populations remained relatively small. In the 1850s, with sugar economies once again expanding, planters requisitioned larger numbers of immigrants, and Indian populations expanded in both absolute and relative terms.

This was most evident in Mauritius. Between 1851 and 1856, the colony's Indian population grew from 84,404 to 134,271—roughly 59 percent of the total. At the same time, the formerly enslaved (or "ex-apprentice") population decreased to 40,730, or 17.5 percent.[175] By the end of 1859, the Indian population exceeded 200,000, roughly two-thirds of what was then the total.[176] The result, according to Governor Stevenson, was that Indian immigrants had "superseded" the formerly enslaved as field workers.[177] In the West Indies, Indian populations remained minorities. But they nonetheless provided an increasingly large proportion of sugar-plantation labor. A report compiled by Trinidad's Agent General of Immigrants in March 1858, for example, suggested that Indians outnumbered freedpeople and others working on the plantations. According to the report, Indians accounted for roughly 37 percent of days worked during the month. Migrant labor together—including Indians, Africans, Chinese, and West Indians—accounted for 79 percent.[178]

All of these factors—increased migration, production, and revenue—marked the consolidation of the indenture system in a material sense. The imposition of free trade unsettled plantation production, which made indentured labor increasingly important in the colonies. During the 1850s, economic growth both fueled and reflected an expansion of the indenture system. Using indentured labor, planters increased production as global sugar prices rose. Rising revenue and profitability, meanwhile, created additional demand for labor migration. Indenture had been a response to decline. It was now a pillar of growth.

This material consolidation affected the way indenture was perceived and discussed. Official skepticism of indenture largely faded in these years, particularly in the colonies. If, amid disease and desertion, indenture had at one point seemed like expensive folly, it now acquired a sense of triumphant necessity. In Mauritius, it was the "very life-blood" and "cornerstone" of prosperity.[179] In British Guiana, it was similarly "of first necessity."[180] Perhaps most notable as a measure of change was the transformation apparent in dispatches sent by Trinidad's governor, Lord Harris. In early 1848, Harris questioned whether Indian labor migration should continue.[181] But during the 1850s, his perspective transformed. "There can be no question," he wrote, "that Oriental immigration is not only beneficial, but that it is also absolutely necessary to sustain this Colony as a Sugar exporting country."[182] Like Harris, other officials came to support indenture steadfastly and without reservation. As Trinidad's Agent General put it in 1858, "all doubts as to the propriety of the introduction of foreign labour have now ceased."[183] Economic growth strengthened this official support for indenture. By the late 1850s, material success—measured solely in terms of export production and profit—cemented the logic of indenture.

At the same time, policy, informed by ideology, was a cause of material change. As officials hailed indenture, the meaning of key terms used to understand the economics of labor migration shifted. That conceptual flexibility, in turn, served to justify indenture policy—and a course of state action committed to ongoing labor migration. Most important in this regard was the concept of "labor shortage," which had been central to justifications for indenture from the beginning. As Madhavi Kale has argued, scholarship on indenture has too often naturalized the notion of labor shortage, treating it straightforwardly as an economic need to which indenture responded.[184] This masks a more complex reality: labor shortage was a category whose meaning was reconfigured over time to produce, not simply respond to, policy imperatives. In the 1840s, the purported withdrawal of Creole populations from the plantations formed the basis of most claims for labor migration. Emancipation caused a labor shortage, critics claimed, and the potential for economic collapse. In the 1850s, the term "labor shortage" took on new meaning, sustaining rather than undermining the rationale for indenture even as underlying economic conditions changed.

Indeed, as the indenture system expanded, colonial officials continued to report that labor shortages necessitated labor migration. In 1856, as export revenue rose, complaints from Trinidad emphasized the colony's "want of labor."[185] Mauritius similarly signaled a "scarcity of labor" even though tens of thousands of new workers had arrived in the previous few years.[186] In other words, labor shortage was a flexible, self-renewing concept. As labor migration facilitated economic growth, increased production created additional demand for new labor. By the mid-1850s, the original economic basis for state-sponsored labor migration—labor shortage spawned by emancipation—no longer existed. But a new kind of shortage, premised on confidence and increased production, did. Growth conferred powers of self-renewal on the economic logic of indenture. This was true in the West Indies and in newer colonies like Natal, far from the originating "crisis" of abolition. In the increasingly triumphant official consensus around indenture, labor migration gained a sense of inevitability.

* * *

By the end of the decade, the indenture system had been solidified. In the 1840s, indenture was precarious. Seen as a betrayal of antislavery, the system faced public criticism and private, official dissent. Competing notions of free labor limited the law's reach in theory, and state weakness, disease, and desertion frustrated attempts to enforce labor discipline in practice. After 1846, the economic dislocation of free trade added to these difficulties, reducing the price of sugar and renewing wage struggles in the Caribbean.

Yet the crisis of free trade was a turning point that set the stage for the indenture system's expansion. Perceptions of economic decline bolstered support for indenture as public opinion turned against the supposed failures of emancipation. New forms of social-scientific analysis similarly reshaped debates on the issue. Replacing older, antislavery conceptions of long-distance migration and trade, political economy and demography made labor migration appear natural, necessary, and mutually beneficial. Prompted by these concerns as well as economic pressures, the Colonial Office sanctioned centralizing and increasingly coercive labor laws. The boundaries of free labor thus shifted in official discourse and practice. Officials "moralized" labor control through the neutral lens of social order. As the laws of indenture became more restrictive, they nonetheless shed their prior association with slavery, gaining instead a sense of progressive utility as a means of directing labor toward ordered development.

Over the course of the decade, meanwhile, indenture reshaped the imperial sugar economy, which grew substantially in spite of abolition. Large-scale migration was both a cause and a product of this growth. As the system expanded, new land was brought under cultivation and sugar production increased dramatically. As prices rose in London, export revenue increased even more quickly. These forms of growth created a renewable "labor shortage" even as the scale of labor migration reached unprecedented heights. Indenture had done more than repair the economic damage done by emancipation and free trade. In Mauritius, British Guiana, and Trinidad, production and revenue now exceeded pre-abolition levels.

By the end of the decade, then, controversy had given way to confidence. Though some criticism remained, economic growth strengthened the public consensus in favor of indenture. As a final measure of conceptual change, supporters appropriated the language of antislavery to their own ends. Mauritius had been a symbol of slavery's intransigence; it now became an exemplar of free labor's power. To the crowning of indenture as a tool rather than a betrayal of antislavery, we turn in the next chapter.

5

Vagrancy, Free Labor, and State Power, 1859–1871

By the early 1860s, the indenture system had won broad public support. As colonial sugar economies expanded, Britons came to see indenture as a force for progressive development. And as new social-scientific discourses displaced antislavery modes of conceptualizing non-European labor and long-distance trade, indenture shed its negative associations with slavery. The final step in this process of normalization was the adaptation of antislavery language in support of indenture. In the early 1840s, critics viewed indenture as a betrayal of emancipation. Twenty years later, a new consensus emerged. No longer controversial, indenture assumed its own antislavery logic. Rather than a subversion, indenture was now a means of saving the project of emancipation, in the empire and abroad.

Though misleading, this ideological consensus had practical importance. In ways we have already begun to see, it undergirded the ongoing expansion of the indenture system. Freed from controversy, the system grew, expanding to new British colonies like Natal and to foreign colonies like Réunion, Guadeloupe, and Suriname. As this occurred, indenture functioned to increase sugar production in British Guiana, Trinidad, and Mauritius. In other words, the large-scale economic pattern traced in the previous chapter continued; by the late 1860s, all three colonies reached new highs in export production and revenue.

If these markers of ideological and material consolidation remained steady, indenture nonetheless continued to change. Problems of labor control, which plagued the indenture system at its inception, intensified as Indian populations grew. In response, colonial authorities introduced new legal and institutional measures designed to police vagrancy. These measures are the subject of much of this chapter. The laws of indenture became increasingly restrictive in the 1860s, as all three colonies heightened penalties associated with unauthorized absence from work. At the level of ideology, these changes followed further shifts in official thinking on the nature of free labor. But they also had a significant impact in practice. While local colonial authorities struggled to enforce the laws of indenture during the late 1840s and early 1850s, rates of prosecution and punishment increased during the 1860s.

The growth of vagrancy law also had unintended consequences, which can only be understood in local context. With particular emphasis on Mauritius, the final section of this chapter argues that efforts to enforce labor discipline broadened in the late 1860s into more generalized forms of discrimination. This transition was the result of a growing collision between state policy aimed at keeping indentured workers on the plantations and changing demographic and economic realities beyond state control. As Indian populations grew, un-indentured "old immigrants" came to outnumber newer arrivals. Many continued to work on plantations, but others left; some bought land, others joined new trades and professions. In sum, the class position of the Indian immigrant diversified beyond the prescribed domain of the docile, "coolie" laborer. As state machinery designed to control illegal absence expanded, it affected increasingly large numbers of un-indentured Indians. Like many workers, labor control left the plantations, and labor law turned from the regulation of indenture to the regulation of Indian populations more broadly.

Appropriating Antislavery: Indenture as Free Labor

As we saw in the previous chapter, the late 1850s witnessed a significant expansion of the indenture system. British public opinion had turned almost entirely in favor of indentured labor migration. And using labor migration on an increasingly large scale, colonial sugar economies boomed, producing more sugar than ever before. At the turn of the decade, a final dynamic solidified the ideological consensus in favor of indenture. From the late 1850s onward, supporters of labor migration appropriated and adapted antislavery language to their own purposes. Antislavery had long been a point of attack. Seen as a covert revival of slavery and the slave trade, labor migration was a betrayal. For radical critics, indenture was also a structural subversion, a means of stymieing social emancipation by reinforcing planters' fixed control over labor.[1] By the 1860s, a significant reversal had taken place. Not only did these older modes of antislavery critique fade, the language of antislavery itself served to justify indenture.

The argument at the heart of this rhetorical shift depended on the relationship between British and foreign sugar-producing colonies. Only by using indentured labor, it was suggested, could British colonies effectively compete with Brazil and Cuba, thereby proving the superiority of free over enslaved labor. If, on the other hand, the experiment of emancipation failed—that is, if sugar production in the West Indies declined—that failure would reinforce slavery in foreign territories. Sustaining this conclusion was the pattern of economic growth seen in the major indenture colonies during the 1850s, and the comparative demographic and economic analysis it produced. In negative comparison with Jamaica, the "success" of Mauritius proved the necessity of labor migration. Casting an eye toward Cuba, it now served to demonstrate that "free labor" could compete with slavery.

Newspapers presented this logic to the British public with increasing frequency at the turn of the decade. According to the *Morning Post*, economic failure was inevitable "without some improved system of immigration." The paper thus concluded that "the interests of the British colonist and of the philanthropist [were] identical." And it adopted dramatic antislavery language to underscore the point: "It is only by proving to the world that tropical cultivation can be successfully carried on by means of free labour that we can hope to rescue the long-suffering children of Ham from the degradation to which the cupidity of the white man has consigned them."[2] For the *Post*, indenture now served a humanitarian function, saving mistreated Africans and other non-Europeans (the "children of Ham") from backwardness and slavery.

As early as 1840, a small group of decidedly pro-West Indian voices had attempted to refigure antislavery language in this manner.[3] As Radhika Mongia has shown, so did some of the official architects of state regulation in 1842.[4] But twenty years later, as Cuba became the largest sugar-producing colony in the Caribbean, the argument circulated widely.[5] Like the *Post*, the *Times* similarly heralded indenture as a means of undermining formal slavery abroad. "Is the Anti-Slavery Society prepared to protect Cuba in its monopoly, for fear an immigrant should get a day's imprisonment too much from a Jamaica magistrate?" an editorial published in February 1859 asked rhetorically. The implied presence underpinning the paper's view was the rapid mid-century rise of Cuban exports. "Europe must have sugar, and has shown plainly enough that if Jamaica cannot produce it Cuba may." In this sense, migration served the cause of antislavery. "If Cuba secures the privilege," the *Times* continued, "not only slavery but the slave trade itself continues to flourish; if Jamaica wins the market, Cuba and the slave trade go down together."[6]

The West India Committee, which had continued throughout the period to lobby the government in favor of labor migration, similarly promoted an antislavery logic for indenture. In the summer of 1860, a policy memorandum sent to the Colonial Office argued that labor migration, indispensable to growth in British Guiana and Trinidad, could be used to combat slavery elsewhere. "Every addition that is made to the production of sugar [in the West Indies] is a check to slavery," the memo concluded, "so that its advantages are not only shared by all classes within these colonies, but are felt in some degree wherever slaves are employed."[7] Stephen Cave, the chairman of the Committee, made the same argument with reference to the United States. "America would gladly rid herself of slavery," he argued before the Association for the Promotion of Social Science, "if they [the British] could teach her to do so without loss."[8] Reframed as a means of discouraging slavery in foreign colonies, labor migration was allied rhetorically with the cause of antislavery.

These comparative arguments remind us that inter-imperial relationships shaped the history of both slavery and freedom during the nineteenth century. The Haitian Revolution, followed some forty years later by the abolition of slavery in the British Caribbean, paved the way for Cuba's rise as a sugar producer.[9] In both Cuba and the United States, slave production intensified between 1830 and 1860, as demand increased for sugar and cotton, respectively.[10] From a British perspective, this was the era of emancipation. Yet the persistence of formal slavery abroad affected the making of post-slavery free labor in the empire. By the 1860s, indenture had become free labor, defined as such in a context in which formal slavery continued to play an important role in the world economy.

Indeed, crucial to all these arguments associating indenture with antislavery was the portrayal of indenture as an unambiguous form of "free labour."[11] No longer a revival of slavery, indenture was now a free-labor competitor. By the turn of the decade, this view was widespread, and not just among lobbyists. It was promoted by the *Times*, which had condemned indenture twenty years earlier. And it held sway in Parliament, where the passage of a controversial Jamaican immigration law stirred debate in 1859. There too arguments in favor of indentured labor migration actively invoked the legacy of the antislavery movement, framing indenture as a means of supporting, not betraying, the project of emancipation. Henry Labouchere, a former colonial secretary, argued that indenture was needed to ensure the triumph of free over slave labor, thus proving that emancipation was sound economic policy. "The question whether free labour can compete in a tropical climate with slave labour," he maintained, "depends upon the sufficiency with which that free labour is supplied." Indentured labor migration, styled unquestioningly as "free labour," thus served an antislavery purpose. By facilitating migration, Labouchere argued, "you are doing far more to put down the slave trade and slavery than can be accomplished by all the squadrons you may fit out and all the treaties you can devise."[12]

Edward Bulwer Lytton, Labouchere's successor as colonial secretary, similarly portrayed indenture *as* antislavery—as a means of discouraging slavery around the world. Addressing the Anti-Slavery Society by name, Bulwer Lytton invoked the legacy of abolition explicitly:

> Let me say, in conclusion, a few words to the friends of the Anti-Slavery Society. I have fought by their side in my youth, and now, when I think they have been mis-informed, I still believe that our object is the same—namely, to give complete and triumphant success to the sublime experiment of negro emancipation. It becomes them above all men to do their best to render prosperous the Colonies in which slavery has been abolished. Every hundred weight of sugar produced by the immigrant at Jamaica is a hundred weight of sugar withdrawn from the market of Cuban slaves. Will slave states follow our example, unless capital flourish under it? Can capital flourish unless it has the right to hire labour wherever labour is willing to be hired? I warn them, that if by any indiscretion of over zeal on our part one West Indian Colony becomes vitally injured, it is we who shall rivet the bonds of negro slavery wherever it yet desecrates a corner of the earth.[13]

Instead of rejecting antislavery, Bulwer Lytton repurposed its moral banner. By competing with Cuban slavery, indenture would promote the "sublime experiment." Such a conclusion he framed as a necessary passage from innocence to experience. If in his "youth" he had misunderstood, he now knew: indenture was a vital means of preserving the legacy of emancipation itself.

These accounts—in Parliament and the press—reprised one of the antislavery movement's key original themes. British abolitionists had claimed that free labor was efficient, not just moral, inherently more efficient than bondage. Abolition would increase productivity, they suggested; liberal theories of labor efficiency were part of antislavery's promise.[14] Years later, in the early 1860s, supporters of indenture made a similar claim, but with a different understanding of freedom. Declining sugar production in the immediate wake of emancipation damaged antislavery's economic credibility. After a decade of sustained growth, it was once again argued that free labor could compete with slavery. But in this new incarnation of the prophecy, indenture had to be seen as a form of free labor—and as a means of promoting the "sublime experiment" of emancipation.

Antislavery and the Ongoing Expansion of the Indenture System

In addition to demonstrating the extent of the pro-immigration consensus that had developed during the 1850s, the exaltation of indenture *as* antislavery had important effects on state policy. Among imperial officials, antislavery arguments rendered formerly contentious aspects of the indenture system increasingly uncontroversial. State funding for Indian labor migration was one such policy. During the 1840s, the use of colonial taxes and imperial loans to pay for immigration faced criticism from freedpeople and radical abolitionists.[15] In 1860, when the Colonial Office reconsidered the issue, officials discounted such criticism and antislavery served to justify continued state aid. Writing privately to his colleagues in the Colonial Office, Frederic Rogers acknowledged that liberal, free-trade principles counseled against intervention in private relations of capital. But he nonetheless argued that state funding was appropriate, so that "sugar made by free labour, may be able to compete with sugar grown by Slave Labour." Like Labouchere and Bulwer Lytton, Rogers framed indenture as a "free labour" competitor. Emphasizing economic growth, he similarly dismissed the argument that funding drawn from colonial taxation unfairly disadvantaged freedpeople. "Immigration does not cheapen labour," he wrote, "but only facilitates and increases production."[16]

Formerly co-chair of the Colonial Land and Emigration Commission, Rogers was in 1860 permanent undersecretary of state for the colonies. As we have seen, he was also a primary negotiator behind the French convention providing for labor migration to Réunion. His view was thus of importance; he was one of several colonial officials who helped produce a new official consensus on the merits of indenture. Indeed, Rogers's minute on immigration funding, and the antislavery logic it relied on, incorporated many of the conceptual shifts traced in the last chapter. Labor migration, he suggested, was mutually beneficial; it was a means of promoting growth in the colonies and of civilizing or improving impoverished workers. "The great anti slavery policy of the Country," he wrote, "seems by means of immigration to have made an effectual movement—a movement which has about it indefinite promise of increase, and which draws in its train the incalculable advantage of transferring (as time proceeds) hundreds of thousands of Indians and Chinese from Countries where misery, and injustice, are at least very common, to competence, and effectual British protection."[17] This brief yet sweeping account revised years of conflict into a singular progressive vision. From this perspective, indenture was neither a break nor a diminishment; it was instead of a piece with abolition. Facing outward, it was part of Britain's "great anti slavery policy" in relation to Cuba and Brazil. Facing inward, it was a form of emancipation—from "misery" to productivity under British "protection." Like many such visions, Rogers's was a defense and celebration of empire.[18] On his recommendation, the Colonial Office approved a plan for the colonial state to continue paying for part of the cost of labor migration to the West Indies.[19]

State funding increased the scale of migration in the Caribbean. But indenture's antislavery logic also helped the system expand to new sites. As we have seen, deterring African migration thought to resemble slavery was a primary motivation underlying Britain's decision to negotiate a labor migration treaty with France.[20] As a result, Indian indenture came to Réunion, Guadeloupe, and Martinique. During the 1860s, more than 43,000 Indian workers arrived in French colonies.[21] Britain signed a similar treaty with the Netherlands in 1870, enabling indentured labor migration to Suriname, where slavery was abolished in 1863.[22] As with France, the Dutch treaty functioned as part of Britain's foreign antislavery policy. In 1873, as full slave emancipation took effect after a ten-year period of apprenticeship, indentured Indians began to arrive in Suriname.[23]

Expansion occurred within the empire as well. Just as statutory precedent smoothed the passage of law, indenture's antislavery logic rendered such expansion uncontroversial. Again Natal is perhaps the clearest example. Natal was a new colony, annexed in 1842, eight years after abolition. The colony's sugar industry was also new, its plantations established in the early 1850s. Early arguments in favor of labor migration to the Caribbean had portrayed indentured labor as a necessary response to economic dislocation caused by emancipation. No such argument could be made for Natal. There, indenture could not be framed as restitution for abolition.[24]

The decision to bring Indian labor to Natal was nonetheless uncontroversial. The economic "necessity" that first justified indenture was gone. But a new, equally powerful presumption took its place. Internally, Frederic Rogers wrote that there was "no reason why the Colonists of Natal should be prevented from availing themselves of the advantages of Indian Labour."[25] As the Colonial Office considered approving Natal's requests for Indian labor between 1857 and 1859, there was no debate on the issue in Parliament. Nor did British newspapers comment on the possibility. Natal—and the significant expansion of the indenture system that began in this era—was a non-event. Therein lies its importance. In the late 1830s, indenture provoked a public scandal whose reverberations haunted imperial officials for twenty years. By 1860, even as migration levels reached previously unmatched highs, the system was a normal, perhaps unremarkable, part of the imperial economy.

In this sense, the appropriation of antislavery language by supporters of indenture marked the triumph of a broader mid-century consensus. The extension of indenture to Natal, where 152,184 indentured Indians would arrive between 1860 and 1917, occurred without controversy.[26] Indentured labor migration had become an internal administrative matter for colonial officials in London and Calcutta. It was no longer an object of public debate.

Anti-Vagrancy Enforcement and the Growing Power of the Colonial State

By the early 1860s, the ideological normalization of indenture was complete. But over the course of the decade, the system continued to change. During the 1840s and early 1850s, local authorities struggled to control working populations rigidly. Conflicts associated with labor discipline persisted and intensified as Indian populations grew in the 1850s and 1860s. In response, local colonial authorities introduced legal and institutional measures aimed at preventing dispersal from the plantations. The laws of indenture thus became substantially more restrictive during the 1860s in both theory and practice. Conceptually, the boundaries of free labor continued to shift, as vagrancy penalties rejected in the late 1830s were imposed and accepted. In practice, expanded state machinery made the enforcement of vagrancy law an increasing social reality.

Despite the gradual approval of longer contracts, labor discipline remained an object of key concern for local authorities. At the turn of the decade, the Protector of Immigrants in Mauritius called desertion "one of the most serious evils that the Agriculture of the Island has to contend against," noting a supposed Indian "propensity to lead an errant life."[27] Similar complaints proliferated. Shortly after becoming governor, Henry Barkly—the former governor of British Guiana—told the Colonial Office that Mauritian plantations suffered from "systematic desertion."[28] More soberly, the colony's annual immigration reports tallied thousands of convictions for absence-related offenses in the early 1860s.[29] In Trinidad, the Agent General of Immigrants estimated in 1858 that roughly 20 percent of the first five-year term of industrial residence was lost to absence.[30] Subsequent reporting similarly concluded that indentured laborers missed an average of two and a half months' work each year because of sickness and "willful absence."[31]

In response, colonial officials introduced a range of new measures designed to keep workers on the plantations. In the Caribbean, where British Guiana and Trinidad remained responsible for providing return passages to India, officials first attempted to encourage "re-indenture," or contract extensions after the termination of the initial five-year indenture period. In Trinidad, legal reform followed the development of re-indenture in practice, which had begun without explicit authorization. In the mid-1850s, some planters began offering "bounties," or one-time cash payments, to encourage time-expired immigrants to sign one-year re-indenture contracts. Between 1855 and 1859, the colony enacted laws gradually legalizing such re-indentures.[32] A consolidated immigration ordinance passed in 1862 retained the rule, authorizing twelve-month re-indenture contracts with or without bounty.[33]

British Guiana went further, legalizing five-year periods of re-indenture. In 1860, the colony enacted a law authorizing time-expired immigrants to contract for a second period of industrial residence in exchange for a fifty-dollar bounty.[34] Under the law, the requirements of the first residence were replicated exactly. Old immigrants were thus made new: bound to a three-year initial contract followed by two more years of work or payment of commutation fees. As in the first period of industrial residence, it would be illegal to return to India before completing the second.

In 1863, after the Colonial Office authorized five-year initial contracts, the terms of re-indenture changed. In exchange for bounty, workers would simply agree to a second five-year contract without the ability to commute the ninth and tenth years.[35] Then, in 1865, a final modification was enacted, making it legal to sign re-indenture agreements before the end of the first period of industrial residence. Again legal change followed social practice. Planters initiated re-indenture before the completion of initial contracts in an attempt to encourage workers to stay on the plantations to which they had originally been assigned. Ordinance No. 5 of 1865 subsequently formalized the process.[36] Unsurprisingly, Governor Hincks justified the new rule as a mutually beneficial means of promoting social order.[37]

In both Trinidad and British Guiana, re-indenture altered labor relations. Many time-expired workers continued to leave the plantations. But large numbers accepted re-indenture and its requirements. In Trinidad, 35 percent of the indentured Indians who completed industrial residence in 1859 agreed to annual re-indenture contracts.[38] The bounties they received in exchange ranged from two to four pounds sterling.[39] The dynamics of control and opportunity intertwined in such payments; over time, some used cash savings to purchase land and gain a foothold outside the sugar economy.[40] But in the medium term, re-indenture lengthened contracts and the penal regime that enforced them. In British Guiana, 5,920 time-expired immigrants entered into five-year re-indenture contracts in 1865, as did 4,825 workers in 1866.[41]

As re-indenture extended contract terms, all three colonies also heightened vagrancy penalties applied to workers convicted of illegally leaving work on the plantations. British Guiana's consolidated immigration ordinance of 1864 made refusal to work an offense punishable by a fine of up to twenty-four dollars or imprisonment with hard labor for up to one month.[42] The law imposed further penalties for "desertion," defined as absence from work for seven days or more. First-time deserters faced fines *and* imprisonment, not to exceed twenty-four dollars and one month with hard labor. The punishment for second-time offenders doubled to forty-eight dollars and two months in jail.[43]

Alongside these penalties the law contained a range of provisions designed to prevent deserters from evading capture. In particular, it authorized police and employers themselves to arrest without a warrant immigrants found more than two miles away from their plantations without a written pass.[44]

These provisions moved the colony's anti-vagrancy law away from the original settlement approved by the Colonial Office in the late 1830s. The same was true of reforms enacted in Mauritius. James Stephen's 1838 orders had limited breach-of-contract punishments to fourteen days of imprisonment.[45] As in British Guiana, Mauritius heightened these penalties substantially. A law passed in 1864 authorized prison sentences of up to twenty-eight days for first-time vagrancy offenders, and between six and nine months for subsequent offenses.[46] Both "deserters" and those convicted of nonperformance of work obligations (through absence, refusal, or neglect) were punishable under the law.[47] In other words, the definition of "vagrancy" broadened. In 1838, Stephen and the Colonial Office insisted on tying the offense to separate forms of criminality, like begging, prostitution, or robbery. By the 1860s, vagrancy covered multiple forms of illegal work stoppage alone.

The following year, Trinidad enacted its own set of heightened penalties. Ordinance No. 3 of 1865 made illegal absence punishable by imprisonment with hard labor for up to sixty days.[48] Separately, the law rendered immigrants who left the plantations unlawfully liable to fine and imprisonment of up to sixty shillings and sixty days, or three months in prison with hard labor.[49] Like the Guiana ordinance, Trinidad's law authorized warrantless arrests for indentured workers found away from the plantations without a certificate of industrial residence or written pass from an employer.[50] These measures Governor Sutton framed as protective social management. Notably absent in his report was any reference to the law's capacity to reinforce economic power. Instead, he moralized the colony's vagrancy restrictions in an ostensibly neutral language: his stated aim was to uphold a mutually beneficial social order. "The prevalence of vagrancy among Indentured Labourers has been quite as injurious to the Immigrants, as a class, as it has been to the Employers," he argued, making the new law advantageous to "the welfare of the Immigrants, as well as to that of the Planters."[51]

In 1866, the colony went further, increasing the mandatory penalty for unauthorized absence to six months in prison with hard labor.[52] Creating a system of penal re-indenture, the amended law also authorized the Agent General to reassign convicted vagrants to new, five-year indenture contracts after the end of their prison sentences.[53] The Colonial Office refused to sanction the ordinance, finding its re-indenture provisions too strict "for a people

FIGURE 7. Vagrant Depot, Grand River North West, Mauritius. Photograph by the author.

so ignorant and prejudiced as Indian Immigrants."[54] But it accepted three-month sentences as well as specified fines as appropriate punishments under an amended version of the law passed later in the year.[55]

Alongside these changes came institutional reforms designed to make vagrancy punishments more effective. In Mauritius, local authorities established a "Vagrant Depot," a special vagrancy prison, in 1864.[56] Motivated in part by overcrowding in the colony's existing prisons, the Vagrant Depot also reflected a desire to intensify prison discipline. That desire, in turn, followed an explicit rejection of antislavery sentiment and the legal orientation of officials like Stephen in the early period of emancipation. According to Governor Barkly, the "Prison Regulations adopted under the influence of the humane reaction which succeeded slavery" were "so scrupulously lenient" that they failed to deter immigrants from breaching their contracts. The result, in his view, was "to efface the line of demarcation between innocence and guilt, to break down every barrier against crime, and gradually to contaminate the whole mass of the labouring population in the Colony."[57]

Barkly's emphasis on "contamin[ation]" suggests a connection between the Vagrant Depot and the broader development of Victorian penal reform. So does his tendency to associate vagrancy with a more general propensity for crime. Regulations issued under Ordinance No. 4 set forth requirements for prison life that clearly recall the "separate system," a product of Benthamite reform, which sought to use silence and solitary confinement as tools of moral reformation.[58] Yet in Mauritius, channeling labor trumped the imperatives of solitude.[59] Convicted vagrants held in the Depot were to work from six a.m. to five p.m., with an hour break for breakfast between nine and ten. Organized in conjunction with the colony's surveyor general, prison labor was devoted largely to public works. A second meal was served after the workday, but rations were limited to rice and salt except on Sundays, when they also included either dhal or vegetables. Prison rules forbade inmates from speaking while working and at night. Those whose employers were known were to be sent back to their plantations after finishing their sentences; others were to be reassigned on new contracts by the Protector.[60]

The result of these legal and institutional reforms was increasing numbers of arrests and prison committals for vagrancy-related offenses. In the 1840s and for much of the 1850s, the colonies struggled to enforce the laws of indenture because of a range of institutional limitations.[61] In the 1860s, that began to change: state capacity expanded and anti-vagrancy enforcement increased. Within months of its opening, more than a thousand Indian immigrants had been jailed in the Mauritian Vagrant Depot. Notices were sent to known employers, but relatively few inmates were "claimed" after finishing their sentences. Those whose status was ambiguous—who were neither under contract nor able to prove completion of industrial residence—were kept on for a further three-month term of paid labor. Others returned to the stipendiary magistrates.[62]

Prison officials imposed strict punishments for infractions within the Depot. One prisoner, Marday, was placed in solitary confinement twice and whipped three times for repeatedly attempting to escape.[63] Illness and a lack of sanitation were also part of prison life. The Protector of Immigrants, H. N. D. Beyts, criticized these conditions after visiting the Depot in the spring of 1864, noting in particular that some inmates appeared too sick to work. One, Migallee, was "subject to epileptic fits" and "in too debilitated a state to be put to labor." Another, Mahadoo Jacko, was "in a deplorably weak and emaciated condition" and "could hardly speak."[64] Beyts requested an inquiry into whether the Depot's meager rations were contributing to "the large number of prisoners incapacitated for labor by excessive weakness."[65] As to those whose vagrancy stemmed from physical incapacity, he concluded that the Depot was "a totally unsuitable place."[66] Despite these concerns, use of the Vagrant Depot grew more extensive. In its first year the prison housed 4,466 first-time vagrants and 588 repeat offenders.[67] In 1868, the combined figure was 7,662.[68] Between 1864 and 1871, more than 40,000 individuals served time at the Depot.[69]

Levels of imprisonment also rose in British Guiana. There, authorities committed 4,620 individuals to prison in 1865. The following year the figure was 6,276, and in 1867 it was 6,346.[70] A large proportion of those jailed comprised indentured immigrants convicted of violating the colony's labor laws. In 1869, more than 40 percent of those in prison were Indian and Chinese workers found to have breached their contracts.[71] Between 1865 and 1870, thousands of immigrants were arrested and convicted of illegal absence or desertion.[72] During the same five-year period, the colony's magistrates heard more than 30,000 labor cases involving immigrant workers. Of these, fewer than 100 were charges brought by immigrant workers against their employers.[73] As Prabhu Mohapatra has shown, rates of conviction and imprisonment remained high for the rest of the century; between 1880 and 1917, more than 20 percent of the indentured populations of British Guiana and Trinidad were prosecuted for labor offenses on an average annual basis, and more than 15 percent were ultimately convicted.[74]

Alongside imprisonment, other kinds of penalties were also used to punish labor infractions. In British Guiana, many workers convicted of illegal absence were fined in accordance with the law (although still imprisoned in cases of default).[75] Other, less formal methods were also put to use. Employers lodged large numbers of complaints with magistrates, only to abandon or withdraw them later. Some observers viewed the practice with suspicion—as a sign that the threat of litigation was being used to harass and coerce informally. In that scenario, there was no intention to gather proof and pursue conviction, and the precise substance of the law was of little importance. Formal adjudication stood as a means of reinforcing customary control and informal bargaining on the estates.[76] Between 1865 and 1869, declining rates of conviction reflected not fewer convictions (in absolute terms) but larger numbers of withdrawn or abandoned complaints.[77]

In Mauritius, contract extensions played an additional role in punishing illegal absence. Such extensions were legal, but they were applied with varying degrees of uniformity. One magistrate in Plaines Wilhems, for example, applied doubling penalties—contract extensions for twice the period of illegal absence.[78] Others simply added missed time to the end of the contract, extending industrial residence.[79] In both cases, the result of prosecution was an extended contract rather than imprisonment. For some indentured workers who had successfully left plantations in the early 1860s, this meant lengthy industrial residence obligations reapplied in the middle and later part of the decade. Peerajee Luximon, an Indian immigrant, was sentenced to 278 days of labor, double the period of an initial absence, as well as 113 days for a subsequent offense.[80] This penalty—adding more than a year to his contract—

was not unique. Combining double and single extensions for absence, the same magistrate added 872 days to the contract of another worker during the same period, and 964 days to that of a third.[81] The Protector of Immigrants questioned the legality of these punishments, arguing that the magistrate had misapplied the law.[82] The procureur general disagreed, however, and the convictions stood.[83]

In Trinidad, too, employers and magistrates used contract extensions, not just imprisonment, to punish absence. There, imprisonment levels rose but remained relatively low in the early 1860s. In 1860, 252 Indian workers were sent to the Royal Gaol for breach of contract, up from 192 in 1859.[84] The figure rose to 500 in 1861 and 721 in 1862, before again decreasing to 453 in 1863.[85] In part, these levels reflected a preference for less formal, alternative modes of addressing illegal absence. In the summer of 1864, the colony's Agent General of Immigrants suggested that magistrates were sending "sturdy vagrants" back to their plantations rather than formally convicting and punishing them. Fees garnered in the process were subsequently deducted from future wages. The decrease in imprisonments seen between 1862 and 1863, the Agent General similarly attributed to a "desire on the part of the employer to escape the trouble of appealing to the Magistrate."[86]

In the later 1860s, however, prison committals rose substantially as the colony's immigrant population grew. In 1866, Trinidad jailed 1,158 Indian and 905 Chinese immigrant workers, most of whom had been convicted of illegal absence and breach of contract.[87] The year 1868 saw similar levels—1,222 Indian, 375 Chinese, and 469 Creole—roughly 73 percent of the year's total prison committals.[88] As in British Guiana, actual imprisonments were only part of the story. Less formally, employers filed and then abandoned large numbers of complaints with magistrates, summoning the power of law without pursuing formal convictions. Surviving records suggest between 1,425 and 1,680 summary convictions for breach of master-and-servant laws in 1872, alongside 1,258 charges dismissed for lack of evidence, and 532 dismissed on the merits.[89]

Overall, then, the laws of indenture changed substantially during the 1860s in response to ongoing resistance to labor control. Trinidad and British Guiana introduced re-indenture provisions designed to keep time-expired workers on the plantations. And all three colonies substantially heightened legal penalties for vagrancy-related offenses. Unlike in previous decades, these reforms had concrete practical effects. That is to say, colonial authorities imposed heightened sanctions—wage penalties, contract extensions, fines, and terms of imprisonment—on increasingly large numbers of indentured workers.

The Imposition of Pass Laws: From Labor Discipline to Discrimination

In addition to imposing increasingly severe penalties, vagrancy laws also came to affect increasingly large groups of people, as pass laws introduced to control illegal absence significantly impacted the lives of formerly indentured workers who remained in the colonies. This was particularly the case in Mauritius, where the Indian population grew dramatically, from 77,996 in 1851 to 208,899 in 1868.[90] By the latter date, "old immigrants"—Indians who had already completed their mandatory period of industrial residence—made up a large portion of the total. According to the Protector of Immigrants' estimates, less than half of the total Indian population still lived and worked on sugar estates.[91]

Pass laws had far-reaching antecedents in slave law. They were also implemented during the transitional apprenticeship phase after abolition.[92] The pass laws enacted in Mauritius in the late 1860s were more comprehensive than these precedents, however. Their origins lay in changing social dynamics, particularly unanticipated population growth. And their effects were different as well. Since the beginning of the indenture system, the aim of vagrancy law had been to enforce labor discipline—to keep indentured workers on the plantations. In the context of population growth, anti-vagrancy efforts broadened into something larger—into a generalized system of registration and control for all Indian immigrants, even those no longer under indenture. In short, pass laws marked a transition from labor discipline to broader forms of discrimination based on race.

Indian population growth had multiple causes. For years, Mauritian authorities had argued that large cohorts of new immigrants were urgently needed, and in 1853, the colony stopped paying for return passage to India.[93] Return migration did continue, but most migrants stayed in Mauritius after completing their indentures. Birth rates, meanwhile, increased. The colony's Indian population remained disproportionately male—the result of years of recruiting male plantation workers alongside relatively few women. But larger numbers of women began to arrive after 1855, when officials in Britain and India instituted rules requiring fixed proportions of men and women on indenture ships.[94] All the while, annual recruitment tallies remained high—more than 7,000 indentured Indians arrived each year during the 1860s.[95]

The result of these factors—new migration, settlement as opposed to return migration, and increasing birth rates—was massive population growth. As scholars of indenture in Mauritius have termed it, the colony experienced a "demographic revolution."[96] The colony's Indian population almost tripled between 1851 and 1871, while other sectors of the population decreased slightly.[97] By the latter date, Indians were the clear majority, representing roughly two-thirds of the colony's total population.[98] Women comprised roughly a third of the Indian population, up from a mere 17 percent in 1851.[99]

With population growth came class diversification. By the late 1860s, many Indian immigrants still living in Mauritius had completed their indentures. Significant numbers of these "old immigrants" continued to work under contract on sugar plantations.[100] But many others, no longer legally required to stay, left for other professions. Census records from 1871 categorized roughly 73,000 Indians as plantation workers belonging to the "agricultural class."[101] An even greater number lived off the plantations, however.[102] Of these, some worked as domestic servants, in commerce and trade, and as skilled industrial workers.[103] Many others worked as small farmers and as craftsmen.[104]

It was in this context that new, more expansive pass laws were drafted. Colonial authorities looked warily at the growing old immigrant population, much of which had moved away from plantation labor. The purpose of labor migration had been to sustain and expand the plantation system. That goal was achieved, but thirty years later indenture had also produced a new kind of society, with an increasingly diffuse working class. This development frustrated local elites whose interests depended on channeling labor to the plantations. It also stoked more general fears regarding the social order. Writing in 1867, Governor Barkly associated old immigrants with rising crime, sickness, and disease. Transposing the issue of labor discipline, Barkly criticized the growing population's "filth" and immorality, contrasting its structure with what he viewed as a "regularly constituted society." His conclusion was that the state should regulate living and working conditions more actively—that too much freedom was dangerous. "There can be little doubt indeed," he argued, "that too entire and uncontrolled liberty has been accorded to these 'old Immigrants,' and that as commonly happens with men unaccustomed to its enjoyment, it is fast degenerating into License."[105]

For Barkly and other prominent local officials, concern surrounding old immigrants derived from increasingly negative assessments of inherently Indian characteristics. J. T. N. O'Brien, the inspector general of police, argued that the Indian immigrant was "much like an ill regulated child" and "incapable of self-government."[106] Deracination, or loss of tradition stemming from migration, played a central role in this assessment. The mixing of "Races and Tribes from every part of Hindostan" left old immigrants "exempt from the influences of Caste" and "unconscious of religious or moral obligations," Barkly asserted.[107] O'Brien, who had spent much of his career in India and viewed himself as having particular expertise on the matter, agreed.

Immigrants drawn "largely of the dregs" lost caste and religion, he wrote, and therefore lacked "higher attributes of cleanliness, honesty, sobriety and obedience."[108]

This anthropology of race, tradition, and migration made it possible to present heightened regulation as necessary protection. As with the moralizing discourses of the mid-1850s, official criticism of old immigrants translated issues of class—class movement away from plantation labor—into a more general language of social order. By the same token, it helped frame particularized social control as a neutral, generally beneficial form of state management. Like Governor Barkly, the Protector of Immigrants argued that new regulations would "benefit the Immigrants themselves." Large numbers of old immigrants, he suggested, lived "under insufficient restraint, and imperfect control." Measures taken to force old immigrants to "employ themselves profitably" would stave off "demoralization."[109] Associated with order, not just interest, industriousness was again exalted as a moral principle, and as a justification for labor control.

With these concerns in mind, the colony's Legislative Council drafted a new consolidated immigration law—Ordinance No. 31—in the fall of 1867.[110] The law required housing and medical care for immigrants under the initial, five-year term of indenture, and it limited work hours in the fields to nine hours per day.[111] But it also forbade indentured workers from traveling away from their assigned residences, authorized warrantless arrests for those suspected of vagrancy, and defined three days' absence as criminal "desertion."[112] Most important, the law required old immigrants not under indenture to carry passes or "registration tickets" at all times.[113] In effect, the entire Indian population was brought under the control of a special system of vagrancy law not applicable to the colony's other inhabitants. Ordinance No. 31 marked an important transition, as efforts to instill labor discipline produced more generalized forms of "class legislation," or discrimination based on race.

Writing to London, Governor Barkly justified this substantial extension of vagrancy law in the now familiar terms of race and civilization. According to Barkly, special legal restrictions were appropriate "for men in the state of civilization of the low caste natives who emigrate to these Colonies." Allowing time-expired Indians to travel and settle without state regulation, he suggested, had produced an "agglomeration of people of dirty habits in wretched and overcrowded huts." Barkly thus viewed "registration"—and the extension of pass laws—as an "essential preliminary" for further legislation.[114]

The Colonial Office's response revealed the extent to which officials in London had come to accept pro-indenture arguments long advocated in the colonies. To be sure, when the consolidated Mauritian ordinance was sent for approval to the Colonial Land and Emigration Board, the legal officer who reviewed it expressed some concern. "These sections are no doubt extraordinarily stringent," he wrote, "and introduce a principle unknown to, and inconsistent with, English Law."[115] But even while acknowledging this inconsistency, the officer—T. W. C. Murdoch—proved unwilling to recommend that the law be disallowed. Indeed, this is the key point: fully aware that the law was discriminatory and "extraordinarily stringent," the Colonial Office nonetheless saw it as a legitimate measure.

Underlying this shift was an apparent acceptance of Governor Barkly's race-based account of the island's social disorder. For Murdoch, the Governor's assessment had "much prima facie probability" since, after all, the "Indians who emigrate to the Colonies must necessarily be of the lower class in their native Country—a class in which habits of truthfulness and honesty are notoriously deficient."[116] Two decades earlier, the Colonial Office had explicitly rejected local descriptions of inherent Indian vagrancy, insisting instead on the universal applicability of liberal theories of economic behavior.[117] Now, the Office evinced a newfound deference toward local expertise—to "those on the spot most capable of forming a judgment."[118] Even though Murdoch concluded that the law contravened "the principles we have been accustomed to consider essential to liberty in this Country," he nonetheless recommended its provisional adoption.[119] Several months later, his superiors did just that, writing to notify the governor of the law's "gracious confirmation and allowance."[120] Gone was London's former insistence on short contracts and free movement as essential conditions of free labor. In its place there emerged an increasing deference to local decision-making, and an apparent acceptance of new and discriminatory restrictions on Indian labor in the colonies.

In 1861, the legal theorist Henry Maine published *Ancient Law*, in which he famously argued that legal development in the modern world was characterized by a progressive movement from "status to contract." In Maine's view, pre-modern legal relations were determined by status—by group membership in fixed, social hierarchies. The modern world, by contrast, witnessed the rise of contract, in which legal obligations stemmed from agreements made by autonomous individuals. Status was associated with feudalism, contract with freedom, progress, and the modern economy.[121]

The legal history of indenture, which is part of the history of modern economic relations in the nineteenth century, tells a very different story. Indenture was of course a contractual relation, and consent had long played a key role in distinguishing indenture from slavery.[122] But over the course of the century, special restrictions justified on the basis of racial difference reinscribed status into nominally voluntary labor obligations. The imposition of pass laws on indentured and un-indentured immigrants alike marked a highpoint in that reverse transition, from contract to status. Indian immigrants had been imported as field labor. As they left the plantations, law followed, past the contractual sphere of indenture to a more generalized realm of race-based social control.

The Pass Laws in Practice

How did the pass laws affect everyday lives? Ordinance No. 31 of 1867 required old immigrants to obtain and carry two separate registration documents. The first was a "ticket" received from the Protector of Immigrants, which certified completion of industrial residence (i.e., five years of contract labor). Old immigrants' tickets listed name, age, immigration number, and date of arrival. They also, for the first time, contained passport-style photographs designed to facilitate identification and impede forgery.[123] Separately, old immigrants who chose not to re-engage under written contracts were required to declare their occupation and place of residence to the police. In return they were to receive a police "pass," which also documented their identity and status.[124]

Under the law, it was illegal to hire an old immigrant without a valid ticket and pass.[125] More generally, old immigrants who failed either to obtain or to display both documents became liable to arrest. The law authorized warrantless arrests for those without valid pass documents as well as those with police passes found outside their declared district of residence.[126] In both cases, those arrested were to be detained and sent to the Immigration Depot.[127] If inquiries made by the Protector of Immigrants revealed no "*bona fide* employment," the old immigrant in question was to be punished as a vagrant or reassigned to a new employer.[128]

Adding to the complexity of these rules were three sets of regulations issued between 1868 and 1869 in accordance with the ordinance. Unlike ordinances, implementing regulations did not require approval from the Colonial Office. In the case of Ordinance No. 31, they nonetheless made the law more stringent. Initial and amended regulations imposed new fees on old immigrants, particularly those seeking to replace lost tickets and passes.[129] They also added new fines and penalties for noncompliance. Old immigrants who failed to declare their intention to move to the police (in order to obtain a new police pass) became liable for a fine of up to two pounds sterling.[130] Final amendments to the regulations, issued in the summer of 1869, increased that penalty to four pounds or fourteen days in prison.[131]

These 1869 amendments, in particular, hardened the pass system's impact. Under the original ordinance, immigrants arrested without a valid pass and

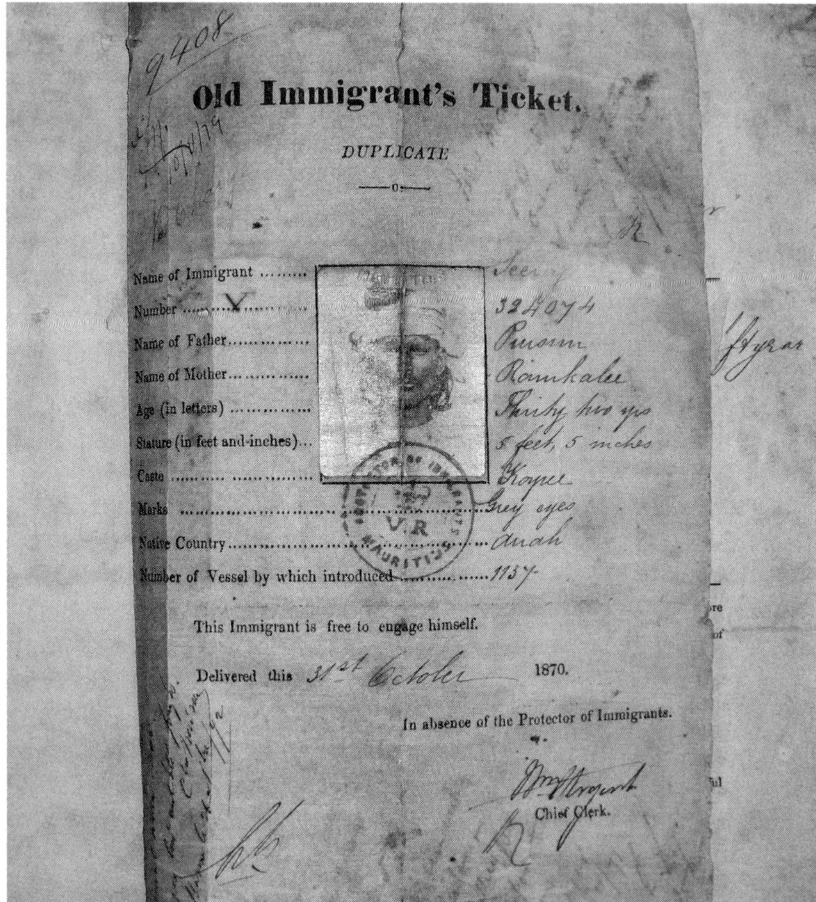

9408

Old Immigrant's Ticket.

DUPLICATE

Name of Immigrant ....

Number 324074

Name of Father ....

Name of Mother .... Ramkalee

Age (in letters) .... Thirty two yrs

Stature (in feet and inches) .... 5 feet, 5 inches

Caste ....

Marks .... Grey eyes

Native Country .... Arrah

Number of Vessel by which introduced 1137

This Immigrant is free to engage himself.

Delivered this 31st October 1870.

In absence of the Protector of Immigrants.

Chief Clerk.

FIGURE 8. Old immigrant's ticket of Seeraj, 324074, 31 October 1870. National Archives Department, Coromandel, Mauritius, PA 38, p. 175.

ticket were to be sent to the Protector of Immigrants for inquiries.[132] The amended regulations instead rendered such immigrants liable to immediate fine or imprisonment.[133] They similarly imposed immediate punishment on those who failed either to re-engage or to obtain a police pass within eight days of having received a duplicate ticket.[134] In both cases, the penalty—a fine of up to two pounds or imprisonment of up to seven days—was separate from and in addition to any punishment subsequently resulting from a formal vagrancy conviction.[135]

In other ways as well, the regulations issued under Ordinance No. 31 expanded the law's substance rather than simply specifying detail. Most notably, the regulations introduced special license fees for old immigrants who claimed to be day laborers—that is, those who worked without entering into fixed, written contracts with specific employers. The annual fee for a "job-work" license was initially set at four shillings per year.[136] In 1869, the fee increased to £1, a substantial sum at a time when average wages for field work stood at sixteen shillings per month.[137] The goal of these rules was to discourage part-time wage labor and to drive old immigrants to sign new long-term contracts.

Like the heightened vagrancy laws enacted earlier in the decade, the pass system had immediate, concrete effects on society. By the summer of 1868, nearly 15,000 old immigrants had registered with the police.[138] The number rose steadily over the course of the next few months, and between June 1868 and May 1869, the police issued close to 30,000 new passes.[139] Nearly a third of these went to field laborers who worked on either a monthly or daily basis. But thousands were issued to servants, salespeople ("hawkers"), and small farmers, and hundreds to workers in a wide range of trades and professions—including coachmen, traders, and artisans, as well as teachers, bakers, and shoemakers.[140] The pass system thus affected not only field workers but also growing classes of old immigrants who had left the plantations for other professions. For more than two decades, local authorities had devised laws designed to tie workers to the plantations. Now, in the late 1860s, immigration law reached beyond the formal indenture relation to regulate the colony's growing and increasingly diverse Indian working population.

As the pass system went into effect, new efforts were made to identify and arrest suspected vagrants. Police authorities organized periodic searches known as "vagrant hunts" to find potential offenders, old and new.[141] Vagrant hunts mobilized the warrantless search and arrest powers conferred by Ordinance No. 31. According to one police inspector, constables moved systematically from regional stations to central meeting points, "stopping and questioning each Indian they me[t]."[142] That is to say, instead of searching for particular individuals suspected of having breached their contracts, police made stops arbitrarily (on the basis of physical appearance) and demanded to see papers. Those without proof of employment were arrested as vagrants and sent in groups to the stipendiary magistrates.[143] Outcomes varied, but vagrant hunts routinely resulted in large numbers of arrests—fifty on average, according to one police inspector from the district of Flacq.[144] Another suggested that as many as 300 had been taken in a single operation—new and old immigrants, some as deserters, some without valid police papers, all seen as "vagrants."[145]

Partly as a result, vagrancy arrests increased dramatically in the first several years of the law's operation. In 1867, slightly fewer than 20,000 individuals were arrested as vagrants. In 1868, the figure was close to 27,000. And in 1869, it exceeded 30,000—an increase of more than 50 percent in two years.[146] The scale of these arrest figures can only be appreciated in relation to the size of the colony's Indian population. In 1869—the highpoint of vagrancy enforcement—roughly 20 percent of the entire male Indian population was arrested.[147]

Many arrests led to formal vagrancy convictions, though the latter did not increase in proportion with the former. Discrepancies in surviving records make it impossible to state with certainty how many individuals were convicted. According to magistrate records, the number was close to 9,000 in 1868 and 1869, and lower in 1870 and 1871.[148] Police records put the figures higher—10,609 in 1869—before dropping to roughly 7,500 in 1870.[149] Resulting prison sentences ranged from seven days to nine months. And not all who escaped conviction were released. In 1868, for example, magistrates sent several thousand either back to their employers or to the Protector for further processing.[150]

Indeed, variation and informality marked individual sentencing. The colony's magistrates did not act in unison. Nor, in all cases, did they apply the law strictly as written. Informality led to a range of inconsistent outcomes. But overall the pass laws—and Ordinance No. 31 as a whole—contributed to the already apparent trend of imposing harsh sentences on those convicted of vagrancy offenses. Sick workers found themselves swept up in the system. One "in so weak a state as to be unable to walk" was sentenced to 112 days in prison soon after his arrival in the colony—for illegally leaving work for a month.[151] The case was not unique. According to the Protector, immigrants suffering from illness were similarly condemned "every day."[152]

Ordinance No. 31 defined "desertion" as illegal absence for three or more days, and authorized, as punishment, prison sentences of up to three months.[153] In so doing, however, the law specifically stated that longer sentences authorized under Ordinance No. 4 of 1864 should not apply to deserters, as newly defined.[154] Nonetheless, some magistrates continued to apply both laws.[155] The result, for some repeat offenders, was lengthy, sequential prison terms beyond the immediate commands of the new consolidated law. One immigrant named Saivock, for instance, was sentenced by a magistrate in Port Louis to nine months in prison under Ordinance No. 4. Several months after his release, he was arrested again as a vagrant and sentenced, by a different magistrate in Pamplemousses, to six more months.[156]

Ambiguity between the ordinance and its implementing regulations similarly amplified the discretion afforded to individual magistrates. Under the law, Indians arrested for leaving their districts of residence were to be sent to the Protector for inquiries before facing punishment.[157] But some magistrates punished directly (for vagrancy), skipping the intermediate step. Asked about the legality of the practice, the magistrate for Black River claimed that he followed the "spirit" rather than the letter of the law, "chapter by chapter."[158]

If some magistrates applied the law flexibly, occasionally ignoring its details, their ability to do so was bolstered by the fact that they decided individual cases in an extremely summary manner.[159] Though cases were decided individually, police took to charging groups of suspected vagrants collectively.[160] Eugene Dupuy, a magistrate in Port Louis, decided more than 2,000 vagrancy cases in the last three months of 1869, an average of 175 per week. The largest number of cases he decided in a single day, he later reported, was 113. Most he decided without witnesses or defense evidence, on the basis of statements made by the police.[161] Asked about standards of proof, another magistrate simply stated: "when a Policeman is before me, and makes out a *prima facie* case against a party, and his statement cannot be contradicted, and when I am satisfied in my own mind that he is right, I apply the law."[162] Under the pass laws, the burden of making such a case was light. As the magistrate of Moka explained, an Indian brought without papers was "*prima facie* . . . a vagabond under the present Law."[163]

As we have seen, Ordinance No. 31 had important effects on "new immigrants," those legally bound to contract labor. Alongside others under contract, many were arrested and punished for desertion as anti-vagrancy enforcement efforts expanded. But the pass laws also affected "old immigrants" no longer under indenture, including many who attempted to comply with the law. Indians who left their registered district of residence were liable to arrest. Yet the boundaries of several districts were unclearly defined—"as if they were non-existent," in the words of one magistrate.[164] Meanwhile, police had difficulty distinguishing new from old immigrants, as well as from Indo-Mauritians born in the colony, who were not technically subject to the pass laws. In some cases, Indians stopped arbitrarily and found without papers were assumed to be new immigrants and arrested as suspected deserters.[165] In other cases, old immigrants with papers were arrested because of "irregularities" and taken to police stations for further inquiry.[166]

One result was that large numbers of old immigrants appear to have been arrested improperly and subsequently released. In 1868, more than 12,000 Indians were arrested on suspicion of vagrancy and/or pass-law violations only to be later discharged without punishment. In 1869, the figure exceeded 13,000. In both cases, more immigrants were arrested and discharged than were actually convicted.[167] In addition to those who were punished, then, large numbers of Indian immigrants were affected by the pass laws in smaller ways. As both contemporary observers and modern scholars have argued, the frequent dropping of charges after arrest appears to suggest police misconduct and clearly indicates, at a more basic level, that many were arrested without cause.[168]

Beginning in 1870, old immigrants recorded complaints regarding the effects of the pass laws on their lives. These testimonies, coupled with scattered references to individual outcomes in police and magistrate records in the Mauritian archives, give some sense of the varied experience of Ordinance No. 31. Some old immigrants complained that their children born in Mauritius and not subject to the pass laws had nonetheless been arrested. Dilloo, for example, an old immigrant who lived and worked on a sugar estate, claimed that four policemen had searched his home without a warrant in the summer of 1868. They subsequently arrested his three children, aged nine, twelve, and thirteen, whose birth certificates had been lost. The children were held for two days and then released, he stated, "having proved to the satisfaction of the Magistrate that they were not vagabonds." The following year, one son was rearrested, again for not having papers, and sentenced to ten days in prison with hard labor.[169]

Others similarly described temporary detention and short prison sentences after being arrested for pass irregularities. Ramchurun, who arrived in Mauritius in the early 1840s, had an old immigrant's ticket but without a photograph as required. He was arrested as a result and sentenced to six days in prison.[170] Another old immigrant, Ramluckhun, claimed to have been arrested at home despite having valid papers. He was held in a police station in Moka for two days only to be released without a formal charge.[171]

Travel within the colony mired other individuals in anti-vagrancy sweeps. An immigrant named Sumassee who worked as a farmer on rented land claimed to have been arrested twice in separate districts for pass infractions. His first arrest came while traveling to attend a funeral without valid paperwork. Separately, he was arrested on his way to apply for a new police pass. Both occasions resulted in prison sentences—one month and five days, respectively.[172] Another old immigrant, Sevoon, stated that he repeatedly tried but failed to obtain a police pass in Pamplemousses. After traveling to Port Louis to obtain a necessary signature, he was arrested and sentenced to one month in jail.[173]

Licensing fees introduced in the law's amended 1869 regulations also impacted daily lives. Of particular importance was the "job-man's" or day-worker license. In 1869, the annual cost of that license rose from 4s. to £1, a significant sum in relation to average wages. The change was in keeping with other efforts to direct labor back toward longer-term contracts on plantations. But it affected a wide swath of the old immigrant population. Indeed this was the crux of the problem. Efforts to maintain labor discipline in the context of rapid population growth streamed past their intended targets and across society as a whole. In addition to young, recently indentured workers, the pass laws and their accompanying regulations touched the old, the very young, the sick, as well as increasing numbers who worked away from the plantations. Though perhaps unique, a petition sent from one Hurry Sing dramatized this dynamic poignantly. Sing was old immigrant number 859; he had arrived in Mauritius among the first waves of indentured Indians, in 1835. In 1870, he was over sixty years old, and he worked, intermittently, on a daily basis. Newly subject to a license fee, Sing was unable to pay. He requested an exemption, a "Job-man's license free of Expense," citing "advanced age and infirmity." His petition, like the indenture contract he likely signed in 1835, was marked with an x.[174]

* * *

Ordinance No. 31 was an ending and a beginning. It was the culmination of a process of legal and ideological development traced over the course of this book. In the late 1830s and 1840s, the Colonial Office set limits on the laws of indenture, disallowing local proposals to legally tie immigrant workers to the plantations for long, fixed periods. From the late 1840s through the 1850s, the laws of indenture became increasingly restrictive in important ways; hiring was centralized, contracts lengthened, and penalties for unauthorized absence made more severe. By the late 1860s, when Ordinance No. 31 was enacted, the Colonial Office had come to accept race-based justifications for legal coercion long advocated in the colonies. Formerly prominent antislavery concerns had faded, as had universalist theories of free-labor efficiency. The conceptual limits of free labor had shifted.

Meanwhile, the 1860s saw significant changes in the ways in which the laws of indenture were actually enforced. As we saw previously, early attempts to enforce labor discipline frequently failed. In the 1860s, that changed. New efforts to punish vagrancy—defined increasingly broadly—had widespread effects on society. New prisons, longer sentences, and other penalties were imposed on large numbers of workers. Alongside laws passed in British Guiana and Trinidad, Ordinance No. 31 marked a turn toward increased labor coercion in practice, not just in theory.

But the law also reflected transformations in society spurred by thirty years of large-scale labor migration. In this context, the problem of labor discipline refracted into broader questions of social order. In Mauritius, the Indian population had grown dramatically and diversified in the process. Alongside thousands under indenture on the plantations, many more no longer under indenture remained in the colony. The introduction of pass laws affected not only plantation labor but also this broader, increasingly mobile and independent class of "old immigrants." In this context, efforts to enforce labor discipline broadened into a more generalized form of discrimination based on race. As society transformed, immigration law became more comprehensive. Initially premised on the logic of contract, anti-vagrancy enforcement extended beyond indenture, reintroducing more generalized, status-based principles of social control.

By the early 1870s, the reach and severity of the pass laws began to attract criticism. The Protector of Immigrants, who had approved their introduction, privately denounced the pass laws in 1871, citing an "overstrained severity . . . bordering on heartless cruelty."[175] Around the same time, more than 9,000 old immigrants signed a petition protesting the application of special "Disabilities or Restrictions" on non-Europeans alone.[176] Alongside other reports of mistreatment in the West Indies, these complaints attracted significant attention in Britain. The indenture system had been consolidated, materially and ideologically. But in the 1870s, after a decade of heightened vagrancy enforcement, indenture once again aroused controversy. We turn to this development and its mixed results in the next chapter.

6

Scandal Revived? Royal Commissions of Inquiry and the Persistence of Labor Control, 1869–1878

In the early 1870s, reports of mistreatment made indenture controversial once again. These reports came from below, from Indian immigrants, in response to the intensification of the system's legal structures. They also came from a small group of colonial officials and intermediaries, who wrote to London to demand reform. In response, the home government launched royal commissions of inquiry in British Guiana and Mauritius. The result of these investigations, which condemned many aspects of the indenture system, was legal change in all three colonies.

The reports generated by these royal commissions are cited frequently in histories of indenture. Generally, they serve as empirical evidence in efforts to reconstruct historical experience. There is good reason for this: the reports summarize developments whose real-time paper trail is scattered across voluminous archives, and their lengthy appendices include statistical information and subaltern testimonies that are undeniably valuable. My aim in what follows, however, is different. Building on scholarship that has sought to illuminate the ideological function of official inquiry in colonial contexts, I treat the royal commissions less as a source and more as a subject.[1] Like the original scandal of indenture analyzed in chapter 1, the renewed controversy of the 1870s was a flash point that revealed conceptual fault lines and political commitments. In this sense, the commissions are themselves part of the story told in this book—about the gradual remaking of both the law of indenture and the category of free labor.

As I will show, official inquiry did not fundamentally undermine the legal and ideological consensus favoring indenture that had developed over the previous thirty years. While the commissioners condemned individual cases of mistreatment, they reaffirmed the ideological principles that underlay the system as a whole. They continued to see indenture as an objectively rational and mutually beneficial means of redistributing labor, and as a tool of economic and civilizational improvement. The new scandal of indenture brought attention to individual acts of mistreatment, but official inquiry reaffirmed imperial power nonetheless.[2]

Like the establishment of state regulation in the 1840s, legal reform in the 1870s was thus protective *and* enabling: by regulating controversial practices, reform made it possible for the economic project of indenture to continue. Colonial authorities implemented new regulations, particularly involving medical care. But they simultaneously upheld a racialized logic of labor coercion. Lobbying pressure diluted reforms concerning labor discipline, particularly regarding maximum working hours and re-indenture practices. Many of the heightened provisions that had reignited controversy, meanwhile, were quietly retained as the colonies drafted new consolidated laws of indenture over the course of the decade.

The royal commissions of the 1870s were thus part of a broader pattern across the history of the British Empire, in which scandal frequently served to justify rather than undermine imperial control.[3] Perhaps the most famous imperial scandal of the eighteenth century, the trial of the governor-general of India, Warren Hastings, resulted in a reformulation rather than a diminishment of East India Company rule.[4] Years later, when the governor of Jamaica was put on trial for abusing martial law during the Morant Bay Rebellion, imperial control was similarly centralized and strengthened.[5] In both cases, scandal led to reform, but reform entrenched imperial power. The renewed scandal of indenture, and the royal commissions that followed, had a similar effect. Rather than drastically changing the system, reform lent indenture new legitimacy.

Controversy Revived: Local Protest and Official Inquiry

The root of renewed protest was the intensification of labor control examined in the previous chapter. As we have seen, British Guiana, Trinidad, and Mauritius all heightened penalties for unauthorized absence from work during the 1860s. Unlike in the 1840s and early 1850s, the colonies also strengthened institutional enforcement mechanisms, making the law more forceful in practice. In the West Indies, longer periods of re-indenture functioned to keep immigrant workers on the estates. In Mauritius, a system of pass laws developed, dramatically expanding the reach of anti-vagrancy patrols to unindentured as well as indentured immigrants.

As these changes occurred, indentured labor migration continued to bolster export production. In the 1850s, British Guiana, Trinidad, and Mauritius experienced economic growth, not just recovery from prior losses. That pattern continued during the 1860s. Average annual sugar production in Trinidad exceeded 77,000,000 lb. between 1864 and 1866, nearly three times the average between 1839 and 1841.[6] In British Guiana, production reached a new all-time high in 1865 and then continued to rise.[7] By the late 1860s, production had increased by between 30 and 50 percent over levels from the late 1850s, and annual export revenue had come to exceed £2,000,000.[8] In Mauritius, export revenue also rose between 1866 and 1870, although in response to increases in price rather than production.[9] Continuing growth reflected further expansions in the indenture system. Nearly 60,000 new Indian workers went to British Guiana and Trinidad during the 1860s, nearly 70,000 to Mauritius.[10]

But even as the system grew, it attracted new forms of protest and controversy. In British Guiana, a strike on a major Demerara plantation prompted, in 1869, the first sustained investigation into the treatment of indentured workers in nearly two decades.[11] Alarmed by the disturbance, a former stipendiary magistrate, George Des Voeux, wrote a lengthy condemnation of indenture to the Colonial Office. Interpreting the workers' grievances, Des Voeux warned of widespread "discontent and disaffection existing throughout the immigrant population." Seeing the strike as a symptom rather than an aberration, he predicted "far more serious calamities" in the absence of significant reform.[12]

Des Voeux's letter was an indictment of plantocracy. He argued that colonial magistrates were beholden to "planting influence," and that the colony's judicial system was a tool of control rather than impartial adjudication. In addition to strict application of the normal penalties for absence—loss of wages, fine, and imprisonment—workers also faced extralegal coercion, including illegal arrests, searches, and corporal punishment. Medical care, he argued, similarly suffered from a lack of independence, as doctors employed by estate managers sent sick workers back to work, and as others wound up in jail.[13]

The report quickly attracted attention in London, setting in motion a process that led to an official investigation. The Colonial Office forwarded Des Voeux's allegations to the India Office, warning that British Guiana's Indian population was "discontented and disaffected to a degree which if not stopped will lead to an outbreak."[14] In early 1870, the colonial secretary, Earl Granville, wrote to the colony's governor similarly expressing alarm. Noting Des Voeux's allegations of "neglect, ill-usage, and mismanagement," Granville described the situation as "manifestly one which calls for enquiry."[15]

The emerging scandal soon spread across imperial circuits crucial to the development of indenture as a whole. Expanding the orbit of the incipient controversy, Granville sent Des Voeux's letter to Trinidad, where it was received by Governor Arthur Gordon. Gordon, who was later appointed governor of Mauritius, subsequently became a vocal critic. After arriving in Mauritius in 1871, he began to argue that the laws of indenture failed to protect the colony's Indian population. Mauritian law did not distinctly require the "non-separation of parents and children" on arrival, he noted. Nor did it define "fitness for habitation" in workers' housing. Whereas failure to meet certain criteria—provision of medical care, for example—could result in a refusal to allot new immigrants in the West Indies, government authorities in Mauritius had no such discretionary power. Meanwhile, Mauritian penalties for illegal absence were harsher than their West Indian equivalents. In this respect, Gordon was particularly critical of the pass system. Explaining the requirements of police registration, he concluded: "Every Indian Immigrant in the Colony as long as he lives is subject to these restrictions."[16]

As Gordon continued to send negative reports, a broader base of protest emerged from below. Ordinance No. 31 of 1867, as we have seen, imposed new restrictions and obligations on Indian immigrants no longer under indenture. Beginning in 1870, many of these "old immigrants" lodged petitions against the law. One, Ramluckhun, reported being arrested at home, imprisoned for several days, and repeatedly summoned to magistrate proceedings before ultimately being released without charge or explanation.[17] Another old immigrant, Suroop, claimed to have been arrested and sentenced to a month in prison with hard labor for leaving his registered district of residence without having his police pass endorsed.[18] Like many others, these voices of protest emphasized not indenture itself but rather the discriminatory legal apparatus built up through the pass system, and the ways in which that system punished *un-indentured* immigrant workers. As labor law left the plantations, protest similarly transcended labor to reach broader questions of status and rights.

In bringing these claims to light, old immigrants found an advocate in Adolphe de Plevitz, the manager of a small plantation in the district of Pamplemousses. Born in Paris, de Plevitz was himself an immigrant; after working for the colony's local government as a forest ranger, he acquired property through marriage and became a planter.[19] De Plevitz lived and worked in Nouvelle Découverte, a "somewhat secluded place . . . inhabited by great numbers of small proprietors, chiefly Old Immigrant Indians."[20] As a neighbor and employer of old immigrants, de Plevitz came to regard their treatment—especially after the enactment of Ordinance No. 31 of 1867—as unjust. In 1869, he began collecting testimonies from old immigrants who claimed to have been mistreated under the law. Acting as an advocate and intermediary, he then drafted a petition, which was translated and circulated across the colony.[21]

Published as a pamphlet in the summer of 1871, the petition was a milestone—the most visible document of Indian protest since the beginning of the indenture system. Citing pass requirements and the possibility of imprisonment for even small irregularities, the petition declared that old immigrants lived "at the mercy of the police," and were "deprived of that freedom which all other inhabitants of Mauritius enjoy." Focusing on the discriminatory nature of the pass system rather than on indenture itself, the petition argued that the colony's Indian residents should not be subjected to special "disabilities or restrictions to which persons of European birth or descent are not also subjected or made liable." Meanwhile, de Plevitz attached a series of "observations" in which he argued that the colony's labor law had created a system of "tyranny and oppression." The pass laws left Indian immigrants "without the pale of humanity," he declared. Nearly 9,500 old immigrants signed the petition.[22]

As Des Voeux's letter had in British Guiana, the old immigrants' petition motivated further inquiry, criticism, and reform. In Mauritius, the petition caused an outcry. De Plevitz was twice attacked in public, and a counterpetition, which roughly 900 people signed, called for his expulsion from the colony.[23] But among higher-ranking officials, the allegations of mistreatment raised a different sort of concern. Governor Gordon declared that the pass system was "unjust and almost unintelligible."[24] He subsequently instituted an official investigation into police conduct.[25] Forwarding Gordon's dispatches to the Indian authorities, the Colonial Office suggested that the threat of suspending emigration should be used to pressure the colony into implementing reforms.[26] Indian officials, meanwhile, responded negatively to the reports they received. The Government of Bengal concluded that the pass laws had "deprive[d] them [the colony's old immigrants] of their freedom."[27] The Government of India similarly decried what it saw as "vexatious and unnecessary restraints upon their personal liberty."[28] Because of local protest, these "restraints" suddenly became visible to the state. For the first time in years, protest generated concern at the highest levels of the imperial administration. What emerged, newly, was a sense that indenture might be incompatible with freedom.

In direct response to the protests and allegations received from the colonies, the home government called royal commissions of inquiry to investigate labor conditions in British Guiana and Mauritius. After considering Des Voeux's letter, the colonial secretary, Granville, wrote to Governor Scott to suggest that an official inquiry would be necessary.[29] The Colonial Office appointed George Young, an English barrister, and Charles Mitchell, a former magistrate from Trinidad, as commissioners.[30] On the recommendation of the India Office, William Edward Frere, a former judge on the High Court of Bombay, was also appointed.[31] Tasked with appraising Des Voeux's claims, the commissioners traveled to British Guiana, where they examined forty-seven witnesses and visited fifty-five of the colony's 124 estates.[32] Their final report, which ran to 203 pages, was published in June 1871.[33]

Soon after publication, Governor Gordon recommended that a similar commission be held for Mauritius.[34] Though separate in time and space, the two processes were connected. William Edward Frere once again served as a commissioner, joined this time by Victor Alexander Williamson, a barrister.[35] Their mandate was broad: to investigate the specific claims made in the Plevitz petition as well as "the condition generally of the Indian labourers employed in the sugar cultivation" of the colony.[36] Active between 1872 and 1874, the commissioners examined sixty-four witnesses, including de Plevitz, and inspected fifty-one of the colony's 210 sugar estates.[37] They also received "about 500 petitions" from Indian immigrants.[38] The commission's final report, published in 1875, was the longest and most comprehensive account of the indenture system produced to that point.

The commissions ultimately confirmed many of the allegations made by Des Voeux and de Plevitz.[39] The Guiana commission concluded, as Des Voeux had claimed, that the colony's magistrate courts disadvantaged immigrant workers systematically.[40] The commissioners condemned the colony's labor laws, which, they stated, "must necessarily appear to immigrants as a mere instrument wielded by the manager for their chastisement, and not as an intelligent arbitration between them and him."[41] They found that wage deferrals and deductions were common and frequently unjustified.[42] Long periods of re-indenture, they further concluded, effectively kept "the immigrant population, as a whole, out of the free labor market."[43] While most observers had come to see indenture as free labor, the Guiana commission suddenly suggested otherwise.

The findings of the Mauritius commission were similarly damning. Its report declared that Ordinance No. 31 of 1867 had been "enforced both by the police and Magistrates in such a reckless and indiscreet manner as to cause cruel hardship."[44] The commissioners found that penalties for absence, vagrancy, and desertion were "confounded" in practice, resulting in "great injustice" to indentured workers as well as "old immigrants not working under indenture."[45] Physical abuse against workers was a "common occurrence," they reported—"systematic and long-continued" on certain estates.[46] Accompanying these critiques of labor-law enforcement were a broader range of observations on working and living conditions. Employers illegally withheld and deducted from wages, increasing workers' dependency.[47] Medical care was inadequate, and some workers' housing was "scarcely fit for human habitation."[48] The Immigration Department was ineffective; its registration systems "utterly useless."[49] So too were estate inspections; no government official, the commission noted, had the power to "order the summary rectification of any abuses or irregularities which may be detected in the course of the visits of inspection."[50]

These criticisms stirred attention in Britain and India. For the first time in decades, the indenture system was questioned as the commissions unearthed evidence of mistreatment. And inquiry created a new impetus for reform. After the publication of the commission for British Guiana, the colonial secretary, the Earl of Kimberley, called for new laws in accordance with the commissioners' recommendations.[51] The Government of India was similarly alarmed. "We feel ourselves compelled to say," they wrote, "that unless we receive speedy assurance that the state of things described in the Report . . . has been effectually remedied, we shall consider it our duty to take into serious consideration the question of suspending emigration from this country to British Guiana."[52] It appeared, at least initially, that change was coming.

In addition to official debate, the rising controversy also sparked concern in a broader public sphere. The year 1871 saw the publication, in London, of new books and pamphlets criticizing indenture.[53] Sheldon Amos, a jurist and professor, wrote an account of British Guiana's labor law, which argued that "coolie immigration" was "a revival of the worst features of slavery, under the cloak of free and untrammeled industry."[54] Joseph Beaumont, the former chief justice of British Guiana, published a similarly scathing description of "oppression and suffering"; his book was titled, quite directly, *The New Slavery*.[55] Both featured prominently at a meeting of the Social Science Association held to discuss the newly controversial question of indenture. Critical media attention followed, in newspapers like the *Times* and *Morning Post*, which had vehemently supported "immigration" for years.[56] Long submerged, the argument that indenture resembled slavery suddenly resurfaced.

The forms of local protest that had led to the commissions, meanwhile, continued, now under greater scrutiny. Even before the publication of the Mauritius commission, strikes in British Guiana generated concern not just locally but across the empire. In 1872, workers on a large Demerara plantation, Devonshire Castle, struck. Their grievance concerned wages and the value of task work; a confrontation ensued and five workers were shot.[57] With the royal commission's comprehensive condemnation in hand, the press reacted forcefully. The *Times* called for a new inquiry into the events at Devonshire Castle, warning against "barbarous treatment." Though the paper had long supported indenture, it suddenly began to criticize the system. "If it be not slavery," the same article declared, "[it] is certainly very far from freedom."[58]

The next day, the *Times* published a letter from Joseph Beaumont, who claimed that the "evils" of indenture were "not only cognate, but in great measure identical with the mischiefs, and even some of the worst horrors of negro slavery."[59] The West India Committee responded with its own letter, arguing that indenture was a "mutual benefit," and that further investigation would only reveal its true "advantages."[60] But it is significant that the comparison between indenture and slavery—so long forgotten—suddenly reemerged in the early 1870s. Local protest was the root cause, official inquiry and criticism the discursive flash point; together, both phenomena sparked indignation across the empire and in Britain. According to the *Times*, there were "signs that the old zeal against slavery, which seemed to have died out for want of an object, [was] reviving and ready to go forth against new enemies."[61] As it turned out, that zeal did revive, but it did not triumph.

Limitations of Reform: British Guiana

The royal commissions of inquiry in British Guiana and Mauritius led to legislative and institutional reform. But while such reform was significant, it did not fundamentally alter the indenture system. Like state regulation in the 1840s, the reformist impulse of the 1870s was protective but also legitimizing: its function was to redeem indenture. Through medical and housing regulation, new steps were taken to keep immigrants healthy. But structures of labor control largely remained in place. The pattern of legal development traced over the course of this book—toward increased labor coercion—was not reversed. Nor was the broader conceptual re-evaluation of indenture as an acceptable and necessary form of economic development.

To start, the commissions did not presage an end to indenture. While they condemned multiple aspects of the system, they did not suggest that labor migration should stop. Nor did they reconsider the basic indenture relation. Like most other imperial observers, the commissioners continued to believe that a formal requirement to labor (in exchange for transportation) was necessary. If they found indenture mired in "injustice," they nonetheless endorsed its continuance.[62] Not until the late nineteenth century would serious calls to end or dramatically limit indenture be made.

British Indian authorities adopted a similarly modest reformist stance after the publication of the royal commission reports. True, the India Office threatened a suspension of emigration. But the threat was temporary and, more important, never acted upon. In 1883, the Government of India modified its existing framework for regulating emigration.[63] A new emigration act set restrictions on recruitment and transportation practices, but did nothing to change the structure of the labor system in the colonies. Rather, regulation legitimized its ongoing operation. Emigration levels to the Caribbean and Indian Ocean remained high throughout the 1870s and into the 1880s.[64]

The position of the Colonial Office was even less ambiguous. It reacted swiftly to the commissions, but its goal was to stabilize the system rather than to end or radically change it. As colonial secretary, the Earl of Kimberley exemplified this position. Writing to British Guiana in the spring of 1872, he argued that reform was needed to "remove all ground of complaint on the part of the Indian authorities, and enable Her Majesty's Government to maintain this system of emigration which has been of so great advantage to the Colonies."[65] Like Lord Stanley thirty years earlier, Kimberley thought that new regulations could ensure "good treatment" for immigrant workers.[66] And for Kimberley as for Stanley, the idea of regulation was legitimizing. For it secured a broader ideal: that indenture was a mutually beneficial form of development, not a system designed to support particular agricultural interests. Properly regulated, Kimberley suggested, indenture would "confer considerable benefits on the emigrants themselves."[67]

As we have seen, the idea of mutual benefit had been central to the logic of indenture since the 1840s. Kimberley was not alone in reaffirming that logic amid calls for reform in the 1870s. Despite their numerous criticisms, the commissioners themselves espoused a series of basic conclusions that underlay the perceived necessity of the indenture system as a whole. The royal commission for British Guiana maintained that the "great experiment" of emancipation had "failed," making indentured labor migration necessary.[68] This was an early history, and as history, the commissioners' report affirmed the consensus built up during the 1840s and 1850s. They further defended the contractual logic of indenture, calling its labor obligations "justifiable, however contrary to English ideas, to insure payment by the immigrant for services rendered."[69] In this sense, too, the commission process was about regulatory reform rather than structural change. The commissioners sustained the basic framework in which indenture was justified even as they condemned the apparent abuses wrought by the system in practice.

In addition, sustained pressure from local officials, planter elites, and lobbyists diluted the reforms the commissioners did propose. The commission for British Guiana called for medical and penal reform, as well as an end to five-year re-indenture contracts.[70] When local officials responded slowly, the Colonial Office had George Young, one of the commissioners, draft a model ordinance.[71] Young's draft incorporated all of the changes recommended by the commission. The draft created new medical officers subject to the control of local government as well as a system of regular medical inspections.[72] It instituted a five-day workweek and a minimum wage of twenty-four cents per day, while making it easier to sue and increasing penalties for nonpayment of wages.[73] Concerned that Indians lacked political representation, Young gave the Immigration Agent General a seat on the colony's legislative body, the Court of Policy.[74] Finally, the draft limited re-indenture to one-year periods.[75] This change Young saw as being "absolutely necessary" to end a "vicious system" of long-term dependency.[76]

Young's draft did not become law, however. Local officials responded negatively, and their counterarguments led to negotiations that ultimately diluted the commission's recommendations. Governor Scott opposed giving the Immigration Agent General a seat on the Court of Policy, stating that the council already represented "all classes of the community, including the immigrants."[77] More generally, he maintained that a "penal labour code" was a "necessity," even while acknowledging the "tyrannical" nature of certain penalties highlighted by the commissioners.[78] If warrantless arrests were potentially "objectionable," he nonetheless argued that "stringent measures [were] necessary to suppress vagrancy, both in the interests of the employer and of the immigrant himself."[79] Similarly, he saw contract extensions for illegal absence as being "in strict accordance with justice."[80]

Behind Scott's partial resistance lay broader opposition to reform among the elected members of the Court of Policy. All plantation owners, the elected members refused to cede control of estate functions to government officials. They thus rejected the commission's proposal for medical reform, arguing that it constituted "unjust interference" with the existing system of estate doctors.[81] In addition, they opposed limiting re-indenture, as well as the requirement that magistrates approve re-indenture contracts.[82] In London, the West India Committee's opposition was similarly comprehensive. Lobbying the Colonial Office, the Committee argued that workers should have the option of entering into five-year re-indenture contracts. An absolute prohibition, they maintained, would unfairly limit workers' "freedom of action."[83] Meanwhile, they decried the work-hours restrictions laid down in Young's draft.

As we saw in chapter 5, imperial and foreign precedent gradually normalized particular indenture regulations, insulating them from criticism. In the 1870s, existing precedent steadied the status quo against drastic change, muddying the waters of reform. Young had proposed a five-day workweek and a seven-hour workday.[84] Citing Jamaican and Dutch laws, the West India Committee counter-proposed six-day weeks and nine-hour days. There was "no reason," they argued, "for placing British Guiana to such great disadvantage as compared not only with Jamaica, but with the neighbouring Dutch Colony of Surinam."[85] In a decentralized imperial legal context, incremental reform was vulnerable to charges of unfairness and comparative disadvantage. In such cases, the metric of fairness was the freedom of colonial councils from imperial control, not the freedom of workers from labor control.

Resistance to reform had concrete effects. Though never articulated as formal policy, imperial authorities in Britain and India moved toward a compromise position. The Colonial Office insisted on reform measures thought to reduce mortality and improve basic living conditions. But the Office repeatedly made concessions when it came to the colony's system of labor control. This dynamic became increasingly clear as negotiations continued over the issue of re-indenture. When the colony began to prepare a revised law, the elected members of the Court of Policy moved to amend Young's draft and allow for multiyear re-indenture contracts.[86] Governor Scott opposed the amendment but privately argued their cause. To the Colonial Office, he suggested a "middle course": optional re-indentures for any period up to five years instead of a fixed, one-year limit.[87] A month later, the West India Committee lobbied for the same rule.[88]

Re-indenture practices were important in this context as a platform for debate on the boundaries of free labor. The royal commission had concluded that five-year re-indenture contracts were used to "keep the immigrant population, as a whole, out of the free labour market."[89] Young was particularly adamant that long re-indentures could not be tolerated. Arguing that re-indenture caused "discontent and demoralization," he petitioned the Secretary of State for India in an attempt to block the Court of Policy's modified proposal. "The great majority," he warned, "will remain as at present, helplessly stumbling from indenture to indenture." The West India Committee had framed optional re-indenture as a question of freedom of contract. Young rejected this logic as preserving the "shadow" rather than the "substance" of freedom.[90]

The Colonial Office ultimately acceded to local demands in spite of the commission's stance.[91] Kimberley's response to the West India Committee made the nature of the government's compromise position clear. While the Office refused to relent on "the appointment and payment of medical officers," it proved willing to "allow reindenture . . . instead of being limited to periods of one year, to be for periods of one, two, or more, not exceeding five years, at the option of the Immigrant."[92] Medical reform was insisted upon; labor reform was not.

Other contested regulations concerning labor control met a similar fate. Governor Scott, among others, argued against limiting work hours as Young had proposed. A five-day workweek would produce "idleness," Scott claimed.[93] He similarly opposed the seven-hour workday, arguing, like the West India Committee, that it would leave British Guiana at a disadvantage in relation to Trinidad and Jamaica.[94] In response, the Colonial Office agreed that Saturday labor should be required.[95] Maximum hours (seven in the fields; ten in the factories) remained, although with semi-compulsory overtime requirements for workers in manufacturing.[96] Later, the Colonial Office would reject proposals to set fixed maximums on factory hours, where in practice averages continued to range between eleven and a half and upwards of eighteen hours per day.[97]

In the end, the revised law British Guiana enacted did not depart radically from what existed before the commissions, at least in terms of labor control. Between the 1840s and the 1860s, the terms of indenture had become increasingly stringent: hiring was centralized, contracts lengthened, and penalties for work absence increased. The new law—Ordinance No. 7 of 1873—did little to reverse that pattern. The five-year initial contract remained, with none of the controversy it had attracted in the 1840s and 1850s.[98] The law likewise sanctioned a centralized allotment system; newly arriving workers would continue to be assigned to plantations of the government's choosing.[99] As before, it remained illegal for indentured immigrants to leave the colony before completing their five-year initial contract.[100] And, following the lobbying process described above, the law continued to allow for re-indenture periods of up to five years.[101]

Penal sanctions for breaches of labor law had been at the heart of the royal commissioners' inquiry. The revised law nonetheless continued to impose strict punishments for unauthorized absence, which were similar if not identical to those enacted in the 1860s. The definition of "desertion" remained seven or more days absent from work, as it had been in the colony's consolidated law of 1864.[102] Under the new law, first-time deserters were liable to be fined ten dollars, imprisoned for a month, or both.[103] For second and subsequent offenses, the maximum penalty increased to twenty-four dollars and two months in jail.[104] The law provided for contract extensions, requiring indentured workers to replace days lost to desertion.[105] And in all cases, the law specified, hard labor was to accompany imprisonment for labor-law violations.[106]

In both British Guiana and Mauritius, the power of the police to arrest and detain suspected vagrants had caused significant controversy in the buildup to the commission process. Nevertheless, Ordinance No. 7 continued to provide for warrantless arrests.[107] Suspected vagrants unable to produce either a certificate of exemption (received on completion of the initial five-year indenture) or a pass from an employer faced prosecution, as well as an immediate punishment (fine or imprisonment) if they refused to identify themselves.[108] Like many immigration laws before it, Ordinance No. 7 also had an anti-harboring provision. Those who hired, housed, or otherwise protected deserters were thus subject to a fine of forty-eight dollars as well as damages paid to the harbored immigrants' original employer.[109]

In addition to absence, the law confronted labor discipline with similarly broad penalties. Drunkenness, property damage, and "abusive or threatening or insulting" language all rendered indentured workers liable to fine and imprisonment.[110] If striking was criminalized as desertion, efforts to "persuade any other indentured immigrants unlawfully to refuse, absent himself from or desist from work" were also made illegal.[111] The punishment for so attempting to persuade others to strike or leave work was the same as that for desertion—a fine of ten dollars or imprisonment for a month, or twenty-four dollars and two months for repeat offenders.[112]

In short, Ordinance No. 7, the result of the reform process in British Guiana, reinstated many of the provisions that had momentarily caused controversy in the late 1860s. The law did make some changes. It became easier, for example, for workers to sue to recover unpaid wages.[113] The law also allowed explicitly for workers, including "heathen immigrant[s]," to give defense testimony under oath in magistrate courts.[114] But core provisions concerning labor control remained largely unreformed. No move was made to release indentured workers from fixed, multiyear contracts—the kinds of contracts that imperial officials had rejected as being unduly coercive in the 1840s. Strict penalties for illegal absence and desertion remained in force, as did broad powers of arrest and detention.[115]

Lobbying pressure was only partially responsible for this result. With important exceptions like re-indenture, the commission itself endorsed the maintenance of a rigid anti-vagrancy regime. Young's draft also called for centralized allotment and five-year initial contracts.[116] The punishments ultimately enacted against illegal absence and desertion mirrored Young's original suggestions exactly.[117] The royal commission called attention to widespread mistreatment in the application of British Guiana's labor law. But it did not fundamentally alter the colony's system of labor control.

Protection and Coercion

Though it left structures of labor discipline intact, the royal commission for British Guiana introduced new regulations governing housing and medicine, as well as harsher sanctions against employers who failed to comply. The aim of these regulations was to make indenture more humane by reducing mortality and improving basic living conditions on the estates. They reflected a growing concern, emerging in the early 1870s, for questions of sickness, habitability, and sanitation. Such concern made basic well-being rather than wages, penalties, or other sites of economic power the measure by which free labor was judged.[118]

Medical reform had meaningful benefits, but it also served to discipline workers.[119] Like heightened anti-vagrancy controls, such reform reflected a paternalistic belief in non-European incapacity, as well as decreasing official concern for what we might consider personal freedom. The attributes of free labor that had been hotly contested in the 1840s—contract length, consent, choice—were no longer central. Instead, reform followed a general impulse toward increasing administrative control over indentured workers. Reforms softened the system of labor control built up over the previous three decades, but they also helped sustain it. To make indenture more humane was to reorder and relegitimize the labor system that had followed abolition. It was a turn toward protection, but not a turn against indenture.

In this sense, we should interpret the reform of indenture in the 1870s alongside earlier efforts to "ameliorate" slavery in the 1820s. In the British Caribbean, amelioration introduced a system of slave registration, new supervisory personnel (the Protector of Slaves, the clear institutional precursor to the Protector of Immigrants), and new rules on rationing, childbirth, and punishment—all designed to lower mortality rates.[120] For radical abolitionists, amelioration was a stepping stone toward abolition, but for many others—in Britain, but also in the US South—amelioration was a means of relegitimizing slavery in the face of criticism.[121] Reform in Trinidad and British Guiana played a similar role: by making the system more humane, it made indenture palatable.

As we have seen, after the publication of the Guiana commission report, the Colonial Office insisted upon medical reform even as it made concessions in areas more directly related to labor control. Ordinance No. 7 of 1873 reflected that compromise. Despite objections from the West India Committee and others, it included new regulatory measures suggested by the commission and initially drafted by Young. The Ordinance called for the appointment of government medical inspectors paid for by the state rather than plantation owners.[122] It required district inspectors to visit the plantations under their supervision every forty-eight hours.[123] To remain eligible to receive new indentured workers, estates would have to build and run hospitals according to specifications issued by the government.[124] Medical officers could further order the removal of sick immigrants from outlying plantations to a central

FIGURE 9. "Medical Examination of New Arrivals," British Guiana, 1900. The National Archives, London, CO 1069/355 (41).

hospital in New Amsterdam.[125] Employers who refused to send their workers to a hospital became liable for fines of up to twenty-four dollars.[126]

New regulations coupled with sanctions for noncompliance also featured in housing reform. Like previous laws, Ordinance No. 7 required employers to provide indentured workers with "suitable dwelling[s]."[127] But the law set out specific space requirements, newly defining the term "suitable"; conversely, it prohibited all housing deemed "unfit for habitation" by visiting medical inspectors.[128] And it empowered the Immigration Agent General to issue additional rules governing workers' housing and grounds.[129] Failure to comply constituted an offense that carried a maximum fine of twenty-four dollars.[130]

The royal commission's medical and housing recommendations drew on policies that originated earlier, in Trinidad. Unlike British Guiana and Mauritius, Trinidad did not have a formal inquiry into the conditions facing indentured workers. But it nonetheless played a role in the reform process that emerged in the 1870s. That process exceeded the boundaries of any one colony; it involved the transposition of norms and practices across multiple jurisdictions. A key figure in this regard was Arthur Gordon, the governor of Trinidad between 1866 and 1870, and then of Mauritius, between 1871 and 1874.[131] In Mauritius, Gordon's criticisms of indenture helped lead to a royal commission of inquiry. But it was in Trinidad, several years earlier, where Gordon oversaw the implementation of medical reforms designed to reduce mortality rates on plantations. If humane reform was the most significant outcome of the Guiana commission, it was an outcome that owed as much to earlier developments in Trinidad as it did to the commission itself.

In 1866, Gordon reorganized Trinidad's system of medical inspections for arriving immigrants.[132] That same year, the colony issued new regulations for plantation hospitals.[133] By early 1867, ninety-two out of 155 estates employing Indian and Chinese workers had built new hospitals to comply with the law.[134] Fifty more, Gordon reported, were either "awaiting inspection or . . . rapidly approaching completion."[135] A revised ordinance enacted around the same time then increased the government's power to force employers to send sick immigrant workers to the hospital.[136] Between 1866 and 1867, then, Trinidad anticipated a central reform ultimately recommended by the Guiana commission: the basic requirement that all estates have hospitals regulated and certified by the local government.

In 1870, before the publication of the Guiana commission, Trinidad enacted a revised indenture law, which included further medical reform.[137] All of the key features enacted later in British Guiana were present. Government medical officials replaced estate doctors.[138] The law set forth minimum standards for licensed estate hospitals, which all plantations employing indentured immigrants were required to maintain.[139] Employers who refused or neglected to send sick workers to the hospital became subject to significant fines—ten pounds sterling for each offense.[140] Finally, the law explicitly prohibited the allotment of new indentured workers to estates where mortality rates exceeded 7 percent in a given year.[141]

These measures marked a new seriousness in the colonial state's effort to improve medical care, and they helped lower death rates on the estates.[142] But Gordon's policy in Trinidad—the precursor to similar reform in British Guiana—was about maintaining, not challenging, the structure of the plantation system. In the interest of protection, the state asserted greater control over workers' lives. Reform did not reflect a resurgent concern for personal autonomy, or a new questioning of the merits of indenture. While improving basic living conditions, its implicit purpose was to stabilize the existing system of wage-labor dependency.

This connection—between protection and control—was most apparent in efforts to guarantee basic food supply for indentured workers. During the late 1860s, calls for improved medical services turned attention to food and nutrition. Some officials became convinced that undernourishment had increased mortality rates, particularly among recently arrived immigrants. There was little discussion of nutrition science, food quality, or malnutrition in the modern sense of the term.[143] But there was, in Trinidad at least, a new conviction that recently arrived immigrants failed to eat enough. That failure, officials argued, made the newly indentured population particularly unhealthy and susceptible to sickness.[144]

The result of these convictions was a reformist push toward mandatory rationing for new indentured workers. In 1869, Trinidad enacted a "feeding ordinance," which required employers to deliver rations to indentured workers for the first year of their contracts.[145] The law specified daily portions of rice, maize, or yams, along with salt fish or meat, oil, and vegetables.[146] But it also called for wage deductions, to pay for the cost of food, at the rate of five pence and one halfpenny per day.[147] In 1870, the ordinance was modified, extending the mandatory rationing period from one to two years.[148]

Though aimed at improving the health of newly arriving immigrants, the feeding ordinance was coercive. When it was initially proposed, the Colonial Office suggested that rationing should be optional—"permissive only, not obligatory"—in deference to workers' preferences.[149] Governor Gordon argued that mandatory rationing was necessary. An Indian "avidity for money" would defeat the law's purpose if workers were allowed to opt out, he asserted.[150] Health came at the expense of choice, which was important because compulsory rationing meant compulsory wage deductions. The Colonial Office eventually agreed with Gordon.[151] The arrangement ultimately sanctioned, as we have already seen, was partial payment in food rather than wages for the first two years of indenture.

Even at the time, mandatory rationing was controversial. Contemporary observers acknowledged that paying workers with food rather than wages appeared potentially coercive. It could increase dependency, creating a "temptation to abuse on the part of the Master," as an emigration commissioner wrote to the Colonial Office. It was, more generally, "an interference with the liberty of the Immigrant," one "calculated to produce discontent and ill feeling" among workers. For years, the Government of India had refused to allow rationing in the West Indies on these grounds.[152]

The Colonial Office approved Trinidad's feeding ordinance nonetheless. Like medical reform, rationing was promoted as a means of saving lives. But its acceptance depended on the same kind of conceptual shift that had underpinned the intensification of anti-vagrancy law. Beneath both developments was a belief that particular Indian deficiencies required particular, or intensified, administrative adjustment. As we saw in the previous chapter, local officials in Mauritius justified heightened pass laws on the view that the Indian immigrant was "much like an ill regulated child" and "incapable of self-government."[153] The political anthropology underlying Trinidad's feeding ordinance was similar. The officials who approved the law discounted the autonomy of the indentured. Personal freedom—"liberty"—was not the point. If the law constituted "exceptional legislative interference with the liberty of the immigrant," it was justified because of particular "Cooly habits and dispositions."[154] Admitting that many immigrants opposed rationing, the Land and Emigration Board argued that the law could be "defended on the ground of humanity."[155] Notably, the multivalent term "humanity" here referred to conscientiousness, not to a unified humankind.[156] Indeed, the opposite was the case: the Board's sense of humaneness implied a humanity differentiated by race. Premised on racial deficiency, the goal of protection resulted in a need for control.

Meanwhile, the feeding ordinance exemplified how efforts to ensure humane treatment served to reinforce, rather than alter, the structure of the labor system built through indenture. Initially, it was suggested that Indian hoarding made rationing necessary—that Indians chose to guard their wages rather than properly feed themselves. But after the ordinance was passed, a different suggestion emerged: some workers did not earn enough to afford basic necessities, particularly during the first year of indenture. One year after the feeding ordinance went into effect, Governor Gordon reported that "a very large number of Immigrants had not earned a sufficient amount to cover the deduction made for their food."[157] Instead of receiving wages, then, the workers went into debt.[158] Beyond nutrition, rationing renewed the cause of the problem it had been designed to address. That is to say, rationing helped sustain a labor market characterized by low wages and high food prices.

Indeed, Gordon's solution was not to raise wages; it was to extend the period of mandatory rationing from one to two years. At that point, Gordon argued, "the Coolie is generally well able to feed himself."[159] But why, before, could he not? Why did food costs exceed wages? The answer had to do with long-term state policy. Indenture had been used deliberately to lower wages after the repeal of the sugar duties and throughout the 1850s. During the same period, food prices rose as a result of changing tax policy. Before abolition, local revenues derived primarily from capitation taxes on the enslaved. In the post-emancipation period, sugar colonies like Trinidad reduced export taxes on sugar products, seeking revenue instead from a range of new import duties. Unlike export taxes, import duties fell on the consuming population at large, the majority of which was working class.[160] Food was central in this regard. Monocultural export production meant that basic food items—including rice, bread, and meat—were all imported. In short, import taxes raised the cost of food as labor migration lowered wages.

Mandatory rationing was thus not simply a protective measure. It was also a means of sustaining particular forms of economic dependency. So too, in a less direct manner, was medical reform. State policy created conditions in which problems of sickness, injury, and undernourishment were endemic. Reform mitigated those problems while maintaining the system that had produced them. Wages below the cost of living threatened productivity, as did sickness amplified by undernourishment. As Trinidad's Agent General, a supporter of the feeding ordinance, noted, rationed workers "averaged a larger amount of work than those who were not fed . . . on some estates in a marked degree."[161] Lauded as a "great saving of life," rationing was also a means of ensuring that work continued.[162] Here the comparison with amelioration is most evident. Reform rescued indenture, like slavery, from charges of inhumanity.

As analysis of Trinidad's policy makes clear, reform was linked to labor control: both depended on decreasing official concern for personal freedom and an increasing conviction that non-European workers could not regulate themselves rationally. The royal commission for British Guiana continued this process. Guiana's medical and housing reforms mirrored hospital laws enacted in Trinidad between 1868 and 1870. Mandatory rationing also became a part of British Guiana's new regime, although for a shorter period, along with wage deductions for food.[163] Both colonies empowered government officials to cancel indentures for mistreatment. In both cases, however, such cancellation resulted in reassignment to a new employer.[164] Regulation centered on housing, medicine, and nutrition—on well-being and against mistreatment—was protective but limited. And it aimed, implicitly, to bolster the existing structure of the indenture system on which plantation economies depended.

Limitations of Reform: Labor Control in Mauritius

What, then, of Mauritius? The royal commission report for Mauritius, published in 1875, was longer and more comprehensive than that of British Guiana. But its effects were similarly limited. As in the West Indies, moderate reforms followed while the basic structure of indenture survived. In Mauritius, too, the legal and ideological consensus surrounding indenture remained intact.

After the publication of the royal commission's report, there were some signs of impending change. Though it had approved it only years earlier, the Colonial Office rejected Ordinance No. 31 of 1867 in direct terms. According to the colonial secretary, Lord Carnarvon, the law was "repugnant in principle to that liberty to which an Immigrant like every other class of Her Majesty's subjects is entitled."[165] Citing the commission, Carnarvon asserted that indentured workers had been "subjected to systematic and continued ill-treatment" on certain estates, and that de Plevitz's allegations against the police had been "shown to be true."[166] With these and other observations, he instructed the colony's governor to prepare new laws of indenture based on the royal commission's recommendations.[167]

New laws did come, but the reforms they instituted were modest. As in British Guiana, the reform process in Mauritius did not fundamentally alter the legal structure of indenture. Despite harshly criticizing mistreatment endured by Indian workers, the royal commission simultaneously endorsed basic presumptions long central to justifying the indenture system as a whole. Like so many officials during the previous twenty years, the royal commissioners maintained that a strict system of labor control was indispensable. They themselves recommended that controversial penalties for illegal absence and desertion be retained. Thus the "double cut"—the practice of deducting two days' wages for each day of illegal absence—survived. So did lengthy prison sentences for extended absence and forced labor for "incorrigible" vagrants. These results were not, strictly speaking, a betrayal of the commission's findings; to the contrary, the commissioners themselves recommended them.[168]

Lord Carnarvon similarly favored retaining principal features of the colony's penal labor code. Despite his insistence on legal reform, he maintained that Indian laborers required special modes of discipline and control. "Imprisonment without hard labour," he wrote to the colony's governor, "has no terrors for an idle Indian, and no good is to be got by a mere extension of the term." Carnarvon warned, rather ambiguously, that prison discipline should not be "unduly severe." But there was no doubt that he supported the use of imprisonment to enforce contracts and punish vagrancy.[169]

The commission's recommendations regarding the pass laws were similarly limited. As we have seen, no aspect of the Mauritian system had attracted more controversy than the pass laws. Their application to Indians no longer under indenture had been the foundation of rising local protest in the colony. Allegations of mistreatment, compiled in the Plevitz petition, motivated imperial officials to institute a formal inquiry. Nonetheless, even though the royal commission criticized the pass laws, it decided not to dismantle them. The commission suggested reforms—imposing a literacy requirement on policemen authorized to demand and inspect immigration papers, for example.[170] But it concluded that old immigrants should continue to carry photographic "tickets" (certifying their identities and the completion of industrial residence), and that mandatory police registration should continue. The commission even proposed a possible extension of these obligations to Indo-Mauritians born in the colony and not formerly required to carry tickets or passes.[171]

The commission's mixed position on passes reflected a broader official consensus. Passes stood out as an exceptional measure, one that potentially contravened English legal principles. But if the "obligation of free Indians to carry a pass" created "a serious and aggravating grievance," imperial officials continued to argue that passes of some kind were "almost indispensable."[172] In Trinidad, some feared that requiring un-indentured Indians to carry passes would potentially discourage permanent settlement. The Colonial Office's response was that passes were necessary. As a letter to the India Office explained: "Although it is undoubtedly desirable that Indian settlers should have all the rights and privileges of other Colonists, and should not be liable to interference on the part of the Police from which other settlers are exempt, it will be found impracticable to dispense with the requirement of a personal pass, the absence of which might render it impossible to exercise the necessary control over the indentured coolies."[173] Thirty years of migration had produced larger, more diffuse Indian populations in the sugar colonies. Despite the renewed controversies of the early 1870s, imperial authorities committed to enforcing labor contracts through penal sanctions continued to believe that passes were needed to distinguish un-indentured "settlers" from indentured "coolies." Acknowledging pass laws as a potential infringement on important "rights and privileges" did little to change that policy. Modified pass laws would remain, in Mauritius as elsewhere.[174]

Many of the reforms the commissioners did propose, meanwhile, faced resistance from local elites and officials. Not until 1878 was a new comprehensive law finally enacted in Mauritius. In the nearly three years between then and the publication of the commission's report, lengthy negotiations further limited the scope of potential reform. In late 1874, Arthur Gordon left the colony to take up a new position as governor of Fiji.[175] His replacement, Arthur Phayre, proved willing to relax various recommendations in response to local protest. The commission had recommended mandatory estate inspections every three months. Phayre found that impractical, and suggested six-month inspections instead.[176] As in British Guiana, local elites objected to proposed one-year limits on terms of re-indenture. Phayre agreed, and in 1876, a draft bill prepared in the colony did away with the limitation.[177]

Local resistance even diluted medical reform—the primary sphere in which the Colonial Office had previously refused to make concessions. As in British Guiana, the royal commissioners for Mauritius recommended that the state control plantation doctors, as government officials rather than private employees. Planters objected, insisting that the colony's existing system, by which owners and managers appointed their own medical personnel, was adequate. As colonial secretary, Carnarvon reluctantly conceded, stipulating only that local government should have "the power of objecting beforehand to any particular appointment."[178] Carnarvon's successor, Michael Hicks Beach, appeared less troubled by the departure from Guiana's precedent. In 1878, as a new law came into being, he told Governor Phayre: "It has been indeed represented to me that the Medical service of Mauritius estates should have been placed on the footing of a Government Department as in British Guiana, but I have not felt called upon to recommend so considerable a change in the Mauritius system nor am I disposed to do so."[179] The Colonial Office would not ultimately insist.

Other protective measures made standard in British Guiana also caused tension—and eventual concessions—in Mauritius. Most notably, local elites resisted attempts to give the government power to remove indentured workers from estates that violated the law. Such powers existed in both British Guiana and Trinidad, and the draft bill initially prepared in Mauritius included discretionary removal provisions for serious breaches of both hospital regulations and labor law.[180] Both provisions met steady opposition. In 1877, a large group of Mauritian planters sent a petition to Queen Victoria, arguing that removal powers violated their property rights.[181] Ten elected members of the colony's Legislative Council drafted a similar protest, which disputed the Guiana commission's findings on the matter.[182] In the aftermath of the commission process, reform proposals remained subject to debate and to less public though equally insistent reaction. Instead of firmly establishing new norms, the commissioners' recommendations were interrogated by those hostile to change.

Imperial officials rejected the legal substance of these protests, but concessions followed nonetheless.[183] Instead of eliminating removal protections altogether, the governor agreed to limit their scope. Removal would only occur for repeated infractions against the law—for violations "of a gross and systematic nature" or a "system of violation of the law," as the procureur general, G. B. Colin, put it.[184] Carnarvon was perhaps more revealing when he said, in defense of the provision, that it would "in practice be seldom if ever called into requisition."[185]

Ultimately, the revised law enacted in 1878 did not radically change the structure of the indenture system. As in British Guiana, the new law did institute protective reforms designed to improve the basic living conditions of indentured immigrants. The law required all estates employing twenty or more immigrants to build hospitals according to specifications issued by the government, and all employers to pay for medical care for resident workers.[186]

Housing reform was similarly enacted. The revised law required "sufficient and wholesome lodging" for indentured workers, did more to define the term through subsidiary regulations, and imposed penalties for noncompliance.[187] It also prohibited the separation of families on arrival—a basic protection long present in the West Indies but missing in Mauritius.[188] And it raised the required proportion of women for new contingents of indentured recruits—to a third as opposed to a quarter of each ship's total.[189]

As in Trinidad and British Guiana, these protective reforms made indenture acceptable and workable without altering labor relations. Medical and housing reform would improve living conditions, but also stabilize a labor system under threat: they would make indentured Indians healthier as individuals and as productive workers. A dual purpose similarly underlay rules designed to bring more Indian women to the colonies. Women would mitigate the perceived inhumanity of disproportionately male migrant societies.[190] But they would also help normalize indenture, justifying the persistence of low-wage agricultural labor. As these reforms took shape, basic living conditions, rather than labor relations, became the prevailing criteria of acceptability—of what could be accepted as freedom and free labor.[191]

Indeed, the revised law did not substantially alter the basic labor structure of indenture or the colony's pre-existing penal system of labor control. Hiring remained centralized, with workers either committing to a specific employer before leaving India or being distributed to a plantation of the government's choosing on arrival.[192] The law continued to permit five-year initial contracts.[193] Strict penalties for various forms of absence from work stayed on the books. Workers who refused or abandoned work during regulated hours were subject to either contract extensions or "double cut" wage deductions.[194] Employers themselves could apply both penalties, without judicial intervention.[195] Workers wishing to contest wage deductions could only do so by bringing a complaint before a magistrate within seven days of the penalty's application.[196]

Penalties for "desertion" similarly remained on the books. Under the new law, indentured workers who left their estates for more than three consecutive days became deserters.[197] The penalty imposed was imprisonment for up to three months as well as a contract extension for the period of absence.[198] In other words, the definition of and punishment for desertion were nearly identical to what they had been under Ordinance No. 31 of 1867, before the royal commission. In addition, the new law defined absence for fourteen days over the course of a month, or twenty-four days over two months, as "habitual idleness," punishable by imprisonment for up to three months.[199]

The law prohibited vagrant hunts, which the commission had condemned.[200] But strict punishments remained for vagrancy, which was defined separately from desertion. Whereas unlawful absence and desertion criminalized breach-of-contract obligations, vagrancy made it illegal not to work in the first place. Thus vagrants were "those who have no fixed domicil, nor any means of subsistence, and who, being able to labour, do not habitually work at any trade or profession."[201] The punishment for first-time offenders was one month in prison with or without hard labor—two months on the second offense.[202] Those who subsequently refused contract labor assignments (from the Protector of Immigrants) became "incorrigible vagrants" subject to imprisonment for up to one year.[203]

Significant pass restrictions also remained. G. B. Colin, the principal author of the law's first draft, claimed that it had achieved "the absolute abolition of the pass system."[204] That was an exaggeration. Identity papers, registration, and warrantless arrests stayed in place. After five years of contract labor ("industrial residence"), indentured workers were to receive an "Old Immigrant's Ticket," which, as before, contained identifying information and a photograph.[205] The law no longer required police passes. But un-indentured Indians remained liable to arrest without their tickets, which documented their status.[206] Qualified police officers could demand to inspect tickets, and Indians who failed or refused to show their papers were liable to fine or imprisonment.[207] First-time offenders faced a maximum fine of fifty rupees or imprisonment for up to fourteen days. The penalty for subsequent offenses committed within the same year increased to three months in prison with or without hard labor.[208] Separately, the law authorized employers, police, and prison guards to arrest suspected deserters without a warrant.[209] The pass system did not disappear, though its requirements became less elaborate. In Mauritius, as in British Guiana and Trinidad, formerly indentured Indians remained subject to arrest for failing to carry and display identity papers.

Some saw this as a betrayal. After the law was enacted, the Aborigines' Protection Society sent letters of protest to the Colonial Office.[210] The Society, established in 1836 and closely associated with the antislavery movement, called for greater medical reform and took aim at the colony's system of labor control.[211] George Campbell, who reviewed the law on the Society's behalf, condemned its anti-vagrancy and illegal absence provisions as an infringement of free-labor principles. He argued that the law's vagrancy clause "restrict[ed] the freedom of men who ought to be free"; criticized the maintenance of the double cut; and found old immigrants' tickets unfairly discriminatory ("Surely this is not equality!").[212] He further argued that contracts longer than three years should not be permitted, since transportation from India to Mauritius was less expensive than it was to the West Indies. In the process, he rejected the frequently made argument that the Mauritian Indian population was particularly deficient or savage, and that it needed special forms of legal control.[213] George Young, the commissioner and author of British Guiana's draft ordinance, echoed Campbell's criticisms. He too argued against "an unfounded, depreciation of the natural character of the immigrant population."[214]

But these were minority views. Despite the Society's protest, the law was approved.[215] Its final version went into effect in January 1879. As the culmination of the royal commission process, the new law left the indenture system largely unchanged. It instituted moderate reforms designed to reduce mortality rates and prevent mistreatment. But protective regulation did little to change hiring, contracts, work requirements, and penal contract enforcement. In other words, it left the structure of the labor system intact.

In this sense, the commission process was like the imposition of state regulation for indenture in the 1840s. It also bore a resemblance to earlier scandals of colonial rule where individual officials stood trial for abusing their powers. Like the Hastings trial or the Governor Eyre controversy in Jamaica, the royal commissions for indenture ultimately reaffirmed imperial power.[216] Reformed laws sought to protect against extreme abuse at the margins, but simultaneously legitimized a much broader sphere of action at the center. Rather than undermining indenture, inquiry and reform steadied the process of normalization begun thirty years earlier.

* * *

The 1870s were a period of trial for the indenture system. Local protest led to two official inquiries, which condemned multiple aspects of the system and reignited public controversy. For the first time in decades, observers in Britain and India questioned the acceptability of indenture, comparing it once again to slavery.

Nonetheless, the official inquiries of the 1870s ultimately reinforced the indenture system. Reformed laws introduced new protections to improve living conditions and lower death rates. In particular, the state sought to regulate medical care and guarantee basic housing and food standards. But these interventions served to legitimize indenture without changing its basic structure. Like the invention of state regulation in 1842, they made indenture acceptable in the face of mounting criticism. They made indenture free by reforming living conditions rather than labor relations.

Indeed, the new labor laws enacted after the royal commissions of inquiry did not significantly alter the structure of the labor system. Despite the apparent controversy they created, five-year contracts, re-indenture provisions, and strict vagrancy penalties all remained. In this sense, the royal commissions revealed just how far the process of normalization traced in this book had come. Official inquiry affirmed state efforts to impose labor discipline as well as the general belief that indenture was mutually beneficial. The racial logic of non-European incapacity underlay both protective reform and labor control. Administrative control had become a part of post-slavery freedom—state regulation would protect, while wage labor would civilize. At a larger scale, both would sustain plantation production and the export economy. Rather than dismantling indenture, reform reinforced it.

Epilogue

Far from ending indenture, the royal commissions of the 1870s stabilized the system against renewed controversy. What they revealed was not a crumbling edifice; on the contrary, they showed just how far the process of normalization had come. Over the next thirty years, the system continued to operate on a large scale. Between 1880 and 1920, more than 520,000 Indian workers emigrated under indenture.[1] They went not just to Mauritius and the West Indies but also to Natal and Fiji, as well as Réunion and Suriname. Labor migration did not stop until 1917, and not until 1920 was indenture finally finished in the colonies.

New economic and political forces brought about that end. First, the global sugar economy changed in ways that diminished the indenture system's profitability. At the height of Atlantic slavery, nearly all of the world's sugar came from the Caribbean. That changed during the nineteenth century as world production exploded. In 1839, just after abolition, total production stood at roughly 820,000 tons. It increased steadily for the next twenty years, to roughly 150,000 tons per year by the late 1850s. But in the last quarter of the century, the figure rose tremendously—to 3,740,210 tons in 1880, and 6,276,800 tons in 1890. By 1900, world production exceeded 11,000,000 tons, and by 1930 it had nearly tripled—to 27,853,321 tons.[2]

As overall production increased, the proportion of the world's sugar grown in colonies formerly dominated by slavery decreased. Cane sugar from tropical plantations had once been Europe's sole supply.[3] But in the later nineteenth century, beet sugar diminished cane's preeminence. By 1870, cane accounted for only 64 percent of the world's sugar. The figure continued to drop after that, to 50.2 percent in 1880 and 41.2 percent in 1890.[4]

Beet sugar came primarily from Europe and Russia, and additionally from the United States. Fueled by state subsidies, production expanded enormously in the second half of the century.[5] These subsidies, called "bounties," paid European producers for exports above predetermined levels.[6] Not only did that boost production, it allowed exporters to sell below cost. By Noël Deerr's estimate, between 60,000,000 and 65,000,000 tons of beet sugar went to market "at less than the cost of production" between 1850 and 1904.[7]

Massive increases in supply alongside low-cost beet sales drove down world sugar prices. Again, this dynamic crystallized during the last quarter of the century. As we have seen, rising prices played a key role in the growth of indenture during the 1850s and 1860s. Between 1880 and 1900, that pattern reversed. In London, the price of raw sugar fell from 25s. 6d. per hundredweight in 1872 to 20s. in 1882. By 1892, the price had nearly halved, to 13s. 6d. By 1902, it was a mere 7s. 3d.[8] Within this overall pattern, sudden increases in European bounties led to particular price drops in 1884 and 1895.[9]

The collapse of sugar prices, alongside general overproduction, made the economic project of the sugar colonies—and of indenture—less viable. Production continued to increase in Mauritius, British Guiana, and Trinidad, but as prices fell, exports became less profitable. In certain years, after an acute drop in 1884, for instance, prices fell below the cost of production.[10] For British consumers, meanwhile, the Caribbean became less important. In an era of cheap, plentiful sugar, the sugar colonies were less central to the British economy. The late nineteenth century saw the beginning of the Caribbean's transformation, without movement, from "center" to "periphery."[11]

On a local level, decreasing sugar prices destabilized labor relations in the colonies. In the later 1880s, new resistance to indenture and the plantation system emerged. When employers lowered wages in response to falling prices, workers began to strike with increasing frequency. British Guiana saw thirty-one strike incidents in 1886, followed by fifteen in 1887 and forty-two in 1888.[12] As Walter Rodney explained, "violent labor confrontation," formerly rare, occurred frequently in these years.[13] Strikes affected Trinidad as well, particularly after wage reductions in the 1880s and 1890s.[14] Efforts to control mass gatherings led to further conflict surrounding religious and cultural life. In 1884, the local government violently suppressed Indo-Trinidadian Hosay celebrations after participants disregarded a partial ban on the ritual procession.[15]

To keep wages low in the face of increasing resistance, planters continued to import large numbers of new indentured workers. Rather than shoring up the system, however, new migration exposed further weakness. Many plantations took on more workers than they needed; for the first time, underemployment became a feature of plantation life. By the 1890s, some officials (the Protector of Immigrants in Trinidad, for example) began to argue that migration levels should be reduced.[16] This too was part of the region's silent movement to the periphery, whereby "underdevelopment" followed monocultural dependency and sugar's eventual decline.

Low wages and underemployment amplified the long-term trend by which Indian workers gradually settled away from the plantations. Settlement, in turn, slowly diversified colonial economic life, reducing dependency on sugar-related wage labor. For most of the indenture period, the colonies imported basic food items consumed by the working classes. That started to change around the turn of the century. In the 1880s, British Guiana imported rice. By 1916, local production met domestic needs.[17] Sugar was still important, to be sure, but its comprehensive grip over local economies loosened.

In this opening, as scholars of the late indenture period have shown, Indian experiences diversified, as "settlers," not simply "coolies." While the exploitation of the plantations continued, many found different futures in late-century societies now changed by five decades of migration. In Mauritius, formerly indentured Indians purchased land in increasingly large quantities during the 1880s and 1890s, in a process known as the *grand morcellement*.[18] In Trinidad, Indian immigrants similarly acquired land through purchase and when the colonial government began offering tracts of Crown land in lieu of return passage to India.[19] Landownership accompanied a broader range of economic possibilities, both within and apart from the sugar economy.[20] Alongside new forms of economic life, the emergence of Black and mixed-race middle classes challenged what abolitionists had formerly decried as "plantocracy." Moderate constitutional reform expanded the franchise, which allowed opponents of indenture into local government.[21] Newly formed political associations—the People's Association in British Guiana and the Working Men's Association in Trinidad—campaigned against further labor migration. Increasingly, so did local newspapers, no longer solely aligned with planting interests.[22]

Together, these dynamics pointed toward something larger: a gradual weakening of the plantation system. Sugar production had dominated most aspects of West Indian life, society and politics included. But at the turn of the century, export production became less profitable and less integral to imperial interests. As a result, sugar's singular economic importance diminished. An expanding middle class complicated island politics, and labor protest reemerged forcefully in response to declining economic conditions. These changes challenged the indenture system in fundamentally new ways, diminishing its economic viability and creating new space for political opposition.

FIGURE 10. Felix Morin, "East Indian Women, Men, and Children," c. 1890–1896. DeGolyer Library, SMU.

Local protest raised concern about indenture but did not end the system on its own. Alongside the diminished economic stature of cane sugar, a second decisive force pushed toward an end to indenture. That force was Indian nationalism. It was no coincidence that Gandhi began his campaign for satyagraha in South Africa. There, he encountered the legacy of indenture: an increasingly discriminatory legal apparatus designed to control Indian immigrants. Frightened by the growth of the Indian population, the white minority in Natal attempted to make re-indenture and repatriation to India compulsory in the 1890s.[23] Gandhi denounced such special restrictions alongside other forms of "class legislation," like pass laws, that applied only to Indians.[24]

By the turn of the century, Indian political leaders associated with the Indian National Congress opposed indenture with increasing stridency.[25] In 1910, G. K. Gokhale campaigned for the Government of India to ban emigration.[26] Books such as *The Indians of South Africa; helots within the Empire* began to appear.[27] Totaram Sanadhya, a former indentured laborer in Fiji, published a firsthand account of indenture in Hindi, which attracted widespread attention across India.[28] As the campaign against indenture grew, it spurred on a popular movement, particularly in the 1910s. Anti-indenture associations formed in Calcutta, Madras, and Allahabad. Public meetings, pamphlets, and songs discouraged potential recruits.[29]

The Indian challenge to indenture differed from the antislavery critique of the immediate post-emancipation period. Anticolonial nationalism, a force virtually unknown to the early nineteenth century, created a new ideological foundation for protest in the early twentieth. Indian attacks on indenture emphasized rights of "imperial citizenship"—representation and civic equality—as much as labor conditions or class relations.[30] Indian nationalists objected to indenture as they made larger claims for political rights within the empire. For this reason, the nationalist campaign against indenture has sometimes been seen as an exogenous force—"totally unrelated to West Indian circumstances," in the words of Walton Look Lai.[31]

Focused on imperial citizenship—on "dignity and self-respect," as Gaiutra Bahadur writes, the Indian anti-indenture movement reproduced its own hierarchies of status and in particular, of gender.[32] In 1913, widely publicized accounts of the sexual mistreatment and subsequent salvation of Kunti, an indentured woman in Fiji, galvanized protest.[33] Privately, officials disputed the story, but publicly, it exemplified a broader, political theme: for nationalist critics, indenture had demeaned Indian womanhood.[34] In making this claim, opponents of indenture sometimes mirrored negative portrayals of sexual and moral ruin that had long circulated among local officials.[35]

Still, rising Indian opposition to indenture was powerful; most scholars describe it as the primary cause of indenture's ultimate end. What had changed, in addition to the articulation of a new critique, was the nature and location of the public sphere. Much of my analysis of public debate has centered on Britain and on London in particular, for this was the debate that most directly shaped imperial indenture policy in the 1840s and 1850s. By the early twentieth century, that was no longer the case. The nationalist movement against indenture circulated and gained attention in Indian newspapers, in English and in Hindi, as the story of "Kunti's Cry" demonstrates most prominently. There was an "expansion," as Mrinalini Sinha has argued, "of what until then had counted as legitimate public opinion in India."[36]

In the context of this increasingly vocal, increasingly visible protest movement, British officials who had continued to support indenture, at least lukewarmly, took notice of the nationalist challenge. By 1914, the viceroy of India, Lord Hardinge, recommended the "total abolition" of the indenture system, arguing that it represented "a racial stigma that India deeply resent[ed]."[37] The First World War, a turning point in the global history of anticolonial nationalism, made managing that resentment—and maintaining stability in India more broadly—ever more urgent.[38] In the fall of 1915, the Government of India echoed the viceroy's call for abolition.[39] New indentured migration from India was banned in 1917, and by 1920, indenture came to a final end in the colonies.[40]

The forces that ended indenture were new and particular to the turn of the century. The story of the immediate post-emancipation period—the story of this book—followed a very different trajectory. Rather than reform, its key theme was normalization. Between 1842 and 1878, the indenture system grew substantially. It sustained and expanded plantation economies and reshaped labor relations. That is to say, it reshaped the "great experiment" and the socio-economic meaning of emancipation. As that occurred, indenture gained legitimacy. Once a scandal, it became normal, acceptable, useful. By the end of the period in question, Britons celebrated indenture as a civilizing project, as a means of development, and as free labor.

The goal of this book has been to explain how and why this process occurred. Early attempts to promote indenture, as we have seen, resulted in public scandal. Through much of the 1840s, the system remained mired in controversy and precarious at the local level. The repeal of the sugar duties lowered sugar prices, threatening to undermine the imperial sugar economy at the decade's close. Locally, colonial authorities struggled to control both freedpeople and newly arriving indentured immigrants. Wage struggles intensified a longer-term process by which the formerly enslaved moved to new villages and renegotiated their relationship to plantation labor. Disease and desertion took indentured laborers from the fields as well. Relatively weak colonial governments proved unable to impose strict labor discipline in practice.

Despite these fragmented beginnings, the 1850s and 1860s witnessed the consolidation of the indenture system. A period of sustained economic growth began in the 1850s, when sugar prices rebounded from the crisis of free trade. With the help of state subsidies, indentured migration continued on a large scale. In Mauritius, British Guiana, and Trinidad, where thousands of Indian workers arrived each year, the result was transformative. Planters put new land under cultivation, production steadily increased, and raw exports and revenues surpassed pre-abolition levels. In this sense, the indenture colonies took part in the economic pattern of the "second slavery"—the expansion of plantation-based commodity production after British abolition, in a global economy characterized by free trade.[41] Contemporaries frequently saw indenture as a response to economic decline—as a means of mitigating the effects of abolition. But in reality it was more. Rather than simply repairing, indenture *grew* the plantation economy.

Bolstering this dynamic were concerted efforts to re-establish labor discipline through law. As I have shown, the legal terms of indenture became more restrictive over time. Initial contracts lengthened from one to five years. Penalties for breach—fine, imprisonment, forced contract extensions—increased, and enforcement became more effective. Vagrancy controls intensified, most dramatically in Mauritius, where pass laws were applied to all Indians regardless of legal status.

Shifting ideological commitments help explain *why* the laws of indenture became increasingly stringent. For much of the 1840s, the Colonial Office disallowed local attempts to tie workers to the plantations. Rejecting assertions of inherent racial inferiority, officials in London insisted that Indians would respond efficiently to liberal economic incentives. Over time, a race-based conception of non-European labor displaced that relatively universalistic vision. Imperial authorities came to accept more direct forms of legal coercion on the view that they were necessary corrections to particular, non-European deficiencies.

Changes in the legal category of free labor reflected a broader ideological shift apparent in public and private discourse. A series of conceptual transformations legitimized indenture, justifying it as an acceptable part of the imperial order. New forms of social-scientific analysis displaced antislavery notions of freedom and emancipation. Liberal political economy recast labor migration and long-distance trade as the natural products of Western economic development. Similarly, it presented indenture as a mutually beneficial enterprise, as a civilizing project for non-European workers and as a means of growth and profit for investors of capital. Increasingly fixed notions of racial incapacity, meanwhile, made indenture appear necessary. From this imperial perspective, particularized social control served to correct a supposedly natural tendency to disorder and "idleness."

This process of transformation, as I have argued throughout, was both ideological and material. Declining sugar production drove support for indenture in the late 1840s. Over time, a growing consensus that emancipation had failed economically led British observers to invest new explanatory significance in race. That, in turn, served to justify indenture. Not only would labor migration increase labor supply, it would also impose labor discipline, forcing freedpeople to conform to the dictates of plantation-based wage labor. From this perspective, the perceived "failure" of emancipation enabled the ideological triumph of indenture. Institutional voices that had once condemned indenture, like the *Times*, now supported it.

At the same time, an ideological acceptance of indenture led to political action that dramatically altered economic conditions. However foundational, by the mid-1850s the crisis of the sugar colonies had abated. Sugar prices rebounded and production increased. The imperial state's decision to allow and help fund large-scale indentured labor migration made the economic growth that subsequently occurred possible. That growth, in turn, created a new basis for ideological support for indenture. Trinidad, British Guiana, and Mauritius proved the "success" of free labor as compared with slave labor in foreign colonies. Indenture adopted its own antislavery mantle. And the process continued: as economic success minimized controversy, acceptance allowed for the expansion of the system to new colonies, furthering its material growth.

As this occurred, particular economic interests found new life and legitimacy in seemingly neutral discourses of social order. This process, which I referred to as "moralization," appeared most clearly in official debates over the laws of indenture. However unsystematic, an accumulation of private, official rationales and demands coalesced over time into an imperial commonsense. Within this consensus, threats to profitability (like competition for labor or rising wages) marked irrational disorder. Labor control stood to benefit the social order generally, rather than planting capital specifically. Such translation—from interest to order—preserved the ideal of free labor by framing economic restructuring as social reform. State regulation, meanwhile, insulated the economic project of indenture from the critique of neoslavery. This was true in the late 1830s, when indenture was first attacked as a "Coolie slave trade," and again in the 1870s, when the royal commissions for British Guiana and Mauritius investigated but ultimately affirmed the system.

All of these changes redefined "freedom" and "free labor" in the post-emancipation period. Indeed, the overlapping arguments in this book illuminate an overarching theme: the shifting, unstable meaning of freedom in the post-emancipation world. Freedom is frequently defined in relation to rule—defined negatively, as a release from control. In this sense, freedom's only meaning is the absence of slavery, the absence of political, social, or economic domination. Such a definition is unsatisfying historically. For freedom's positive content is historically unfixed. To say that abolition confers freedom is really to ask a question: when slavery and freedom cease to define each other, what does freedom become?

The history of emancipation can be seen as the history of freedom's positive content—its meaning in the world. Indenture reveals many of the limits imposed on freedom in the early post-emancipation period. Though economic relations were by no means static, indenture allowed the plantation-based export economy to survive. Its demands led the imperial state to restructure labor relations, importing hundreds of thousands of new workers, and legally tying them to the plantations. The concept of freedom evolved to accommodate these dynamics. Racial hierarchy structured freedom, as did class-bound notions of civilization. Indenture became free labor, filling, temporarily, the void of emancipation.

Acknowledgments

I am deeply grateful to those who helped me research and write this book over the course of many years. The project began at Stanford University, and I am indebted to the Department of History as a whole, as well as to Stanford Law School. For teaching and inspiration, I thank Keith Baker, Jim Campbell, David Como, Tamar Herzog, Paul Robinson, Peter Stansky, Lisa Surwillo, and Amir Weiner, as well as Michelle Anderson, Bob Gordon, Bernadette Meyler, and Norman Spaulding. Most of all, I thank Priya Satia for guidance and inspiration, and for engaging so insightfully with every draft of every chapter. I am similarly grateful to J. P. Daughton and Richard Roberts, who deeply influenced my thinking, and to Amalia Kessler for brilliant close readings and years of generous mentorship.

From an early stage, a number of scholars shared expertise and offered encouragement, often on the basis of little more than an unsolicited email or chance archival encounter. For these conversations, I remain very grateful to Richard Allen, Sunil Amrith, Clare Anderson, the late Christopher Bayly, Amitava Chowdury, Richard Drayton, Malick Ghachem, Thomas Holt, and Christopher Tomlins. And to James Vernon, for inspiring and incisive advice.

Postdoctoral fellowships at the Mahindra Humanities Center at Harvard University and the Shelby Cullom Davis Center at Princeton University allowed the project to grow. From my time at Harvard, I thank Homi Bhabha, Mary Halpenny-Killip, and my co-Mahindra fellows: Valeria Castelli, Onur Gunay, Sumayya Kassamali, Matthew Kruer, and Anooradha Iyer Siddiqi. I am similarly grateful to Sunil Amrith, Sven Beckert, Kelly Brignac, Vincent Brown, Caroline Elkins, Mary Lewis, Orlando Patterson, Catherine Peters, and Emma Rothschild for responding to drafts and offering invaluable advice. At Princeton, I thank Angela Creager and Natasha Wheatley for leading the Law and

Legalities program, and then-Davis fellows George Aumoithe, Tatiana Borisova, Tom Johnson, Lena Salaymeh, Franziska Seraphim, Mitra Sharafi, Liz Thornberry, and Barbara Welke for their advice and comradery. Conversations with Jeremy Adelman, Michael Blaakman, Graham Burnett, Vera Candiani, Linda Colley, Fara Dabhoiwala, Jacob Dlamini, Dirk Hartog, Matthew Karp, Michael Laffan, Isadora Moura Mota, Phil Nord, Dan Rodgers, Keith Wailoo, the late Eric Weitz, and Peter Wirzbicki helped immensely. And I thank Christopher Brown, Angela Creager, and participants in the Davis Seminar for engaging with my project in an especially stimulating workshop the following year.

Since I joined the University of Illinois at Chicago, my incredible colleagues have supported this book in numerous ways. I thank the Department of History for welcoming me in the midst of the pandemic, for their intellectual community, and for their friendship. Thank you to Jennifer Brier, Lilia Fernández, Gosia Fidelis, Adam Goodman, Kirk Hoppe, Laura Hostetler, Lynn Hudson, Michael Jin, Robert Johnston, Ralph Keen, Clare Kim, Rama Mantena, Ellen McClure, Marina Mogilner, Hayley Negrin, Ivón Padilla-Rodríguez, Junaid Quadri, James Sack, Jeffrey Sklansky, Keely Stauter-Halsted, and Elizabeth Todd-Breland. I am especially grateful to Marina, Jeff, Rama, and Gayatri Reddy for commenting on portions of the manuscript, and to Kevin Schultz for intellectual and professional guidance as department chair. I finished writing the book as a fellow at UIC's Institute for the Humanities, and I thank both the Institute and Mark Canuel for that exceptional opportunity.

I am indebted to the many archivists who facilitated my research. In the UK, my appreciation for The National Archives grows with each visit, and I am similarly grateful to the Asian and African Studies Reading Room at the British Library, the Senate House Library, the School of Oriental and African Studies, and the Bodleian Library of Commonwealth and African Studies. I thank the National Archives of Trinidad and Tobago, and the Parliament Library of Trinidad and Tobago, for welcoming me and working so hard to find useful materials for my project. With equal fondness, I thank the National Archives of Mauritius for providing access to a treasure trove of unique records, and the Aapravasi Ghat Trust Fund (in particular, Satyendra Peerthum) for helping me navigate Mauritian archival materials and guiding me through important historical and archaeological sites. Generous financial support from the Stanford Interdisciplinary Graduate Fellowship, the Mellon Foundation, Princeton University, and the University of Illinois at Chicago made this and subsequent research possible.

As successive drafts took shape, the Hurst Summer Institute for Legal History gave me the chance to workshop several chapters. I am grateful to the

American Society for Legal History and University of Wisconsin Law School for this opportunity, and to Lauren Benton and Sally Gordon for leading our conversations so brilliantly in spite of the pandemic. Over the course of the next year, Hardeep Dhillon, Lisa Ford, Riyad Koya, Jake Subryan Richards, Geneva Smith, and Barbara Welke read sections of the manuscript, and I am deeply grateful for their insights. I am especially grateful to Radhika Mongia for reading a full draft and offering generous suggestions.

Portions of this book appeared in other forms in "Indentured Labour Migration and the Meaning of Emancipation: Free Trade, Race, and Labour in British Public Debate," *Past & Present*, no. 238 (2018): 85–119; and "Indenture as Compensation: State Funding for Labor Migration in the Era of Emancipation," *Slavery & Abolition* 40, no. 3 (2019): 448–71. I am grateful to both journals for permission to republish and, more substantively, to Matthew Hilton and Anna Bayman, to Gad Heuman, and to a number of anonymous reviewers for their enormously constructive suggestions. I similarly thank Catherine Hall and Nicholas Draper for engaging with my second article in draft, and for advice that stayed with me as I wrote the book. While it does not appear as directly here, I also thank David Akin and three wonderfully engaged reviewers for their work on "Antislavery, 'Native Labour,' and the Turn to Indenture in British Colonial Natal," *Comparative Studies in Society and History* 65, no. 3 (2023): 500–525, a distinct but thematically related piece.

At the University of Chicago Press, my deepest thanks go to Dylan Montanari and Fabiola Enríquez Flores for bringing the book to life, as well as to Mary Al-Sayed for her contributions to the project, Marianne Tatom for copyediting, and Derek Gottlieb for the index. I also thank the Press's anonymous reviewers for their encouragement and astute suggestions, which undoubtedly improved the book.

The pandemic renewed my appreciation for the kinds of scholarly exchange that begin at conferences and stay with us as the seemingly solitary process of writing continues. I feel very fortunate, looking back, for moments of intellectual connection that led to lasting correspondence and influenced this work directly and indirectly. Thank you to Tim Alborn, Sascha Auerbach, Chris Bischof, Phil Harling, Richard Huzzey, Susan Pennybacker, and Michelle Tusan; Eddie Bruce-Jones, Riyad Koya, and Renisa Mawani; Catherine Evans, Padraic Scanlan, and Sonia Tycko; and Manuel Barcia, Adriana Chira, Kristin Mann, Rebecca Scott, Randy Sparks, and Alessandro Stanziani. Closer to home, many thanks to Fredrik Albritton Jonsson, Antoinette Burton, Deborah Cohen, Kate Masur, and Dana Rabin for intellectual exchange in and around Chicago as I finished writing.

As my categories happily break down, there are still others I wish to thank, for insight and friendship across many drafts in many different places, including David Baillargeon, Nishant Batsha, Ian Beacock, Edward Cerullo, Alex Chase-Levenson, Maggie Doherty, Liz Evans, Annie Hollister, Ryan Jobson, Tom Johnson, Sienna Kang, Hannah Marcus, Jamie Martin, Kaneesha Parsard, Janina Powells, Claire Rydell Arcenas, Tehila Sasson, and Yan Slobodkin.

I am so grateful to my family for reading and cheering on this project, like so many other endeavors before it. Not to mention for showing up at the occasional conference presentation ("Is that your brother?" "Yes."). Thanks beyond words to Jamie Stern, Michael Connolly, and Alex Connolly. Finally and most of all, I thank Valeria Castelli for her immense, unwavering support for this book (and me), and Valeria and Sofia *per la gioia inaspettata e meravigliosa*.

Abbreviations

ASSP: Bodleian Library of Commonwealth and African Studies, Oxford, Anti-Slavery Society Papers

CO: The National Archives, London, Colonial Office Records

FO: The National Archives, London, Foreign Office Records

HANSARD: *Hansard's Parliamentary Debates*, 3rd ser., 350 vols. (1830–1981)

IOR: British Library, London, India Office Records

NAM: National Archives of Mauritius, Coromandel

NATT: National Archives of Trinidad and Tobago, Port of Spain

PLTT: Parliament Library of Trinidad and Tobago, Port of Spain

PP: UK Parliamentary Papers

RCBG: *Report of the Committee Appointed to Enquire into the Treatment of Immigrants in British Guiana*, PP, 1871, xx (C. 393 I–III)

RCM: *Report of the Royal Commissioners Appointed to Enquire into the Treatment of Immigrants in Mauritius*, PP, 1875, xxiv (C. 1115)

SOAS: School of Oriental and African Studies Special Collections, London

WIC: Senate House Library Historical Collections, London, West India Committee Papers

Notes

Introduction

1. Trinidad Ordinance No. 3 of 1849, The National Archives, London, Colonial Office Records (hereafter CO) 297/4.

2. Earl Grey, Minute, 7 April 1849, restated in Grey to Harris, 28 April 1849, both in CO 295/166.

3. Harris to Grey, 5 September 1849, No. 68, CO 295/168.

4. Harris to Grey, 19 June 1848, No. 71, CO 295/162 (discussing emancipation and the "rights and privileges and *duties* of civilized society") (emphasis added).

5. Harris to Grey, 21 February 1848, No. 21, CO 295/160.

6. "An Act for the Abolition of Slavery throughout the British Colonies," 3 & 4 Will. IV, c. 73 (1833). Beyond the Caribbean and Indian Ocean, abolition applied across the British Empire, though not in British India (then controlled by the East India Company), Ceylon, or Saint Helena.

7. Intense debate surrounds this point. Among arguments that slavery remained profitable, a key text is Seymour Drescher, *Econocide: British Slavery in the Era of Abolition* (Chapel Hill: University of North Carolina Press, 1977). For an overview, see Christopher Leslie Brown, *Moral Capital: Foundations of British Abolitionism* (Chapel Hill: University of North Carolina Press, 2006), 3–22. On the centrality of Eric Williams to this and related debates, see Barbara L. Solow and Stanley L. Engerman, eds., *British Capitalism and Caribbean Slavery: The Legacy of Eric Williams* (Cambridge: Cambridge University Press, 1987).

8. David Brion Davis, *The Problem of Slavery in Western Culture* (Ithaca, NY: Cornell University Press, 1966); Brown, *Moral Capital*; Seymour Drescher, *Abolition: A History of Slavery and Antislavery* (Cambridge: Cambridge University Press, 2009), chap. 9.

9. David Northrup, *Indentured Labor in the Age of Imperialism, 1834–1922* (Cambridge: Cambridge University Press, 1995), 159–61. The total exceeded 1 million for British colonies alone and 1.3 million including French and Dutch colonies. For related estimates, see Colin Clarke, Ceri Peach, and Steven Vertovec, eds., *South Asians Overseas: Migration and Ethnicity* (Cambridge: Cambridge University Press, 1990), 9.

10. Northrup, *Indentured Labor*, 159–61.

11. Russell to Light, 15 February 1840, No. 56, UK Parliamentary Papers (hereafter PP), 1840, xxxiv (151), 43; famously cited in Hugh Tinker, *A New System of Slavery: The Export of Indian Labour Overseas* (London: Oxford University Press, 1974), epigraph.

12. *Hansard*, 3rd ser., clii, col. 1232 (3 March 1859).

13. Grey to Harris, 28 April 1849, CO 295/166; Grey to Harris, 14 January 1850, PP, 1850, xl (643), 242.

14. Key works include Richard Allen, *Slaves, Freedmen, and Indentured Laborers in Colonial Mauritius* (Cambridge: Cambridge University Press, 1999); Clare Anderson, "Convicts and Coolies: Rethinking Indentured Labour in the Nineteenth Century," *Slavery and Abolition* 30, no. 1 (2009): 93–109; Gaiutra Bahadur, *Coolie Woman: The Odyssey of Indenture* (Chicago: University of Chicago Press, 2014); Marina Carter, *Servants, Sirdars and Settlers: Indians in Mauritius, 1834–1874* (Delhi: Oxford University Press, 1995); Ashwin Desai and Goolam Vahed, *Inside Indian Indenture: A South African Story, 1860–1914* (Cape Town: HSRC Press, 2010); William A. Green, *British Slave Emancipation: The Sugar Colonies and the Great Experiment, 1830–1865* (Oxford: Clarendon, 1976); Maurits S. Hassankhan, Brij V. Lal, and Doug Munro, eds., *Resistance and Indian Indenture Experience: Comparative Perspectives* (New Delhi: Manohar, 2014); Madhavi Kale, *Fragments of Empire: Capital, Slavery, and Indian Indentured Labor Migration in the British Caribbean* (Philadelphia: University of Pennsylvania Press, 1998); Ashutosh Kumar, *Coolies of the Empire: Indentured Indians in the Sugar Colonies, 1830–1920* (Cambridge: Cambridge University Press, 2017); K. O. Laurence, *A Question of Labour: Indentured Immigration into Trinidad and British Guiana, 1875–1917* (New York: St. Martin's Press, 1994); Walton Look Lai, *Indentured Labor, Caribbean Sugar: Chinese and Indian Migrants to the British West Indies, 1838–1918* (Baltimore: Johns Hopkins University Press, 1993); Basdeo Mangru, *Benevolent Neutrality: Indian Government Policy and Labour Migration to British Guiana, 1854–1884* (London: Hansib, 1987); Radhika Mongia, *Indian Migration and Empire: A Colonial Genealogy of the Modern State* (Durham, NC: Duke University Press, 2018); Northrup, *Indentured Labor*; Walter Rodney, *A History of the Guyanese Working People, 1881–1905* (Baltimore: Johns Hopkins University Press, 1981); Lomarsh Roopnarine, *Indo-Caribbean Indenture: Resistance and Accommodation, 1838–1920* (Mona: University of the West Indies Press, 2007); Kay Saunders, ed., *Indentured Labour in the British Empire, 1834–1920* (London: Croom Helm, 1984); Rachel Sturman, "Indian Indentured Labor and the History of International Rights Regimes," *American Historical Review* 119, no. 5 (2014): 1439–65; Tinker, *New System of Slavery*.

15. Tinker, *New System of Slavery*.

16. Stanley L. Engerman, "Contract Labor, Sugar, and Technology in the Nineteenth Century," *Journal of Economic History* 43, no. 3 (1983): 635–59; P. C. Emmer, "The Meek Hindu: The Recruitment of Indian Indentured Labourers for Service Overseas, 1870–1916," in *Colonialism and Migration: Indentured Labour Before and After Slavery*, ed. P. C. Emmer (Dordrecht: M. Nijhoff, 1986).

17. Northrup, *Indentured Labor*, x, 5–6. For a brief restatement, see David Northrup, "Overseas Movements of Slaves and Indentured Workers," in *The Cambridge World History of Slavery: Volume 4, AD 1804–AD 2016*, ed. David Eltis, Stanley L. Engerman, Seymour Drescher, and David Richardson (Cambridge: Cambridge University Press, 2017), 49–70. For additional analysis of these debates, see Amit Kumar Mishra, "Indian Indentured Labourers in Mauritius: Reassessing the 'New System of Slavery' vs. Free Labour Debate," *Studies in History* 25, no. 2 (2009): 229–51, 234–38.

18. Key work on Mauritius has emphasized change over time. See, in particular, Allen, *Slaves, Freedmen, and Indentured Laborers*, and Carter, *Servants, Sirdars and Settlers*, and, more recently, Nandini Boodia-Canoo, *Slavery, Indenture and the Law: Assembling a Nation in Colonial Mauritius* (London: Routledge, 2023).

19. As does important work that has critically assessed the categories previously used to study indenture, including Anderson, "Convicts and Coolies"; Kale, *Fragments of Empire*; and Mongia, *Indian Migration and Empire*.

20. Mongia, *Indian Migration and Empire*, 39.

21. Northrup, *Indentured Labor*, 144.

22. Key works include Frederick Cooper, Thomas C. Holt, and Rebecca J. Scott, *Beyond Slavery: Explorations of Race, Labor, and Citizenship in Postemancipation Societies* (Chapel Hill: University of North Carolina Press, 2000); Seymour Drescher, *The Mighty Experiment: Free Labor versus Slavery in British Emancipation* (Oxford: Oxford University Press, 2002); Catherine Hall, *Civilising Subjects: Metropole and Colony in the English Imagination, 1830–1867* (Chicago: University of Chicago Press, 2002); Thomas C. Holt, *The Problem of Freedom: Race, Labor, and Politics in Jamaica and Britain, 1832–1938* (Baltimore: Johns Hopkins University Press, 1992). Relatedly, Frederick Cooper, *From Slaves to Squatters: Plantation Labor and Agriculture in Zanzibar and Coastal Kenya, 1890–1925* (New Haven, CT: Yale University Press, 1980); Rebecca J. Scott, *Degrees of Freedom: Louisiana and Cuba after Slavery* (Cambridge, MA: Harvard University Press, 2005).

23. On Indian indenture in Jamaica, see Verene A. Shepherd, *Transients to Settlers: The Experience of Indians in Jamaica 1845–1950* (Leeds: Peepal Tree, 1993).

24. Cooper, Holt, and Scott, *Beyond Slavery*, 9, 3.

25. Holt, *Problem of Freedom*.

26. Drescher, *Mighty Experiment*, 158–230.

27. Rodney, *History of the Guyanese Working People*, 31–59.

28. For an overview, see Lawrence M. Friedman, "The Law and Society Movement," *Stanford Law Review* 38, no. 3 (1986): 763–80.

29. Eric Foner, *Nothing but Freedom: Emancipation and Its Legacy*, rev. ed. (Baton Rouge: Louisiana State University Press, 2007), 3.

30. As in Natal, beginning in 1860.

31. Edward Said, *Orientalism* (New York: Vintage, 1978); Michel Foucault, *The Archaeology of Knowledge*, 1969 (New York: Vintage, 2010), and *Discipline and Punish*, 1975 (New York: Vintage, 1995). For an introduction to the many ways in which the cultural turn influenced imperial history, see Catherine Hall, ed., *Cultures of Empire, A Reader: Colonizers in Britain and the Empire in the Nineteenth and Twentieth Centuries* (New York: Routledge, 2000); Kathleen Wilson, ed., *A New Imperial History: Culture, Identity, and Modernity in Britain and the Empire, 1660–1840* (Cambridge: Cambridge University Press, 2004); Ann Laura Stoler and Frederick Cooper, "Between Metropole and Colony: Rethinking a Research Agenda," in *Tensions of Empire: Colonial Cultures in a Bourgeois World*, ed. Frederick Cooper and Ann Laura Stoler (Berkeley: University of California Press, 1997), 1–56.

32. On the term "political culture," as used by cultural historians to analyze the linguistic construction and contestation of political meaning, see Keith Michael Baker, *Inventing the French Revolution* (Cambridge: Cambridge University Press, 1990), 4–7.

33. Priya Satia, *Spies in Arabia: The Great War and the Cultural Foundations of Britain's Covert Empire in the Middle East* (Oxford: Oxford University Press, 2008), 5.

34. See Kale, *Fragments of Empire*, 5–6; Mongia, *Indian Migration and Empire*, 3–5, 9 (articulating related critiques).

35. Eric Williams, *Capitalism and Slavery* (Chapel Hill: University of North Carolina Press, 1944).

36. Davis, *Problem of Slavery in Western Culture*; Drescher, *Econocide*; Seymour Drescher, *Capitalism and Antislavery: British Mobilization in Comparative Perspective* (Oxford: Oxford University Press, 1987).

37. Thomas Bender, ed., *The Antislavery Debate: Capitalism and Abolitionism as a Problem in Historical Interpretation* (Berkeley: University of California Press, 1992); David Brion Davis, *The Problem of Slavery in the Age of Revolution, 1770–1823* (Ithaca, NY: Cornell University Press, 1975).

38. On connections between Atlantic slavery and the rise of capitalism, see, among others, Sven Beckert, *Empire of Cotton: A Global History* (New York: Knopf, 2014); Joseph E. Inikori, *Africans and the Industrial Revolution in England: A Study in International Trade and Economic Development* (Cambridge: Cambridge University Press, 2002); Walter Johnson, *River of Dark Dreams: Slavery and Empire in the Cotton Kingdom* (Cambridge, MA: Belknap, 2013); Sidney W. Mintz, *Sweetness and Power: The Place of Sugar in Modern History* (New York: Penguin, 1985); Barbara L. Solow, *The Economic Consequences of the Atlantic Slave Trade* (Lanham, MD: Lexington Books, 2014). For related analysis and caution, see Trevor Burnard and Giorgio Riello, "Slavery and the New History of Capitalism," *Journal of Global History* 15, no. 2 (2020): 225–44.

39. Relatedly, see Stuart Hall, "Race—The Sliding Signifier," in *The Fateful Triangle: Race, Ethnicity, Nation*, ed. Kobena Mercer (Cambridge, MA: Harvard University Press, 2017), 31, 46 (on "discourse," ideas, and practice), and "The Problem of Ideology: Marxism without Guarantees," in *Selected Writings on Marxism*, ed. Gregor McLennan (Durham, NC: Duke University Press, 2021), 136; Richard Huzzey, *Freedom Burning: Anti-Slavery and Empire in Victorian Britain* (Ithaca, NY: Cornell University Press, 2012), 206 (ideologies as "belief systems through which economic realities or interests are created, imagined, and pursued"); Karuna Mantena, *Alibis of Empire: Henry Maine and the Ends of Liberal Imperialism* (Princeton, NJ: Princeton University Press, 2010), 2–10 (on "imperial ideology").

40. Gareth Stedman Jones, *Languages of Class: Studies in English Working Class History, 1832–1982* (Cambridge: Cambridge University Press, 1983), 7–8, 94–95. Separately, I will at times attribute a more specific theoretical meaning to the term "ideology" in my discussions, first, of law, and second, of the naturalizing effects of certain discourses. These more specific meanings will be elaborated when relevant.

41. While some of the connections described in this book involve a crossing of imperial borders (in relation to the Spanish and French empires), many others cut across conventionally defined regions (in particular, the Caribbean and Indian Ocean) within a British imperial sphere. In this sense, my use of the term "connected" is adjacent to but not coterminous with Sanjay Subrahmanyam's influential approach in *Explorations in Connected History: From the Tagus to the Ganges* (Oxford: Oxford University Press, 2005).

42. For a trans-colonial approach to indenture focused on return and onward migration by indentured migrants from the 1870s onward, see Reshaad Durgahee, *The Indentured Archipelago: Experiences of Indian Labour in Mauritius and Fiji, 1871–1916* (Cambridge: Cambridge University Press, 2021).

43. On the movement of officials across the empire, see David Lambert and Alan Lester, eds., *Colonial Lives Across the Empire: Imperial Careering in the Long Nineteenth Century* (Cambridge: Cambridge University Press, 2006); Hall, *Civilising Subjects*, 23–65.

44. Richard B. Allen, "Suppressing a Nefarious Traffic: Britain and the Abolition of Slave Trading in India and the Western Indian Ocean, 1770–1830," *William and Mary Quarterly*, 3rd ser., 66, no. 4 (2009): 873–94.

45. Stoler and Cooper, "Between Metropole and Colony," 21–28.

46. In analyzing the imperial state in this way, I have in mind both Thomas Metcalf's work on India as an imperial center and Lauren Benton and Lisa Ford's work on "middle power" and imperial legal ordering. See Thomas R. Metcalf, *Imperial Connections: India in the Indian Ocean Arena, 1860–1920* (Berkeley: University of California Press, 2008); Lauren Benton and Lisa Ford, *Rage for Order: The British Empire and the Origins of International Law, 1800–1850* (Cambridge, MA: Harvard University Press, 2016).

47. Northrup, *Indentured Labor*, 159. Between 1831 and 1917, some 429,454 indentured Indians arrived in the British Caribbean. The corresponding figure for Mauritius was 451,786.

48. Modern-day Guyana is 83,000 square miles, but the borders of British Guiana were contested throughout the nineteenth century. On mapping and border-making in the colony, see D. Graham Burnett, *Masters of All They Surveyed: Exploration, Geography, and a British El Dorado* (Chicago: University of Chicago Press, 2000).

49. Richard H. Grove, *Green Imperialism: Colonial Expansion, Tropical Island Edens and the Origins of Environmentalism, 1600–1860* (Cambridge: Cambridge University Press, 1996), 210; Vijayalakshmi Teelock, *Mauritian History: From Its Beginnings to Modern Times*, rev. ed. (Moka, Mauritius: Mahatma Gandhi Institute, 2009), 81–83.

50. Kale, *Fragments of Empire*, 56–65.

51. Brij V. Lal, *Chalo Jahaji: On a Journey through Indenture in Fiji* (Canberra: ANU Press, 2012); Surendra Bhana and Joy B. Brain, *Setting Down Roots: Indian Migrants in South Africa, 1860–1911* (Johannesburg: Witwatersrand University Press, 1990); Desai and Vahed, *Inside Indian Indenture*, 173–319; David Dabydeen and Brinsley Samaroo, eds., *Across the Dark Waters: Ethnicity and Indian Identity in the Caribbean* (London: Macmillan Caribbean, 1996).

52. Carter, *Servants, Sirdars and Settlers*; Kumar, *Coolies of the Empire*. Beyond post-slavery indenture, see Sunil S. Amrith, *Crossing the Bay of Bengal: The Furies of Nature and the Fortunes of Migrants* (Cambridge, MA: Harvard University Press, 2013).

53. On women, gender, and indenture, see Bahadur, *Coolie Woman*; Marina Carter, *Voices from Indenture: Experiences of Indian Migrants in the British Empire* (London: Leicester University Press, 1996); Arunima Datta, *Fleeting Agencies: A Social History of Indian Coolie Women in British Malaya* (Cambridge: Cambridge University Press, 2021). On Indian nationalism and indenture, see Kumar, *Coolies of the Empire*, chap. 7; Radica Mahase, *Why Should We Be Called "Coolies"? The End of Indian Indentured Labour* (New Delhi: Manohar, 2020); Mrinalini Sinha, "Premonitions of the Past," *Journal of Asian Studies* 74, no. 4 (2015): 821–41; Sturman, "Indian Indentured Labor."

54. Hannah Franziska Augstein, ed., *Race: The Origins of an Idea* (Bristol: Thoemmes Press, 1996); Michael Banton, *Racial Theories*, rev. ed. (Cambridge: Cambridge University Press, 1998); Colin Kidd, *The Forging of Races: Race and Scripture in the Protestant Atlantic World, 1600–2000* (Cambridge: Cambridge University Press, 2006); George Mosse, *Toward the Final Solution: A History of European Racism* (New York: H. Fertig, 1978), 65–76; Nancy Stepan, *The Idea of Race in Science: Great Britain 1800–1960* (London: Macmillan, 1982). As Philip Curtin wrote, race before the nineteenth century was "a *mark* identifying the group—not a *cause* of the group's other characteristics." Philip D. Curtin, *The Image of Africa: British Ideas and Action, 1780–1850* (Madison: University of Wisconsin Press, 1973), 36.

55. Hall, *Civilising Subjects*; Richard Price, *Making Empire: Colonial Encounters and the Creation of Imperial Rule in Nineteenth-Century Africa* (Cambridge: Cambridge University Press, 2008); Andrew C. Ross, "Christian Missions and Mid-Nineteenth Century Change in Attitudes to Race: The African Experience," in *The Imperial Horizons of British Protestant Missions*, ed. Andrew Porter (Grand Rapids, MI: Eerdmans, 2003), 85–105.

56. Christine Bolt, *Victorian Attitudes to Race* (London: Routledge, 1971), 75–108; Thomas R. Metcalf, *Ideologies of the Raj* (Cambridge: Cambridge University Press, 1995); Holt, *Problem of Freedom*; Karuna Mantena, "The Crisis of Liberal Imperialism," in *Victorian Visions of Global Order: Empire and International Relations in Nineteenth-Century Political Thought*, ed. Duncan Bell (Cambridge: Cambridge University Press, 2007), 113–35. For an important dissenting view to the nineteenth-century "hardening" of racial attitudes thesis, see Richard Drayton, *Nature's Government: Science, Imperial Britain, and the "Improvement" of the World* (New Haven, CT: Yale University Press, 2000), 225 ("Biology merely provided a new vocabulary with which to express old explanations for dominance, subordination, and violence.").

57. John A. Hobson, *Imperialism: A Study* (London, 1902); V. I. Lenin, *Imperialism, the Highest Stage of Capitalism*, 1917 (London: Penguin, 2010); Joseph Schumpeter, "The Sociology of Imperialism," 1919, in *Imperialism, Social Classes: Two Essays* (New York: Meridian, 1955).

58. John Gallagher and Ronald Robinson, "The Imperialism of Free Trade," *Economic History Review*, new ser., 6, no. 1 (1953): 1–15. See also John Darwin, *The Empire Project: The Rise and Fall of the British World System, 1830–1970* (Cambridge: Cambridge University Press, 2009).

59. Uday Singh Mehta, *Liberalism and Empire: A Study in Nineteenth-Century British Liberal Thought* (Chicago: University of Chicago Press, 1999).

60. Jennifer Pitts, *A Turn to Empire, The Rise of Imperial Liberalism in Britain and France* (Princeton, NJ: Princeton University Press, 2005). Relatedly, Mantena, *Alibis of Empire*; Metcalf, *Ideologies of the Raj.*

61. Mantena, *Alibis of Empire*, 9. On liberalism and empire "beyond the rarified domains of self-conscious political theory or jurisprudence into wider worlds of normative social and political discourse," see also Andrew Sartori, *Liberalism in Empire: An Alternative History* (Oakland: University of California Press, 2014), quote on 7.

62. Dipesh Chakrabarty, *Provincializing Europe: Postcolonial Thought and Historical Difference* (Princeton, NJ: Princeton University Press, 2008), 7, 8, 16. See also Priya Satia, *Time's Monster: How History Makes History* (Cambridge, MA: Belknap, 2020).

63. On free trade and free-trade ideals, see among others Philip Harling, *The Waning of "Old Corruption": The Politics of Economical Reform in Britain, 1779–1846* (Oxford: Clarendon, 1996); Anthony Howe, *Free Trade and Liberal England, 1846–1946* (Oxford: Clarendon, 1997); Boyd Hilton, *The Age of Atonement: The Influence of Evangelicalism on Social and Economic Thought, 1785–1865* (Oxford: Clarendon, 1986); Frank Trentmann, *Free Trade Nation: Commerce, Consumption, and Civil Society in Modern Britain* (Oxford: Oxford University Press, 2008).

64. To be clear, such power was never absolute, as discussed in chapters 2, 3, and 6.

65. Karl Polanyi, *The Great Transformation: The Political and Economic Origins of Our Time*, 1944 (Boston: Beacon Press, 2001), esp. 75–76, 171–86.

Chapter 1

1. Secretary to the Government of Bengal to G. F. Dick, Chief Secretary to the Government of Mauritius, 20 May 1835, National Archives of Mauritius, Coromandel (hereafter NAM), RA 341.

2. McFarlan, Chief Magistrate of Calcutta, to Torrens, Officiating Secretary to the Government of India, 3 May 1835, and enclosed contract between John Shaw Sampson and 151 Indian laborers, NAM, RA 341.

3. The indenture system also operated, on a smaller scale, in St. Lucia, St. Vincent, and Grenada. In addition, Indian indenture featured in the French colonies of Réunion, Guadeloupe,

and Martinique, and the Dutch colony of Suriname. While I do not focus on these aspects of the indenture system, I do address Indian migration to French colonies and the treaty relations ultimately brokered to regulate indenture in that context in chapter 4.

4. Smyth to Glenelg, 7 August 1836, and Young to Smyth, 27 July 1836, CO 111/146; Smyth to Glenelg, 8 August 1836, CO 111/146.

5. Glenelg to Smyth, 29 September 1836, CO 111/146; William A. Green, "Emancipation to Indenture: A Question of Imperial Morality," *Journal of British Studies* 22, no. 2 (1983), 102–4.

6. Free Labor Association to Campbell, 14 May 1840, NAM, IA 26; Free Labor Association to Anderson, 28 August 1840, NAM, IA 26.

7. David Northrup, *Indentured Labor in the Age of Imperialism, 1834–1922* (Cambridge: Cambridge University Press, 1995), 22–23. This is not to suggest that European migration was unimportant throughout the period. Large numbers of Portuguese migrants arrived in British Guiana during the 1840s and 1850s after harvest failures in Madeira. On failed efforts to recruit European and African workers, see also J. H. Galloway, *The Sugar Cane Industry: An Historical Geography from Its Origins to 1914* (Cambridge: Cambridge University Press, 1989), 125–26; Marina Carter, *Servants, Sirdars and Settlers: Indians in Mauritius, 1834–1874* (Delhi: Oxford University Press, 1995), 18–19.

8. Prinsep, Secretary to the Government of India, to Dick, Chief Secretary to the Government of Mauritius, 22 September 1834, NAM, RA 341 (reporting a contract signed by 36 Indian workers with G. C. Arbuthnot); Prinsep to Dick, 29 December 1834, NAM, RA 341 (reporting that 480 Indians had "entered into engagements with Mr. Henderson Agent of Mr. W. W. West"). See also Satyendra Peerthum, *"They Came to Mauritian Shores": The Life-Stories and the History of the Indentured Labourers in Mauritius (1826–1937)* (Coromandel, Mauritius: Aapravasi Ghat Trust Fund, 2017), 44–48.

9. See, for example, McFarlan to Prinsep, 19 September 1834, and attached contract, NAM, RA 341. See also Seiguette and Anderson to the Colonial Secretary of Mauritius, 25 January 1838, enclosed in Nicolay to Glenelg, 9 March 1838, CO 167/202.

10. Lushington and Galloway (Court of Directors) to the Government of India, Legislative Department, 20 September 1848, British Library, London, India Office Records (hereafter IOR) L/PJ/3/1199.

11. Northrup, *Indentured Labor*, 156.

12. Kaushik Ghosh, "A Market for Aboriginality: Primitivism and Race Classification in the Indentured Labour Market of Colonial India," in *Subaltern Studies X: Writing on South Asian History and Society*, ed. Gautam Bhadra, Gyan Prakash, and Susie Tharu (New Delhi: Oxford University Press, 1999), 8–48; Uday Chandra, "Kol, Coolie, Colonial Subject: A Hidden History of Caste and the Making of Modern Bengal," in *The Politics of Caste in West Bengal*, ed. Uday Chandra, Geir Heierstad, and Kenneth Bo Nielsen (New Delhi: Routledge, 2015): 19–34; Carter, *Servants, Sirdars and Settlers*, 104–5. Here and throughout this book, I use the term "coolie" when analyzing colonial discourses of racial difference but not as a general descriptor for those who migrated under indenture. That said, some scholars have embraced the term for both creative and intellectual reasons. For an elegant discussion of the term's origins and potential uses in contemporary scholarship, see Gaiutra Bahadur, *Coolie Woman: The Odyssey of Indenture* (Chicago: University of Chicago Press, 2014), xix–xxi.

13. Andrea Major, "'Hill Coolies': Indian Indentured Labour and the Colonial Imagination, 1836–38," *South Asian Studies* 33, no. 1 (2017): 23–36; Rose Cullen, "Empire, Indian Indentured Labour and the Colony: The Debate Over 'Coolie' Labour in New South Wales, 1836–1838," *History Australia* 9, no. 1 (2012): 84–109; Ghosh, "A Market for Aboriginality."

14. Major, "'Hill Coolies,'" 32.

15. Gladstone to Hobhouse, 23 February 1837, CO 111/161 (explaining the influence of Mauritius).

16. Gillanders, Arbuthnot & Co. to Gladstone, 6 June 1836, PP, 1837–38, lii (232), 2–3. On Gladstone's correspondence and mercantile networks, see Madhavi Kale, *Fragments of Empire: Capital, Slavery, and Indian Indentured Labor Migration in the British Caribbean* (Philadelphia: University of Pennsylvania Press, 1998), 16–17; Purba Hossain, "'A Matter of Doubt and Uncertainty': John Gladstone and the Post-Slavery Framework of Labour in the British Empire," *Journal of Imperial and Commonwealth History* 50, no. 1 (2022): 52–80.

17. Gladstone to Grey, 23 March 1837, PP, 1837–38, lii (180), 25. See also Gladstone to Hobhouse, 23 February 1837, CO 111/161.

18. Kale, *Fragments of Empire*, 52.

19. Richard B. Allen, "Slaves, Convicts, Abolitionism and the Global Origins of the Post-Emancipation Indentured Labor System," *Slavery & Abolition* 35, no. 2 (2014): 328–48, 332; Marina Carter, "The Transition from Slave to Indentured Labour in Mauritius," in *The Wages of Slavery: From Chattel Slavery to Wage Labour in Africa, the Caribbean and England*, ed. Michael Twaddle (London: Frank Cass, 1993), 115–18; M. D. North-Coombes, "From Slavery to Indenture: Forced Labour in the Political Economy of Mauritius, 1834–1867," in *Indentured Labour in the British Empire, 1834–1920*, ed. Kay Saunders (London: Croom Helm, 1984), 81–82.

20. Kale, *Fragments of Empire*, 59.

21. On this usage of the term "ideology," see Hannah Arendt, *The Origins of Totalitarianism*, new ed. (New York: Harcourt, 1977), 468–74. Here, like Arendt, I see ideology not simply as a set of political ideas, but rather as a "logicality" that purports to explain past and future deterministically—as an idea or set of ideas whose inner logic makes a particular course of political action appear necessary and inevitable.

22. See Lisa Lowe, *The Intimacies of Four Continents* (Durham, NC: Duke University Press, 2015), 24–25 (discussing the "instability and multivalence of the term *coolie*").

23. Brij V. Lal's *Girmitiyas: The Origin of the Fiji Indians* (Canberra: Journal of Pacific History, 1983) was pioneering in this regard, as was Surendra Bhana's *Indentured Indian Emigrants to Natal, 1860–1902: A Study Based on Ships' Lists* (New Delhi: Promilla & Co., 1991). For Mauritius, see Peerthum, *"They Came to Mauritian Shores,"* 26–44. As Arunima Datta argues in *Fleeting Agencies: A Social History of Indian Coolie Women in British Malaya* (Cambridge: Cambridge University Press, 2021) at 8–9, the notion of the coolie remained male-centric even during the late nineteenth and early twentieth centuries, at which point larger numbers of women had also migrated under indenture.

24. Moon-Ho Jung, *Coolies and Cane: Race, Labor, and Sugar in the Age of Emancipation* (Baltimore: Johns Hopkins University Press, 2006).

25. B. W. Higman, "The Chinese in Trinidad, 1806–1838," *Caribbean Studies* 12, no. 3 (1972): 21–44; Allen, "Slaves, Convicts, Abolitionism"; James Epstein, *Scandal of Colonial Rule: Power and Subversion in the British Atlantic during the Age of Revolution* (Cambridge: Cambridge University Press, 2012), 205–21.

26. Allen, "Slaves, Convicts, Abolitionism," 335; Clare Anderson, "Convicts and Coolies: Rethinking Indentured Labour in the Nineteenth Century," *Slavery and Abolition* 30, no. 1 (2009): 93–109; Clare Anderson, *Convicts in the Indian Ocean: Transportation from South Asia to Mauritius, 1815–53* (Basingstoke: Palgrave, 2000).

27. Richard B. Allen, *European Slave Trading in the Indian Ocean, 1500–1850* (Athens: Ohio University Press, 2014), 197; Satyendra Peerthum, "'A Cheap Reservoir of Mankind for Labour':

The Genesis of the Indentured Labour System in Mauritius, 1826–1843," in *Angaje: Explorations into the History, Society and Culture of Indentured Immigrants and Their Descendants in Mauritius*, vol. 1, *Early Years*, ed. Vijayalakshmi Teelock et al. (Port Louis, Mauritius: Aapravasi Ghat Trust Fund, 2012), 159.

28. Anderson, "Convicts and Coolies."

29. Allen, "Slaves, Convicts, Abolitionism," 332; Higman, "The Chinese in Trinidad," 32–35.

30. Allen, *European Slave Trading*, 197.

31. Anderson, *Convicts in the Indian Ocean*, 111–23; Hamish Maxwell-Stewart, "Transportation from Britain and Ireland, 1615–1875," in *A Global History of Convicts and Penal Colonies*, ed. Clare Anderson (London: Bloomsbury, 2018), 202.

32. John Scoble, *Hill Coolies: A Brief Exposure of the Deplorable Condition of the Hill Coolies, in British Guiana and Mauritius, and of the Nefarious Means by which they were Induced to Resort to these Colonies (London, 1840)*, 4.

33. Scoble, *Hill Coolies*, 4.

34. Clarkson to Beaumont, 8 March 1842, Bodleian Library of Commonwealth and African Studies, Oxford, Anti-Slavery Society Papers (hereafter ASSP), MSS Brit Emp S 18, C 107/19.

35. "The Slave-Trade Revival," *British Emancipator*, 31 January 1838 (italics in original).

36. Purba Hossain, "Protests at the Colonial Capital: Calcutta and the Global Debates on Indenture, 1836–42," *South Asian Studies* 33, no. 1 (2017): 37–51. On antislavery thought in colonial India, see Andrea Major, *Slavery, Abolitionism and Empire in India, 1772–1843* (Liverpool: Liverpool University Press, 2012); Allen, *European Slave Trading*, 179–220; Howard Temperley, *British Antislavery, 1833–1870* (London: Longman, 1972), 93–110.

37. "Transportation of Labourers to the Sugar Colonies," *Friend of India*, 1 February 1838; "Exportation of Coolies from India," *Friend of India*, 7 June 1838. See also "Progress of the Abolition of the Cooly Trade," *Friend of India*, 5 July 1838; "The Cooly Trade," *Friend of India*, 9 August 1838; "Lord Glenelg's Protection Bill," *Friend of India*, 30 August 1838. The paper continued to print similar articles between 1838 and 1843, as did several other Indian newspapers, like the *Christian Observer* and the *Englishman* (which was published in Calcutta). For additional examples, see I. M. Cumpston, *Indians Overseas in British Territories, 1834–1854* (London: Oxford University Press, 1953), 21, 67.

38. "Petition of the Inhabitants of Calcutta to the Honorable Alexander Ross, President of the Council of India in Council," Calcutta Town Hall, 10 July 1838, IOR F/4/1725, No. 69489.

39. "Petition of the Inhabitants of Calcutta," 10 July 1838.

40. *Times*, 29 July 1839, 4. See also *Times*, 12 July 1838 (calling indenture a "novel abomination"), cited in Cumpston, *Indians Overseas*, 22.

41. *Times*, 29 June 1842, 6.

42. *Hansard*, 3rd ser., xli, col. 421 (6 March 1838).

43. Auckland to the Court of Directors, 9 July 1838, Public No. 5, in *Further Papers respecting East-Indian Labourers*, 7, IOR V/27/820/4.

44. Ross, Morison, and Bird (Government of India) to the Court of Directors, 22 August 1838, Public No. 27, in *Further Papers respecting East-Indian Labourers*, 10–15, IOR V/27/820/4.

45. Ross, Morison, and Bird to the Court of Directors, 22 August 1838.

46. Major, "Hill Coolies," 27.

47. Major, "Hill Coolies," 27; Crispin Bates and Marina Carter, "Enslaved Lives, Enslaving Labels: A New Approach to the Colonial Indian Labor Diaspora," in *New Routes for Diaspora Studies*, ed. Sunkanya Banerjee, Aims McGuinness, and Seven C. McKay (Bloomington: Indiana University Press, 2012), 67–92.

48. Bates and Carter, "Enslaved Lives"; Carter, *Servants, Sirdars and Settlers*; Ashutosh Kumar, *Coolies of the Empire: Indentured Indians in the Sugar Colonies, 1830–1920* (Cambridge: Cambridge University Press, 2017), 20–54.

49. Light to Normanby, 8 May 1839, PP, 1839, xxxix (463), 79.

50. "Report of the Committee appointed by the Supreme Government of India to inquire into the Abuses alleged to exist in exporting from Bengal Hill Coolies and Indian Labourers, of various Classes, to other Countries" (hereafter Calcutta Committee), PP, 1841 Session I, xvi (45), 4–12, 5. The committee's majority report is often referred to as the Dickens Report, after the committee's chair, Theodore Dickens.

51. Calcutta Committee, 7. See also Kale, *Fragments of Empire*, 79–84; Radhika Mongia, *Indian Migration and Empire: A Colonial Genealogy of the Modern State* (Durham, NC: Duke University Press, 2018), 33–37.

52. Lushington and Jenkins (Court of Directors) to the Governor General of India in Council, 1 August 1838, Legislative No. 9, IOR F/4/1769, No. 72747.

53. Morison, Robertson, Bird, and Amos (Government of India) to the Court of Directors, 27 May 1839, IOR L/PJ/3/279.

54. Morison, Robertson, Bird, and Amos to the Court of Directors, 27 May 1839.

55. *Times*, 29 July 1839, 4.

56. Northrup, *Indentured Labor*, 63.

57. Northrup, *Indentured Labor*, 156–57.

58. Radhika Mongia similarly argues that state regulation played a crucial role in legitimizing indenture in this early period in *Indian Migration and Empire*, 43–55.

59. Light to Normanby, 21 May 1839, PP, 1839, xxxix (463), 88.

60. Basdeo Mangru, "Indian Government Policy towards Indentured Labour Migration to the Sugar Colonies," in *Across the Dark Waters: Ethnicity and Indian Identity in the Caribbean*, ed. David Dabydeen and Brinsley Samaroo (London: Macmillan Caribbean, 1996), 162.

61. Prinsep, Minute, 9 May 1841, IOR F/4/1909, No. 81645; Amos, Minute, 11 May 1841, IOR, F/4/1909, No. 81645.

62. Amos, Minute, 11 May 1841, IOR, F/4/1909, No. 81645.

63. Riyad Sadiq Koya, "Slavery, Abolitionism, Indentured Labour: The Problem of Exit and the Border Between Land and Sea in Colonial India," in *South Asian Migrations in Global History: Labour, Law, and Wayward Lives*, ed. Neilesh Bose (London: Bloomsbury, 2021), 120. For a detailed account of dissent within the committee, see Mongia, *Indian Migration and Empire*, 34–36.

64. Minute by the Governor General (Auckland), 25 April 1841, IOR/F/4/1909, No. 81645.

65. Isaiah Berlin, "Two Concepts of Liberty," in *Four Essays on Liberty* (Oxford: Oxford University Press, 1969); Richard Huzzey, "Concepts of Liberty: Freedom, Laisse-Faire and the State after Britain's Abolition of Slavery," in *Emancipation and the Remaking of the British Imperial World*, ed. Catherine Hall, Nicholas Draper, and Keith McClelland (Manchester: Manchester University Press, 2014), 150–51.

66. Kale, *Fragments of Empire*, 8; Drescher, *Mighty Experiment*.

67. Cited in Kale, *Fragments of Empire*, 82. See also Koya, "Slavery, Abolitionism, Indentured Labour," 118–20 (analyzing related free-labor claims).

68. Mike Davis, *Late Victorian Holocausts: El Niño Famines and the Making of the Third World* (London: Verso, 2001); Sunil Amrith, *Unruly Waters: How Rains, Rivers, Coasts, and Seas Have Shaped Asia's History* (New York: Basic Books, 2018), 65–89.

69. *Hansard*, 3rd ser., lx, col. 1333 (1 March 1842).

70. *Hansard*, 3rd ser., lx, cols. 1333, 1335. In his minute dissenting from the report of the Calcutta Committee, James Grant made a similar argument. J. P. Grant, "Minute on the Cooly Question," PP, 1841, xvi (427), 1–32.

71. Bernard Semmel, *The Rise of Free Trade Imperialism: Classical Political Economy the Empire of Free Trade and Imperialism 1750–1850* (Cambridge: Cambridge University Press, 1970), 76–129; Donald Winch, *Classical Political Economy and Colonies* (Cambridge, MA: Harvard University Press, 1965), 73–143; Peter Burroughs, *Colonial Reformers and Canada, 1830–1849* (Toronto: McClelland and Stewart, 1969), vii–xxxii. Wakefield's publications included *A Sketch of a Proposal for Colonizing Australasia* (London, 1829), and *A View of the Art of Colonization, in Letters between a Statesman and a Colonist* (London, 1849).

72. Jane Lydon, "A Secret Longing for a Trade in Human Flesh: The Decline of British Slavery and the Making of the Settler Colonies," *History Workshop Journal* 90 (2020): 189–210.

73. J. R. Ward, *British West Indian Slavery, 1750–1834: The Process of Amelioration* (Oxford: Clarendon, 1988), 190–232; Christa Dierksheide, *Amelioration and Empire: Progress and Slavery in the Plantation Americas* (Charlottesville: University of Virginia Press, 2014), esp. 180–209; Caroline Quarrier Spence, "Ameliorating Empire: Slavery and Protection in the British Colonies, 1783–1865," PhD diss., Harvard University, 2014), esp. 138–243; Lauren Benton and Lisa Ford, "Magistrates in Empire: Convicts, Slaves, and the Remaking of the Plural Legal Order in the British Empire," in *Legal Pluralism and Empires, 1500–1850*, ed. Lauren Benton and Richard J. Ross (New York: New York University Press, 2013), 176–80; Trevor Burnard and Kit Candlin, "Sir John Gladstone and the Debate over the Amelioration of Slavery in the British West Indies in the 1820s," *Journal of British Studies* 57, no. 4 (2018): 760–82; Hossain, "A Matter of Doubt," 66–69; Mary Turner, "The 11 O'Clock Flog: Women, Work, and Labour Law in the British Caribbean," *Slavery & Abolition* 20, no. 1 (1999): 38–58; Eric Williams, *Capitalism and Slavery* (Chapel Hill: University of North Carolina Press, 1944), 197–98.

74. Spence, "Ameliorating Empire," 247.

75. Diana Paton, *No Bond but the Law: Punishment, Race, and Gender in Jamaican State Formation, 1780–1870* (Durham, NC: Duke University Press, 2004).

76. For a related argument about the assertion of imperial power as against local or private despotisms, see Lauren Benton and Lisa Ford, *Rage for Order: The British Empire and the Origins of International Law, 1800–1850* (Cambridge, MA: Harvard University Press, 2016), 28–84.

77. *Hansard*, 3rd ser., lx, col. 1337 (1 March 1842).

78. Lushington and Galloway (Court of Directors) to the Government of India, Legislative Department, 20 September 1848, IOR L/PJ/3/1199.

79. Elliot to Stephen, 14 October 1845, CO 167/265 (Colonial Land and Emigration Board report describing the history of labor migration to Mauritius).

80. On the pitfalls of ignoring pre-emancipation histories of indenture, see Allen, "Slaves, Convicts, Abolitionism," 329, and Nandini Boodia-Canoo, *Slavery, Indenture and the Law: Assembling a Nation in Colonial Mauritius* (London: Routledge, 2023), 105.

81. Gladstone to Grey, 23 March 1837, Glenelg to Gladstone, 3 May 1837, and Order in Council, 12 July 1837, PP, 1837–38, lii (180), 25–32; Hugh Tinker, *A New System of Slavery: The Export of Indian Labour Overseas* (London: Oxford University Press, 1974), 63–64.

82. Government of India to the Court of Directors, 18 October 1837, in *Papers respecting the East-India Labourers' Bill*, 177–9, IOR V/27/820/4, (on India Act V of 1837).

83. Mauritius Ordinance No. 17 of 1835, CO 169/2.

84. I base this contention on individual petitions filed under the ordinance that remain in the National Archives of Mauritius, most of which were approved. See, for example, Troberville Griffiths to Dick, 11 November 1835, NAM, RC 34 (approved on 18 November); and other petitions contained in NAM, RC 34.

85. Minute by the Governor General (Auckland), 25 April 1841, IOR F/4/1909, No. 81645.

86. Minute by W. W. Bird, 6 May 1841, IOR F/4/1909, No. 81645.

87. Emigration Committee to Nicolay, 17 December 1839, NAM, RD 60.

88. Emigration Committee to Nicolay, 6 January 1840, NAM, RD 60.

89. Emigration Committee to Nicolay, 17 December 1839, NAM, RD 60; Emigration Committee to Nicolay, 11 January 1840, NAM, RD 60.

90. Emigration Committee to Messrs Barclay Bros. & Co., Reid Irving & Co., A. D'Epinay, Hugh Hunter, Baring Bros. & Co., Cockerall & Co., Gower Nephews & Co., and Arbuthnot and Latham, 11 January 1840, NAM, RD 60. The companies/individuals addressed here were absentee landowners.

91. Free Labor Association to Hugon, 2 September 1840, NAM, IA 26.

92. Emigration Committee to Barclay Bros. & Co., et al., 11 January 1840, NAM, RD 60; Free Labor Association to Hugon, 2 September 1840, NAM, IA 26.

93. Emigration Committee to Barclay Bros. & Co. et al., 11 January 1840.

94. "Plan pour l'introduction de Travailleurs," articles 3, 5–6, 10, 12, Free Labor Association Procès Verbal, 28 May 1840, NAM, IA 29.

95. Emigration Committee to Anderson, 11 January 1840, NAM, RD 60. The Committee agreed to pay Anderson £1500 for his services with a possible bonus of £500 if the mission succeeded. Free Labor Association Proceedings, 11 January 1840, NAM, IA 28. For additional discussion of Anderson, see Mongia, *Indian Migration and Empire*, 46–47, 50–51.

96. Free Labor Association to Hugon, 2 September 1840, NAM, IA 26. For an example of Hugon's reporting and advocacy in favor of regulated migration in India, see "Report of T Hugon upon the subject of Indian Emigration to Mauritius," 29 July 1839, IOR F/4/1847, No. 77655.

97. Emigration Committee to Anderson, 11 January 1840, NAM, RD 60.

98. Anderson to Russell, 1 May 1840, PP, 1840, xxxvii (331), 194–97, 196.

99. Free Labor Association to Smith, 14 January 1841, NAM, IA 26.

100. Free Labor Association to Arbuthnot and Barlow, 12 April 1841, NAM, IA 26. While not focused on the Free Labor Association, Cumpston's discussion of Lord Stanley's correspondence with Indian officials in 1841–42 can be read as additional evidence linking lobbying pressure to the state's ultimate embrace of regulated migration. See *Indians Overseas*, 58–64.

101. Douglas Hall, *A Brief History of the West India Committee* (Barbados: Caribbean Universities Press, 1971), 4.

102. Hall, *Brief History of the West India Committee*, 7, 14.

103. "Memorial of the Standing Committee of West India Planters and Merchants," Acting Committee Minutes, 11 July 1843, Senate House Library Historical Collections, London, West India Committee Papers (hereafter WIC) M 915, Reel 7.

104. "Memorial of the Standing Committee," Acting Committee Minutes, 11 July 1843, WIC, M 915, Reel 7.

105. Cave to Stanley, 19 October 1843, in Acting Committee Minutes, 19 October 1843, WIC, M 915, Reel 7.

106. "Memorandum of a Plan of Emigration from the East to the West Indies," in Acting Committee Minutes, 24 May 1844, WIC, M 915, Reel 7.

107. Acting Committee Minutes, 11 June 1844, WIC, M 915, Reel 7.

108. "Proposed Emigration of Laborers from the East to the West Indies," 5 June 1844, sub-enclosed in Stanley to the Commissioners for the Affairs of India, 5 June 1844, enclosed in Stark (Board of Control) to Melvill (Court of Directors), 7 June 1844, IOR, L/PJ/2/189.

109. Tony Ballantyne, *Orientalism and Race: Aryanism in the British Empire* (Basingstoke: Palgrave, 2002), and *Webs of Empire: Locating New Zealand's Colonial Past* (Vancouver: UBC Press, 2014); Alan Lester, *Imperial Networks: Creating Identities in Nineteenth-Century South Africa and Britain* (London: Routledge, 2001); Zoë Laidlaw, *Colonial Connections 1815–45: Patronage, the Information Revolution and Colonial Government* (Manchester: Manchester University Press, 2005); David Lambert and Alan Lester, eds., *Colonial Lives Across the Empire: Imperial Careering in the Long Nineteenth Century* (Cambridge: Cambridge University Press, 2006).

110. Laidlaw, *Colonial Connections*, 14.

111. For two relevant examples, see Catherine Hall, *Civilising Subjects: Metropole and Colony in the English Imagination, 1830–1867* (Chicago: University of Chicago Press, 2002), 23–65; Laurence Brown, "Inter-Colonial Migration and the Refashioning of Indentured Labour: Arthur Gordon in Trinidad, Mauritius and Fiji (1866–1888)," in Lambert and Lester, *Colonial Lives*, 204–27.

112. "Proposed Emigration of Laborers from the East to the West Indies," 5 June 1844, IOR L/PJ/2/189.

113. Acting Committee Minutes, 27 August 1844, WIC, M 915, Reel 7.

114. Free Labor Association to Smith, 14 January 1841, NAM, IA 26.

115. Free Labor Association to Smith, 14 January 1841.

116. Cave to Stanley, 9 July 1844, in Standing Committee Minutes, 10 July 1844, WIC, M 915, Reel 5.

117. Free Labor Association to Anderson, 28 August 1840, NAM, IA 26; Boodia-Canoo, *Slavery, Indenture and the Law*, 147 (on Ordinance No. 7 of 1842, authorizing this tax).

118. PP, 1860, xlv (250), 3. See also Jonathan Connolly, "Indenture as Compensation: State Financing for Indentured Labor Migration in the Era of Emancipation," *Slavery & Abolition* 40, no. 3 (2019): 448–71.

119. Tinker, *New System of Slavery*, 81, 70.

120. Walton Look Lai, *Indentured Labor, Caribbean Sugar: Chinese and Indian Migrants to the British West Indies, 1838–1918* (Baltimore: Johns Hopkins University Press, 1993), 276. The exact figure given is 17,972.

121. John Brewer, *The Sinews of Power: War, Money, and the English State, 1688–1783* (Cambridge, MA: Harvard University Press, 1988), 221–49; Paula E. Dumas, *Proslavery Britain: Fighting for Slavery in an Era of Abolition* (New York: Palgrave, 2016).

122. Richard Huzzey, *Freedom Burning: Anti-Slavery and Empire in Victorian Britain* (Ithaca, NY: Cornell University Press, 2012), 8.

123. Kale, *Fragments of Empire*, 22–37, 88–108; Tinker, *New System of Slavery*, 64–70, 77–82, 236–40; Look Lai, *Indentured Labor, Caribbean Sugar*, 156–65; Green, "Emancipation to Indenture," 98–105.

124. Walter Rodney, *A History of the Guyanese Working People, 1881–1905* (Baltimore: Johns Hopkins University Press, 1981).

125. "The Immigration Question," *Anti-Slavery Reporter*, 11 March 1840, 42.

126. On Sturge, see Alex Tyrrell, *Joseph Sturge and the Moral Radical Party in Early Victorian Britain* (London: C. Helm, 1987). On Sturge, the British and Foreign Anti-Slavery Society, and

the Society's relationship to prior antislavery organizations, see Temperley, *British Antislavery*, 36, 64–84.

127. "The Immigration Question," *Anti-Slavery Reporter*, 29 January 1840, 9.

128. "The Immigration Question," *Anti-Slavery Reporter*, 26 February 1840, 32.

129. "The Immigration Question," *Anti-Slavery Reporter*, 26 February 1840, 32.

130. "Memorial of the Anti-Slavery Committee on the Exportation of Coolies to Mauritius," *Anti-Slavery Reporter*, 11 March 1840, 46.

131. "The Immigration Question," *Anti-Slavery Reporter*, 11 March 1840, 42.

132. Kate Boehme, Peter Mitchell, and Alan Lester, "Reforming Everywhere and All at Once: Transitioning to Free Labor across the British Empire, 1837–1838," *Comparative Studies in Society and History* 60, no. 3 (2018): 710–15.

133. Joseph Sturge and Thomas Harvey, *The West Indies in 1837: Journal of a Visit to Antigua, Montserrat, Barbados, St. Lucia and Jamaica* (London, 1838).

134. *Hansard*, 3rd ser., xi, col. 1306 (20 February 1838).

135. *British Emancipator*, 14 March 1838, 36.

136. *British Emancipator*, 14 March 1838, 36.

137. Resolution of the London Anti-Slavery Society, 6 July 1838, in *British Emancipator*, 11 July 1838, 132.

138. *British Emancipator*, 2 April 1838, 52.

139. Hossain, "Protests at the Colonial Capital," 43.

140. Calcutta Committee, 9.

141. "The Cooly Trade," *Friend of India*, 26 March 1840.

142. "The Cooly Trade," *Friend of India*, 8 November 1838.

143. "Progress of the Abolition of the Cooly Trade," *Friend of India*, 5 July 1838. See also "The Cooly Trade," *Friend of India*, 9 August 1838.

144. Connolly, "Indenture as Compensation," 453–60.

145. "Memorial of the Undersigned, being Ministers of the Gospel, residing in the County of Demerara, in the Colony of British Guiana," 18 May 1844, enclosed in Light to Stanley, 18 May 1844, No. 111, PP, 1846, xxx (321), 101–3.

146. "The Immigration Question," *Anti-Slavery Reporter*, 26 February 1840, 32. See also "The Immigration Question," *Anti-Slavery Reporter*, 11 March 1840, 42–44; "Emigration from Africa to the West Indies," *Anti-Slavery Reporter*, 20 April 1842, 57–58.

147. "Emigration from Africa to the West Indies," *Anti-Slavery Reporter*, 20 April 1842, 58.

148. Thomas Clarkson, "Emigration to the British Colonies," *Anti-Slavery Reporter*, 11 December 1844, 226.

149. *Anti-Slavery Reporter*, 13 November 1844, 210; 27 November 1844, 218–19; 19 March 1845, 50; 1 January 1847, 9; 1 March 1847, 40; 1 April 1847, 56–57; 1 May 1848, 79 (reprinting a petition signed by 540 freeholders and laborers in the parish of St. Ann, Jamaica).

150. See, for example, Thomas L. Haskell, "Convention and Hegemonic Interest in the Debate over Antislavery," in *The Antislavery Debate: Capitalism and Abolitionism as a Problem in Historical Interpretation*, ed. Thomas Bender (Berkeley: University of California Press, 1992), 200–260.

151. "The Immigration Question," *Anti-Slavery Reporter*, 11 March 1840, 42. See also "On Free Immigration," *Anti-Slavery Reporter*, 25 March 1840, 58 (arguing for "an equality of social and civil rights").

Chapter 2

1. Mauritius Ordinance No. 16 of 1835, preamble, CO 169/2; Nicolay to Glenelg, 21 January 1837, PP, 1837–38, lii (180), 103–4.

2. Britain first captured the Dutch Guianese colonies (which were not yet united as a single entity) in 1796. They were temporarily returned in 1802 but recaptured in 1803 and officially ceded in 1814.

3. William A. Green, *British Slave Emancipation: The Sugar Colonies and the Great Experiment, 1830–1865* (Oxford: Clarendon, 1976), 76–77.

4. British Guiana's constitutional structure derived partly from Dutch law and practice. An electoral college called the College of Keizers elected both unofficial members of the colony's legislative body, the Court of Policy, as well as the financial representatives who, together with the Court of Policy, formed the "Combined Court." Green, *British Slave Emancipation*, 77–78.

5. Radhika Mongia, *Indian Migration and Empire: A Colonial Genealogy of the Modern State* (Durham, NC: Duke University Press, 2018), 59 (explaining that nineteen separate Indian emigration acts went into force between 1842 and 1864); Riyad Sadiq Koya, "The Regulation, Division, and Multiplication of Emigrant Labor: The Border between Land and Sea in Colonial India, 1834–1922," *Journal of World History* 32, no. 1 (2021): 45–63, 52–56.

6. In this respect, it is important to see India as a center of imperial power with influence over neighboring British colonies in the Indian Ocean and beyond, as argued by Thomas Metcalf in *Imperial Connections: India in the Indian Ocean Arena, 1860–1920* (Berkeley: University of California Press, 2008).

7. I make a detailed argument about statutory precedent and legal borrowing in chapter 4.

8. Renisa Mawani and Iza Hussin, "The Travels of Law: Indian Ocean Itineraries," *Law and History Review* 32, no. 4 (2014): 733–47. Though less focused on jurisdictional politics, I join work on legal pluralism in examining the complexity and multiplicity of "state" and "imperial" law. On approaches to legal pluralism, see Lauren Benton and Richard J. Ross, eds., *Legal Pluralism and Empires, 1500–1850* (New York: New York University Press, 2013).

9. Such reconstruction is archivally complex. British colonial archives are organized geographically and chronologically, not thematically. This structure reinforces a disciplinary tendency toward geographic specialization and discourages trans-colonial analysis, as Lisa Lowe notes in *The Intimacies of Four Continents* (Durham, NC: Duke University Press, 2015), at 5. In addition, official discussions of colonial law are not stored alongside the statutes and regulations to which they refer but are kept instead in voluminous chronological files of general correspondence. Thus, while much prior scholarship has discussed the law of indenture, this larger body of material concerning official thinking on the law has rarely been subjected to analysis.

10. On apprenticeship (primarily in Jamaica), see, among others, W. L. Burn, *Emancipation and Apprenticeship in the British West Indies* (London: Jonathan Cape, 1937); D. G. Hall, "The Apprenticeship Period in Jamaica, 1834–1838," *Caribbean Quarterly* 3, no. 3 (1953): 142–66; Thomas C. Holt, *The Problem of Freedom: Race, Labor, and Politics in Jamaica and Britain, 1832–1938* (Baltimore: Johns Hopkins University Press, 1992), 55–79; Kenneth Morgan, "Labour Relations during and after Apprenticeship: Amity Hall, Jamaica, 1834–1840," *Slavery & Abolition* 33, no. 3 (2012): 457–78; Diana Paton, *No Bond but the Law: Punishment, Race, and Gender in Jamaican State Formation, 1780–1870* (Durham, NC: Duke University Press, 2004), 53–120.

11. Glenelg to the Governors of British Guiana, Trinidad, St. Lucia, and Mauritius, 15 September 1838, PP, 1839, xxxv (107–I), 4–6; Green, *British Slave Emancipation*, 163.

12. Green, *British Slave Emancipation*, 164; William A. Green, "James Stephen and British West India Policy, 1834–1847," *Caribbean Studies* 13, no. 4 (1974): 33–56, 38; Glenelg to Nicolay, 25 May 1836, PP, 1837–38, lii (180), 62–66 (disallowing Mauritius Ordinance No. 16 of 1835).

13. Glenelg to the Governors of British Guiana, Trinidad, St. Lucia, and Mauritius, 15 September 1838, PP, 1839, xxxv (107–I), 4–6.

14. Thomas C. Holt, "The Essence of the Contract: The Articulation of Race, Gender, and Political Economy in British Emancipation Policy, 1838–1866," in Frederick Cooper, Thomas C. Holt, and Rebecca J. Scott, *Beyond Slavery: Explorations of Race, Labor, and Citizenship in Postemancipation Societies* (Chapel Hill: University of North Carolina Press, 2000), 34 (second and third quotations citing Glenelg to Governors of the West India Colonies, 6 November 1837, PP, 1837–38, xlix [154-I], 9–11).

15. Glenelg to the Governors of British Guiana, Trinidad, St. Lucia, and Mauritius, 15 September 1838, PP, 1839, xxxv (107–I), 5.

16. Paul Knaplund, "Mr. Oversecretary Stephen," *Journal of Modern History* 1, no. 1 (1929): 40–66. On Stephen and the Colonial Office during the 1830s, see Zoë Laidlaw, *Colonial Connections 1815–45: Patronage, the Information Revolution and Colonial Government* (Manchester: Manchester University Press, 2005), 51–54, 169–99.

17. Paul Knaplund, *James Stephen and the British Colonial System, 1813–1847* (Madison: University of Wisconsin Press, 1953), 98.

18. Green, "James Stephen," 35.

19. Stephen to Stanley, 20 May 1834, CO 323/50, cited in Knaplund, *James Stephen*, 111. Stephen was writing about the Bahamas abolition act.

20. Green, "James Stephen," 36.

21. Order in Council, 7 September 1838, in Glenelg to the Governors of British Guiana, Trinidad, St. Lucia, and Mauritius, 15 September 1838, PP, 1839, xxxv (107–I), 7–10. As Christopher Tomlins has explained, the scope of master-servant doctrine changed over time and was frequently limited, in England before the eighteenth century and in North America before the nineteenth, to specific contracts (particularly indenture and apprenticeship), trades, and groups (often young people). See Christopher L. Tomlins, *Law, Labor, and Ideology in the Early American Republic* (Cambridge: Cambridge University Press, 1993), 232–92. In the post-emancipation context at issue here, however, the scope of master-servant law was broader and clearly aimed at formerly enslaved majority populations, who were expected (in imperial eyes) to continue working on plantations as wage workers.

22. Order in Council, 7 September 1838, cap. I, preamble.

23. Order in Council, 7 September 1838, cap. IV, § 7.

24. Order in Council, 7 September 1838, cap. IV, § 8. The order also empowered magistrates to seize and sell goods "for making such compensation" and, optionally, to imprison offending employers for up to one month in the event of nonpayment.

25. Order in Council, 7 September 1838, cap. IV, § 1. On the stipendiary magistracy in Jamaica, see Holt, *Problem of Freedom*, 57–60; Paton, *No Bond but the Law*, 59–61, 71–78; Padraic X. Scanlan, "Slaves and Peasants in the Era of Emancipation," *Journal of British Studies* 59, no. 3 (2020): 516–18.

26. Order in Council, 7 September 1838, cap. IV, § 5.

27. Glenelg to the Governors of British Guiana, Trinidad, St. Lucia, and Mauritius, 15 September 1838, PP, 1839, xxxv (107–I), 4–6.

28. Order in Council, 7 September 1838, § I, in Glenelg to the Governors of British Guiana, Trinidad, St. Lucia, and Mauritius, 15 September 1838, PP, 1839, xxxv (107–I), 10–13. One could also be convicted as an "idle and disorderly" person for deliberately refusing work when capable of working, and when such a refusal resulted in public poor relief for one's wife and children.

29. Order in Council, 7 September 1838, § II.

30. The maximum punishment for repeat offenders, categorized as "incorrigible rogues," was six months. Order in Council, 7 September 1838, §§ III, VII.

31. Stephen, Report on Grenada Act No. 217, 28 October 1828, CO 323/45, cited in Knaplund, *James Stephen*, 116.

32. Order in Council, 15 January 1842, enclosed in Stanley to Light, 22 January 1842, PP, 1842, xxx (26), 34–37.

33. Order in Council, 15 January 1842, §§ 3–14; Mongia, *Indian Migration and Empire*, 57–58.

34. Order in Council, 15 January 1842, § 18.

35. Order in Council, 15 January 1842, § 20.

36. Government of India to the Court of Directors, 9 March 1844, PP, 1844, xxxv (284), 1–3 (authorizing labor migration to the West Indies on the model of Mauritius with certain modifications); *Fifth General Report of the Colonial Land and Emigration Commission*, appendices 15–17, PP, 1845, xxvii (617), 43–51 (reproducing regulatory plans for emigration from India to the West Indies).

37. Robert J. Steinfeld, *The Invention of Free Labor: The Employment Relation in English and American Law and Culture, 1350–1870* (Chapel Hill: University of North Carolina Press, 1991), 22. Douglas Hay and Paul Craven, "Introduction," in *Masters, Servants, and Magistrates in Britain and the Empire, 1562–1955*, ed. Douglas Hay and Paul Craven (Chapel Hill: University of North Carolina Press, 2004), 33.

38. Steinfeld, *Invention of Free Labor*, 23.

39. Steinfeld, *Invention of Free Labor*, 23.

40. Hay and Craven, "Introduction," 2. I say "seemingly criminal" because in modern Anglo-American law, physical penalties like imprisonment are reserved for criminal, as opposed to civil, offenses.

41. Steinfeld, *Invention of Free Labor*, 113–14; Robert J. Steinfeld, *Coercion, Contract, and Free Labor in the Nineteenth Century* (Cambridge, 2001), 39–84. See also Hay and Craven, "Introduction," 32; Paul Johnson, *Making the Market: Victorian Origins of Corporate Capitalism* (Cambridge: Cambridge University Press, 2010), 100–101.

42. Steinfeld, *Invention of Free Labor*, 115 (discussing 7 Geo. I, c. 13 [1720]).

43. Steinfeld, *Invention of Free Labor*, 115 (discussing 6 Geo. III, c. 25 [1766]).

44. Steinfeld, *Invention of Free Labor*, 115–16; Christopher Frank, *Master and Servant Law: Chartists, Trade Unions, Radical Lawyers and the Magistracy in England, 1840–1865* (Farnham: Ashgate, 2010), 5; Johnson, *Making the Market*, 71–84; Alessandro Stanziani, *Bondage: Labor and Rights in Eurasia from the Sixteenth to the Early Twentieth Centuries* (New York: Berghahn, 2014), 56, 156; Tomlins, *Law, Labor and Ideology*, 232–39.

45. Abbot Emerson Smith, *Colonists in Bondage: White Servitude and Convict Labor in America, 1607–1776* (Chapel Hill: University of North Carolina Press, 1947), 336; David W. Galenson, *White Servitude in Colonial America: An Economic Analysis* (Cambridge: Cambridge University Press, 1981), 3–4; Steinfeld, *Invention of Free Labor*, 10. On European indenture in Barbados during the seventeenth century, see Simon P. Newman, *A New World of Labor: The*

Development of Plantation Slavery in the British Atlantic (Philadelphia: University of Pennsylvania Press, 2013), 60–107.

46. Christopher Tomlins, *Freedom Bound: Law, Labor, and Civic Identity in Colonizing English America, 1580–1865* (Cambridge: Cambridge University Press, 2010), 35, 573–82.

47. For recent treatment, see Anna Suranyi, *Indentured Servitude: Unfree Labor and Citizenship in the British Colonies* (Montreal: McGill-Queen's University Press, 2021).

48. Stanziani, *Bondage*, 11, 147–64, 175–98; Alessandro Stanziani, "Debt, Labour and Bondage: English Servants versus Indentured Immigrants in Mauritius, from the Late Eighteenth to Early Twentieth Century," in *Bonded Labour and Debt in the Indian Ocean World*, ed. Gwyn Campbell and Alessandro Stanziani (London: Pickering & Chatto, 2013), 75–86.

49. Doug Munro, "Conclusion: On Resistance and Accommodation," in *Resistance and Indian Indenture Experience: Comparative Perspectives*, ed. Maurits S. Hassankhan, Brij V. Lal, and Doug Munro (New Delhi: Manohar, 2014), 294.

50. Steinfeld, *Invention of Free Labor*, 8, 163–72.

51. Frank, *Master and Servant Law*, 35–36.

52. Frank, *Master and Servant Law*, 27, 44–89.

53. Frank states that between 7,500 and 17,000 workers were prosecuted annually for breach of contract between 1855 and 1875. Frank, *Master and Servant Law*, 5. Stanziani estimates approximately 10,000 prosecutions and 7,000 convictions annually during the same period. Stanziani, *Bondage*, 165.

54. Seymour Drescher, *The Mighty Experiment: Free Labor versus Slavery in British Emancipation* (Oxford: Oxford University Press, 2002), 74–75; Richard S. Dunn, *Sugar and Slaves: The Rise of the Planter Class in the English West Indies, 1624–1713* (Chapel Hill: University of North Carolina Press, 1972), 264; Green, *British Slave Emancipation*, 263.

55. Glenelg to the Governors of British Guiana, Trinidad, St. Lucia, and Mauritius, 15 September 1838, PP, 1839, xxxv (107–I), 5.

56. One can certainly contest this view; some historians have argued that it marked an ideological blindness among abolitionists toward labor coercion in industrial society. In *Capitalism and Slavery* (Chapel Hill: University of North Carolina Press, 1944), Eric Williams famously argued that antislavery served the interests of capital and industry by legitimizing "free" wage labor in contrast to slavery. David Brion Davis later developed a different version of this argument, suggesting that antislavery ideology unintentionally supported the rising hegemony of industrial wage labor by diverting attention from the coerciveness of domestic labor conditions, in *The Problem of Slavery in the Age of Revolution, 1770–1823* (Ithaca, NY: Cornell University Press, 1975). On this issue and the scholarly debates surrounding it, see Thomas Bender, ed., *The Antislavery Debate: Capitalism and Abolitionism as a Problem in Historical Interpretation* (Berkeley: University of California Press, 1992).

57. *The Labour and Indian Immigration Question at Mauritius* (*Report of the Committee of the Legislative Council*), 15 July 1845, enclosed in Gomm to Stanley, 19 August 1845, No. 149, CO 167/263. Mauritian efforts to enact heightened vagrancy laws began even earlier. In 1841, for example, the colony enacted a new vagrancy ordinance tacitly undermining Stephen's 1838 order on the subject. The Colonial Office rejected the ordinance, which it deemed "manifestly improper." Mauritius Ordinance No. 10 of 1841, discussed in Smith to Russell, 11 June 1841, CO 167/231; Minute, 5 October 1841, CO 167/231; Stanley to Smith, 30 October 1841, No. 26, CO 167/231.

58. Russell to Metcalfe, 14 July 1840, cited in *Labour and Indian Immigration*, CO 167/263.

59. *Labour and Indian Immigration*, CO 167/263.

60. William A. Green, "Emancipation to Indenture: A Question of Imperial Morality," *Journal of British Studies* 22, no. 2 (1983): 98 (noting that historians of indenture have tended to make this assumption). Hugh Tinker, *A New System of Slavery: The Export of Indian Labour Overseas* (London: Oxford University Press, 1974); Madhavi Kale, *Fragments of Empire: Capital, Slavery, and Indian Indentured Labor Migration in the British Caribbean* (Philadelphia: University of Pennsylvania Press, 1998), 6.

61. Elliot and Wood to Stephen, 14 October 1845, CO 167/265.

62. Lyttleton to Macgregor, 28 March 1846, PP, 1846, xxviii (691–II), 4–5.

63. Lyttleton to Macgregor, 22 April 1846, PP, 1846, xxviii (691–II), 8.

64. Lyttleton to Macgregor, 22 April 1846.

65. By 1846, Indians comprised roughly 35 percent of the colony's total population (56,245 out of 158,462). By 1851, the figure was 77,996, or 43 percent of the total. Higginson to Pakington, 21 January 1853, No. 5, CO 167/343.

66. Higginson to Pakington, 21 January 1853.

67. Gladstone to Gomm, 14 May 1846, PP, 1846, xxviii (691–II), 216–22.

68. Marina Carter, *Servants, Sirdars and Settlers: Indians in Mauritius, 1834–1874* (Delhi: Oxford University Press, 1995), 91–94; Arunima Datta, *Fleeting Agencies: A Social History of Indian Coolie Women in British Malaya* (Cambridge: Cambridge University Press, 2021), 27–41; Prabhu P. Mohapatra, "'Restoring the Family': Wife Murders and the Making of a Sexual Contract for Indian Immigrant Labour in the British Caribbean Colonies, 1860–1920," *Studies in History* 11, no. 2 (1995): 227–60; Rachel Sturman, "Indian Indentured Labor and the History of International Rights Regimes," *American Historical Review* 119, no. 5 (2014): 1450–52.

69. Gladstone to Gomm, 14 May 1846, PP, 1846, xxviii (691–II), 217–19. On the relation between evangelicalism and Gladstone's political thought, see Boyd Hilton, *The Age of Atonement: The Influence of Evangelicalism on Social and Economic Thought, 1785–1865* (Oxford: Clarendon, 1986), 340–50, 357–58. On Gladstone's moral conscience in relation to liberal imperialism, see Priya Satia, *Time's Monster: How History Makes History* (Cambridge, MA: Belknap, 2020), 119–24.

70. Peel's government fell after his decision to support the repeal of the corn laws split the Conservative Party. This event—and the effects of free-trade policy on indenture debate more broadly—will be discussed in the next chapter.

71. Green, *British Slave Emancipation*, 89–90 (on Grey's general influence on colonial policy in relation to that of prior colonial secretaries).

72. Even earlier, in 1845, Trinidad had covertly attempted to legalize contracts signed in India, departing from the Colonial Office's orders in council. The Colonial Office rejected the proposed legislation. Trinidad Ordinance No. 6 of 1845, discussed in MacLeod to Stanley, 3 February 1845, No. 13, CO 295/146; Stanley to MacLeod, 30 April 1845, PP, 1846, xxviii (691–III), 88–90.

73. Harris to Gladstone, 18 July 1846, No. 30, CO 295/151.

74. Stephen to Hawes, 22 August 1846, CO 295/151.

75. "Coolie Regulations," enclosed in Harris to Gladstone, 30 July 1846, No. 34, CO 295/151.

76. "Coolie Regulations," §§ 2, 10. Wages were to be paid monthly.

77. "Coolie Regulations," § 4, 6.

78. "Coolie Regulations," § 8.

79. "Coolie Regulations," § 9.

80. Harris to Gladstone, 30 July 1846, No. 34, CO 295/151. On the appointment of Fagan, at the recommendation of the Court of Directors of the East India Company, see Gladstone to MacLeod, 25 March 1846, CO 295/146.

81. Harris to Gladstone, 30 July 1846, No. 34, CO 295/151.

82. Harris to Gladstone, 30 July 1846.

83. Harris to Grey, 4 September 1846, No. 58, CO 295/151.

84. Grey to Harris, 15 September 1846, CO 295/151. Because the "Coolie Regulations" had clearly changed the state of the law, they could not be passed by the executive outside the normal legislative process as mere explanatory "regulations."

85. Grey to Harris, 24 October 1846, CO 295/151. This dispatch was based on a lengthy memorandum Grey wrote, also included in the volume: Grey, Minute, 12 October 1846, CO 295/151.

86. Grey to Harris, 24 October 1846, CO 295/151.

87. Grey to Harris, 24 October 1846.

88. Grey to Harris, 24 October 1846. Grey did not categorically reject the idea of using law to encourage wage labor. As his dispatch continued, it proposed modified land and squatting regulations designed to make it more difficult for laborers to become landowners. Around the same time, he suggested in Mauritius a series of labor taxes designed to keep workers on the plantations. I discuss these proposals and their underlying causes more fully in the next chapter.

89. Gomm to Stanley, 7 March 1846, No. 54, CO 167/268.

90. Grey to Gomm, 29 September 1846, No. 38, CO 167/268.

91. Grey to Gomm, 29 September 1846.

92. Grey to Gomm, 29 September 1846. Though Grey consistently rejected laws directly requiring plantation labor, he did, as this quotation suggests, expect workers to accept wage labor on their own. On this point, see Holt, *Problem of Freedom*, 46–53; Richard Huzzey, "Concepts of Liberty: Freedom, Laisse-Faire and the State after Britain's Abolition of Slavery," in *Emancipation and the Remaking of the British Imperial World*, ed. Catherine Hall, Nicholas Draper, and Keith McClelland (Manchester: Manchester University Press, 2014).

93. Grey to Gomm, 29 September 1846, No. 38, CO 167/268.

94. British Guiana Ordinance No. 3 of 1848, CO 113/2.

95. British Guiana Ordinance No. 3 of 1848, § 19.

96. British Guiana Ordinance No. 3 of 1848, § 21.

97. British Guiana Ordinance No. 3 of 1848, § 21.

98. Grey, Minute, 10 May 1848, CO 111/251.

99. Grey to Light, 23 May 1848, No. 338, CO 111/251.

100. Grey to Light, 23 May 1848.

101. See Thomas R. Metcalf, *Ideologies of the Raj* (Cambridge: Cambridge University Press, 1995), 29 (arguing, while describing the age of reform in Britain and India, that "liberals conceived that human nature was intrinsically the same everywhere, and that it could be totally and completely transformed").

102. Walker to Grey, 18 July 1848, Private, CO 111/255.

103. Trinidad Ordinance No. 3 of 1849, § VII, CO 297/4.

104. Trinidad Ordinance No. 3 of 1849, § VI.

105. Harris to Grey, 6 February 1849, No. 21, CO 295/166.

106. Taylor, Minute, 18 March 1849, CO 295/166. On Taylor, see Holt, *Problem of Freedom*, 42–47, 284–85.

107. Grey, Minute, 7 April 1849, CO 295/166.

108. Scoble to Grey, 23 January 1849, CO 295/169. On the term "human rights" in antislavery discourse, see Manisha Sinha, *The Slave's Cause: A History of Abolition* (New Haven, CT: Yale University Press, 2016), esp. 246–56, 299–330.

109. "Report of the Committee of Council called to report on Grey's dispatch 28 April 1849 relative to Ordinance No. 3," enclosed in Harris to Grey, 5 September 1849, No. 68, CO 295/168.

110. The theme of "moralization" in legal ideology is pursued in greater detail in chapter 4.

111. Harris to Grey, 5 September 1849, No. 68, CO 295/168.

112. In several contexts, scholars of indenture have analyzed absence and desertion as forms of everyday resistance alongside broader discussions of resistance and accommodation. See Hassankhan, Lal, and Munro, *Resistance and Indian Indenture*; Radica Mahase, *Why Should We Be Called "Coolies"? The End of Indian Indentured Labour* (New Delhi: Manohar, 2020), chap. 3; Lomarsh Roopnarine, *Indo-Caribbean Indenture: Resistance and Accommodation, 1838–1920* (Mona: University of the West Indies Press, 2007), chap. 2.

113. Gomm to Stanley, 16 February 1846, No. 34, CO 167/267.

114. Harris to Grey, 12 June 1847, No. 52, CO 295/157.

115. Allen, *Slaves, Freedmen, and Indentured Laborers*, 66.

116. "Comparative Statement of Labourers Employed, Absent, and Sick for the Quarters ended 30th September and 31st December 1848," in Gomm to Grey, 13 February 1849, No. 44, CO 167/309. Quarterly returns for 1847 similarly showed rates of absence and sickness at between 15 and 19 percent of the total contract labor force. "Abstract of the Quarterly Returns of Labourers Employed, Absent and Sick in the Year 1847," in Gomm to Grey, 8 April 1848, PP, 1847–48, xlvi (749), 358–62.

117. "General Statement of Labourers employed, absent and sick on 31st December 1849, according to the Statements furnished," 12 February 1850, in Anderson to Grey, 12 February 1850, No. 29, CO 167/319. These records consistently underestimated the number of Indian workers employed, absent, and sick because they relied on information filed by employers, some of whom failed to comply with reporting requirements. For this reason, the percentages of absences and sickness stated in the returns are more valuable than the absolute numbers of absences and sicknesses reported.

118. Anderson to the Colonial Secretary [of Mauritius], 2 April 1845, NAM, RA 828.

119. Anderson to the Colonial Secretary [of Mauritius], 2 April 1845.

120. Harris to Grey, 1 July 1848, No. 75, CO 295/163. References like this to "bands" may point to forms of collective action invisible to the colonial state, perhaps not unlike the Creole task and "jobbing" gangs described by Walter Rodney in *A History of the Guyanese Working People, 1881–1905* (Baltimore: Johns Hopkins University Press, 1981), 43.

121. Harris to Grey, 1 July 1848, No. 75, CO 295/163.

122. Walker to Grey, 4 December 1848, No. 151, CO 111/260.

123. Walker to Grey, 4 December 1848.

124. My interest in the surprising coexistence of state strength and weakness stems from longstanding debates over the nature of the colonial state in Africa. Compare Crawford Young, *The African Colonial State in Comparative Perspective* (New Haven, CT: Yale University Press, 1994), and Jeffrey Herbst, *States and Power in Africa: Comparative Lessons in Authority and Control* (Princeton, NJ: Princeton University Press, 2000). See also Bruce Berman and John Lonsdale, *Unhappy Valley: Conflict in Kenya and Africa*, vol. 1 (Oxford: James Currey, 1992); Sara Berry, *No Condition Is Permanent: The Social Dynamics of Agrarian Change in Sub-Saharan Africa* (Madison: University of Wisconsin Press, 1993).

125. Acting Chief Commissary of Police to the Colonial Secretary [of Mauritius], 3 March 1847, NAM, RA 929.

126. Green, *British Slave Emancipation*, 137; Holt, *Problem of Freedom*, 288.

127. Herbst, *States and Power in Africa*, esp. chaps. 2–3.

128. The National Archives of Mauritius contains some records of individual vagrancy cases from this period, which reveal significant variation among different stipendiary magistrates in the enforcement of penalties under the law. See for example, *District of Port Louis. Report of Proceedings for the Second Week of September 1848*, Case 1524 (sentencing 16 vagrants to temporary labor while awaiting transfer to the Immigration Department); Case 1526 (sentencing two vagrants to twenty days' imprisonment with hard labor); Case 1533 (sending two vagrants back to their employers), NAM, RA 977.

129. "Statement of the number of Deserters arrested by the Police, under Ordinance No. 7 of 1849, between the 1st October and 31st December 1849," 11 January 1850, in Anderson to Grey, 14 January 1850, No. 11, CO 167/318.

130. "General Statement of Labourers employed, absent and sick," in Anderson to Grey, 12 February 1850, No. 29, CO 167/319.

131. Harris to Grey, 21 February 1848, No. 21, CO 295/160.

132. Harris to Grey, 21 February 1848.

133. Green, *British Slave Emancipation*, 278.

134. Harris to Grey, 21 February 1848, No. 21, CO 295/160.

135. Mitchell, 16 January 1851, enclosed in Harris to Grey, 24 January 1851, No. 13, CO 295/173.

136. Mitchell, 16 January 1851.

137. On reading archives "against the grain," see Ann Laura Stoler, "Colonial Archives and the Arts of Governance," *Archival Science* 2, no. 1–2 (2002): 87–109; Ann Laura Stoler, *Along the Archival Grain: Epistemic Anxieties and Colonial Common Sense* (Princeton, NJ: Princeton University Press, 2009). Michel-Rolph Trouillot, *Silencing the Past: Power and the Production of History* (Boston: Beacon Press, 1995).

138. Harris to Grey, 1 July 1848, No. 75, CO 295/163.

139. Mitchell, 16 January 1851, enclosed in Harris to Grey, 24 January 1851, No. 13, CO 295/173 ("There appears to exist among them some kind of affiliation by means of which the news of one district is immediately communicated to all the others."). Walton Look Lai also cites this material in *Indentured Labor, Caribbean Sugar: Chinese and Indian Migrants to the British West Indies, 1838–1918* (Baltimore: Johns Hopkins University Press, 1993), 112. While the networks of "affiliation" mentioned by Mitchell frequently remain obscure in colonial records, Marina Carter's work on labor brokering by sirdars in Mauritius suggests modes of further interpretation, as does, more broadly, recent scholarship on enslaved communication networks before abolition. See Carter, *Servants, Sirdars and Settlers*; and Julius S. Scott, *The Common Wind: Afro-American Currents in the Age of the Haitian Revolution* (New York: Verso, 2018); Vincent Brown, *Tacky's Revolt: The Story of an Atlantic Slave War* (Cambridge, MA: Harvard University Press, 2020); Miles Ogborn, *The Freedom of Speech: Talk and Slavery in the Anglo-Caribbean World* (Chicago: University of Chicago Press, 2019).

140. Harris to Grey, 21 February 1848, No. 21, CO 295/160.

141. Harris to Grey, 8 March 1848, No. 23, CO 295/160.

142. Light to Grey, 4 April 1848, No. 60, CO 111/252 ("The distress of some of the planters may perhaps cause the Creoles to hold back their labor for fear of non-payment of Wages."). See also Walker to Grey, 13 June 1848, No. 20, CO 111/254 (also discussing nonpayment of wages in the context of Creole labor). On estate debts and bankruptcy in this period, see Alan H. Adamson, *Sugar Without Slaves: The Political Economy of British Guiana, 1838–1904* (New Haven, CT: Yale University Press, 1972), 160–63; Green, *British Slave Emancipation*, 43, 218–22, 234–38.

143. Chief Commissary of Police, Report No. 929, 17 August 1843, NAM, RD 62.

144. "The Coolie and Madeira Immigrants," *Trinidad Spectator*, 23 December 1846, in CO 300/12. See also Harris to Grey, 15 August 1846, No. 45, CO 295/151.

145. Harris to Grey, 12 June 1847, No. 52, CO 295/157.

146. On the term "agency" and its conceptualization in relation to resistance and domination, see Walter Johnson, "On Agency," *Journal of Social History* 37, no. 1 (Autumn, 2003): 113–24; Datta, *Fleeting Agencies*, 15–19.

147. Bonyun to Light, 6 January 1848, CO 111/250. The exact arrivals figure was 15,699, including 429 who arrived in 1835.

148. Bonyun to Light, 6 January 1848. George Bonyun, the official responsible for the inquiry, reported that of the 3,985 immigrants who had arrived from Madras since 1845, some 1,249 had since "died or receded from field labor."

149. Barkly to Grey, 28 November 1851, No. 170, CO 111/284.

150. Barkly to Grey, 28 November 1851. See also Adamson, *Sugar Without Slaves*, 50.

151. Allen, *Slaves, Freedmen, and Indentured Laborers*, 56; Marina Carter, *Voices from Indenture: Experiences of Indian Migrants in the British Empire* (London: Leicester University Press, 1996), 104–5.

152. Fagan to Grey, n.d., enclosed in Fagan to Under Secretary of State for the Colonies, 14 March 1852, CO 295/179; Harris to Grey, 5 October 1846, No. 75, CO 295/153; White to Walkinshaw, 11 September 1846, CO 295/153.

153. Fagan to Grey, n.d., enclosed in Fagan to Under Secretary of State for the Colonies, 14 March 1852.

154. Fagan to Harris, 8 September 1847, enclosed in Harris to Grey, 7 December 1847, No. 102, CO 295/158.

155. Fagan to Harris, 8 September 1847.

156. Grey to Harris, 2 July 1848, CO 295/161.

157. Harris to Grey, 5 October 1846, No. 75, CO 295/153.

158. *Trinidad Spectator*, 26 April 1848, CO 300/13; *Trinidadian*, 18 August 1849, CO 300/13. The *Spectator* was renamed the *Trinidadian* in 1849. The paper had a particular perspective: it was part of a reformist movement that opposed Crown colony government and petitioned for greater representation. As such, the paper tended to be critical of government policy, including indenture, and it was often hostile to Governor Harris.

159. Joseph Waddington, Letter to the Editor, *Leeds Mercury*, 27 November 1847, CO 111/257.

160. Walker to Grey, 23 September 1848, No. 112, CO 111/257.

161. Harris to Grey, 21 February 1848, No. 21, CO 295/160. A later estimate made by Harris in 1849 stated that of the 5,300 who arrived between 1845 and 1848, 3,700 remained on the island and 2,400 continued to work as "good laborers." Harris to Grey, 6 September 1849, No. 69, CO 295/168.

162. Barkly to Grey, 28 November 1851, No. 170, CO 111/284.

163. *Report of the Committee Appointed to Enquire into the Treatment of Immigrants in British Guiana*, PP, 1871, xx (C. 393 I–III) (hereafter RCBG), 42.

164. Census of 1851, 31 March 1851, Population Return, CO 116/220. Roughly 1,170 had returned to India, leaving approximately 3,000 unaccounted for. See Look Lai, *Indentured Labor, Caribbean Sugar*, 117.

165. Response of John Croal, in "Queries relative to the results of Emancipation in the British Colonies," enclosed in Light to Stanley, 18 April 1845, No. 83, CO 111/227. These West Indian

workers were not indentured; many returned to the islands from which they came in cyclical patterns. See Look Lai, *Indentured Labor, Caribbean Sugar*, 13–14.

166. Bonyun to Light, 6 January 1848, CO 111/250. The exact figure was 15,699, including 429 who arrived in 1835.

167. RCBG, 39.

168. Harris to Grey, 1 July 1848, No. 75, CO 295/163.

169. In 1848, the Court of Policy demanded reductions in government salaries and subsequently refused to authorize fixed appropriations, creating a temporary financial and political crisis. See Green, *British Slave Emancipation*, 78, 240–42.

170. RCBG, 40–41. Tinker, *New System of Slavery*, 81.

171. Gomm to Stanley, 16 February 1846, No. 34, CO 167/267.

172. See p. 50, above.

173. Allen, *Slaves, Freedmen, and Indentured Laborers*, 23.

Chapter 3

1. Boyd Hilton, *The Age of Atonement: The Influence of Evangelicalism on Social and Economic Thought, 1785–1865* (Oxford: Clarendon, 1986), esp. 3–70; Boyd Hilton, *Corn, Cash, Commerce: The Economic Policies of the Tory Governments 1815–1830* (Oxford: Oxford University Press, 1977), 69–82, 217–314; Norman McCord, *The Anti-Corn Law League, 1838–1846*, 2nd ed. (London: Allen & Unwin, 1968), 15; Anthony Howe, *Free Trade and Liberal England, 1846–1946* (Oxford: Clarendon, 1997), 34; D. P. O'Brien, *The Classical Economists Revisited* (Princeton, NJ: Princeton University Press, 2004), 1–19; Eugenio Biagini, *Liberty, Retrenchment and Reform: Popular Liberalism in the Age of Gladstone, 1860–1880* (Cambridge: Cambridge University Press, 1992), 93–102.

2. On the political consequences of repeal, see Philip Harling, *The Waning of "Old Corruption": The Politics of Economical Reform in Britain, 1779–1846* (Oxford: Clarendon, 1996), 228–66; Biagini, *Liberty, Retrenchment and Reform*, 103–47; Howe, *Free Trade and Liberal England*. On free trade and the world economy, see Dale W. Tomich, *Through the Prism of Slavery: Labor, Capital, and World Economy* (Lanham, MD: Rowman & Littlefield, 2004), 58–71; Jürgen Osterhammel, *The Transformation of the World: A Global History of the Nineteenth Century*, trans. Patrick Camiller (Princeton, NJ: Princeton University Press, 2014), 427, 452–55.

3. P. S. Atiyah, *The Rise and Fall of Freedom of Contract* (Oxford: Clarendon, 1979), 299–305; Harling, *Waning of "Old Corruption,"* 9; Howe, *Free Trade and Liberal England*, 12, 19–20, 42, 51; Paul Johnson, *Making the Market: Victorian Origins of Corporate Capitalism* (Cambridge: Cambridge University Press, 2010), 31–32; Bernard Semmel, *The Rise of Free Trade Imperialism: Classical Political Economy the Empire of Free Trade and Imperialism 1750–1850* (Cambridge: Cambridge University Press, 1970), 7; Frank Trentmann, *Free Trade Nation: Commerce, Consumption, and Civil Society in Modern Britain* (Oxford: Oxford University Press, 2008), 2–3, 5–6. The phrase "assumptive world" comes from Johnson, *Making the Market*, 32. On laissez-faire and the idea of the self-regulating economy, see also Karl Polanyi, *The Great Transformation: The Political and Economic Origins of Our Time*, 1944 (Boston: Beacon Press, 2001), 116–35, 141–57.

4. John Gallagher and Ronald Robinson, "The Imperialism of Free Trade," *Economic History Review*, new ser., 6, no. 1 (1953): 1–15; C. A. Bayly, *The Birth of the Modern World, 1780–1914: Global Connections and Comparisons* (Malden: Blackwell, 2004), 128–38.

5. Julia Lovell, *The Opium War: Drugs, Dreams and the Making of China* (New York: Overlook Press, 2014); Stephen R. Platt, *Imperial Twilight: The Opium War and the End of China's Last Golden Age* (New York: Knopf, 2018).

6. William A. Green, *British Slave Emancipation: The Sugar Colonies and the Great Experiment, 1830–1865* (Oxford: Clarendon, 1976), 229–60; Seymour Drescher, *The Mighty Experiment: Free Labor versus Slavery in British Emancipation* (Oxford: Oxford University Press, 2002), 179–201; Douglas Hall, *Five of the Leewards 1834–1870: The Major Problems of the Post-Emancipation Period in Antigua, Barbuda, Montserrat, Nevis and St. Kitts* (Barbados: Caribbean Universities Press, 1971); Philip Harling, "Sugar Wars: the Culture of Free Trade versus the Culture of Anti-Slavery in Britain and the British Caribbean, 1840–50," in *The Cultural Construction of the British World*, ed. Barry Crosbie and Mark Hampton (Manchester: Manchester University Press, 2016).

7. Alan H. Adamson, *Sugar Without Slaves: The Political Economy of British Guiana, 1838–1904* (New Haven, CT: Yale University Press, 1972), 34–103; Richard Allen, *Slaves, Freedmen, and Indentured Laborers in Colonial Mauritius* (Cambridge: Cambridge University Press, 1999); Jay R. Mandle, *The Plantation Economy: Population and Economic Change in Guyana, 1838–1960* (Philadelphia: Temple University Press, 1973), 19–25; Thomas C. Holt, *The Problem of Freedom: Race, Labor, and Politics in Jamaica and Britain, 1832–1938* (Baltimore: Johns Hopkins University Press, 1992), 115–76.

8. Semmel, *Free Trade Imperialism*.

9. On the distinction between labor as commodity and labor as human activity shaped by social expectations and practices, see Polanyi, *Great Transformation*, esp. 75–76, 171–86.

10. Green, *British Slave Emancipation*, 246; Noël Deerr, *The History of Sugar*, 2 vols. (London: Chapman and Hall, 1949–50), 2:193–203.

11. *Morning Chronicle*, 19 March 1840.

12. *Morning Chronicle*, 26 December 1839.

13. *Times*, 23 September 1840, 4.

14. *Report of the Select Committee on the West India Colonies*, PP, 1842, xiii (479), iv–v.

15. *Report of the Select Committee on the West India Colonies*, iii, vii–viii.

16. Madhavi Kale, *Fragments of Empire: Capital, Slavery, and Indian Indentured Labor Migration in the British Caribbean* (Philadelphia: University of Pennsylvania Press, 1998), 66–87, esp. 79–87.

17. Russell's famous Edinburgh letter announcing this policy was published in several daily newspapers. See for example "Lord John Russell to the Electors of the City of London," *Times*, 27 November 1845, 5.

18. [Petition of the Agricultural Society of Trinidad], 17 January 1848, enclosed in Harris to Grey, 20 January 1848, No. 9, CO 295/160; Petition, 18 September 1846, enclosed in Harris to Grey, 3 October 1846, No. 73, CO 295/152.

19. "Petition to Parliament, General Meeting of Planters, Merchants and Others interested in the British West India Colonies," 5 May 1841, WIC, M915 Reel 5.

20. [Petition of the West India Committee to Parliament], Minutes of the Standing Committee, 26 January 1848, WIC, M915 Reel 5.

21. Simon Morgan, "The Anti-Corn Law League and British Anti-Slavery in Transatlantic Perspective, 1838–1846," *Historical Journal* 52, no. 1 (2009): 87–107.

22. Committee report, enclosed in Harris to Grey, 3 February 1847, No. 12, CO 295/156.

23. "Petition to the Queen, made by the Inhabitants of Berbice interested in the cultivation of sugar," enclosed in Light to Grey, 6 March 1848, No. 41, CO 111/251.

24. Cave to Stanley, 9 July 1844, Minutes of the Standing Committee, 10 July 1844, WIC, M915 Reel 5.

25. Minutes of the Standing Committee, 10 July 1844, WIC, M915 Reel 5.

26. Catherine Hall, Nicholas Draper, Keith McClelland, Katie Donington, and Rachel Lang, *Legacies of British Slave-Ownership: Colonial Slavery and the Formation of Victorian Britain* (Cambridge: Cambridge University Press, 2014), 6; Nicholas Draper, *The Price of Emancipation: Slave-Ownership, Compensation and British Society at the End of Slavery* (Cambridge: Cambridge University Press, 2010).

27. Draper, *Price of Emancipation*, 270. On compensation, see also Kris Manjapra, *Black Ghost of Empire: The Long Death of Slavery and the Failure of Emancipation* (New York: Scribner, 2022), 101–9.

28. Public meeting, 29 December 1848, enclosed in Walker to Grey, 4 January 1849, Separate, CO 111/263.

29. Jonathan Connolly, "Indenture as Compensation: State Financing for Indentured Labor Migration in the Era of Emancipation," *Slavery & Abolition* 40, no. 3 (2019): 448–71, 450–51.

30. Anna Gambles, *Protection and Politics: Conservative Economic Discourse, 1815–1852* (Bury St. Edmunds, Suffolk: Royal Historical Society, 1999).

31. A total of 21,760 indentured Indian workers reached the Caribbean colonies between 1845 and 1848, at which point migration stopped temporarily, until 1851. In Mauritius, by contrast, the scale was much greater: between 1842 and 1850, some 93,690 indentured Indians arrived. David Northrup, *Indentured Labor in the Age of Imperialism, 1834–1922* (Cambridge: Cambridge University Press, 1995), 159.

32. *Standard*, 7 March 1844.

33. *Standard*, 3 November 1847.

34. *Standard*, 22 November 1847; 23 November 1847.

35. *Morning Post*, 19 June 1844, 4. See also *Morning Post*, 24 June 1844, 3.

36. *Morning Post*, 28 July 1846, 4.

37. Mercator, "The Sugar Colonies and the Fallacy of Immigration Without Additional Protection," *Morning Post*, 23 November 1847, 2. "Mercator" was a pen name used by Samuel Jones Lloyd, who became Lord Overstone. See O'Brien, *Classical Economists Revisited*, 6, 16.

38. *Standard*, 3 November 1847 (italics removed); 22 November 1847. The paper continued to compare indenture to slavery: *Standard*, 24 November 1847; 27 January 1848; 24 February 1848.

39. "Cheap Sugar and Slave Trade," *Quarterly Review* 88, no. 175 (1850): 132–34.

40. Before abolition, the *Quarterly Review* frequently contested antislavery positions, often in debate with the Whig and abolitionist *Edinburgh Review*. See Paula E. Dumas, "*The Edinburgh Review*, *The Quarterly Review*, and the Contributions of the Periodical to the Slavery Debates," *Slavery & Abolition* 38, no. 3 (2017): 559–76.

41. "Cheap Sugar and Slave Trade," *Quarterly Review* 88, no. 175 (1850): 132–34.

42. Grey to Gomm, 29 September 1846, No. 38, CO 167/268, discussed in chapter 2, pp. 50–51.

43. Grey to Gomm, 29 September 1846.

44. Grey to Gomm, 29 September 1846.

45. "Heads of an Ordinance for Promoting Immigration into the Island of Mauritius, and the Industry of Immigrants," § 2, enclosed in Grey to Gomm, 29 September 1846, No. 38, CO 167/268 (italics in original).

46. "Heads of an Ordinance for Promoting Immigration into the Island of Mauritius," § 3.

47. "Heads of an Ordinance for Promoting Immigration into the Island of Mauritius," § 3. Grey's model included a third recommendation not discussed here: stamp duties imposed on indenture contracts, whose purpose was to defray transportation costs and discourage employers from "enticing," or hiring away, workers already under contract on other plantations.

48. Holt, *Problem of Freedom*, 203.

49. Mauritius Ordinance No. 22 of 1847, § 5, CO 169/7.

50. Mauritius Ordinance No. 22 of 1847, § 28.

51. For example, if the worker's monthly wage was ten shillings, the fine would amount to five pence for each day absent. At that rate, twenty-four days of absence would result in a fine equal to the total monthly wage. Separately, the law also imposed additional restrictions associated with industrial residence, which were sanctioned in Grey's model. Free return passage to India, for example, was conditioned on the completion of industrial residence. Those wanting and able to pay their own return passage were only allowed to do so after paying a fee of one pound and ten shillings for each year of industrial residence left outstanding. Mauritius Ordinance No. 22 of 1847, § 8.

52. Melvill (Court of Directors) to Byng (Board of Control), 29 April 1847, IOR L/PJ/2/193.

53. Melvill to Byng, 29 April 1847. The reference is to Grey's dispatch to Governor Gomm, 29 September 1846, discussed on p. 51, above.

54. Melvill to Byng, 29 April 1847.

55. Hawes to Wyse, 3 November 1847, enclosed in Wyse to Melvill, 6 November 1847, IOR L/PJ/2/193.

56. On admixtures of hierarchy, liberalism, and laissez-faire in this period, see Huzzey, "Concepts of Liberty."

57. Merivale to Hyde, 6 July 1848, enclosed in Hyde (Board of Control) to Melvill (Court of Directors), 8 July 1848, IOR L/PJ/2/193.

58. Earl Grey, *The Colonial Policy of Lord John Russell's Administration*, 2 vols. (London, 1853), 1:54–55 (on the conditions needed for "steady and continuous labour"), 74 (on his model ordinance for indenture and the ways in which it created an "effective obligation to work").

59. Herman Merivale, *Lectures on Colonies and Colonization, delivered at the University of Oxford in 1839, 1840 and 1841*, 1861 (London, 1928), 320.

60. Merivale, *Lectures on Colonies and Colonization*, esp. 312–22; Denis M. Benn, *The Caribbean: An Intellectual History, 1774–2003* (Kingston, Jamaica: Ian Randle, 2004), 37–39.

61. Karl Marx, *Capital: A Critique of Political Economy*, vol. 1, trans. Ben Fowkes (New York: Vintage, 1977), 935–40 (commenting on Edward Gibbon Wakefield's program for "systematic colonization" and Merivale's *Lectures on Colonies and Colonization*).

62. Merivale, *Lectures on Colonies and Colonization*, 318; Benn, *The Caribbean*, 37.

63. Mauritius Ordinance No. 25 of 1848, CO 169/8.

64. Mauritius Ordinance No. 25 of 1848, §§ 8, 22.

65. Court of Directors to Wyse (Board of Control), 2 December 1847, IOR L/PJ/2/193; Dickinson (Court of Directors), 3 August 1848, IOR L/PJ/2/193.

66. Circular Dispatch, 23 October 1846, enclosed in Gomm to Stanley, 7 March 1846, CO 167/268.

67. Trinidad Ordinance No. 5 of 1850, CO 297/4. See also Harris to Grey, 20 April 1850, No. 31, and Grey to Harris, 25 July 1850 (confirming the ordinance), CO 295/170.

68. British Guiana Ordinance No. 21 of 1850, §§ 9, 15, CO 113/2. The monthly tax was raised to $1.50.

69. Melvill (Court of Directors) to Elliot (Board of Control), 14 November 1850, IOR L/PJ/2/194.

70. Melvill to Elliot, 24 December 1851, and Melvill to Baillie (Board of Control), 25 November 1852, both in IOR L/PJ/2/195; Basdeo Mangru, *Benevolent Neutrality: Indian Government Policy and Labour Migration to British Guiana, 1854–1884* (London: Hansib, 1987), 143. For Guiana's revised laws, see British Guiana Ordinances Nos. 20, 21, and 22 of 1851, CO 113/2.

71. Murdoch and Rogers to Merivale (Colonial Office), 16 December 1852, enclosed in Stark (Board of Control) to Melvill (Court of Directors), 18 January 1853, IOR L/PJ/2/195.

72. Murdoch and Rogers to Merivale, 16 December 1852.

73. Atiyah, *Freedom of Contract*, 388–405.

74. Murdoch and Rogers to Merivale, 16 December 1852, enclosed in Stark to Melvill, 18 January 1853, IOR L/PJ/2/195. On the relation between this kind of paternalism and distinctions drawn by colonial officials between European and non-European migrants during this period, see also Adam M. McKeown, *Melancholy Order: Asian Migration and the Globalization of Borders* (New York: Columbia University Press, 2008), 70–71.

75. Merivale to Stark, 29 December 1852, enclosed in Stark (Board of Control) to Melvill (Court of Directors), 18 January 1853, IOR L/PJ/2/195.

76. Grey to Barkly, 1 January 1852, CO 111/284.

77. Barkly to Grey, 29 January 1851, No. 17, CO 111/280.

78. Barkly to Grey, 29 January 1851.

79. Extract, White to Barkly, 8 November 1850, CO 111/280. White's view, specifically his insistence that indentured Indians were naturally prone to authoritarian command and thus incapable of self-rule, recalls notions of "Oriental despotism," which marked British perceptions of pre-colonial Indian societies from the eighteenth century onward. See Erik Stokes, *The English Utilitarians and India* (Oxford: Clarendon, 1959), 31–2, 53–54; Bernard S. Cohn, *Colonialism and its Forms of Knowledge: The British in India* (Princeton, NJ: Princeton University Press, 1996), 62–65; Nasser Hussain, *The Jurisprudence of Emergency: Colonialism and the Rule of Law* (Ann Arbor: University of Michigan Press, 2003), 31–32, 39–55.

80. Higginson to Pakington, 17 May 1852, No. 301, CO 167/335.

81. Harris to Grey, 21 February 1848, No. 21, CO 295/160.

82. Harris to Grey, 5 September 1849, No. 68, CO 295/168, discussed on pp. 1, 54, above.

83. British Guiana Ordinance No. 3 of 1853, § 31, CO 113/2.

84. Colonial Office to Barkly, 14 May 1853, CO 111/293; Newcastle to Barkly, 14 May 1853, PP, 1852–53, lxvii (986), 115–18.

85. Grey to Anderson, 23 October 1849, CO 167/313; Mauritius Ordinance No. 3 of 1849, § 1, CO 169/8. The law was permissive rather than mandatory; it did not require new immigrants to accept three-year contracts. But in undermining the former prohibition, it set the stage for mandatory multiyear contracts, which would be introduced in 1854.

86. Colonial Office to Wilson (Board of Control), 6 October 1849, responding to Anderson to Grey, 10 July 1849, No. 113, CO 167/313.

87. Grey to Harris, 15 April 1848, PP, 1847–48, xlv (399), 200–201 (stating "I doubt not that your Lordship will perceive the serious difficulties under which we labour in the treatment of immigrants belonging to savage or half-civilized races, whose unfitness for unrestrained liberty is not generally understood or acknowledged in this country").

88. Mauritius Ordinance No. 7 of 1849, enclosed in Anderson to Grey, 3 October 1849, No. 62, CO 167/315.

89. W. W. West, E. Desmarais, Allard, et al., Address to Governor Anderson, 30 August 1849, PP, 1850, xxxix (741), 183.

90. Anderson to Grey, 20 September 1849, No. 58, CO 167/314; Grey to Anderson, 20 January 1850, No. 127, CO 167/314.

91. British Guiana Ordinance No. 20 of 1851, § 30, CO 113/2.

92. Ordinance No. 21 of 1850, §§ 21 and 22, modified and re-enacted as Ordinance No. 21 of 1851, CO 113/2.

93. In keeping with contemporary usage, the term "Creole" refers here to the colonies' Black populations, including both the formerly enslaved and their descendants, but not indentured African (post-emancipation) migrants or mixed-race people of color. In other contexts, the term had different and more expansive meanings and could include free people of color as well as (particularly in Spanish-speaking contexts) colonial-born whites. See Edward Brathwaite, *The Development of Creole Society in Jamaica, 1770–1820* (Oxford: Clarendon, 1971), xiv–xvi.

94. Wallbridge to Scoble, 1 September 1841, ASSP, MSS Brit Emp S 18, C 22/112; Minutes of the British and Foreign Anti-Slavery Society, 21 January 1840, ASSP, MSS Brit Emp S 20, E 2/6; John Scoble, *Hill Coolies: A Brief Exposure of the Deplorable Condition of the Hill Coolies, in British Guiana and Mauritius, and of the Nefarious Means by which they were Induced to Resort to these Colonies* (London, 1840), 23.

95. "Petition of the Undersigned Inhabitants of British Guiana," enclosed in Light to Gladstone, 13 July 1846, No. 136, CO 111/234; "Memorial of the Undersigned, being Ministers of the Gospel, residing in the County of Demerara, in the Colony of British Guiana," 18 May 1844, enclosed in Light to Stanley, 18 May 1844, No. 111, PP, 1846, xxx (321), 101–3.

96. See for example Gallagher to Holligan, 9 October 1867, enclosed in Hincks to Buckingham and Chandos, 17 October 1867, No. 143, CO 111/364; Hincks to Buckingham and Chandos, 22 June 1868, No. 85, CO 111/367; Scott to Kimberley, 21 December 1871, No. 180, CO 111/387; Frederic Rogers, Minute, 20 June 1860, attached to Keate to Newcastle, 9 February 1860, No. 24, CO 295/208; RCBG, 73.

97. See for example Harris to Newcastle, 23 January 1854, No. 10, CO 295/184; Mitchell to Johnston, 1 June 1858, enclosed in Keate to Bulwer Lytton, 26 September 1858, No. 131, CO 295/200; Keate to Newcastle, 9 August 1859, No. 123, CO 295/205; D. W. D. Comins, *Note on the Abolition of Return Passages to East Indian Immigrants from the Colonies of Trinidad and British Guiana* (Calcutta, 1892), 8, IOR, V/27/820/11. For a critique of wage savings data colonial officials used to make these claims, see Mangru, *Benevolent Neutrality*, 146–49.

98. Modern historians have to a certain extent followed this pattern. Tinker argued that wages were nominal as part of his broader claim that indenture perpetuated the conditions of slavery. Seizing on savings data from the later nineteenth century, others have argued that some workers managed to earn and save significant sums. Compare Hugh Tinker, *A New System of Slavery: The Export of Indian Labour Overseas* (London: Oxford University Press, 1974), 21, 178, 183–91, with Northrup, *Indentured Labor*, 135–39.

99. The Sugar Duties Act called for a gradual reduction of duties and full equalization in 1851. Ongoing political negotiation, however, ultimately delayed full equalization until 1854. Green, *British Slave Emancipation*, 229; Richard Huzzey, "Free Trade, Free Labour, and Slave Sugar in Victorian Britain," *Historical Journal* 53, no. 2 (2010): 359–79, 362.

100. Deerr, *History of Sugar*, 2:531.

101. [Untitled sugar production return], Christopher Bagot, Comptroller, 4 February 1852, enclosed in Barkly to Pakington, 21 April 1852, No. 86, CO 111/289. A "hogshead" was a unit of

measure frequently used to record sugar exports. It equated to between 17 and 20 hundredweight (cwt.), that is, between 1,904 and 2,240 lb. The hogshead was thus close to, though not always the same as, the imperial ton, which was 2,240 lb. or 20 cwt.

102. Allen, *Slaves, Freedmen, and Indentured Laborers*, 23. According to Allen, average annual production was 56,069 tons between 1845 and 1849, and 33,784 tons between 1830 and 1834.

103. Trinidad Blue Book for 1846, CO 300/57.

104. Trinidad Blue Book for 1847, CO 300/58.

105. Trinidad Blue Book for 1848, CO 300/59; Trinidad Blue Book for 1849, CO 300/60.

106. British Guiana Blue Book for 1844, CO 116/213.

107. British Guiana Blue Book for 1847, CO 116/216. These figures refer to sugar exported to Britain and exclude small amounts exported to other West Indian islands and to North America.

108. British Guiana Blue Book for 1848, CO 116/217. In 1849, the figures were 38,150 hogsheads with a value of £493,284. British Guiana Blue Book for 1849, CO 116/218.

109. Harris to Grey, 21 February 1848, No. 21, CO 295/160.

110. Harris to Grey, 19 June 1848, No. 71, CO 295/162.

111. Adamson, *Sugar Without Slaves*, 160–63; Green, *British Slave Emancipation*, 218–22, 234–38; Walton Look Lai, *Indentured Labor, Caribbean Sugar: Chinese and Indian Migrants to the British West Indies, 1838–1918* (Baltimore: Johns Hopkins University Press, 1993), 10–11; Donald Wood, *Trinidad in Transition: The Years after Slavery* (London: Oxford University Press, 1968), 121–24.

112. Barkly to Grey, 28 February 1849, No. 36, CO 111/264.

113. See, for example, "Abstract Statement, Administration of the Sugar Plantation Great Diamond, on the East Bank of the river Demerary, from the date of being placed under Sequestration, 17 August 1847, to the date of sale on 4th October 1848," enclosed in Walker to Grey, 18 January 1849, No. 13, CO 111/263; as well as other enclosures in the same dispatch.

114. Adamson, *Sugar Without Slaves*, 160. Adamson explains that there were at least 201 execution sales of estates in British Guiana between 1838 and 1853, and that "almost half" occurred between 1847 and 1850.

115. Gomm to Gladstone, 10 August 1846, No. 149, CO 167/271.

116. "Petition to the Queen, made by the Inhabitants of Berbice interested in the cultivation of sugar," enclosed in Light to Grey, 6 March 1848, No. 41, CO 111/251. Governor Light reported similar demands from other parts of the colony, not just Berbice. See Light to Grey, 18 January 1848, Private, CO 111/249.

117. "Petition of the Court of Policy and of the Financial Representatives in Combined Court," 3 June 1847, enclosed in Light to Grey, 3 June 1847, No. 114, CO 111/244. See also Extract from the Minutes of the Court of Policy, 1 March 1847, enclosed in Light to Grey, 3 March 1847, No. 46, CO 111/242.

118. Barkly to Grey, 2 February 1850, No. 25, CO 111/272.

119. Gomm to Stanley, 31 January 1844, No. 13, CO 167/252.

120. Gomm to Stanley, 24 August 1844, No. 124, CO 167/254. See also Unofficial Members of Council to Gomm, 16 March 1844, enclosed in Gomm to Stanley, 21 March 1844, No. 37, CO 167/252 ("We have stated that the supply is not equal to the demand; the proof of which is, that those labourers who have finished their first year of engagement re-engaged during the month of February at $2½, $3, and $3½ per month, while now demanding $4½ and $5 per month, instead of five rupees; rates of wages which no prudent man can possibly give . . .").

121. George Ross, "A Review of the Prospects of the Sugar Cultivation in British Guiana," 18 February 1845, in Light to Stanley, 19 February 1845, No. 38, CO 111/220; Adamson, *Sugar Without Slaves*, 166.

122. Light to Stanley, 19 February 1845, No. 38, CO 111/220.

123. British Guiana Blue Book for 1844, CO 116/213; British Guiana Blue Book for 1845, CO 116/214.

124. Trinidad Blue Book for 1846, CO 300/57.

125. The wage records I rely on to make this argument did not distinguish between male and female workers, but separate evidence (largely from a later time period) from Fiji, Trinidad, and Jamaica suggests that indentured women were frequently paid less than men. Arunima Datta, *Fleeting Agencies: A Social History of Indian Coolie Women in British Malaya* (Cambridge: Cambridge University Press, 2021), 48–60; Rhoda Reddock, "The Indentureship Experience: Indian Women in Trinidad and Tobago 1845–1917," and Verene A. Shepherd, "Indian Migrant Women and Plantation Labour in Nineteenth and Twentieth Century Jamaica: Gender Perspectives," both in *Women Plantation Workers: International Experiences*, ed. Shobita Jain and Rhoda Rheddock (Oxford: Berg, 1998).

126. Trinidad Blue Book for 1848, CO 300/59; Trinidad Blue Book for 1849, CO 300/60; Trinidad Blue Book for 1850, CO 300/61.

127. Trinidad Blue Book for 1857, CO 300/68. This was true for 1855 as well: Trinidad Blue Book for 1855, CO 300/66.

128. British Guiana Blue Book for 1845, CO 116/214; British Guiana Blue Book for 1848, CO 116/217. In 1846, the average wage was 3l. 10s. per month, or roughly 2s. 4d. per day. British Guiana Blue Book for 1846, CO 116/215. On declining wages, see also Adamson, *Sugar Without Slaves*, 167; Heather Cateau, "Re-Examining the Labour Matrix in the British Caribbean 1750–1850," in *Emancipation and the Remaking of the British Imperial World*, ed. Catherine Hall, Nicholas Draper, and Keith McClelland (Manchester: Manchester University Press, 2014), 98–112, 108.

129. British Guiana Blue Book for 1849, CO 116/218 (1s. 5d. to 2s.); British Guiana Blue Book for 1850, 116/219 (1s. 4d.); British Guiana Blue Book for 1853, CO 116/222.

130. Gomm to Grey, 4 October 1847, No. 218, CO 167/287.

131. The figures in this paragraph come from Rawson W. Rawson (Immigration Committee), 30 March 1853, enclosed in Higginson to Newcastle, 20 May 1853, No. 93, CO 167/345.

132. Light to Grey, 31 December 1871, No. 224, CO 111/246.

133. Walker, Government Secretary, to [Stipendiary Magistrates], 24 December 1847, Private, enclosed in Light to Grey, 31 December 1847, No. 224, CO 111/246.

134. Grey to Light, 12 February 1848, No. 293, CO 111/246.

135. *Eighth Report from the Select Committee on Sugar and Coffee Planting*, PP, 1847–48, xxiii (361-II), iii–iv.

136. Cave to Stanley, 9 July 1844, in Minutes of the Standing Committee, 10 July 1844, WIC M915 Reel 5; Memorial of the Acting Committee of West India Planters and Merchants to Lord John Russell, 25 October 1847, PP, 1847–48, xlv (17), 1–4.

137. Act 11 & 12 Vict. c. 130 authorized these loans. Of the total amount, £250,000 was allocated to British Guiana; £125,000 to Trinidad; £100,000 to Jamaica; £18,000 and £7,000 to St. Lucia and Grenada, respectively. *Return of Loans by British Government to W. Indian Colonies, British Guiana, and Mauritius for Immigration*, PP, 1860, xlv (250), 3.

138. £70,000 to British Guiana and £64,073 0s. 8d. to Trinidad, as authorized by Act 11 & 12 Vict. c. 22. *Return of Loans*, 3. For a more detailed account of the private loans raised by British Guiana to fund migration, see Connolly, "Indenture as Compensation."

139. *Return of Loans*, 10; Connolly, "Indenture as Compensation," 454–55.

140. "Memorial of the Undersigned, being Ministers of the Gospel, residing in the County of Demerara," 18 May 1844, PP, 1846, xxx (321), 101–3; "Petition of the Undersigned Inhabitants of British Guiana," enclosed in Light to Gladstone, 13 July 1846, No. 36, CO 111/234.

141. On this theme, see also Eric Foner, *Nothing but Freedom: Emancipation and Its Legacy*, rev. ed. (Baton Rouge: Louisiana State University Press, 2007), 23–25. On regressive taxation after abolition, see Adamson, *Sugar Without Slaves*, 12, 107, 239–42; Bridget Brereton, *A History of Modern Trinidad, 1783–1962* (Kingston, Jamaica: Heinemann), 141; Woodville K. Marshall, "The Emergence and Survival of the Peasantry," in *General History of the Caribbean, IV, The Long Nineteenth Century: Nineteenth Century Transformations*, ed. K. O. Laurence (Paris: UNESCO, 2011), 149–90, 188–89; James Rose, " 'Behold the Tax Man Cometh': Taxation as a Tool of Oppression in Early Post-Emancipation British Guiana, 1838–48," in *In the Shadow of the Plantation: Caribbean History and Legacy*, ed. Alvin O. Thompson (Kingston, Jamaica: Ian Randle, 2002), 297–313. On the extent to which colonial revenues depended on import and sales taxes rather than export taxes, see also Colonial Estimates, 1848–1873, Parliament Library of Trinidad and Tobago, Port of Spain, Trinidad; Colonial Estimate for 1850 (British Guiana), enclosed in Barly to Grey, 4 May 1850, No. 73, PP, 1851, xxix (624), 112–13.

142. Mitchell to Bushe, 19 September 1859, PP, 1860, xlv (250), 8–9; Connolly, "Indenture as Compensation," 454, 458; Look Lai, *Indentured Labor, Caribbean Sugar*, 276.

143. Stanley, Inspector of Police, to Waterschoodt, Inspector-General of Police, Leguan, 15 September 1846, and Light to Grey, 18 September 1846, No. 192, CO 111/236.

144. Light to Grey, 18 January 1848, Private, CO 111/249; Light to Grey, 31 January 1848, No. 17, CO 111/249. Separately and in a later period, indentured Indians similarly used arson as a tool of protest on a localized, intermittent basis. See Kusha Haraksingh, "Control and Resistance among Indian Workers: A Study of Labour on the Sugar Plantations of Trinidad 1875–1917," in *India in the Caribbean*, ed. David Dabydeen and Brinsley Samaroo (London: Hansib, 1987), 75.

145. Light to Grey, 31 January 1848, No. 17, CO 111/249.

146. See Grey to Light, 28 February 1848, Confidential, CO 111/249.

147. Harris to Grey, 6 October 1849, No. 79, PP, 1852–53, lxvii (936), 13–18; Harris to Grey, 12 November 1849, Confidential, CO 295/168. These dispatches describe estate burnings and anti-government riots, which Harris attributed to a number of different factors, including dissatisfaction over reduced wages, rumors regarding the imposition of new taxes, rules regarding debtors' prison, and republican ideals imported partly from the French Caribbean colonies.

148. Carbery, District G, enclosed in Walker to Grey, 13 June 1848, No. 20, CO 111/254. See also "Government Notice and Reports of the Stipendiary Magistrates," enclosed in Walker to Grey, 13 June 1848; "Abstract of Reports made to the Governor on the state of the Rural Districts of this Colony from the 24th of January to the 17th of February 1848," enclosed in Light to Grey, 18 February 1848, No. 32, CO 111/249; Mangru, *Benevolent Neutrality*, 28–29.

149. Light to Grey, 18 February 1848, No. 32, CO 111/249.

150. Scott to Tidman, 13 January 1848, School of Oriental and African Studies Special Collections, London (hereafter SOAS), CWM/LMS British Guiana Incoming Correspondence, Demerara, Box 7, Folder 3. See also Kenyon to Tidman, 16 February 1848, SOAS, CWM/LMS British Guiana, Incoming Correspondence, Berbice, Box 6, Folder 4 (describing a "general strike" in Berbice and Demerara).

151. Scott to Tidman, 13 January 1848, SOAS, CWM/LMS British Guiana Incoming Correspondence, Demerara, Box 7, Folder 3.

152. "Abstract Report of progress of resumption of Creole Labour in this Colony during the first three months of 1848," enclosed in Light to Grey, 4 April 1848, No. 61, CO 111/252.

153. Walter Rodney, *A History of the Guyanese Working People, 1881–1905* (Baltimore: Johns Hopkins University Press, 1981). For related analysis building on Rodney, see Malcolm Cross, "East Indian-Creole Relations in Trinidad and Guiana in the Late Nineteenth Century," in *Across the Dark Waters: Ethnicity and Indian Identity in the Caribbean*, ed. David Dabydeen and Brinsley Samaroo (London: Macmillan Caribbean, 1996), 14–38.

154. Prabhu P. Mohapatra, "Assam and the West Indies, 1860–1920: Immobilizing Plantation Labor," in *Masters, Servants, and Magistrates in Britain and the Empire, 1562–1955*, ed. Douglas Hay and Paul Craven (Chapel Hill: University of North Carolina Press, 2004), 455–80, 458.

155. Mimi Sheller, *Citizenship from Below: Erotic Agency and Caribbean Freedom* (Durham, NC: Duke University Press, 2012), 99.

156. Light to Gladstone, 30 July 1846, No. 153, CO 111/234.

157. Rodney, *History of the Guyanese Working People*, esp. 39–42.

158. Ferrier to Tidman, 4 May 1849, SOAS, CWM/LMS British Guiana Incoming Correspondence, Demerara, Box 7, Folder 4.

159. Adamson, *Sugar Without Slaves*, 34–103; Green, *British Slave Emancipation*, 296–306; Mandle, *Plantation Economy*, 19–25; Woodville K. Marshall, "Notes on Peasant Development in the West Indies Since 1838," *Social and Economic Studies* 17, no. 3 (1968): 252–63; Holt, *Problem of Freedom*, 115–76; Clive Y. Thomas, *Plantations, Peasants, and State: A Study of the Mode of Sugar Production in Guyana* (Mona, Jamaica: University of the West Indies, 1984), 18–20.

160. Jean Besson, "Freedom and Community: The British West Indies," in *The Meaning of Freedom: Economics, Politics, and Culture after Slavery*, ed. Frank McGlynn and Seymour Drescher (Pittsburgh: University of Pittsburgh Press, 1992), 193–219. On land purchases for new villages, see "Queries Relative to the results of Emancipation in the British Colonies," enclosed in Light to Stanley, 18 April 1845, No. 83, CO 111/227.

161. Consolidated Return, 31 December 1845, Table A, CO 116/166.

162. Consolidated Half Yearly Return, 31 December 1853, Table A, CO 116/169. These figures are clearly approximate. See also Adamson, *Sugar Without Slaves*, 37–39.

163. Harris to Grey, 7 January 1851, No. 2, CO 295/173.

164. O. Nigel Bolland, "The Politics of Freedom of Freedom in the British Caribbean," in McGlynn and Drescher, *The Meaning of Freedom*, 113–46; Holt, *Problem of Freedom*, 143–76; Mimi Sheller, *Democracy After Slavery: Black Publics and Peasant Radicalism in Haiti and Jamaica* (Gainesville: University of Florida Press, 2000), 147–61. For related analysis of Antigua, Natasha Lightfoot, *Troubling Freedom: Antigua and the Aftermath of British Emancipation* (Durham, NC: Duke University Press, 2015).

165. W. J. Sandiford (Stipendiary Magistrate), report from District L, enclosed in Light to Stanley, 2 August 1845, CO 111/224.

166. See "Return of all lots of land transported and advertised to be transported in the County of Berbice to individuals of the labouring class during the year 1847" and "Return of lots of land transported to Individuals of the Labouring Class in the Counties of Demerary and Essequebo in the Colony of British Guiana between the First day of January and Thirty first day of December 1847," enclosed in Walker to Grey, 13 June 1848, No. 20, CO 111/254 (showing hundreds of individual land purchases by laborers, mostly between half an acre and an acre in size, all from land that was formerly part of estates). On patterns of Creole landownership in Jamaica during this period, see Holt, *Problem of Freedom*, 143–68; Sidney W. Mintz, *Caribbean*

Transformations (Chicago: Aldine Publishing, 1974), 158–66; Sheller, *Democracy after Slavery*, 50–52.

167. See, for example, Governor Light's description of Creole villages, including Litchfield and Hope Town, built on former estates. Light to Gladstone, 31 March 1846, Separate, CO 111/232. See also Mitchell, Superintendent of Immigrants, report dated 16 January 1851, enclosed in Harris to Grey, 24 January 1851, No. 13, CO 295/173.

168. Bridget Brereton, "Family Strategies, Gender, and the Shift to Wage Labor in the British Caribbean," in *Gender and Slave Emancipation in the Atlantic World*, ed. Pamela Scully and Diana Paton (Durham, NC: Duke University Press, 2005), 143–61.

169. See, for example, William Ware (Stipendiary Magistrate, District D, British Guiana), 29 April 1848, sub-enclosed in Government Notice and Reports of the Stipendiary Magistrates, enclosed in Walker to Grey, 13 June 1848, No. 20, CO 111/254.

170. Rattray to Tidman, 21 March 1849, SOAS, CWM/LMS British Guiana Incoming Correspondence, Demerara, Box 7, Folder 4.

171. Barkly to Grey, 17 April 1850, No. 60, CO 111/273.

172. Barkly to Grey, 17 April 1850.

173. Barkly to Grey, 24 September 1850, No. 136, CO 111/276.

174. Mintz, *Caribbean Transformations*, 157–79, 206–13.

175. Allen's work is particularly valuable for the often forgotten histories of Mauritian freedpeople and *gens de couleur* because of his substantial research with the voluminous notarial records that survive in the Mauritian archives. Allen, *Slaves, Freedmen, and Indentured Laborers*, chap. 5, esp. 126–27.

176. Allen, *Slaves, Freedmen, and Indentured Laborers*, 129.

177. Allen, *Slaves, Freedmen, and Indentured Laborers*, 133.

178. Allen, *Slaves, Freedmen, and Indentured Laborers*, 110–11. Between 1835 and 1846, Allen explains, the average mortality rate was 3.2 percent per year. Large outbreaks of cholera and smallpox in the early 1850s, moreover, disproportionately affected the ex-apprentice population. On the use of archaeology to understand historical patterns of disease incidence in Mauritius and the wider Indian Ocean world, see Krish Seetah, "Climate and Disease in the Indian Ocean: An Interdisciplinary Study from Mauritius," in *Connecting Continents: History and Archaeology in the Indian Ocean World*, ed. Krish Seetah (Athens: Ohio University Press, 2018). On freedpeople leaving the plantations, see also Martin A. Klein, "The Emancipation of Slaves in the Indian Ocean," in *Abolition and Its Aftermath in Indian Ocean Africa and Asia*, ed. Gwyn Campbell (London: Routledge, 2005), 198–218, 201.

179. Allen, *Slaves, Freedmen, and Indentured Laborers*, 134.

180. Rawson, Wilson, and Hugon (Census Commissioners) to Higginson, 30 December 1852, enclosed in Higginson to Pakington, 21 January 1853, No. 5, CO 167/343.

181. Rawson, Wilson, and Hugon to Higginson, 30 December 1852.

182. Rawson, Wilson, and Hugon to Higginson, 30 December 1852. Allen gives a lower figure of 4,461 ex-apprentices who "lived or worked on a sugar estate." *Slaves, Freedmen, and Indentured Laborers*, 107.

183. "Abstract of Returns of Population," Census Return of 1851, National Archives of Trinidad and Tobago, Port of Spain, Trinidad (hereafter NATT). By 1861, the figure had risen to 15.97 percent. Between 1851 and 1861, 14,338 Indians arrived and 2,252 returned to India. In 1861, then, Indians comprised 15.97 percent of Trinidad's total population. D. W. D. Comins, *Note on Emigration from India to Trinidad* (Calcutta, 1893), Appendix A, i–ii, NATT.

184. British Guiana Blue Book for 1851, Census of 1851, CO 116/220.

185. Look Lai, *Indentured Labor, Caribbean Sugar*, 118.

186. Harris to Newcastle, 20 August 1853, No. 97, CO 295/181.

187. Look Lai, *Indentured Labor, Caribbean Sugar*, 117.

188. Heyliger to the Colonial Secretary of Mauritius, 4 August 1847, NAM, RA 928; Heyliger to the Colonial Secretary of Mauritius, 5 October 1847, NAM, RA 928; "Indians arrested under Ordinance No. 22 of 1847 for non Payment of Taxes and how disposed of by stipendiary magistrate Maguire, From 14 July 1847 to 23 May 1848," 25 May 1848, enclosed in Maguire to the Colonial Secretary of Mauritius, 25 May 1848, NAM, RA 977.

189. Self to the Colonial Secretary of Mauritius, 4 August 1847, NAM, RA 928.

190. Hervey to the Colonial Secretary of Mauritius, 2 August 1848, NAM, RA 979.

191. Self to the Colonial Secretary of Mauritius, 4 August 1847, NAM, RA 928.

192. Self to the Colonial Secretary of Mauritius, 4 August 1847.

193. Self to the Colonial Secretary of Mauritius, 4 August 1847.

194. Maguire to the Colonial Secretary of Mauritius, 25 May 1848, NAM, RA 977. The stipendiary magistrate from Savanne made a similar argument, suggesting that through payment of the tax immigrants would "acquire the right of roaming about the Country." Elliot to the Colonial Secretary of Mauritius, 2 October 1847, NAM, RA 928.

195. Self to the Colonial Secretary of Mauritius, 6 March 1848, NAM, RA 977; Regnard, "Report on Ordinance 22 of 1847," 1 June 1848, NAM, RA 978.

196. Randall to the Colonial Secretary of Mauritius, 29 May 1848, NAM, RA 977.

197. Heliger to the Colonial Secretary of Mauritius, 22 April 1848, NAM, RA 977. One of these three had been in the colony since the early 1840s, meaning that he had likely already completed industrial residence and should not have been subject to the tax regardless of his employment status.

198. Maguire to the Colonial Secretary of Mauritius, 25 May 1848, NAM, RA 977. Maguire gave the following example, claiming that "an Indian who owes a simple Debt, in the shape of Tax, amounting to 4 shillings, suffers for Non Payment of same an Imprisonment of 96 days . . . accompanied with Hard labour."

199. "Indians arrested under Ordinance No. 22 of 1847 for non Payment of Taxes and how disposed of by stipendiary magistrate Maguire, From 14 July 1847 to 23 May 1848," 25 May 1848, enclosed in Maguire to the Colonial Secretary of Mauritius, 25 May 1848, NAM, RA 977.

200. Randall to the Colonial Secretary of Mauritius, 29 May 1848, NAM, RA 977.

201. "District of Port Louis. Report of Proceedings for the Second Week of September 1848," NAM, RA 977. Some 37.5 percent of the claims brought before Maguire in this period were for unpaid wages.

202. Self to the Colonial Secretary of Mauritius, 14 August 1848, NAM, RA 977; Self to the Colonial Secretary of Mauritius, 27 October 1848, NAM, RA 977.

203. "Report of the Procureur General," 22 August 1848, NAM, RA 977.

204. Case No. 1533, 11 September 1848, and Case No. 1561, 14 September 1848, in "District of Port Louis, Report of Proceedings for the Second week of September 1848," NAM, RA 977.

205. Case No. 1526, 11 September 1848, in "District of Port Louis. Report of Proceedings for the Second Week of September 1848," NAM, RA 977.

206. Regnard, "Report on Ordinance 22 of 1847," 1 June 1848, NAM, RA 978. The ordinance allowed for the deduction of an additional halfpenny for each shilling of monthly wages for each day of unauthorized absence. Mauritius Ordinance No. 22 of 1847, § 28, CO 169/7.

207. Article 28 called for monetary penalties while Article 30 allowed for imprisonment with hard labor when an immigrant owing fines for absence proved unable to pay. The law did not, however, authorize fine *and* imprisonment. Mauritius Ordinance No. 22 of 1847, CO 169/7.

208. Case No. 1564, 14 September 1848, in "District of Port Louis. Report of Proceedings for the Second Week of September 1848," NAM, RA 977.

209. Regnard, 8 September 1847, NAM, RA 928. Regnard, who was writing from Flacq, stated that workers recruited in Port Louis "without numbers or any other means of identifying them" would later abandon their contracts, leaving the authorities with few means of finding them.

210. Government Notices, 8 and 10 July 1852, enclosed in Barkly to Pakington, 19 July 1852, No. 126, CO 111/290, f. 250.

211. "Memorandum as to the duties of the officers about to be appointed to carry out the immigration ordinances, enclosed in Barkly to Pakington," 19 July 1852, No. 126, CO 111/290; Barkly to Pakington, 19 July 1852, No. 126, CO 111/290. Three more stipendiary magistrates were added in 1853, increasing the total from 9 to 12. Barkly to Newcastle, 14 March 1853, No. 44, CO 111/293.

212. Barkly to Pakington, 19 July 1852, No. 126, CO 111/290.

213. John Bisset, District G, 30 September 1852, enclosed in Minutes of the Proceedings of the Honorable the Court of Policy of the Colony of British Guiana, 26 November 1852, CO 114/18. Bisset was a subagent and collector, here discussing the instructions he received from his supervising stipendiary magistrate, Carbery, and the "object of the Government" in enacting the law.

214. John Brummell, District H, 2 October 1852, enclosed in Minutes of the Proceedings of the Honorable the Court of Policy of the Colony of British Guiana, 26 November 1852, CO 114/18.

215. J. V. Aanzorg, District F, 8 October 1852, enclosed in Minutes of the Proceedings of the Honorable the Court of Policy of the Colony of British Guiana, 26 November 1852, CO 114/18.

216. J. V. Mittelholzer, 2 October 1852, enclosed in Minutes of the Proceedings of the Honorable the Court of Policy of the Colony of British Guiana, 26 November 1852, CO 114/18.

217. J. V. Mittelholzer, 2 October 1852.

218. Abraham Garnett, 2 October 1852, enclosed in Minutes of the Proceedings of the Honorable the Court of Policy of the Colony of British Guiana, 26 November 1852, CO 114/18.

219. Abraham Garnett, 2 October 1852.

220. Abraham Garnett, 2 October 1852, and Edward French, 29 September 1852, enclosed in Minutes of the Proceedings of the Honorable the Court of Policy of the Colony of British Guiana, 26 November 1852, CO 114/18.

221. John Bissett, District G, 30 September 1852, enclosed in Minutes of the Proceedings of the Honorable the Court of Policy of the Colony of British Guiana, 26 November 1852, CO 114/18.

222. J. V. Aanzorg, District F, 8 October 1852, enclosed in Minutes of the Proceedings of the Honorable the Court of Policy of the Colony of British Guiana, 26 November 1852, CO 114/18.

223. Financial Statement No. 2 of 1852, 21 January 1853, enclosed in Barkly to Newcastle, 26 April 1853, No. 69, CO 111/294.

224. RCBG, 68. The exact figures given were $8,854.48 in costs and $604.68 in receipts.

225. Protest of the Elective Members, enclosed in Walker to Newcastle, 9 August 1853, No. 56, CO 111/296.

226. RCBG, 68.

227. The Court of Policy's critique of labor taxes, cited above, was made in the context of debate on Ordinance No. 3 of 1853, which permitted five-year contracts and which the Colonial Office disallowed.

228. Protest of the Elective Members, enclosed in Walker to Newcastle, 9 August 1853, No. 56, CO 111/296.

229. Barkly to Grey, 21 March 1849, No. 53, CO 111/264.

230. Minutes of the Proceedings of the Honorable the Court of Policy of the Colony of British Guiana, 19 June 1850, CO 114/17.

231. Minutes of the Proceedings of the Court of Policy, 19 June 1850.

Chapter 4

1. *Hansard*, 3rd ser., xli, col. 470 (6 March 1838).

2. On the founding and subsequent history of the *Economist*, see Ruth Dudley Edwards, *The Pursuit of Reason: The Economist, 1843–1993* (London: Hamish Hamilton, 1993); Alexander Zevin, *Liberalism at Large: The World According to the Economist* (London: Verso, 2019).

3. Seymour Drescher, *The Mighty Experiment: Free Labor versus Slavery in British Emancipation* (Oxford: Oxford University Press, 2002), 5–8, 121–201.

4. According to the *Spectator*, Britain's slave-trade suppression efforts were a "costly failure" and a "deadly farce." "The African Squadron," *Spectator*, 23 March 1850, 277. The *Examiner* condemned the policy in similar terms. See, for example, "The African Blockade and the Slave Trade," *Examiner*, 8 July 1848, 433. On Britain's slave-trade suppression policy and its effects, see also David Eltis, *Economic Growth and the Ending of the Transatlantic Slave Trade* (Oxford: Oxford University Press, 1987); Richard Huzzey, *Freedom Burning: Anti-Slavery and Empire in Victorian Britain* (Ithaca, NY: Cornell University Press, 2012), 42–51, 113–24; Robert Burroughs and Richard Huzzey, eds., *The Suppression of the Atlantic Slave Trade: British Policies, Practices and Representations of Naval Coercion* (Manchester: Manchester University Press, 2015).

5. "Can the Slave Trade Be Suppressed?," *Economist*, 2 September 1848, 993.

6. For instance, Thomas Clarkson, *The History of the Rise, Progress, and Accomplishment of the Abolition of the African Slave-Trade by the British Parliament* (London, 1808). See also David Brion Davis, *The Problem of Slavery in Western Culture* (Ithaca, NY: Cornell University Press, 1966), 291–390; Eric Herschthal, *The Science of Abolition: How Slaveholders Became the Enemies of Progress* (New Haven, CT: Yale University Press, 2021).

7. "Can the Slave Trade Be Suppressed?," *Economist*, 2 September 1848, 994.

8. Matthew Karp, *This Vast Southern Empire: Slaveholders at the Helm of American Foreign Policy* (Cambridge, MA: Harvard University Press, 2016), 123–72. "A Few Thoughts on Slavery," *Southern Literary Messenger*, April 1854, 204, cited in Karp, *Vast Southern Empire*, 157.

9. *Charleston Mercury*, 4 October 1854, cited in Karp, *Vast Southern Empire*, 156. On proslavery thought in the South, see also Drew Gilpin Faust, ed., *The Ideology of Slavery: Proslavery Thought in the Antebellum South, 1830–1860* (Baton Rouge: Louisiana State University Press, 1981); Manisha Sinha, *The Counterrevolution of Slavery: Politics and Ideology in Antebellum South Carolina* (Chapel Hill: University of North Carolina Press, 2000); Elizabeth Fox-Genovese and Eugene D. Genovese, *The Mind of the Master Class: History and Faith in the Southern Slaveholders' Worldview* (Cambridge: Cambridge University Press, 2005).

10. Howard Temperley, *British Antislavery, 1833–1870* (London: Longman, 1972), 116–18.

11. Relatedly, Zach Sell, *Trouble of the World: Slavery and Empire in the Age of Capital* (Chapel Hill: University of North Carolina Press, 2021), 28–36. By contrast, on Northern and Brazilian discourses linking antislavery to capitalist modernization, see Roberto Saba, *American*

Mirror: The United States and Brazil in the Age of Emancipation (Princeton, NJ: Princeton University Press, 2021).

12. "Can the Slave Trade Be Suppressed?," *Economist*, 2 September 1848, 994.

13. "The Planter and Immigration," *Economist*, 18 May 1844, 807–8.

14. "The Planter and Immigration," 808. See also *Economist*, 6 June 1846, 729–30; 15 August 1846, 1051; 6 November 1847, 1270.

15. "A System of Free African Emigration," *Economist*, 13 November 1847, 1299.

16. "A System of Free African Emigration," 1299.

17. On the relationship between fixed conceptions of social development and nineteenth-century ideologies of imperial rule, see Uday Singh Mehta, *Liberalism and Empire: A Study in Nineteenth Century British Liberal Thought* (Chicago: University of Chicago Press, 1999); Jennifer Pitts, *A Turn to Empire, The Rise of Imperial Liberalism in Britain and France* (Princeton, NJ: Princeton University Press, 2005); Dipesh Chakrabarty, *Provincializing Europe: Postcolonial Thought and Historical Difference* (Princeton, NJ: Princeton University Press, 2008).

18. "Coolies at the Mauritius," *Friend of India*, 14 August 1845.

19. "Coolies at the Mauritius," *Friend of India*, 14 August 1845. See also "Coolies at the Mauritius," *Friend of India*, 21 August 1845.

20. "The Slave Trade and the West Indies," *Examiner*, 22 January 1848, 49.

21. "The Slave Trade and the West Indies," 49.

22. *Times*, 5 February 1848, 5.

23. This was one of several moments when the London press paid greater attention to the possibility of migration to the Caribbean than the actuality of migration to the Indian Ocean. For useful political context, see I. M. Cumpston, *Indians Overseas in British Territories, 1834–1854* (London: Oxford University Press, 1953), 127–37. On the indenturing of "liberated Africans" generally, see Monica Schuler, *"Alas, Alas, Kongo": A Social History of Indentured African Immigration into Jamaica, 1841–1865* (Baltimore: Johns Hopkins University Press, 1980); Beatriz G. Mamigonian, "In the Name of Freedom: Slave Trade Abolition, the Law and the Brazilian Branch of the African Emigration Scheme (Brazil-British West Indies, 1830s–1850s)," *Slavery & Abolition* 30, no. 1 (2009): 41–66; Padraic X. Scanlan, *Freedom's Debtors: British Antislavery in Sierra Leone in the Age of Revolution* (New Haven, CT: Yale University Press, 2017), 167–209; Jake Christopher Richards, "Anti-Slave-Trade Law, 'Liberated Africans' and the State in the South Atlantic World, c. 1839–1852," *Past & Present*, no. 241 (2018): 179–219.

24. *Hansard*, 3rd ser., xcvi, col. 18 (3 February 1848).

25. *Morning Chronicle*, 5 August 1851; *Morning Post*, 24 June 1852, 4; *Times*, 13 April 1850, 5. See also Drescher, *Mighty Experiment*, 34–53.

26. Bernard Semmel, *The Rise of Free Trade Imperialism: Classical Political Economy the Empire of Free Trade and Imperialism 1750–1850* (Cambridge: Cambridge University Press, 1970), 111.

27. *Morning Chronicle*, 5 August 1851.

28. *Morning Post*, 24 June 1852, 4.

29. *Morning Chronicle*, 5 August 1851.

30. *Times*, 13 April 1850, 5.

31. *Times*, 13 April 1850, 5.

32. "The Future of the West Indies," *Spectator*, 12 February 1848, 152. See also "Anti-Slavery and Free Trade," *Spectator*, 3 June 1848, 538.

33. Frederick Cooper, *From Slaves to Squatters: Plantation Labor and Agriculture in Zanzibar and Coastal Kenya, 1890–1925* (New Haven, CT: Yale University Press, 1980), 29–31; Drescher,

Mighty Experiment, 217–18; Thomas C. Holt, *The Problem of Freedom: Race, Labor, and Politics in Jamaica and Britain, 1832–1938* (Baltimore: Johns Hopkins University Press, 1992), 278–86; Natasha Lightfoot, *Troubling Freedom: Antigua and the Aftermath of British Emancipation* (Durham, NC: Duke University Press, 2015), 183–93.

34. Dror Wahrman, *The Making of the Modern Self: Identity and Culture in Eighteenth-Century Britain* (New Haven, CT: Yale University Press, 2004); Roxann Wheeler, *The Complexion of Race: Categories of Difference in Eighteenth-Century England* (Philadelphia: University of Pennsylvania Press, 2000); Nicholas Hudson, "From 'Nation' to 'Race': The Origin of Racial Classification in Eighteenth-Century Thought," *Eighteenth-Century Studies* 29, no. 3 (1996): 247–64.

35. Michael Banton, *Racial Theories*, rev. ed. (Cambridge: Cambridge University Press, 1998); Philip D. Curtin, *The Image of Africa, British Ideas and Action, 1780–1850* (Madison: University of Wisconsin Press, 1973), chaps. 2, 15; George Mosse, *Toward the Final Solution: A History of European Racism* (New York: H. Fertig, 1978), 65–76; Nancy Stepan, *The Idea of Race in Science: Great Britain 1800–1960* (London: Macmillan, 1982).

36. Catherine Hall, *Civilising Subjects: Metropole and Colony in the English Imagination, 1830–1867* (Chicago: University of Chicago Press, 2002), 174–208; Richard Price, *Making Empire: Colonial Encounters and the Creation of Imperial Rule in Nineteenth-Century Africa* (Cambridge: Cambridge University Press, 2008); Andrew C. Ross, "Christian Missions and Mid-Nineteenth-Century Change in Attitudes to Race: The African Experience," in *The Imperial Horizons of British Protestant Missions*, ed. Andrew Porter (Grand Rapids, MI: Eerdmans, 2003), 85–105.

37. Karuna Mantena, *Alibis of Empire: Henry Maine and the Ends of Liberal Imperialism* (Princeton, NJ: Princeton University Press, 2010), and "The Crisis of Liberal Imperialism," in *Victorian Visions of Global Order: Empire and International Relations in Nineteenth-Century Political Thought*, ed. Duncan Bell (Cambridge: Cambridge University Press, 2007); Thomas R. Metcalf, *Ideologies of the Raj* (Cambridge: Cambridge University Press, 1995), 43–65; Christine Bolt, *Victorian Attitudes to Race* (London: Routledge, 1971), 75–108; Hall, *Civilising Subjects*, 209–64; Holt, *Problem of Freedom*, 263–309.

38. Stuart Hall, "Race, Articulation, and Societies Structured in Dominance," in *Black British Cultural Studies: A Reader*, ed. Houston A. Baker Jr. et al. (Chicago: University of Chicago Press, 1996), 18. Hall's term "sociological" reflects an effort to speak across the social sciences; within the discipline of history, his point refers to revisionist rejections of orthodox Marxism and the subsequent "cultural turn."

39. On the study of "race relations" apart from economic and political life, see Rebecca J. Scott, *Degrees of Freedom: Louisiana and Cuba after Slavery* (Cambridge, MA: Harvard University Press, 2005), 1–2; Karen E. Fields and Barbara J. Fields, *Racecraft: The Soul of Inequality in American Life* (London: Verso, 2012), chaps. 4–5.

40. As modeled by Frederick Cooper, Thomas C. Holt, and Rebecca J. Scott in *Beyond Slavery: Explorations of Race, Labor, and Citizenship in Postemancipation Societies* (Chapel Hill: University of North Carolina Press, 2000).

41. Hall, "Race, Articulation, and Societies Structured in Dominance," 52.

42. Anthony J. Barker, *The African Link: British Attitudes to the Negro in the Era of the Atlantic Slave Trade* (London: Frank Cass, 1978); Winthrop D. Jordan, *White over Black: American Attitudes toward the Negro 1550–1812*, 2nd ed. (Chapel Hill: University of North Carolina Press, 2012); Trevor Burnard, *Mastery, Tyranny, and Desire: Thomas Thistlewood and His Slaves in the Anglo-Jamaican World* (Chapel Hill: University of North Carolina Press, 2005), 129–36; Jennifer L.

Morgan, *Laboring Women: Reproduction and Gender in New World Slavery* (Pennsylvania: University of Pennsylvania Press, 2004), esp. 12–49.

43. Long, a Jamaican proprietor and early proponent of polygenesis, published a three-volume *History of Jamaica* (London, 1774). Of sustained interest to scholars of Caribbean slavery and the history of racism, Long is the subject of new work by Catherine Hall, *Edward Long and Lucky Valley: Racial Capitalism and the History of Jamaica* (forthcoming).

44. Inasmuch as this perceived failure was conceived in relation to an emerging capitalist norm of "free" wage labor, this argument and much other work on the history of British emancipation potentially speaks to a growing literature on racial capitalism, particularly as such work continues to expand beyond the primarily US context in which interest in the concept was initially revived. For a sense of these possibilities and an argument that does explicitly connect imperial discourses around Indian labor to the notion of racial capitalism, see Destin Jenkins and Justin Leroy, "Introduction: The Old History of Capitalism," and Mishal Khan, "The Indebted among the 'Free': Producing Indian Labor through the Layers of Racial Capitalism," both in *Histories of Racial Capitalism*, ed. Destin Jenkins and Justin Leroy (New York: Columbia University Press, 2021), 1–26, 85–110.

45. *Morning Chronicle*, 30 September 1850; *Morning Chronicle*, 5 August 1851.

46. Thomas Carlyle, "Occasional Discourse on the Negro Question," *Fraser's Magazine* 40 (1849), 670–79. See also Hall, *Civilising Subjects*, 347–63.

47. *Times*, 5 February 1848, 5.

48. *Times*, 5 February 1848, 5.

49. *Times*, 18 July 1857, 9.

50. *Times*, 29 July 1839, 4.

51. *Times*, 18 July 1857, 9.

52. David Northrup, *Indentured Labor in the Age of Imperialism, 1834–1922* (Cambridge: Cambridge University Press, 1995), 159.

53. Alan H. Adamson, *Sugar Without Slaves: The Political Economy of British Guiana, 1838–1904* (New Haven, CT: Yale University Press, 1972), 178; Noël Deerr, *The History of Sugar*, 2 vols. (London: Chapman and Hall, 1949–50), 2:531.

54. Higginson to Labouchere, 31 May 1856, No. 94, CO 167/376; Higginson to Labouchere, 13 June 1857, No. 116, CO 167/387.

55. Sutherland to Newcastle, 22 July 1854, No. 61, CO 167/359; Stevenson to Bulwer Lytton, 26 August 1858, No. 187, CO 167/402. The figure given for 1852 (£1,110,546) is total revenue, including other goods and specie, while the figures given for 1856 and 1857 are sugar revenue only. But the vast majority of export revenue in Mauritius was sugar revenue. In 1856, total export revenue was £1,804,123, and in 1857 it was £2,303,786.

56. Keate to Bulwer Lytton, 26 September 1858, No. 131, CO 295/200.

57. Some 6,672 indentured Indians arrived in Jamaica between 1845 and 1860, as compared with 38,561 in British Guiana. Walton Look Lai, *Indentured Labor, Caribbean Sugar: Chinese and Indian Migrants to the British West Indies, 1838–1918* (Baltimore: Johns Hopkins University Press, 1993), 276. Jamaican sugar production decreased from 71,584 tons in 1832 to 31,366 tons in 1848. Deerr, *History of Sugar*, 2:366.

58. *Morning Post*, 29 December 1857, 4.

59. On this conception of free labor, see Kale, *Fragments of Empire*, 5 ("free labor was, for capitalists, mobile labor"); Adam M. McKeown, *Melancholy Order: Asian Migration and the Globalization of Borders* (New York: Columbia University Press, 2008), 72.

60. *Hansard*, 3rd ser., clii, col. 1227 (3 March 1859). The *Morning Chronicle* also cited Mauritius as evidence of the importance of immigration. *Morning Chronicle*, 30 September 1850; 10 August 1860.

61. *Morning Post*, 24 June 1854, 4; 27 September 1854, 4; 16 August 1855, 4; 24 December 1857, 4; 29 December 1857, 4; 2 January 1858, 4; 29 January 1859, 4; 31 January 1859, 4.

62. *Standard*, 10 January 1860, 4. See also *Standard*, 27 January 1859, 4.

63. *Anti-Slavery Reporter*, 1 July 1857, 165; 1 August 1857, 177; 1 September 1857, 209–11; "Immigration to the West Indies," 1 February 1859, 32–39; "Revival of the Slave-Trade," 1 August 1859, 183–84.

64. *Daily News*, 4 July 1857; 21 July 1857; 30 December 1857; 7 September 1858; 31 January 1859; 25 October 1859; 9 January 1860.

65. *Daily News*, 31 January 1859.

66. *Daily News*, 31 January 1859.

67. McKeown, *Melancholy Order*, 14.

68. My argument about moralization implicitly engages a Marxian conception of ideology of longstanding interest to scholars of law and society. There is no single "Marxist" theory of ideology, since Marx himself never defined the term and generations of subsequent interpreters have elaborated a variety of different meanings. See John Torrance, *Karl Marx's Theory of Ideas* (Cambridge: Cambridge University Press, 1995), 1–28, 191. However, in *The German Ideology*, Marx suggested, in terms that went beyond his immediate polemic against philosophical idealism, that ideology serves to legitimate "ruling ideas," specifically by reframing the particular interests of the ruling class "as the common interest of all the members of society." *The Marx-Engels Reader*, 2nd ed., ed. Robert C. Tucker (New York: Norton, 1978), 172–74. Such a reframing is false or "illusory" in Marx's view; it obscures the true nature of social relations. *Marx-Engels Reader*, 161. The idea that legal ideology conceals and legitimates—that it "masks" class structure by representing itself in universal terms—remains important to the social history of law even as scholars rightly refuse to *reduce* law to that function alone. See, for an influential example, E. P. Thompson, *Whigs and Hunters: The Origin of the Black Act* (New York: Pantheon Books, 1975). My argument about interest and order affirms one possible reading of Marx on ideology, in that it demonstrates a process of translation that reframed particular economic interests as the general or common interest. Like Marx, I view such translation as masking the reality of social relations in the colonies. But I do not see this process as a mere reflection of clearly defined "ruling ideas," or as an intentional attempt by colonial officials to use the law for their personal gain. Instead, I see it in linguistic terms as a prevailing discourse, centered on notions of civilization and order, which structured official thinking. We might consider this a form of limited hegemony, espoused by a range of British thinkers, some but not all of whom stood to gain directly by plantation production, while acknowledging that such thinking was brought to bear on a colonial world in which consent played only a minor role in legitimating governance. See Ranajit Guha, *Dominance Without Hegemony: History and Power in Colonial India* (Cambridge, MA: Harvard University Press, 1997) (on rule without consent), and Lauren Benton, *Law and Colonial Cultures: Legal Regimes in World History, 1400–1900* (Cambridge: Cambridge University Press, 2002), 254–62 (on Guha as a response to Thompson's *Whigs and Hunters*).

69. Higginson to Pakington, 17 June 1852, No. 320, CO 167/336.

70. British Guiana Ordinance No. 3 of 1853, CO 113/2; Barkly to Newcastle, 11 February 1853, CO 111/293.

71. Newcastle to Barkly, 14 May 1853, PP, 1852–53, lxviii (986), 115–18. On the disallowance of Ordinance No. 3, see also Newcastle to Walker, 16 January 1854, No. 175, PP, 1859, xvi (2452), 1–4.

72. Draft Immigration Act, § 17, enclosed in Newcastle to Wodehouse, 10 March 1854, PP, 1859, xvi (2452), 13–17.

73. Draft Immigration Act, § 17. The commutation fee was five pounds sterling after the third year or two pounds ten shillings after the fourth.

74. Draft Immigration Act, §§ 27, 29.

75. Elliot to Grey, 20 February 1855, No. 18, CO 295/187; British Guiana Ordinance No. 7 of 1854, CO 113/3; Wodehouse to Newcastle, 7 June 1854, CO 111/300.

76. Newcastle to Walker, 16 January 1854, No. 175, PP, 1859, xvi (2452), 1–4.

77. Minute by B. Peacock, 18 July 1853, IOR F/4/2534, No. 146,926. See also Government of India to the Court of Directors, 2 September 1853, Legislative No. 16, IOR F/4/2534, No. 146,926.

78. Government of India to the Court of Directors, 11 February 1853, Legislative No. 1, IOR F/4/2485, No. 142038 (responding to proposal from Mauritius to abolish the right of free return passage and agreeing with respect to new immigrants); Government of India to the Court of Directors, 30 April 1852, No. 8, IOR L/PJ/3/291 (confirming decision).

79. Petition from the Chamber of Agriculture to the Duke of Newcastle, 3 April 1854, enclosed in Sutherland to Newcastle, 2 August 1854, No. 61a, CO 167/360.

80. Sutherland to Grey, 8 January 1855, No. 7, CO 167/366.

81. Sutherland to Grey, 8 January 1855.

82. Wodehouse to Newcastle, 7 June 1854, No. 21, CO 111/300.

83. Christopher Leslie Brown, *Moral Capital: Foundations of British Abolitionism* (Chapel Hill: University of North Carolina Press, 2006), 209–58; Lauren Benton and Lisa Ford, *Rage for Order: The British Empire and the Origins of International Law, 1800–1850* (Cambridge, MA: Harvard University Press, 2016), esp. 1–55.

84. Benton and Ford, *Rage for Order*, 28–55; Lauren Benton and Lisa Ford, "Island Despotism: Trinidad, the British Imperial Constitution and Global Legal Order," *Journal of Imperial and Commonwealth History* 46, no. 1 (2018): 21–46.

85. Diana Paton, *No Bond but the Law: Punishment, Race, and Gender in Jamaican State Formation, 1780–1870* (Durham, NC: Duke University Press, 2004), 2. Relatedly, see Clare Anderson, "After Emancipation: Empires and Imperial Formations," in *Emancipation and the Remaking of the British Imperial World*, ed. Catherine Hall, Nicholas Draper, and Keith McClelland (Manchester: Manchester University Press, 2014), 120–21.

86. Order in Council, 15 January 1842, § 18, enclosed in Stanley to Light, 22 January 1842, PP, 1842, xxx (26), 34–7.

87. Order in Council, 15 January 1842, § 18. See also Mongia, *Indian Migration and Empire*, 57.

88. See chapter 2, esp. p. 43.

89. Marina Carter, *Servants, Sirdars and Settlers: Indians in Mauritius, 1834–1874* (Delhi: Oxford University Press, 1995), 154–59.

90. Amit Kumar Mishra, "Sardars, Kanganies and Maistries: Intermediaries in the Indian Labour Diaspora during the Colonial Period," in *The History of Labour Intermediation: Institutions and Finding Employment in the Nineteenth and Early Twentieth Centuries*, ed. Sigrid Wadauer et al. (London: Berghahn, 2015).

91. Crispin Bates and Marina Carter, "Sirdars as Intermediaries in Nineteenth-Century Indian Ocean Indentured Labour Migration," *Modern Asian Studies* 51, no. 2 (2017): 462–84.

92. Bates and Carter, "Sirdars as Intermediaries," 471.

93. Petition from the Chamber of Agriculture to the Duke of Newcastle, 3 April 1854, enclosed in Sutherland to Newcastle, 2 August 1854, No. 61a, CO 167/360.

94. Mauritius Ordinance No. 9 of 1851, CO 169/9; Mauritius Ordinance No. 15 of 1854, CO 169/10.

95. Both laws called for the governor to apportion new immigrants in relation to past sugar production. Thus larger plantations would be entitled from the outset to hire a greater number of immigrants than smaller plantations. Mauritius Ordinance No. 9 of 1851, § 3, CO 169/9; Mauritius Ordinance No. 15 of 1854, § 3, CO 169/10.

96. Mauritius Ordinance No. 30 of 1858, CO 169/12.

97. Mauritius Ordinance No. 30 of 1858, § I.

98. Mauritius Ordinance No. 30 of 1858, § XIII.

99. Melvill to Merivale, 7 July 1859, No. 4336 (draft response), IOR L/PJ/2/4.

100. Governor Stevenson, Proclamation, 12 November 1858 (stating regulations issued under Ordinance No. 30 of 1858), § XXIX, CO 169/12.

101. Governor Stevenson, Proclamation, 12 November 1858, §§ LIII, LIV.

102. Mauritius Ordinance No. 65 of 1860, CO 169/12; "Report of the Procureur General, W. G. Dickson, on Ordinance No. 65," 31 January 1861, enclosed in Stevenson to Newcastle, 1 March 1861, No. 38, CO 167/427.

103. Petition from the Chamber of Agriculture to the Duke of Newcastle, 3 April 1854, enclosed in Sutherland to Newcastle, 2 August 1854, No. 61a, CO 167/360.

104. Bascom to Hincks, 19 June 1862, enclosed in Hincks to Newcastle, 23 June 1862, No. 103, CO 111/335. Bascom was a planter and an elected member of British Guiana's Combined Court.

105. Bascom to Hincks, 19 June 1862.

106. British Guiana Ordinance No. 7 of 1854, § 19, CO 113/3; British Guiana Ordinance No. 1 of 1860, §§ 6, 7, 38, CO 113/3. Mauritius Ordinance No. 65 of 1860, CO 169/12; "Report of the Procureur General, W. G. Dickson, on Ordinance No. 65," 31 January 1861, enclosed in Stevenson to Newcastle, 1 March 1861, No. 38, CO 167/427.

107. Trinidad Ordinance No. 16 of 1862, § XXV, CO 297/7.

108. Stevenson to Labouchere, 30 January 1858, No. 22, CO 167/394.

109. Governor Stevenson, Proclamation, 12 November 1858, §§ XLII, LIX, CO 169/12. Such efforts call to mind what were perhaps parallel efforts developed in the United States and elsewhere to minimize the role played by non-state brokers in Asian (specifically Chinese) migration during the late nineteenth century. McKeown, *Melancholy Order*, 10, 249–58. Yet in Mauritius, sirdars continued to play an important role in spite of state efforts, particularly as Indian migrants, now settlers, began to purchase land during the 1860s. See Bates and Carter, "Sirdars as Intermediaries," 480–81.

110. Wodehouse to Newcastle, 25 February 1860, No. 31, CO 111/326.

111. This paragraph derives from Alessandro Stanziani, *Bondage: Labor and Rights in Eurasia from the Sixteenth to the Early Twentieth Centuries* (New York: Berghahn, 2014), 187, 181–91. On *engagement* in Senegal and Madagascar, see Kelly Brignac, "African Indentured Labor in Senegal and Ste. Marie, Madagascar, 1817–1830," *Slavery & Abolition* 43, no. 4 (2022): 779–97.

112. Bernard to Elliot, 20 May 1856, enclosed in Elliot to Labouchere, 6 July 1856, No. 59, CO 295/192.

113. Elliot to Labouchere, 6 July 1856, No. 59, CO 295/192.

114. See for example Wodehouse to Labouchere, 10 July 1856, No. 89, CO 111/311 (arguing that transportation regulations were more stringent for British rather than French colonies); Wodehouse to Labouchere, 13 August 1856, No. 104, CO 111/312 (forwarding resolutions drafted at a public meeting in British Guiana, complaining of "the advantages enjoyed by the French West

Indian Colonies in respect to the number of Immigrants permitted to be carried in each vessel"); Wodehouse to Newcastle, 23 March 1860, No. 48, CO 111/327 (arguing that concessions made to the French, particularly the five-year contract, should be conceded to the British colonies); Wodehouse to Newcastle, 8 December 1860, No. 135, CO 111/328 (arguing that French colonies were allowed a more favorable [lower] ratio of women to men among Indian immigrants, and that the British colonies should be granted a similar privilege).

115. Government of India to the Court of Directors, 4 May 1853, Legislative No. 5, IOR/F/4/2534, No. 146,910.

116. On this 1850s surge in migration, see Alessandro Stanziani, *Sailors, Slaves, and Immigrants: Bondage in the Indian Ocean World, 1750–1914* (New York: Palgrave, 2014), 101.

117. Russell to Rogers, 15 September 1859, enclosed in Hammond to Clerk, 19 September 1859, IOR L/PJ/2/7. See also Russell to Cowley, 24 December 1859, enclosed in Hammond to Clerk, 28 December 1859, IOR L/PJ/2/7. For new insight into the French illegal slave trade, see Joseph la Hausse de Lalouvière, "A Business Archive of the French Illegal Slave Trade in the Nineteenth Century," *Past & Present*, no. 252 (2021): 139–77.

118. Russell to Cowley, 2 February 1861, enclosed in Hammond to Merivale, 7 February 1861, IOR L/PJ/2/132.

119. On Britain's antislavery foreign policy, see Leslie Bethell, *The Abolition of the Brazilian Slave Trade* (Cambridge: Cambridge University Press, 1970), 88–266; Eltis, *Economic Growth*, 81–122; Huzzey, *Freedom Burning*, 51–74; Jenny S. Martinez, *The Slave Trade and the Origins of International Human Rights Law* (Oxford: Oxford University Press, 2012), 22–37.

120. Richards, "Anti-Slave-Trade Law," 183–85; Mamigonian, "In the Name of Freedom," 42–4; Bethell, *Abolition*, 155–66, 242–84.

121. The final convention did not mention African migration explicitly. But after its ratification, Napoleon III issued a separate declaration, dated 1 July 1862, prohibiting the practices at issue. Wodehouse to Merivale, 31 July 1861, IOR L/PJ/2/132.

122. "Convention between Her Majesty and the Emperor of the French, relative to the Emigration of Labourers from India to the Colony of Réunion, ratified 10 August 1860," The National Archives, London, Foreign Office Records (hereafter FO) 881/448A.

123. "Convention between Her Majesty and the Emperor of the French," § IX.

124. "Convention between Her Majesty and the Emperor of the French," § XV.

125. Rogers to Malmesbury, 31 December 1858, enclosed in Hammond to Merivale, 6 January 1859, CO 318/222.

126. Rogers to Malmesbury, 31 December 1858.

127. Grey, Minute, 7 April 1849, CO 295/166, ff. 199–206, discussed in chapter 2, p. 53.

128. Stevenson to Newcastle, 1 May 1862, No. 81, CO 167/439.

129. Stevenson to Newcastle, 1 May 1862.

130. British Guiana Ordinance No. 30 of 1862, CO 113/4; Trinidad Ordinance No. 23 of 1862, CO 297/7.

131. Stevenson to Newcastle, 1 May 1862, No. 81, CO 167/439. The same was true in Trinidad and British Guiana. See Keate to Newcastle, 20 December 1862, No. 211, CO 295/220; and Hincks to Newcastle, 19 January 1863, No. 19, CO 111/339.

132. Alan Watson, *Legal Transplants: An Approach to Comparative Law*, 2nd ed. (Athens: University of Georgia Press, 1993); Alan Watson, *Slave Law in the Americas* (Athens: University of Georgia Press, 1989).

133. Watson, *Legal Transplants*, esp. 107–18.

134. Renisa Mawani and Iza Hussin, “The Travels of Law: Indian Ocean Itineraries,” *Law and History Review* 32, no. 4 (2014): 733–47; Renisa Mawani, *Across Oceans of Law: The Komagata Maru and Jurisdiction in the Time of Empire* (Durham, NC: Duke University Press, 2018), esp. 6–14.

135. Mawani and Hussin, “Travels of Law,” engaging explicitly with Tony Ballantyne, “Race and the Webs of Empire: Aryanism from India to the Pacific,” *Journal of Colonialism and Colonial History* 2, no. 3 (2001); Metcalf, *Imperial Connections*; Kerry Ward, *Networks of Empire: Forced Migration in the Dutch East India Company* (Cambridge: Cambridge University Press, 2009).

136. On the movement of imperial officials across multiple colonies, see David Lambert and Alan Lester, eds., *Colonial Lives Across the Empire: Imperial Careering in the Long Nineteenth Century* (Cambridge: Cambridge University Press, 2006); Hall, *Civilising Subjects*, 23–65; Zoë Laidlaw, *Colonial Connections 1815–45: Patronage, the Information Revolution and Colonial Government* (Manchester: Manchester University Press, 2005), 13–57; Benton and Ford, *Rage for Order*, 15–16. Relatedly, Ward, *Networks of Empire*, 24.

137. For detailed treatment, see Jonathan Connolly, “Antislavery, ‘Native Labour,’ and the Turn to Indenture in British Colonial Natal, 1842–1860,” *Comparative Studies in Society and History* 65, no. 3 (2023): 500–525.

138. Rogers to Merivale, 19 February 1856, CO 179/44.

139. Scott to Bulwer Lytton, 28 June 1859, No. 51, CO 179/51. Natal’s laws were numbered 13, 14, and 15 of 1859. They were modeled on Mauritius Ordinance No. 23 of 1857, St. Lucia Ordinances No. 3 of 1854 and No. 2 of 1857, and Mauritius Ordinance No. 12 of 1855.

140. Scott to Bulwer Lytton, 28 June 1859, No. 51, CO 179/51.

141. Minute, 28 October 1859, CO 179/51 (summarily approving Natal Laws Nos. 13, 14, and 15 of 1859).

142. Deerr, *History of Sugar*, 2:531. “Hundredweight,” abbreviated “cwt,” was a unit of measure equivalent in this context to 112 lb.

143. Adamson, *Sugar Without Slaves*, 178; Deerr, *History of Sugar*, 2:531.

144. Deerr, *History of Sugar*, 2:531.

145. Stevenson to Bulwer Lytton, 26 August 1858, No. 187, CO 167/402. This assertion is based on rough estimates that showed 39,300 acres devoted to sugar planting in 1851 and between 75,000 and 90,000 acres so devoted in 1857.

146. Look Lai, *Indentured Labor, Caribbean Sugar*, 275.

147. Look Lai, *Indentured Labor, Caribbean Sugar*, 275.

148. Trinidad’s average annual production for the years 1826, 1828, 1829, 1832, and 1834 was 39,438,813 lb. The parallel average for the years 1847–1851 was higher, at 42,644,908 lb. Harris to Pakington, 7 August 1852, No. 49, CO 295/178.

149. “Return of articles exported from the Colony during the years 1852, 1853, and 1854,” enclosed in Elliot to Russell, 1 June 1855, No. 50, CO 295/188.

150. Keate to Newcastle, 9 August 1859, No. 123, CO 295/205.

151. Report of the Agent General of Immigrants, 1 June 1859, enclosed in Keate to Newcastle, 9 August 1859, No. 123, CO 295/205. This estimate by the Agent General assumes a production level of roughly 40,000 hogsheads annually, compared with roughly 20,000 produced in 1842. The year 1858 was exceptional, however. Comparing 1842 production with that of 1857 would produce an estimated increase of closer to 75 percent. See Mitchell to Johnston, 1 June 1858, enclosed in Keate to Bulwer Lytton, 26 September 1858, No. 131, CO 295/200.

152. British Guiana Blue Book for 1844, CO 116/213.

153. British Guiana Blue Book for 1852, CO 116/221; British Guiana Blue Book for 1854, CO 116/223.

154. Hincks to Newcastle, 4 February 1862, No. 12, CO 111/334. For additional statistics showing the increase in sugar production in British Guiana and Trinidad, see Deerr, *History of Sugar*, 2:377; J. H. Galloway, *The Sugar Cane Industry: An Historical Geography from Its Origins to 1914* (Cambridge: Cambridge University Press, 1989), 151.

155. Richard Allen, *Slaves, Freedmen, and Indentured Laborers in Colonial Mauritius* (Cambridge: Cambridge University Press, 1999), 23.

156. Higginson to Labouchere, 31 May 1856, No. 94, CO 167/376.

157. Stevenson to Newcastle, 6 August 1860, No. 132, CO 167/422.

158. Allen, *Slaves, Freedmen, and Indentured Laborers*, 23. According to Allen's calculations, Mauritius produced 8.6 percent of the world's cane sugar between 1855 and 1859, and 9 percent between 1860 and 1864.

159. Sutherland to Newcastle, 22 July 1854, No. 61, CO 167/359; Higginson to Labouchere, 31 May 1856, No. 94, CO 167/376; Stevenson to Bulwer Lytton, 18 June 1859, No. 91, CO 167/411. These figures refer to total export revenue, including specie, not just sugar revenue. But sugar was by far the most significant component of total revenue. In 1856, for example, sugar revenue was £1,687,826 while total revenue was £1,804,123. Stevenson to Bulwer Lytton, 26 August 1858, No. 187, CO 167/402.

160. Stevenson to Newcastle, 6 August 1860, No. 132, CO 167/422.

161. Keate to Bulwer Lytton, 26 September 1858, No. 131, CO 295/200.

162. British Guiana Blue Book for 1848, CO 116/217.

163. British Guiana Blue Book for 1855, CO 116/224.

164. Hincks to Newcastle, 28 July 1862, No. 140, CO 111/335. These increases reflect higher prices, not just increased production. In 1848, Guiana produced 46,914 hogsheads, versus 62,198 hogsheads in 1860. Thus, while production increased by roughly 30 percent, revenue nearly doubled.

165. See chapter 3, pp. 76–77.

166. In Mauritius, for example, revenue increased by more than £350,000 between 1856 and 1857 even though raw production declined in the latter year. Stevenson to Bulwer Lytton, 26 August 1858, No. 187, CO 167/402.

167. Higginson to Labouchere, 13 June 1857, No. 116, CO 167/388.

168. Deerr, *History of Sugar*, 2:377.

169. *Voyages: The Trans-Atlantic Slave Trade Database*, http://www.slavevoyages.org/assessment/estimates (accessed July 10, 2023) (estimating that 468,575 enslaved Africans arrived in Cuba between 1831 and 1870). On the expansion of slavery and the intensification of sugar production in Cuba, see Ada Ferrer, *Freedom's Mirror: Cuba and Haiti in the Age of Revolution* (Cambridge: Cambridge University Press, 2014), 17–43; Franklin W. Knight, *Slave Society in Cuba during the Nineteenth Century* (Madison: University of Wisconsin Press, 1970), 3–22; Manuel Moreno Fraginals, *El ingenio: Complejo económico-social cubano del azúcar*, 3 vols., rev. ed. (Havana: Editorial de Sciencias Sociales, 2014); Rebecca J. Scott, *Slave Emancipation in Cuba: The Transition to Free Labor, 1860–1899* (Princeton, NJ: Princeton University Press, 1985), 3–41.

170. On this point, see Dale W. Tomich, *Through the Prism of Slavery: Labor, Capital, and World Economy* (Lanham, MD: Rowman & Littlefield, 2004), 56–71 (describing the growth of slave production in Cuba, the United States, and Brazil during the nineteenth century as a "second slavery"); Ferrer, *Freedom's Mirror*, 12–13. On the concept of "second slavery," see also

Dale W. Tomich, ed., *The Politics of the Second Slavery* (Albany: State University of New York Press, 2016); Dale Tomich, "The Second Slavery and World Capitalism: A Perspective for Historical Inquiry," *International Review of Social History* 63, no. 3 (2018): 477–501.

171. This assertion is based on the following figures: 16,796 Indians arrived in 1852; 11,674 in 1853; 16,318 in 1854; 12,915 in 1855; and 13,723 in 1857. Sutherland to Newcastle, 22 July 1854, No. 61, CO 167/359; Hay to Herbert, 3 May 1855, No. 60, CO 167/367; Higginson to Labouchere, 31 May 1856, No. 94, CO 167/376; Stevenson to Bulwer Lytton, 26 August 1858, No. 187, CO 167/402. Immigration to Mauritius was temporarily suspended in 1856 because of disease outbreaks attributed to the colony's quarantine policy.

172. Stevenson to Bulwer Lytton, 6 May 1859, No. 68, CO 167/411; Stevenson to Newcastle, 5 March 1860, No. 42, CO 167/419.

173. Look Lai, *Indentured Labor, Caribbean Sugar*, 276.

174. Northrup, *Indentured Labor*, 162. Emigration "seasons" did not correspond with calendar years. The figure above refers to two seasons, 1858–59 and 1859–60, that is, to two rather than three years of migration.

175. Higginson to Labouchere, 13 June 1857, No. 116, CO 167/388.

176. Stevenson to Newcastle, 6 August 1860, No. 132, CO 167/422.

177. Stevenson to Bulwer Lytton, 26 August 1858, No. 187, CO 167/402.

178. Report of the Agent General of Immigrants (Henry Mitchell), 1 June 1859, enclosed in Keate to Newcastle, 9 August 1859, No. 123, CO 295/205. To account for labor consistency, Mitchell tallied not only the number of workers employed but also the number of days worked during the month according to group. My figures are based on this tally, which showed 115,370 days worked by Indians, 64,812 by Trinidad Creoles, 71,162 by immigrant Creoles, 49,285 by Africans, and 7,588 by Chinese. In other words, immigrant workers provided the great majority of plantation labor at this point, and Indians were the largest single immigrant group. Some of the "immigrant Creoles" or West Indian immigrants recorded as working in March 1858 (during the harvest) did not live in the colony permanently and did not arrive under indenture. Indian, African, and Chinese migrants did.

179. Higginson to Earl Grey, 15 May 1852, No. 297, CO 167/335.

180. Barkly to Pakington, 21 April 1852, No. 86, CO 111/289.

181. Harris to Grey, 21 February 1848, No. 21, CO 295/160.

182. Harris to Pakington, 7 August 1852, No. 49, CO 295/178.

183. General Immigration Report for 1857, 20 January 1858, enclosed in Keate to Labouchere, 11 February 1858, No. 11, CO 295/198.

184. Kale, *Fragments of Empire*, 7, 59.

185. Elliot to Labouchere, 5 May 1856, No. 40, CO 295/191.

186. Higginson to Labouchere, 15 November 1856, No. 199, CO 167/379.

Chapter 5

1. See chapter 1, pp. 34–37.

2. *Morning Post*, 2 January 1858, 4.

3. *Morning Chronicle*, 26 December 1839; 19 March 1840; 13 May 1840; 27 June 1840; 2 January 1841; 8 February 1842. See also Madhavi Kale, *Fragments of Empire: Capital, Slavery, and Indian Indentured Labor Migration in the British Caribbean* (Philadelphia: University of Pennsylvania Press, 1998), 54–55.

4. Radhika Mongia, *Indian Migration and Empire: A Colonial Genealogy of the Modern State* (Durham, NC: Duke University Press, 2018), 53. Relatedly, I. M. Cumpston, *Indians Overseas in British Territories, 1834–1854* (London: Oxford University Press, 1953), 40–42 (on the Indian official Major Archer's 1840 pamphlet "Free Labour versus Slave Labour").

5. On increasing sugar production in Cuba between 1820 and 1865, see David Eltis, *Economic Growth and the Ending of the Transatlantic Slave Trade* (Oxford: Oxford University Press, 1987), 190, 285; J. H. Galloway, *The Sugar Cane Industry: An Historical Geography from Its Origins to 1914* (Cambridge: Cambridge University Press, 1989), 159, 162–68; Manuel Moreno Fraginals, *El ingenio: Complejo económico-social cubano del azúcar*, 3 vols., rev. ed. (Havana: Editorial de Sciencias Sociales, 2014), 1:165–75, 3:1–64; Dale W. Tomich, *Through the Prism of Slavery: Labor, Capital, and World Economy* (Lanham, MD: Rowman & Littlefield, 2004), 64–65, 75–94.

6. *Times*, 22 February 1859, 9. The *Morning Post* also criticized the Society on antislavery grounds, stating, in 1859, that it was "clearly the interest of the Anti-Slavery Society to promote [indenture] as the very best means of successfully combating and finally destroying, not only the slave trade, but slavery itself." *Morning Post*, 29 January 1859, 4.

7. West India Committee, "Memorandum relative to Immigration into British Guiana and Trinidad," 6 June 1860, WIC, M 915, Reel 7.

8. Stephen Cave, "The West Indian Labour Question," in *Transactions of the National Association for the Promotion of Social Science*, 1858, ed. George W. Hastings (London, 1859), 704. On the National Association for the Promotion of Social Science, see Laurence Goldman, *Science, Reform and Politics in Victorian Britain: The Social Science Association, 1857–1886* (Cambridge: Cambridge University Press, 2002).

9. Ada Ferrer, *Freedom's Mirror: Cuba and Haiti in the Age of Revolution* (Cambridge: Cambridge University Press, 2014).

10. Tomich, *Through the Prism of Slavery*, 56–94. On Cuba, see Rebecca J. Scott, *Slave Emancipation in Cuba: The Transition to Free Labor, 1860–1899* (Princeton, NJ: Princeton University Press, 1985), 3–41; Ada Ferrer, "Cuban Slavery and Atlantic Antislavery," in *Slavery and Antislavery in Spain's Atlantic Empire*, ed. Josep M. Fradera and Christopher Schmidt-Nowara (New York: Berghahn, 2013), 134–57. On the United States, see Sven Beckert, *Empire of Cotton: A Global History* (New York: Knopf, 2014), 98–135; Walter Johnson, *River of Dark Dreams: Slavery and Empire in the Cotton Kingdom* (Cambridge, MA: Belknap, 2013), 22–47, 244–302. On the persistence of the illegal slave trade in this period, see Leonardo Marques, *The United States and the Transatlantic Slave Trade to the Americas, 1776–1867* (New Haven, CT: Yale University Press, 2016).

11. *Morning Post*, 29 January 1859, 4.

12. *Hansard*, 3rd ser., clii, col. 1235 (3 March 1859).

13. *Hansard*, 3rd ser., clii, col. 1232 (3 March 1859).

14. For a useful recapitulation of antislavery arguments concerning the economic superiority of free over slave labor, see *Proceedings of the General Anti-slavery Convention: called by the Committee of the British and Foreign Anti-slavery Society, and held in London, from Friday, June 12th, to Tuesday, June 23rd, 1840* (London, 1841), 334–62, esp. 335 ("The superiority of free over slave-labour, is a fact now so generally known, and the evidence on which it rests is so indisputable, that your committee think it needless to occupy the time of the Convention."). See also Seymour Drescher, *The Mighty Experiment: Free Labor versus Slavery in British Emancipation* (Oxford: Oxford University Press, 2002), 149–52; Howard Temperley, "Capitalism, Slavery, and Ideology," *Past & Present* 75, no. 1 (1977), 94–118, 107–13, 117–18.

15. See chapter 1, p. 37; Jonathan Connolly, "Indenture as Compensation: State Financing for Indentured Labor Migration in the Era of Emancipation," *Slavery & Abolition* 40, no. 3 (2019), 450.

16. Frederic Rogers, Minute, 20 June 1860, attached to Keate to Newcastle, 9 February 1860, No. 24, CO 295/208.

17. Rogers, Minute, 20 June 1860.

18. Priya Satia, *Time's Monster: How History Makes History* (Cambridge, MA: Belknap, 2020), 3.

19. Newcastle to Walker [draft response], 7 July 1860, CO 295/208. The approved plan was for Trinidad's local government to pay one-third of all immigration costs using general revenue. The remaining two-thirds would be paid through charges levied directly on planters.

20. See chapter 4, pp. 108–9.

21. David Northrup, *Indentured Labor in the Age of Imperialism, 1834–1922* (Cambridge: Cambridge University Press, 1995), 159 (stating that 43,860 Indian workers arrived in Réunion and the French Caribbean between 1861 and 1870).

22. Rosemarijn Hoefte, *In Place of Slavery: A Social History of British Indian and Javanese Laborers in Suriname* (Gainesville: University Press of Florida, 1998), 30–32. Signed in 1870, the treaty was ratified by the Dutch parliament in 1872.

23. Hoefte, *In Place of Slavery*, 61–62. Between 1873 and 1916, some 34,304 Indian workers arrived in the colony. See also Maurits S. Hassankhan, "The Indian Indentured Experience in Suriname: Control, Accommodation and Resistance 1873–1916," in *Resistance and Indian Indenture Experience: Comparative Perspectives, ed.* Maurits S. Hassankhan, Brij V. Lal, and Doug Munro (New Delhi: Manohar, 2014), 199–240.

24. Jonathan Connolly, "Antislavery, 'Native Labour,' and the Turn to Indenture in British Colonial Natal, 1842–1860," *Comparative Studies in Society and History* 65, no. 3 (2023): 500–525; Thomas Metcalf, *Imperial Connections: India in the Indian Ocean Arena, 1860–1920* (Berkeley: University of California Press, 2008), chap. 4.

25. Rogers to Merivale, 19 February 1856, CO 179/44.

26. Arrival figure from Northrup, *Indentured Labor*, 160.

27. H. N. D. Beyts, "Report on Immigration of 1860," 15 January 1861, CO 172/86.

28. Barkly to Cardwell, 18 July 1864, Separate, CO 167/464.

29. Richard Allen, *Slaves, Freedmen, and Indentured Laborers in Colonial Mauritius* (Cambridge: Cambridge University Press, 1999), 66–67. Such figures consistently underreported unauthorized absences because some employers chose to apply wage deductions (which could by law exceed wages due) instead of bringing cases to the stipendiary magistrates. See H. N. D. Beyts, "Report on Immigration of 1861," 31 March 1862, enclosed in Sevenson to Newcastle, 3 May 1862, No. 84, CO 167/439; Hugh Tinker, *A New System of Slavery: The Export of Indian Labour Overseas* (London: Oxford University Press, 1974), 188 (on "double cut" wage deductions in excess of wages due).

30. Report of the Agent General of Immigrants (Henry Mitchell), 1 June 1859, enclosed in Keate to Newcastle, 9 August 1859, No. 123, CO 295/205.

31. Mitchell to Bushe, 1 April 1860, enclosed in Walker to Newcastle, 5 May 1860, No. 68, CO 295/209. Aggregate estimates of illegal absence remained high in the early 1860s. See Mitchell to Cuyler, 1 February 1863, enclosed in Keate to Newcastle, 20 June 1863, No. 101, CO 295/222.

32. Trinidad Ordinance No. 7 of 1855, § I, CO 297/5; Trinidad Ordinance No. 13 of 1859, § I, CO 297/6. Ordinance No. 7 of 1855 applied to Indian immigrants who had arrived before 1854; Ordinance No. 13 of 1859 extended the rule to those who had arrived after.

33. Trinidad Ordinance No. 16 of 1862, § LX, CO 297/7.

34. British Guiana Ordinance No. 1 of 1860, §§ 25, 27, CO 113/3.

35. British Guiana Ordinance No. 3 of 1863, §§ 1, 2, CO 113/4; Hincks to Newcastle, 22 May 1863, No. 90, CO 111/340.

36. British Guiana Ordinance No. 5 of 1865, CO 113/5; Hincks to Cardwell, 6 July 1865, No. 111, CO 111/351.

37. Hincks to Cardwell, 6 July 1865, No. 111, CO 111/351.

38. Mitchell to Bushe, 1 April 1860, enclosed in Walker to Newcastle, 5 May 1860, No. 68, CO 295/209.

39. Mitchell to Bushe, 1 April 1860.

40. This was particularly the case in Trinidad, where authorities offered land grants in lieu of return passage to India to time-expired migrants starting in 1869. Bridget Brereton, *A History of Modern Trinidad, 1783–1962* (Kingston, Jamaica: Heinemann), 105–8; Northrup, *Indentured Labor*, 134.

41. Gallagher (Acting Immigration Agent General), 13 January 1866, enclosed in Hincks to Cardwell, 20 January 1866, No. 24, CO 111/355; Crosby to Halligan, 19 April 1867, enclosed in Mundy to Buckingham and Chandos, 22 April 1867, CO 111/362.

42. British Guiana Ordinance No. 4 of 1864, § 116, CO 113/4. Alongside these punishments, the ordinance also authorized wage forfeitures not to exceed one week's wages, at the discretion of the presiding magistrate.

43. British Guiana Ordinance No. 4 of 1864, § 118.

44. British Guiana Ordinance No. 4 of 1864, § 107. The law also imposed fines on employers who "harboured" or employed immigrants contracted to work on other plantations (§ 104) and on employers who failed to report unauthorized absences to police within forty-eight hours (§ 106).

45. See chapter 2, p. 42.

46. Mauritius Ordinance No. 4 of 1864, § XIII, CO 169/14.

47. Mauritius Ordinance No. 4 of 1864, §§ XVI, XVII.

48. Trinidad Ordinance No. 3 of 1865, § XLVIII, CO 297/7.

49. Trinidad Ordinance No. 3 of 1865, § LXII.

50. Trinidad Ordinance No. 3 of 1865, §§ LX, LXI.

51. Sutton to Cardwell, 23 March 1865, No. 42, CO 295/230.

52. Trinidad Ordinance No. 3 of 1866, § I, CO 297/7.

53. Trinidad Ordinance No. 3 of 1866, § II.

54. Murdoch to Rogers, 17 April 1866, CO 386/99.

55. Trinidad Ordinance No. 6 of 1866, CO 297/7; Rushworth to Cardwell, 6 July 1866, No. 78, CO 295/235; Murdoch to Rogers, 10 August 1866, CO 386/99.

56. Mauritius Ordinance No. 4 of 1864, CO 169/14. On the Vagrant Depot, see Satteeanund Peerthum and Satyendra Peerthum, "'Incorrigible, Defiant and Determined': Vagrancy, Worker Agency, Resistance, and the Experiences of the Vagrants in Colonial Mauritius, 1829–1890," in Hassankhan, Lal, and Munro, *Resistance and Indian Indenture*, 51–94; Vijayalakshmi Teelock, ed., *The Vagrant Depot of Grand River: Its Surroundings and Vagrancy in British Mauritius* (Port Louis: Aapravasi Ghat Trust Fund, 2004).

57. Barkly, Minute, 20 January 1864, enclosed in Barkly to Newcastle, 5 May 1864, No. 120, CO 167/462.

58. On the separate system, see Michel Foucault, *Discipline and Punish: the Birth of the Prison*, trans. Alan Sheridan (New York: Vintage, 1977); U. R. Q. Henriques, "The Rise and

Decline of the Separate System of Prison Discipline," *Past & Present*, no. 54 (1972): 61–93; Michael Ignatieff, *A Just Measure of Pain: The Penitentiary in the Industrial Revolution, 1750–1850* (New York: Pantheon Books, 1978). On related penal reform initiatives in post-emancipation Jamaica, see Diana Paton, *No Bond but the Law: Punishment, Race, and Gender in Jamaican State Formation, 1780–1870* (Durham, NC: Duke University Press, 2004), 123–55.

59. Relevant here is Diana Paton's argument regarding the interplay in post-emancipation Jamaica between reformist impulses influenced by metropolitan and North American penitentiary design and specifically colonial dynamics concerning agricultural labor and race. Paton, *No Bond but the Law*, esp. 147–55.

60. Regulations for the Depot for Vagrant Prisoners, §§ 20, 21, 10, 24 and 6, 42, enclosed in Barkly to Newcastle, 5 May 1864, No. 120, CO 167/462.

61. See chapters 2 and 3, pp. 54–61, 84–89.

62. Inspector General of Police, Report on the Vagrant Depot Grand River, n.d., NAM, RA 1749.

63. Inspector General of Police, Report on the Vagrant Depot Grand River. See also Protector of Immigrants to the Colonial Secretary [of Mauritius], 9 July 1864, No. 5D, NAM, RA 1749 (stating punishments meted out in June 1864, including floggings, restricted rations, and solitary confinement); Peerthum and Peerthum, "Incorrigible, Defiant, Determined," 77–78 (describing punishments imposed on Dabee, an "incorrigible" or repeat offender).

64. Beyts to Rushworth, 31 May 1864, No. 1D, NAM, RA 1749.

65. Protector of Immigrants to the Colonial Secretary [of Mauritius], 9 July 1864, No. 5D, NAM, RA 1749.

66. Beyts to Rushworth, 31 May 1864, No. 1D, NAM, RA 1749. See also Inspector General of Police to the Colonial Secretary [of Mauritius], 14 July 1865, No. 168, NAM, RA 1799 (reporting that "there were not sufficient medicines for the use of the Depot, that the Medical Officer had applied for them but could not get them").

67. "Interrogatories respecting the Construction, State, Discipline, and Management of each prison, House of Correction, Lock-up House, Convict Depot, Penal Settlement, or other place of Confinement in the Colony of Mauritius: Vagrant Depot," interrogatory XXIX, enclosed in Barkly to Cardwell, 4 October 1865, No. 261, CO 167/481. This figure refers to the period from February 1864 to February 1865. I have grouped as "repeat offenders" those convicted twice (494), three times (63), four times (26), and five times (5).

68. Examination of Robert Martenson, Inspector of Police, 26 January 1872, "Minutes of the Proceedings of the Police Force Commission," 387, enclosed in Gordon to Kimberley, 6 March 1872, No. 88, CO 167/542.

69. Examination of Robert Martenson, 26 January 1872. The Depot was designed to hold 450 prisoners at a time, but imprisonment levels frequently exceeded that mark. (The largest number imprisoned at one time was 1,282, in 1869.) When the Depot overcrowded, inmates were redistributed to other holding points in Petite Rivière, Port Louis, and Bois Marchand. As Satteeanund and Satyendra Peerthum showed in "Incorrigible, Defiant, Determined," 75, more than 60,000 individuals had been imprisoned in the Depot by 1886.

70. Scott to Kimberley, 23 February 1871, No. 25, CO 111/383 (discussing five years of prison statistics previously reported in annual blue books). On prison building between 1868 and 1875, see Clare Anderson, Kellie Moss, and Shammane Joseph Jackson, "Coloniality and the Criminal Justice System: Empire and Its Legacies in Guyana," *Slavery & Abolition* 43, no. 4 (2022): 682–704, 691.

71. Scott to Kimberley, 23 February 1871, No. 25, CO 111/383. According to Scott, 2,202 Indian and Chinese workers were jailed out of a total of 5,340, or 41 percent. These figures are revised down from what was originally stated in the colony's 1869 blue book.

72. RCBG, appendices K4 and K5. These appendices give partial estimates; they cite returns from between six and nine districts, not the whole colony. They report an annual average of 1,162 convictions for illegal absence during the five-year period, and roughly 500 convictions per year for desertion.

73. RCBG, 103 and appendix K. Appendix K shows 32,876 recorded immigration-related cases. In the text of the report itself, the commissioners write "certainly not a hundred, perhaps not a score, were cases by immigrants, or by others on their behalf, against employers." In this same passage, the commissioners cite a higher total (82,876), but I have used the lower number listed in the appendix because it appears more reliable: it is the total achieved by adding up recorded cases by type of offense, as listed in subappendices.

74. Prabhu P. Mohapatra, "Assam and the West Indies, 1860–1920: Immobilizing Plantation Labor," in *Masters, Servants, and Magistrates in Britain and the Empire, 1562–1955*, ed. Douglas Hay and Paul Craven (Chapel Hill: University of North Carolina Press, 2004), 467–68.

75. See RCBG, appendices K6 (showing average fines in Demerara ranging from roughly 5 dollars to roughly 7 dollars between 1866 and 1870) and K7–K10 (showing sentences passed, including a range of fines, by magistrates in Berbice).

76. Mohapatra, "Assam and the West Indies," 466.

77. RCBG, 105 (suggesting that as many as half of all complaints brought under the immigration laws between 1865 and 1870 were withdrawn or abandoned, resulting in dismissal but not acquittal).

78. Martindale, Stipendiary Magistrate of Plaines Wilhems, to the Protector of Immigrants, 16 September 1864, enclosed in Beyts to Rushworth, 19 September 1864, No. 140A, NAM, RA 1750.

79. Gautier to Beyts, 14 September 1864, No. 39, enclosed in Beyts to Rushworth, 20 September 1864, No. 141A, NAM, RA 1750.

80. Martindale to the Protector of Immigrants, 16 September 1864, enclosed in Beyts to Rushworth, 19 September 1864, No. 140A, NAM, RA 1750.

81. Martindale to the Protector of Immigrants, 16 September 1864.

82. Beyts to Rushworth, 19 September 1864, No. 140A, NAM, RA 1750.

83. Minute, Procureur General, 27 September 1864, attached to Beyts to Rushworth, 19 September 1854, No. 140A, NAM, RA 1750.

84. "Return of Indian Immigrants committed to the Royal Gaol in 1859, 1860, 1861, 1862, and 1863, with particulars of Crimes and Offences," enclosed in Mitchell to Bushe, 27 April 1864, enclosed in Keate to Newcastle, 21 May 1864, No. 79, CO 295/227.

85. "Return of Indian Immigrants committed to the Royal Gaol."

86. "Notes on the Annual Return of Indentured Immigrants in Trinidad for the Year 1863," enclosed in Keate to Cardwell, 4 June 1864, No. 84, CO 295/227. Under Trinidad Ordinance No. 16 of 1862, indentured workers who illegally missed ten or more days of work during a given year could have their contracts extended to compensate for absence. Trinidad Ordinance No. 16 of 1862, § XLII, CO 297/7.

87. Gordon to Buckingham and Chandos, 8 November 1867, No. 144, CO 295/241.

88. Gordon to Granville, 31 December 1869, No. 170, CO 295/248. These figures include imprisonments for non-labor offenses, but according to Governor Gordon, "Of the immigrants a

very large proportion were imprisoned for being absent from work without leave and for breach of contract." In this context, the term "Creole" refers to the colony's Afro-Caribbean population.

89. Trinidad Blue Book for 1872, CO 300/83.

90. Mauritius Blue Book of 1860, CO 172/86; Mauritius Blue Book of 1868, CO 172/94. During this period, the Indian population came to greatly outnumber the "general" or non-Indian population. The total population in 1868 was estimated at 324,402.

91. "Report of the Protector of Immigrants, 1868," 31 May 1869, CO 172/94.

92. Mary Turner, "The British Caribbean, 1823–1838: The Transition from Slave to Free Legal Status," in Hay and Craven, *Masters, Servants, and Magistrates*, 317; Bhavani Raman, "Oceanic Mobility and the Empire of the Pass," *Law and History Review* (2023): 1–21, 17.

93. Marina Carter, *Servants, Sirdars and Settlers: Indians in Mauritius, 1834–1874* (Delhi: Oxford University Press, 1995), 165; *Report of the Royal Commissioners Appointed to Enquire into the Treatment of Immigrants in Mauritius*, PP, 1875, xxiv (C. 1115) (hereafter RCM), 98.

94. Carter, *Servants, Sirdars and Settlers*, 88–94.

95. Northrup, *Indentured Labor*, 159.

96. Carter, *Servants, Sirdars and Settlers*, 7; Allen, *Slaves, Freedmen, and Indentured Laborers*, 58–59.

97. The colony's Indian population rose from 77,996 in 1851 to 216,258 in 1871. Mauritius Blue Book for 1871, CO 172/97. The general population was 102,217 in 1851, and 99,784 in 1871.

98. Mauritius Blue Book for 1871. The total population in 1871 was 316,042.

99. Mauritius Blue Book for 1871. In 1871, there were 74,454 Indian women and 141,804 Indian men. In 1851, the figures were 13,714 and 64,282. The precise percentage in 1851 was thus 17.58.

100. In his Blue Book report for 1864, Governor Barkly stated that 61,000 old immigrants re-engaged on sugar estates during the year. Barkly to Cardwell, 5 July 1865, Separate, CO 167/479.

101. Testimony of H. N. D. Beyts, "Minutes of the Proceedings of Her Majesty's Commissioners appointed to enquire into the condition of the Indian Immigrants in the Colony of Mauritius" (hereafter Royal Commission Minutes), 29 June 1872, ¶ 3797 (testifying as to the size of the Indian population, based on the census of 1871), enclosed in Gordon to Kimberley, 23 August 1872, No. 270, CO 167/545.

102. Testimony of H. N. D. Beyts, ¶¶ 3797–99. Beyts stated that there were 68,673 Indian immigrants not living and working on the plantations, as well as roughly 29,000 Indo-Mauritians (Indians born in the colony).

103. Testimony of H. N. D. Beyts, ¶ 3799. According to Beyts, there were "831 males and 7 females employed in the professional class; 11,373 males and 1,209 females as domestic servants; 8,423 males and 374 females in the commercial class; [and] 3,256 males and 331 females in the industrial class."

104. Allen, *Slaves, Freedmen, and Indentured Laborers*, 73, 137–38, 140–43, 154–56.

105. Barkly to Buckingham and Chandos, 23 September 1867, Separate, CO 167/500.

106. O'Brien to the Private Secretary to His Excellency the Governor, 13 December 1867, NAM, RA 1955.

107. Barkly to Buckingham and Chandos, 23 September 1867, Separate, CO 167/500.

108. O'Brien to the Colonial Secretary of Mauritius, 30 July 1868, No. 140, NAM, RA 1956. As Karuna Mantena has argued, theories of social dissolution—like the one exemplified by O'Brien here—had profound effects on British law and policy in India during the late nineteenth century. According to Mantena, a long-term transition from a liberal, reformist outlook toward

an authoritarian, hierarchical theory of rule in British India depended on the consolidation of a fixed notion of "traditional society," a "cohesive, cultural whole that . . . was seen to resist the logic of modern society." Such a view then justified authoritarian legal measures (implemented through indirect rule) designed to prevent the dissolution of "traditional" social structures. Karuna Mantena, *Alibis of Empire: Henry Maine and the Ends of Liberal Imperialism* (Princeton, NJ: Princeton University Press, 2010), 2.

109. Beyts to Barkly, 16 December 1867, enclosed in Beyts to Bedingfeld, 16 December 1867, NAM, RA 1954.

110. Mauritius Ordinance No. 31 of 1867, CO 169/14.

111. Mauritius Ordinance No. 31 of 1867, §§ XXII, XXIV.

112. Mauritius Ordinance No. 31 of 1867, §§ XLVIII, L.

113. Mauritius Ordinance No. 31 of 1867, § XLVI; Tinker, *New System of Slavery*, 107–8.

114. Barkly to Buckingham and Chandos, 30 December 1867, CO 167/501.

115. Murdoch to Rogers, 25 February 1868, CO 167/511.

116. Murdoch to Rogers, 25 February 1868.

117. See chapter 2, pp. 46–54.

118. Murdoch to Rogers, 25 February 1868, CO 167/511.

119. Murdoch to Rogers, 25 February 1868.

120. Colonial Office to Governor Barkly [draft response], 15 May 1868, CO 167/511.

121. Henry Maine, *Ancient Law: Its Connection with the Early History of Society, and Its Relation to Modern Ideas* (London, 1861).

122. Mongia, *Indian Migration and Empire*, 22–48. On the relationship between vagrancy law and contract ideology in the postbellum United States, see Amy Dru Stanley, *From Bondage to Contract: Wage Labor, Marriage, and the Market in the Age of Slave Emancipation* (Cambridge: Cambridge University Press, 1998), chap. 3.

123. Mauritius Ordinance No. 31 of 1867, § XXXIX, CO 169/14. This was well before photographs became a standard feature of passports used for international travel. See John C. Torpey, *The Invention of the Passport: Surveillance, Citizenship and the State*, 2nd ed. (Cambridge: Cambridge University Press, 2018).

124. Mauritius Ordinance No. 31 of 1867, § XLIII.

125. Mauritius Ordinance No. 31 of 1867, §§ XLI, XLV. It was valid for old immigrants to re-engage without applying for a police pass if they did so within eight days of the expiration of the prior labor contract. Conversely, old immigrants who chose not to re-engage were required to apply for a police pass within eight days.

126. Mauritius Ordinance No. 31 of 1867, §§ XLVI, XLVIII.

127. Mauritius Ordinance No. 31 of 1867, §§ XLVI, XLVIII.

128. Mauritius Ordinance No. 31 of 1867, § XLVI.

129. A four-shilling fee was charged for the photograph attached to the initial old immigrant's ticket issued by the Protector, and the replacement fee for duplicate tickets was set at £1. Amended regulations added similar replacement fees for duplicate police passes—two shillings for a first and four shillings for second and subsequent replacements. Regulations Under Ordinance No. 31 of 1867, 14 May 1868, Table O (Table of Fees), in *Government Gazette*, 16 May 1868, CO 171/35; Amended Regulations under Ordinance No. 31 of 1867, 11 November 1868, Table T, in *Government Gazette*, 14 November 1868, CO 171/36. For a comparison of the three sets of regulations issued between 1868 and 1869, see RCM, appendix F.

130. Amended Regulations, 11 November 1868, § 43.

131. Amended Regulations Under Ordinance No. 31 of 1867, 24 August 1869, § 4, in *Government Gazette*, 28 August 1869, CO 171/38.

132. Mauritius Ordinance No. 31 of 1867, § XLVI, CO 169/14.

133. Amended Regulations, 24 August 1869, § 13.

134. Amended Regulations, 24 August 1869, § 3.

135. Amended Regulations, 24 August 1869, §§ 13, 3.

136. Amended Regulations, 11 November 1868, § 54.

137. Amended Regulations, 24 August 1869, § 11; "Eleventh Annual Report of the Protector of Immigrants," 23 April 1870, 8, in Mauritius Blue Book for 1869, CO 172/95. This average wage estimate is approximate. For additional analysis of the regulations issued under Ordinance No. 31, see Nandini Boodia-Canoo, *Slavery, Indenture and the Law: Assembling a Nation in Colonial Mauritius* (London: Routledge, 2023), 155.

138. O'Brien to the Colonial Secretary [of Mauritius], 30 July 1868, No. 140, NAM, RA 1956. The figure was 14,239.

139. O'Brien to the Colonial Secretary [of Mauritius], 16 September 1868, No. 183, NAM, RA 1956; O'Brien, "Return shewing the number of Passes issued, and to whom, from 1st June 1868 to 31st May 1869," enclosed in Barkly to Granville, 16 October 1869, No. 271, CO 167/519. Between May 1868 and December 1871, local police issued 75,462 police passes to old immigrants. F. T. Blunt, Acting Inspector General of Police, "Report in Explanation of the Statistical Returns for 1871," Appendix M, NAM, RA 2120.

140. O'Brien, "Return shewing the number of Passes issued, and to whom, from 1st June 1868 to 31st May 1869," enclosed in Barkly to Granville, 16 October 1869, No. 271, CO 167/519. Of the 29,993 passes listed in this return, 6,011 went to monthly laborers, 3,701 to day laborers, 3,681 to servants, 308 to licensed washermen, 451 to licensed coachmen, 3,573 to hawkers, 580 to licensed traders, 7,724 to gardeners (small farmers), 303 to proprietors, 585 to cattle owners, 292 to artisans, 106 to peons, 11 to teachers, 37 to bakers, 36 to priests, 31 to licensed shoemakers, and 52 to wood sellers.

141. Carter, *Servants, Sirdars and Settlers*, 204.

142. Testimony of Inspector Seed, 22 December 1871, "Minutes of the Proceedings of the Police Force Commission" (hereafter Police Commission Minutes), 97, enclosed in Gordon to Kimberley, 6 March 1872, No. 88, CO 167/542.

143. Testimony of Inspector Seed, 22 December 1871.

144. Testimony of Inspector O'Connor, 12 December 1871, Police Commission Minutes, 48, enclosed in Gordon to Kimberley, 6 March 1872, No. 88, CO 167/542.

145. Testimony of Mounted Sergeant Adam, 18 December 1871, Police Commission Minutes, 73, enclosed in Gordon to Kimberley, 6 March 1872, No. 88, CO 167/542.

146. F. T. Blunt, "Report in explanation of the Statistical Returns of the Police Department for the Year 1871," 12 February 1872, NAM, RA 2120. The exact figures given here for vagrancy arrests are: 19,970 in 1867, 26,904 in 1868, and 30,904 in 1869. In 1870 and 1871, the figure once again decreased, to 22,892 and 14,884, respectively. Evidentiary minutes recorded by the royal commission of inquiry in 1872 suggest somewhat lower vagrancy figures. Royal Commission Minutes, ¶¶ 1849–51, enclosed in Gordon to Kimberley, 26 July 1872, No. 244, CO 167/544.

147. According to the census of 1871 (two years later, of course), the colony's male Indian population numbered 141,804. Mauritius Blue Book for 1871, CO 172/97. Using this as an approximate figure for 1869, 30,904 arrests gives an arrest rate of 21.8 percent. Using different figures, evidentiary minutes recorded by the royal commission suggest that the figure was 16 percent.

Royal Commission Minutes, ¶ 6718, enclosed in Gordon to Kimberley, 13 November 1872, No. 326, CO 167/547. See also Peerthum and Peerthum, "Incorrigible, Defiant, Determined," 81 (estimating a figure of 17 percent).

148. Convictions for Vagrancy 1864–71 [multiple returns from individual magistrates], NAM, RA 2134. The exact totals given here are 8,958 for 1868, 8,534 for 1869, 6,144 for 1870, and 3,740 for 1871.

149. RCM, appendix G (no. 46) (stating totals from police records and demonstrating discrepancy with magistrate records). The exact figures given here are 9,804 for 1868, 10,609 for 1869, 7,564 for 1870, and 4,818 for 1871.

150. RCM, appendix G (no. 45) (showing 1,760 arrested vagrants sent back to employers in 1868, and 1,535 in 1869).

151. "Report from the Protector, H. N. D. Beyts," 23 March 1871, enclosed in Gordon to the Colonial Secretary [of Mauritius], 21 March 1871, No. 91, NAM, RA 2084.

152. "Report from the Protector, H. N. D. Beyts," 23 March 1871 (emphasis removed).

153. Mauritius Ordinance No. 31 of 1867, § L, CO 169/14.

154. Mauritius Ordinance No. 31 of 1867, § L. Article 13 of Ordinance No. 4 of 1864 had authorized an initial punishment for vagrancy of 28 days, followed by an additional punishment of between six and nine months for repeat offenses. Mauritius Ordinance No. 4 of 1864, § XIII, CO 169/14.

155. Examination of Charles Renouf, Stipendiary Magistrate for Pamplemousses, 5 January 1872, Police Commission Minutes, 184–85, enclosed in Gordon to Kimberley, 6 March 1872, No. 88, CO 167/542; Testimony of Charles Renouf, 8 November 1872, Royal Commission Minutes, ¶¶ 10,945–46, enclosed in Newton to Kimberley, 28 March 1873, CO 167/551; Examination of Edward Steven Messiter, Stipendiary Magistrate for Grand Port, 15 January 1872, Police Commission Minutes, 249, enclosed in Gordon to Kimberley, 6 March 1872, No. 88, CO 167/542.

156. Examination of Charles Renouf, Stipendiary Magistrate for Pamplemousses, 5 January 1872, Police Commission Minutes, 184, enclosed in Gordon to Kimberley, 6 March 1872, No. 88, CO 167/542.

157. Ordinance No. 31 of 1867, §§ XLVI, XLVIII, CO 169/14.

158. Examination of Paul Francois Oscar D'Emmerez de Charmoy, District and Stipendiary Magistrate of Black River, 26 January 1872, Police Commission Minutes, 369, enclosed in Gordon to Kimberley, 6 March 1872, No. 88, CO 167/542.

159. Carter, *Servants, Sirdars and Settlers*, 208–9.

160. Examination of Eugene Dupuy, Police and Stipendiary Magistrate of Port Louis, 21 December 1871, Police Commission Minutes, 88, enclosed in Gordon to Kimberley, 6 March 1872, No. 88, CO 167/542.

161. Examination of Eugene Dupuy, 21 December 1871, 88–89. In 1870, Dupuy decided 8,219 vagrancy cases. The largest number he decided in a single day was 93. In 1871, his figures were 5,681 and 43.

162. Testimony of Charles Renouf, 12 November 1872, Royal Commission Minutes, ¶ 11,379, enclosed in Newton to Kimberley, 28 March 1873, CO 167/551.

163. Examination of Ernest Didier St. Amand, District and Stipendiary magistrate of Moka, 5 January 1872, Police Commission Minutes, 188, enclosed in Gordon to Kimberley, 6 March 1872, No. 88, CO 167/542. St. Amand also stated that he allowed Indians so arrested who claimed to have either lost their papers or have been born in Mauritius to seek evidence to rebut the prima facie case against them.

164. Examination of Magistrate D'Emmerez (Continued), 26 January 1872, Police Commission Minutes, 381, enclosed in Gordon to Kimberley, 6 March 1872, No. 88, CO 167/542.

165. Superintendent of Police to the Inspector General of Police, 13 February 1877, NAM, PA 25 (citing a legal opinion issued to the police department in 1864 stating that suspected vagrants without documentary proof of completion of industrial residence should be treated as new immigrants). Even at this point, in 1877, the superintendent stated that the police struggled to distinguish old from new immigrants: "I should be glad to know how the Police are expected to determine whether an Immigrant is old or new, when he has no papers of any kind in his possession."

166. Examination of John Alphonso Spencer, Superintendent of Police, n.d., Police Commission Minutes, 18, enclosed in Gordon to Kimberley, 6 March 1872, No. 88, CO 167/542.

167. RCM, Appendix G (No. 44). According to statistics compiled by the royal commission, 12,553 immigrants were arrested and discharged in 1868, and 13,307 in 1869. In those years, 9,801 and 10,609 immigrants were convicted of vagrancy-related offenses, respectively. These figures differ from those given in police records in the Mauritian archives, which suggest larger numbers of total arrests in both years, and a smaller number of discharges. In particular, they state that of those arrested in 1869, some 9,319 were either discharged or sent to the Protector of Immigrants. F. T. Blunt, Acting Inspector General of Police, "Report in explanation of the Statistical Returns of the Police Department for the Year 1871," 12 February, 1872, NAM, RA 2120.

168. RCM, 162 ("It is distressing to think of the amount of annoyance, irritation, and inconvenience which must have been caused to hundreds of inoffensive persons by the inevitable operation of the law, apart from the too many cases of positive oppression, such as we have hereinbefore described in detail.").

169. Statement of Dilloo, Old Immigrant, No. 82,500, Police Commission Minutes, vii–viii, enclosed in Gordon to Kimberley, 6 March 1872, No. 88, CO 167/542. See also Carter, *Servants, Sirdars and Settlers*, 205. On children arrested for vagrancy during the 1880s, see Reshaad Durgahee, *The Indentured Archipelago: Experiences of Indian Labour in Mauritius and Fiji, 1871–1916* (Cambridge: Cambridge University Press, 2021), 73–75.

170. Statement of Ramchurun, Old Immigrant, No. 15,673, Police Commission Minutes, ix, enclosed in Gordon to Kimberley, 6 March 1872, No. 88, CO 167/542.

171. Statement of Ramluckhun, Police Commission Minutes, x, enclosed in Gordon to Kimberley, 6 March 1872, No. 88, CO 167/542. See also Mishra, "Indian Indentured Labourers," 242.

172. Examination of Sumassee, No. 80,567, 8 January 1872, Police Commission Minutes, 214–15, enclosed in Gordon to Kimberley, 6 March 1872, No. 88, CO 167/542.

173. Statement of Sevoon, Old Immigrant, No. 257,105, Police Commission Minutes, xii, enclosed in Gordon to Kimberley, 6 March 1872, No. 88, CO 167/542.

174. Petition of Hurry Sing, Old Immigrant No. 859, 23 February 1870, NAM, RA 2041. The petition was addressed formally to Henry Barkly, the colony's governor. It was received by the Protector of Immigrants, H. N. D. Beyts, who included his own report, dated 3 March 1870, which recommended that Sing's request be granted. It is unclear who wrote the petition on Sing's behalf.

175. "Report from the Protector, H.N.D. Beyts," 23 March 1871, enclosed in Gordon, Acting Inspector General of Police, to the Colonial Secretary [of Mauritius], 21 March 1871, No. 91, NAM, RA 2084.

176. "The Old Immigrants of Mauritius," [Plevitz Petition], enclosed in Gordon to Kimberley, 17 November 1871, CO 167/536.

Chapter 6

1. For the context of indenture, see Madhavi Kale, *Fragments of Empire: Capital, Slavery, and Indian Indentured Labor Migration in the British Caribbean* (Philadelphia: University of Pennsylvania Press, 1998), and in particular, Radhika V. Mongia, "Impartial Regimes of Truth: Indentured Indian Labour and the Status of the Inquiry," *Cultural Studies* 18, no. 5 (2004): 749–68. For broader contexts, see Lauren Benton and Lisa Ford, *Rage for Order: The British Empire and the Origins of International Law, 1800–1850* (Cambridge, MA: Harvard University Press, 2016), 56–84; Stephen Doherty, Lisa Ford, et al., "Inquiring into the Corpus of Empire," *Journal of World History* 32, no. 2 (2021): 219–40; Zoë Laidlaw, "Investigating Empire: Humanitarians, Reform and the Commission of Eastern Inquiry," *Journal of Imperial and Commonwealth History* 40, no. 5 (2012): 749–68; Lisa Lowe, *The Intimacies of Four Continents* (Durham, NC: Duke University Press, 2015), 4; Ann Laura Stoler, *Along the Archival Grain: Epistemic Anxieties and Colonial Common Sense* (Princeton, NJ: Princeton University Press, 2009), 28–31, 141–78.

2. Relatedly, James Epstein, *Scandal of Colonial Rule: Power and Subversion in the British Atlantic during the Age of Revolution* (Cambridge: Cambridge University Press, 2012), 12 ("while scandals have the capacity to stir awareness and political action, they also have the potential to divert public attention from systemic ruling practices and deeper histories of violence and abuse").

3. Nicholas B. Dirks, *The Scandal of Empire: India and the Creation of Imperial Britain* (Cambridge, MA: Belknap, 2006); Epstein, *Scandal of Colonial Rule*; Priya Satia, *Time's Monster: How History Makes History* (Cambridge, MA: Belknap, 2020); Sara Suleri, *The Rhetoric of English India* (Chicago: University of Chicago Press, 1992).

4. Dirks, *Scandal of Empire*.

5. Jonathan Connolly, "Re-Reading Morant Bay: Protest, Inquiry, and Colonial Rule," *Law and History Review* 41, no. 1 (2023): 193–216; Catherine Hall, *Civilising Subjects: Metropole and Colony in the English Imagination, 1830–1867* (Chicago: University of Chicago Press, 2002), 411–15; Gad Heuman, *"The Killing Time": The Morant Bay Rebellion in Jamaica* (London: Macmillan Caribbean, 1994), 158–60, 177–80; Thomas C. Holt, *The Problem of Freedom: Race, Labor, and Politics in Jamaica and Britain, 1832–1938* (Baltimore: Johns Hopkins University Press, 1992), 295–309.

6. The average for 1864–66 was 77,640,700 lb., while the average for 1839–41 was 26,856,600 lb. Gordon to Buckingham and Chandos, 8 November 1867, No. 144, CO 295/241.

7. Hincks to Cardwell, 18 January 1866, No. 22, CO 111/355; Hincks to Buckingham and Chandos, 31 August 1868, No. 135, CO 111/369.

8. In 1857, British Guiana produced 58,766 hogsheads of sugar. In 1866, the figure was 91,580, and in 1867 it was 82,726. Hincks to Buckingham and Chandos, 31 August 1864, No. 135, CO 111/369. On export revenue in these years, see Mundy to Buckingham and Chandos, 10 September 1867, No. 125, CO 111/364.

9. Smyth to Kimberley, 18 September 1871, No. 16, CO 167/535 (presenting corrected export figures). Both production and revenue dropped in 1867 due to draught and disease but then increased again between 1868 and 1870. Export revenue thus went from £2,650,539 in 1866, to £2,156,950 in 1867, back up to £2,599,815 in 1869.

10. David Northrup, *Indentured Labor in the Age of Imperialism, 1834–1922* (Cambridge: Cambridge University Press, 1995), 156–57. These figures (59,577 and 69,669, respectively) reflect departures between 1861 and 1870.

11. Walter Rodney, *A History of the Guyanese Working People, 1881–1905* (Baltimore: Johns Hopkins University Press, 1981), 153; Hugh Tinker, *A New System of Slavery: The Export of Indian*

Labour Overseas (London: Oxford University Press, 1974), 240 (both referring to the outbreak of violence on the plantation *Leonora*). See also Antoinette Burton, *The Trouble with Empire: Challenges to Modern British Imperialism* (Oxford: Oxford University Press, 2015), 87–144 (setting late nineteenth-century Caribbean labor protest in wider imperial contexts).

12. Des Voeux to Granville, 25 December 1869, RCBG, 1.

13. Des Voeux to Granville, 25 December 1869, RCBG, 3, 1–8.

14. Murdoch (Emigration Board) to Rogers (Colonial Office), 9 February 1870, enclosed in Rogers (Colonial Office) to Merivale (India Office), 9 March 1870, No. 8/28f, IOR/L/PJ/2/63.

15. Granville to Scott, 10 March 1870, ASSP, MSS Brit Emp S 22, G 38/A.

16. Gordon to Kimberley, 18 August 1871, No. 135, CO 167/534.

17. Petition of Ramluckhun, enclosed in "The Petition of the Old Immigrants of Mauritius," 6 June 1871, RCM, 4.

18. Petition of Suroop, enclosed in "The Petition of the Old Immigrants of Mauritius," 6 June 1871, RCM, 5.

19. Gordon to Kimberley, 17 November 1871, [No. 197], CO 167/536; also reprinted in RCM, 16.

20. RCM, 16.

21. RCM, 16–17; Marina Carter, *Servants, Sirdars and Settlers: Indians in Mauritius, 1834–1874* (Delhi: Oxford University Press, 1995), 204–5. We might situate de Plevitz alongside other colonial intermediaries—missionaries, humanitarians, and indigenous functionaries—who in different ways reported and thereby structured (for a metropolitan audience) local grievances. Suggestive examples include Alan Lester and Fae Dussart, *Colonization and the Origins of Humanitarian Governance: Protecting Aborigines across the Nineteenth-Century British Empire* (Cambridge: Cambridge University Press, 2014); Benjamin N. Lawrence, Emily Lynn Osborn, and Richard L. Roberts, eds., *Intermediaries, Interpreters, and Clerks: African Employees in the Making of Colonial Africa* (Madison: University of Wisconsin Press, 2006).

22. "The Petition of the Old Immigrants of Mauritius," 6 June 1871, RCM, 2–7; Adolphe de Plevitz, "Observations," 3 August 1871, RCM, 7–14.

23. Gordon to Kimberley, 17 November 1871, [No. 197], CO 167/536.

24. Gordon to [Kimberley], 11 November 1871, No. 184, CO 167/536.

25. On the formation of the police enquiry commission, see RCM, 22.

26. Herbert (Colonial Office) to Under Secretary of State, India Office, 21 December 1871, No. 11/23, IOR/L/PJ/2/100.

27. Bernard, Secretary to the Government of Bengal, to the Secretary to the Government of India, 7 May 1872, No. 1933, IOR/P/691.

28. Government of India to the Duke of Argyll (India Office), 15 July 1872, Emigration No. 23, IOR/L/PJ/3/70. See also India Office, Draft Letter to the Colonial Office, n.d. [1872], No. 11/23d, IOR/L/PJ/2/100 (responding to the police enquiry commission in Mauritius and reporting on critical accounts sent from the Government of India).

29. Granville to Scott, n.d. [April 1870], enclosed in Rogers (Colonial Office) to Merivale (India Office), 9 March 1870, No. 8/28f, IOR/L/PJ/2/63.

30. Rogers (Colonial Office) to Under-Secretary of State, India Office, 1 July 1870, No. 8/28o, IOR/L/PJ/2/63.

31. Rogers to Under-Secretary of State, 1 July 1870.

32. RCBG, 15–16. This chain again emphasizes the importance of intermediaries like Des Voeux, English-speaking colonial observers who not only compiled but also processed and interpreted diffuse subaltern demands. In this case, Des Voeux's interpretation structured the

remit of the royal commission; its charge was to investigate the forms of exploitation he had alleged.

33. RCBG (excluding appendices).

34. Gordon to Kimberley, 10 November 1871, Confidential, CO 167/536.

35. RCM, 1.

36. RCM, 1.

37. RCM, 15.

38. RCM, 15–16.

39. The commissioners did criticize Des Voeux and de Plevitz for exaggerating in certain instances. RCBG, 85; RCM, 577.

40. RCBG, 103.

41. RCBG, 105.

42. RCBG, 112–14.

43. RCBG, 72.

44. RCM, 579.

45. RCM, 582.

46. RCM, 583, 420–63.

47. RCM, 581.

48. RCM, 582–83, quote on 582.

49. RCM, 580.

50. RCM, 580.

51. Kimberley to Scott, 31 October 1871, No. 201, and Kimberley to Scott, 16 May 1872, No. 295, PP, 1872, xliii (C. 641), 27, 86–89.

52. Government of India to the Duke of Argyll (India Office), 22 March 1872, No. 10, sub-enclosed in Holland (Colonial Office) to Under Secretary of State, India Office, 31 May 1872, IOR/L/PJ/2/65.

53. Sheldon Amos, *The Existing Laws of Demerara for the Regulation of Coolie Immigration* (London, 1871); Joseph Beaumont, *The New Slavery: An Account of the Indian and Chinese Immigrants in British Guiana* (London, 1871); John Edward Jenkins, *The Coolie: His Rights and Wrongs. Notes of a Journey to British Guiana, with a Review of the System and of the Recent Commission of Inquiry* (London, 1871).

54. Amos, *Existing Laws of Demerara*, 3.

55. Beaumont, *New Slavery*, 13.

56. "Coolie Oppression in Demerara," *Morning Post*, 28 February 1871, 8 (reporting on the aforementioned meeting of the Social Science Association in London, 27 February 1871); "The Demerara Coolie," *Times*, 17 October 1871, 4 (discussing the allegations made by Des Voeux as well as Jenkins's *The Coolie, his Rights and Wrongs*). Both papers also reported on advocacy meetings held by the Aborigines Protection Society after the publication of the Mauritius commission. See "Indian Coolies in the Mauritius," *Morning Post*, 4 August 1875, 3; "Deputation: Indian Coolies in the Mauritius," *Times*, 5 August 1875, 6.

57. Sascha Auerbach, "Of Rights and Riots: Indenture and (Mis)Rule in the Late Nineteenth-Century British Caribbean," *English Historical Review* 137, no. 589 (2022): 1662–92; Rodney, *History of the Guyanese Working People*, 153.

58. *Times*, 5 November 1872, 7.

59. J. Beaumont, Letter to the Editor, *Times*, 6 November 1872, 10.

60. J. L. Ohlson, Letter to the Editor, *Times*, 12 November 1872, 10.

61. *Times*, 5 November 1872, 7.

62. RCM, 582.

63. India Act XXI of 1883, discussed in Tinker, *New System of Slavery*, 266–69, and Mongia, *Indian Migration and Empire*, 114–16.

64. Northrup, *Indentured Labor*, 156–57.

65. Kimberley to Scott, 16 May 1872, No. 295, PP, 1872, xliii (C. 641), 86–89, 89.

66. Kimberley to Scott, 16 May 1872. On Stanley and the imposition of state regulation for indenture, see chapter 1, pp. 25–27.

67. Kimberley to Scott, 16 May 1872, No. 295, PP, 1872, xliii (C. 641), 89.

68. RCBG, 63.

69. RCBG, 72.

70. RCBG, 54, 110–12, 115, 120, 123, 174, 203.

71. Kimberley to Scott, 31 October 1871, No. 201, PP, 1872, xliii (C. 641), 27.

72. "Draft Ordinance to Consolidate and Amend the Law relating to Immigrants, 1872," §§ 12, 110, 117, enclosed in Young to Herbert, 8 March 1872, PP, 1872, xliii (C. 641), 54–82.

73. "Draft Ordinance to Consolidate and Amend the Law relating to Immigrants, 1872," §§ 89, 91, 93, 96.

74. "Draft Ordinance to Consolidate and Amend the Law relating to Immigrants, 1872," § 7.

75. "Draft Ordinance to Consolidate and Amend the Law relating to Immigrants, 1872," § 73.

76. Young to Herbert, 8 March 1872, PP, 1872, xliii (C. 641), 51–53, 53.

77. Scott to Kimberley, 10 January 1872, No. 5, PP, 1872, xliii (C. 641), 46–50, 50.

78. Scott to Kimberley, 21 December 1871, No. 180, CO 111/387.

79. Scott to Kimberley, 21 December 1871.

80. Scott to Kimberley, 21 December 1871.

81. As reported by Governor Scott. Scott to Kimberley, 5 August 1872, No. 109, CO 111/391.

82. Scott to Kimberley, 29 September 1872, No. 123, CO 111/391.

83. West India Committee to Kimberley, 16 October 1872, CO 111/394.

84. "Draft Ordinance to Consolidate and Amend the Law relating to Immigrants, 1872," § 89. The seven-hour day applied only to field workers. Factory workers (who handled sugar manufacturing) were to work ten hours per day.

85. West India Committee to Kimberley, 16 October 1872, CO 111/394.

86. Scott to Kimberley, 29 September 1872, No. 123, CO 111/391.

87. Scott to Kimberley, 29 September 1872.

88. West India Committee to Kimberley, 16 October 1872, CO 111/394.

89. RCBG, 72.

90. Young to Argyll, 4 March 1873, No. 8/36n, IOR L/PJ/2/65. Rushworth, who succeeded Scott as governor of British Guiana, also opposed long re-indentures, although he found little support for his position in the colony. To the Colonial Office, he argued that re-indenture gave employers "an undue control over the labour market," and that large numbers of Indian immigrants had "never enjoyed real freedom." Rushworth to Kimberley, 26 September 1873, No. 149, CO 111/398.

91. Kimberley to Scott, 14 November 1872, response to Scott to Kimberley, 29 September 1872, No. 123, CO 111/391; Kimberley to Scott, n.d. [21 November 1872], response to Scott to Kimberley, 29 September 1872, No. 123, CO 111/391.

92. Colonial Office to the West India Committee, 21 November 1872, CO 111/394.

93. Scott to Kimberley, 29 September 1872, No. 123, CO 111/391.

94. Scott to Kimberley, 29 September 1872.

95. Kimberley to Scott, n.d. [21 November 1872], response to Scott to Kimberley, 29 September 1872, No. 123, CO 111/391.

96. British Guiana Ordinance No. 7 of 1873, §§ 94, 113, CO 113/5.

97. Rushworth to Kimberley, 6 December 1873, No. 189, CO 111/400 (showing averages of fifteen hours per day for boiler-men, sixteen and a half for cane throwers, and "over 18" for firemen). On the defeated proposal to limit factory hours, with overtime, to thirteen per day, see Rushworth to Kimberley, 6 December 1873, No. 189, CO 111/400.

98. British Guiana Ordinance No. 7 of 1873, § 48, CO 113/5.

99. British Guiana Ordinance No. 7 of 1873, §§ 26, 36. The law did stipulate that families were not to be separated (§ 37) and empowered the Immigration Agent General to refuse applications from employers deemed to be unsuitable (§ 31).

100. British Guiana Ordinance No. 7 of 1873, §§ 144, 145.

101. British Guiana Ordinance No. 7 of 1873, §§ 72, 73.

102. British Guiana Ordinance No. 7 of 1873, § 84; British Guiana Ordinance No. 4 of 1864, § 118, CO 113/4.

103. British Guiana Ordinance No. 7 of 1873, § 86, CO 113/5.

104. British Guiana Ordinance No. 7 of 1873, § 86. In both cases, these penalties were similar to those authorized under Ordinance No. 4 of 1864. Maximum fines decreased, from twenty-four and forty-eight dollars to ten and twenty-four dollars. But the prison sentences authorized—one month for first and two months for subsequent offenses—were the same.

105. British Guiana Ordinance No. 7 of 1873, § 87.

106. British Guiana Ordinance No. 7 of 1873, § 166. Separately, Ordinance No. 7 also criminalized unauthorized absence for fewer than seven days (simple "unlawful absence" rather than "desertion"). The initial punishment for unlawful absence was a fine of five dollars or imprisonment for up to fourteen days. Both punishments were doubled for second and subsequent convictions (§ 105).

107. British Guiana Ordinance No. 7 of 1873, § 88.

108. British Guiana Ordinance No. 7 of 1873, §§ 88, 89. The immediate punishment for refusing to identify oneself was a fine of up to five dollars or imprisonment for up to fourteen days.

109. British Guiana Ordinance No. 7 of 1873, § 90. As discussed in chapter 5, the purpose of such provisions was not only to prevent desertion, but also to stop competition for labor from raising wages; the law made it illegal for one employer to hire away workers contracted to another employer.

110. British Guiana Ordinance No. 7 of 1873, § 109.

111. British Guiana Ordinance No. 7 of 1873, § 109.

112. British Guiana Ordinance No. 7 of 1873, § 109.

113. British Guiana Ordinance No. 7 of 1873, §§ 99, 102.

114. British Guiana Ordinance No. 7 of 1873, § 162.

115. The contrast here between colonial and metropolitan legal development, discussed in chapter 2, appears stark by the 1870s. As noted, penal sanctions for breaches of labor contracts were repealed in England in 1875. In British Guiana, by contrast, they were affirmed in 1873, as they would be again in Mauritius in 1878.

116. "Draft Ordinance to Consolidate and Amend the Law relating to Immigrants, 1872," §§ 27, 48, PP, 1872, xliii (C. 641), 58, 61.

117. Compare "Draft Ordinance to Consolidate and Amend the Law relating to Immigrants, 1872," §§ 99, 80, 82, with British Guiana Ordinance No. 7 of 1873, §§ 105, 84, 86.

118. Rachel Sturman, "Indian Indentured Labor and the History of International Rights Regimes," *American Historical Review* 119, no. 5 (2014): 1453–54.

119. Drawing on Foucault's concept of governmentality, post-structuralist historians of Victorian Britain have argued that this dual function—linking protection and coercion, safety and discipline—characterized the rise of the modern administrative state. While less directly engaged with debates surrounding the term "liberal governmentality," my argument here similarly aims to reveal connections between state protection and social control and, in particular, the extent to which efforts toward the former legitimate the latter. On "liberal governmentality," see Simon Gunn and James Vernon, "Introduction: What Was Liberal Modernity and Why Was It Peculiar in Imperial Britain," in *The Peculiarities of Liberal Modernity in Imperial Britain*, ed. Simon Gunn and James Vernon (Berkeley: University of California Press, 2011); Patrick Joyce, *The State of Freedom: A Social History of the British State since 1800* (Cambridge: Cambridge University Press, 2013); Michel Foucault, "Governmentality," in *Essential Works of Foucault, 1954–1984*, vol. 3, *Power*, ed. James D. Faubion (New York: New Press, 2000), 201–22; Michel Foucault, *Naissance de la Biopolitique: Cours au Collège de France, 1978–1979* (Paris: Gallimard; Seuil, 2004), esp. 3–75. On "colonial governmentality," see David Scott, "Colonial Governmentality," *Social Text*, no. 43 (1995): 191–220.

120. On amelioration, see chapter 1, p. 26 and n73. On the importance of Trinidad as an early laboratory for this process, see Claudius Fergus, "The 'Siete Partidas': A Framework for Philanthropy and Coercion during the Amelioration Experiment in Trinidad, 1823–34," *Caribbean Studies* 36, no. 1 (2008): 75–99; Benton and Ford, "Island Despotism."

121. Trevor Burnard and Kit Candlin, "Sir John Gladstone and the Debate over the Amelioration of Slavery in the British West Indies in the 1820s," *Journal of British Studies* 57, no. 4 (2018): 760–82; Dierksheide, *Amelioration and Empire*, 14–18.

122. British Guiana Ordinance No. 7 of 1873, §§ 9, 10, 19, CO 113/5.

123. British Guiana Ordinance No. 7 of 1873, § 123.

124. British Guiana Ordinance No. 7 of 1873, §§ 115, 119.

125. British Guiana Ordinance No. 7 of 1873, § 126.

126. British Guiana Ordinance No. 7 of 1873, § 130.

127. British Guiana Ordinance No. 7 of 1873, § 132.

128. British Guiana Ordinance No. 7 of 1873, § 133 (calling for at least "fifty feet of superficial space" for each resident and declaring that dwellings "unfit for habitation" will not be permitted).

129. British Guiana Ordinance No. 7 of 1873, § 135.

130. British Guiana Ordinance No. 7 of 1873, § 136.

131. On Gordon, see Laurence Brown, "Inter-Colonial Migration and the Refashioning of Indentured Labour: Arthur Gordon in Trinidad, Mauritius, and Fiji (1866–1880)," in Lambert and Lester, *Colonial Lives across the British Empire*, 204–27; Nishant Batsha, "The Currents of Restless Toil: Colonial Rule and Indian Indentured Labor in Trinidad and Fiji," (PhD diss., Columbia University, 2017), 139–41.

132. Gordon to Carnarvon, 24 November 1866, No. 135, CO 295/236.

133. Gordon to Carnarvon, 26 January 1867, No. 9, CO 295/238; Trinidad Ordinance No. 8 of 1866, CO 297/7.

134. Gordon to Carnarvon, 26 January 1867, No. 9, CO 295/238.

135. Gordon to Carnarvon, 26 January 1867.

136. Gordon to Carnarvon, 8 February 1867, No. 17, CO 295/238 (discussing Ordinance No. 3 of 1867).

137. Trinidad Ordinance No. 13 of 1870, CO 297/8.

138. Gordon to Granville, 25 June 1870, No. 97, CO 295/251.

139. Trinidad Ordinance No. 13 of 1870, § XXX, XXXI, XXXIII, CO 297/8.

140. Trinidad Ordinance No. 13 of 1870, § XXXVII.

141. Trinidad Ordinance No. 13 of 1870, § LXVII.

142. Northrup, *Indentured Labor*, 122. Northrup records an annual death rate among adult indentured laborers of 45.3 deaths per 1,000 adults, and states that the rate declined to 30.9 between 1871 and 1880, and 22.7 between 1881 and 1890. The corresponding figures for British Guiana were 44.8 (1868–1870), 23.0 (1871–1880), and 24.1 (1881–1890). Reduced incidence of disease explains much of this change, but medical reform played a role. On declining death rates, see also Ralph Shlomowitz and Lance Brennan, "Epidemiology and Indian Labor Migration at Home and Abroad," *Journal of World History* 5, no. 1 (1994): 47–67, 56, 60–62.

143. On the emergence of nutrition science and the concept of malnutrition, see Yan Slobodkin, "Famine and the Science of Food in the French Empire, 1900–1939," *French Politics, Culture, and Society* 36, no. 1 (2018): 52–75; James Vernon, *Hunger: A Modern History* (Cambridge, MA: Belknap, 2007), 81–117.

144. Gordon to Buckingham and Chandos, 24 May 1867, No. 73, CO 295/239.

145. Trinidad Ordinance No. 3 of 1869, CO 297/8. See also Batsha, "Currents of Restless Toil," 156–62.

146. Trinidad Ordinance No. 3 of 1869, § I, CO 297/8.

147. Trinidad Ordinance No. 3 of 1869, § II. Deductions were not made against parents for the cost of food provided to children under ten years of age.

148. Trinidad Ordinance No. 3 of 1870, CO 297/8.

149. Buckingham and Chandos to Gordon (draft response), 9 July 1867, enclosed in Gordon to Buckingham and Chandos, 24 May 1867, No. 73, CO 295/239.

150. Gordon to Buckingham and Chandos, 28 August 1867, No. 108, CO 295/240.

151. Gordon to Buckingham and Chandos, 10 February 1868, No. 19, CO 295/243 (acknowledging permission to enact a mandatory feeding ordinance).

152. Murdoch to Rogers, 26 June 1867, CO 386/99.

153. O'Brien to the Colonial Secretary of Mauritius, 30 July 1868, No. 140, NAM, RA 1956.

154. Walcott to Rogers, 20 May 1870, CO 386/99.

155. Walcott to Rogers, 20 May 1870.

156. See Raymond Williams, *Keywords: A Vocabulary of Culture and Society*, new ed. (Oxford: Oxford University Press, 2015), 102–5.

157. Gordon to Granville, 6 April 1870, No. 38, CO 295/250.

158. Gordon to Granville, 6 April 1870.

159. Gordon to Granville, 6 April 1870.

160. Alan H. Adamson, *Sugar Without Slaves: The Political Economy of British Guiana, 1838–1904* (New Haven, CT: Yale University Press, 1972), 241–42; Bridget Brereton, *A History of Modern Trinidad, 1783–1962* (Kingston, Jamaica: Heinemann), 141; Holt, *Problem of Freedom*, 202–6; Woodville K. Marshall, "The Emergence and Survival of the Peasantry," in *General History of the Caribbean, IV, The Long Nineteenth Century: Nineteenth Century Transformations*, ed. K. O. Laurence (Paris: UNESCO, 2011), 188–89.

161. Agent General of Immigrants, Speech in the Legislative Council, 29 March 1870, enclosed in Gordon to Granville, 6 April 1870, No. 38, CO 295/250.

162. Gordon to Granville, 6 April 1870, No. 38, CO 295/250.

163. British Guiana Ordinance No. 7 of 1873, § 139, CO 113/5 (making rationing mandatory from date of allotment "until the first day of October then next following at earliest"; stipulating wage deductions at the rate of 8 cents per day, which was one-third of the stipulated minimum wage of 24 cents per day).

164. British Guiana Ordinance No. 7 of 1873, § 67; Trinidad Ordinance No. 13 of 1870, §§ XXIII, XXV, CO 297/8.

165. Carnarvon to Phayre, 11 March 1875, No. 45, NAM, SA 112.

166. Carnarvon to Phayre, 11 March 1875.

167. Carnarvon to Phayre, 2 February 1876, No. 24, NAM, SA 114.

168. RCM, 587 (on suggested penalties for unlawful absence), 588 (on suggested penalties for incorrigible vagrancy).

169. Carnarvon to Phayre, 11 March 1875, No. 45, NAM, SA 112.

170. RCM, 586.

171. RCM, 586–87.

172. T. W. C. Murdoch, Minute, 23 May 1873, enclosed in Herbert (Colonial Office) to the Under Secretary of State, India Office, 4 June 1873, IOR L/PJ/2/74, No. 8/68.

173. Herbert (Colonial Office) to the Under Secretary of State, India Office, 4 June 1873, IOR L/PJ/2/74, No. 8/68.

174. For examples of vagrancy convictions based solely on a failure to present required identity documents in the 1880s, that is, after the royal commission and apparent reform of Mauritian law, see Durgahee, *Indentured Archipelago*, 75–76.

175. Gordon left Mauritius in August 1874 and became governor of Fiji in June 1875.

176. Phayre to Carnarvon, 20 June 1876, No. 183, NAM, SD 129.

177. Phayre to Carnarvon, 20 June 1876; "Report by the Procureur and Advocate General," 18 May 1876, enclosed in Phayre to Carnarvon, 20 June 1876, No. 183, NAM, SD 129.

178. Carnarvon to Phayre, 22 June 1877, No. 109, NAM, SA 116. Phayre supported the idea, as did the colony's procureur general. Phayre to Carnarvon, 20 June 1876, No. 183, NAM, SD 129.

179. Hicks Beach to Phayre, 27 June 1878, No. 146, NAM, SA 119.

180. Phayre to Carnarvon, 26 May 1875, No. 130, CO 167/564; Hicks Beach to Phayre, 29 June 1878, No. 145, NAM, SA 119.

181. "Petition to Queen Victoria, by Inhabitants of Mauritius," 29 December 1877, enclosed in Newton to Carnarvon, 31 January 1878, No. 33, NAM, SD 136. The petition was signed by 1,812 individuals; "by far the greater number [were] more or less directly or indirectly connected with the production of sugar." Newton to Carnarvon, 31 January 1878, No. 33, NAM, SD 136.

182. "New Labor Law Code. Dissent," 28 December 1877, enclosed in Newton to Carnarvon, 31 January 1878, No. 33, NAM, SD 136.

183. Hicks Beach to Phayre, 29 June 1878, No. 145, NAM, SA 119.

184. Confidential Report of G. B. Colin, 24 January 1878, enclosed in Newton to Carnarvon, 31 January 1878, No. 33, NAM, SD 136.

185. Carnarvon to Phayre, 22 June 1877, No. 109, NAM, SA 116.

186. Mauritius Ordinance No. 12 of 1878, §§ 184, 185, 191, 192, enclosed in Phayre to Hicks Beach, 5 November 1878, No. 385, NAM, SD 139.

187. Mauritius Ordinance No. 12 of 1878, § 222, 229.

188. Mauritius Ordinance No. 12 of 1878, § 53.

189. Mauritius Ordinance No. 12 of 1878, § 51. There were no fixed rules governing the proportion of men and women transported until 1855, when the colonial secretary,

Labouchere, directed the colony to import no more than three times as many men as women, that is, 25 percent of the total. An attempt was subsequently made to raise the required proportion to 50 percent. The colony never managed to achieve that goal, and the decision was soon reversed. The 25 percent rule was reinstated in 1860, after that proportion was stipulated in Britain's treaty with France to allow and regulate Indian emigration to Réunion. RCM, 82, 92.

190. On contemporary fears regarding the negative social consequences of creating disproportionately male societies in the indenture colonies, see Gaiutra Bahadur, *Coolie Woman: The Odyssey of Indenture* (Chicago: University of Chicago Press, 2014), 78–80; Basdeo Mangru, "The Sex-Ratio Disparity and its Consequences under the Indenture in British Guiana," in *India in the Caribbean*, ed. David Dabydeen and Brinsley Samaroo (London: Hansib, 1987), 211–30; Prabhu P. Mohapatra, "'Restoring the Family': Wife Murders and the Making of a Sexual Contract for Indian Immigrant Labour in the British Caribbean Colonies, 1860–1920," *Studies in History* 11, no. 2 (1995): 227–60; Sturman, "Indian Indentured Labor," 1450–52.

191. I am influenced here by Rachel Sturman's suggestion that welfare became a primary lens through which freedom was understood. But I see living conditions and labor relations as separate considerations and think that in this period reform focused on the former rather than the latter. See Sturman, "Indian Indentured Labor," esp. 1453–54.

192. Mauritius Ordinance No. 12 of 1878, § 47, NAM, SD 139.

193. Mauritius Ordinance No. 12 of 1878, §§ 48, 93. These contracts were not mandatory, but all new immigrants remained subject to the requirement of completing a five-year "industrial residence." Thus, new immigrants initially hired for shorter periods would have to continue working under contract for five years unless they commuted a period of their industrial residence by paying a fee (§ 136).

194. Mauritius Ordinance No. 12 of 1878, § 113. The regulated workweek for field workers was nine hours per day, six days per week (§ 112).

195. Mauritius Ordinance No. 12 of 1878, §§ 113, 115. Employers were to determine themselves when their workers were illegally absent, and to select which penalty to apply. Reports were subsequently to be sent to a stipendiary magistrate, who would officially prolong the immigrant's contract if the double cut had not already been applied.

196. Mauritius Ordinance No. 12 of 1878, § 114.

197. Mauritius Ordinance No. 12 of 1878, § 119.

198. Mauritius Ordinance No. 12 of 1878, § 123.

199. Mauritius Ordinance No. 12 of 1878, § 116.

200. Mauritius Ordinance No. 12 of 1878, § 130. The law did allow police to search, with a warrant, homes suspected of sheltering deserters.

201. Mauritius Ordinance No. 12 of 1878, § 128.

202. Mauritius Ordinance No. 12 of 1878, § 128.

203. Mauritius Ordinance No. 12 of 1878, §§ 128, 133.

204. "Report by the Procureur and Advocate General," 18 May 1876, enclosed in Phayre to Carnarvon, 20 June 1876, No. 183, NAM, SD 129.

205. Mauritius Ordinance No. 12 of 1878, § 154, NAM, SD 139.

206. Mauritius Ordinance No. 12 of 1878, §§ 156, 158.

207. Mauritius Ordinance No. 12 of 1878, § 156.

208. Mauritius Ordinance No. 12 of 1878, § 158.

209. Mauritius Ordinance No. 12 of 1878, § 124. Section 125 also imposed penalties for wrongful arrest in this context, but it provided shelter to police who arrested suspected deserters

by specifying that "any officer or constable of police shall be deemed to have been justified in arresting or detaining a servant upon a charge of desertion, if he shall have acted *bona fide* in conformity with the provisions of the preceding articles."

210. F. H. Chesson, Secretary of the Aborigines Protection Society, to E. Hicks Beach, 10 April 1878, enclosed in Hicks Beach to Phayre, 27 June 1878, No. 147, NAM, SA 120.

211. Among the Society's founders were Thomas Fowell Buxton and Thomas Hodgkin. The Society was linked to the British and Foreign Anti-Slavery Society, and in 1909 the two groups merged. See James Heartfield, *The Aborigines' Protection Society: Humanitarian Imperialism in Australia, New Zealand, Fiji, Canada, South Africa, and the Congo, 1836–1909* (London: Hurst, 2011).

212. George Campbell, "Note," 8 April 1878, sub-enclosed in Hicks Beach to Phayre, 27 June 1878, No. 147, NAM, SA 120.

213. George Campbell, "Note," 8 April 1878. Only a month earlier, Lord Carnarvon, the former colonial secretary, had asserted in the House of Lords that Indian migrants to Mauritius "were of a lower class than those generally sent to other Colonies," and that that difference was "one cause of the difficulty which had arisen in the Mauritius." *Hansard*, 3rd. ser., ccxxxix, col. 652 (5 April 1878).

214. George Young, 9 April 1878, sub-enclosed in Hicks Beach to Phayre, 27 June 1878, No. 147, NAM, SA 120.

215. Minutes and Draft Letter, IOR L/PJ/2/100, No. 11/24w.

216. See nn3–5 above, as well as Epstein, *Scandal of Colonial Rule*, and Benton and Ford, *Rage for Empire*, 28–43 (on the trial of Thomas Picton, governor of Trinidad, in 1806).

Epilogue

1. David Northrup, *Indentured Labor in the Age of Imperialism, 1834–1922* (Cambridge: Cambridge University Press, 1995), 156. The exact figure Northrup gives is 520,599.

2. Noël Deerr, *The History of Sugar*, 2 vols. (London: Chapman and Hall, 1949–50), 2:490–91.

3. In 1839, cane sugar still made up more than 95 percent of world supply. Deerr, *History of Sugar*, 2:490–91.

4. Deerr, *History of Sugar*, 2:490–91.

5. J. H. Galloway, *The Sugar Cane Industry: An Historical Geography from Its Origins to 1914* (Cambridge: Cambridge University Press, 1989), 131–32.

6. The specifics of national bounty systems differed, but all involved payments to producers for exports. In Germany, for example, bounties were tax rebates that could (and did) exceed tax owed, resulting in "unearned profit" for producers. Deerr, *History of Sugar*, 2:503.

7. Deerr, *History of Sugar*, 2:504.

8. Deerr, *History of Sugar*, 2:505.

9. Bridget Brereton, *A History of Modern Trinidad, 1783–1962* (Kingston, Jamaica: Heinemann), 87–88.

10. Brereton, *History of Modern Trinidad*, 87. On the sugar crisis of 1884–1885, see also Michael Fakhri, *Sugar and the Making of International Trade Law* (Cambridge: Cambridge University Press, 2014), 41–43.

11. There is a large literature connecting slavery and the plantation economy with modern forms of economic "underdevelopment." See, for example, George L. Beckford, *Persistent Poverty: Underdevelopment in Plantation Economies of the Third World* (New York: Oxford

University Press, 1972). On the conceptual peripheralization of the region in accounts of Western modernity, see Mimi Sheller, *Consuming the Caribbean: from Arawaks to Zombies* (London: Routledge, 2003).

12. Walter Rodney, *A History of the Guyanese Working People, 1881–1905* (Baltimore: Johns Hopkins University Press, 1981), 154.

13. Rodney, *History of the Guyanese Working People*, 154. See also Walton Look Lai, *Indentured Labor, Caribbean Sugar: Chinese and Indian Migrants to the British West Indies, 1838–1918* (Baltimore: Johns Hopkins University Press, 1993), 145.

14. Look Lai, *Indentured Labor, Caribbean Sugar*, 146.

15. Nishant Batsha, "The Currents of Restless Toil: Colonial Rule and Indian Indentured Labor in Trinidad and Fiji," (PhD diss., Columbia University, 2017), 205–30; Madhavi Kale, *Fragments of Empire: Capital, Slavery, and Indian Indentured Labor Migration in the British Caribbean* (Philadelphia: University of Pennsylvania Press, 1998), 150–54; Prabhu P. Mohapatra, "The Hosay Massacre of 1884: Class and Community among Indian Immigrant Labourers in Trinidad," in *Work and Social Change in Asia: Essays in Honour of Jan Breman*, ed. Arvind N. Das and Marcel van der Linden (New Delhi: Manohar, 2003), 187–230; Kelvin Singh, *Bloodstained Tombs: The Muharram Massacre 1884* (Basingstoke: Macmillan Caribbean, 1988). Hosay derived from Muharram but was celebrated in Trinidad by both Muslims and Hindus.

16. This paragraph derives from Look Lai, *Indentured Labor, Caribbean Sugar*, 171.

17. Look Lai, *Indentured Labor, Caribbean Sugar*, 247.

18. Richard Allen, *Slaves, Freedmen, and Indentured Laborers in Colonial Mauritius* (Cambridge: Cambridge University Press, 1999), 136–60; Satyendra Peerthum, *"They Came to Mauritian Shores": The Life-Stories and the History of the Indentured Labourers in Mauritius (1826–1937)* (Coromandel, Mauritius: Aapravasi Ghat Trust Fund, 2017), 54–57. *Morcellement*, or partitioning, refers to the subdividing of large estates.

19. K. O. Laurence, *A Question of Labour: Indentured Immigration into Trinidad and British Guiana, 1875–1917* (New York: St. Martin's Press, 1994), 386–97; David Vincent Trotman, *Crime in Trinidad: Conflict and Control in a Plantation Society, 1838–1900* (Knoxville: University of Tennessee Press, 1986), 199–200; Robinson to Knutsford, 21 July 1890, No. 217, CO 295/329.

20. Laurence, *Question of Labour*, 384–431; Prabhu P. Mohapatra, "'Following Custom'? Representations of Community among Indian Immigrant Labour in the West Indies, 1880–1920," in *Coolies, Capital, and Colonialism: Studies in Indian Labour History*, ed. Rana P. Behal and Marcel van der Linden (Cambridge: Cambridge University Press, 2006), 179–80; Lomarsh Roopnarine, *Indo-Caribbean Indenture: Resistance and Accommodation, 1838–1920* (Mona: University of the West Indies Press, 2007), 80–84. Relatedly, Surendra Bhana and Joy B. Brain, *Setting Down Roots: Indian Migrants in South Africa, 1860–1911* (Johannesburg: Witwatersrand University Press, 1990), 45–55.

21. Look Lai, *Indentured Labor, Caribbean Sugar*, 173–75, 182.

22. Look Lai, *Indentured Labor, Caribbean Sugar*, 172–73; Laurence, *Question of Labour*, 433–42; Radica Mahase, *Why Should We Be Called "Coolies"? The End of Indian Indentured Labour* (New Delhi: Manohar, 2020), 136–41.

23. Hugh Tinker, *A New System of Slavery: The Export of Indian Labour Overseas* (London: Oxford University Press, 1974), 281.

24. See, for example, "Notes on the Grievances of the British Indians in South Africa," 22 September 1896, "Address in Bombay," 26 September 1896, "Address in Madras," 26 October 1896, in *The Collected Works of Mahatma Gandhi*, 90 vols. (Delhi: Ministry of Information and

Broadcasting, Government of India, 1958), 2:53–84, 2:94–121. On Gandhi's role in anti-indenture protest (and the extent to which it did and did not focus on labor relations per se), see Sugata Bose, *A Hundred Horizons: The Indian Ocean in the Age of Global Empire* (Cambridge, MA: Harvard University Press, 2006), 152–70; Ashutosh Kumar, *Coolies of the Empire: Indentured Indians in the Sugar Colonies, 1830–1920* (Cambridge: Cambridge University Press, 2017), 206–10, 222–26.

25. Karen A. Ray, "The Abolition of Indentured Emigration and the Politics of Indian Nationalism, 1894–1917," (PhD diss., McGill University, 1980); Rachel Sturman, "Indian Indentured Labor and the History of International Rights Regimes," *American Historical Review* 119, no. 5 (2014), 1462; Look Lai, *Indentured Labor, Caribbean Sugar*, 176–78; Northrup, *Indentured Labor*, 144.

26. Kumar, *Coolies of the Empire*, 210–11; Riyad Sadiq Koya, "The Regulation, Division, and Multiplication of Emigrant Labor: The Border between Land and Sea in Colonial India, 1834–1922," *Journal of World History* 32, no. 1 (2021): 58–59.

27. Henry Polak, *The Indians of South Africa; helots within the Empire, and how they are treated* (Madras, 1909). Polak was an associate of Gandhi and an editor of *Indian Opinion*, which advocated against the discriminatory treatment of Indians in South Africa between 1903 and 1915. Discussed in Laurence, *Question of Labour*, 456; Goolam Vahed, "Gokhale, Polak and the End of Indian Indenture in South Africa, 1909–1911," in *South Asian Migrations in Global History: Labour, Law, and Wayward Lives*, ed. Neilesh Bose (London: Bloomsbury, 2021), 37–62; Tinker, *New System of Slavery*, 312.

28. Totaram Sanadhya, *Fiji Mein Mere Ekkis Varsh* (Agra, 1914). On Sanadhya and *Fiji Mein Mere Ekkis Varsh* (My Twenty-One Years in Fiji), see Mrinalini Sinha, "Totaram Sanadhya's Fiji Mein Mere Ekkis Varsh: A History of Empire and Nation in a Minor Key," in *Ten Books That Shaped the British Empire: Creating an Imperial Commons*, ed. Antoinette Burton and Isabel Hofmeyr (Durham, NC: Duke University Press, 2014), 168–89.

29. Batsha, "Currents of Restless Toil," chap. 10; Kumar, *Coolies of the Empire*, 206–34; Laurence, *Question of Labour*, 478–79; Mahase, *Why Should We Be Called "Coolies"?*, 148–55; Mrinalini Sinha, "Premonitions of the Past," *Journal of Asian Studies* 74, no. 4 (2015): 828–30; Sturman, "Indian Indentured Labor," 1462.

30. Sturman, "Indian Indentured Labor," 1464.

31. Look Lai, *Indentured Labor, Caribbean Sugar*, 178. Relatedly, Sturman, "Indian Indentured Labor," 1464 ("While elite nationalists deplored the exploitation and oppression of Indian laborers abroad, their criticism of the system nonetheless focused on the fact that it created a global image of Indians as 'coolies.' ").

32. Gaiutra Bahadur, *Coolie Woman: The Odyssey of Indenture* (Chicago: University of Chicago Press, 2014), 155.

33. Brij V. Lal, "Kunti's Cry: Indentured Women on Fiji Plantations," *Indian Economic and Social History Review* 22, no. 1 (1985): 55–71; Kumar, *Coolies of the Empire*, 214–16.

34. Bahadur, *Coolie Woman*, 158–60; Kumar, *Coolies of the Empire*, 216–22; Radhika Mongia, "Gender and the Historiography of Gandhian Satyagraha in South Africa," *Gender & History* 18, no. 1 (2006): 130–49.

35. Compare, for instance, the abolitionist and official reporting surveyed in Lal, "Kunti's Cry."

36. Sinha, "Premonitions of the Past," 830.

37. Cited in Tinker, *New System of Slavery*, 339–40. See also Basdeo Mangru, "Indian Government Policy towards Indentured Labour Migration to the Sugar Colonies," in *Across the Dark*

Waters: Ethnicity and Indian Identity in the Caribbean, ed. David Dabydeen and Brinsley Samaroo (London: Macmillan Caribbean, 1996), 171–72.

38. A vast literature explores the effects of the First World War on anticolonial thought and European responses to nationalist demands. See, among others, Erez Manela, *The Wilsonian Moment: Self-Determination and the International Origins of Anticolonial Nationalism* (Oxford: Oxford University Press, 2007); Cemil Aydin, *The Politics of Anti-Westernism in Asia: Visions of World Order in Pan-Islamic and Pan-Asian Thought* (New York: Columbia University Press, 2007); Heather Streets-Salter, *World War One in Southeast Asia: Colonialism and Anticolonialism in an Era of Global Conflict* (Cambridge: Cambridge University Press, 2017).

39. Tinker, *New System of Slavery*, 340.

40. Tinker, *New System of Slavery*, 357, 367; Radhika Singha, *The Coolie's Great War: Indian Labour in a Global Conflict, 1914–1921* (New York: Oxford University Press, 2020), 35–36, 114–16.

41. On the term "second slavery," see Dale W. Tomich, *Through the Prism of Slavery: Labor, Capital, and World Economy* (Lanham, MD: Rowman & Littlefield, 2004), 56–71.

Index

Page numbers in italics refer to figures.